HAROLD C. SCHONBERG

The Great Pianists

REVISED AND UPDATED

SIMON & SCHUSTER PAPERBACKS
New York   London   Toronto   Sydney

SIMON & SCHUSTER PAPERBACKS
Rockefeller Center
1230 Avenue of the Americas
New York, New York 10020

First Simon & Schuster paperback edition 2006

SIMON & SCHUSTER PAPERBACKS and colophon are registered
trademarks of Simon & Schuster, Inc.

For information about special discounts for bulk purchases,
please contact Simon & Schuster Special Sales:
1-800-456-6798 or business@simonandschuster.com.

Manufactured in the United States of America

25   27   29   30   28   26   24

The Library of Congress has cataloged the Fireside edition as follows:

Schonberg, Harold C.
The Great Pianists.

"A Fireside Book."
Includes index.
Pianists—biography.   I. Title.
ML397.S3   1987   786.1'092'2   [B]   87-341

ISBN-13: 978-0-671-64200-6
ISBN-10:   0-671-64200-6
ISBN-13: 978-0-671-63837-5 (Pbk)
ISBN-10:   0-671-63837-8 (Pbk)

Acknowledgments

To the Music Division of the New York Public Library, and especially to the willing and strong-armed page boys who, relentlessly summoned by me, staggered under load after load of bound copies of old magazines.

To Dr. Bernard Amsterdam, Harry L. Anderson, the late Jan Holcman, Jerrald Moore and Robert Staub, who let me hear as many records as I desired from their great collections. Mr. Holcman also brought to my attention and translated for me several articles in Polish.

To Eric Schaal, who generously let me reproduce many of the items in his extraordinary collection of pictures of musicians.

To Arthur Loesser, for having written *Men, Women, and Pianos*. Anybody working in the field of pianos and pianists must be beholden to him for his pioneer work and for the brilliant book that resulted.

To Leopold Mannes, who read the manuscript and offered many valuable suggestions.

To my wife, Rosalyn, who supplied constant aid, comfort, encouragement, and many of the illustrations in this book.

To Henry Simon, my editor at Simon and Schuster, who supervised the progress of the book, patiently helped clarify detail after detail, and went through every word with the care and concern of a psychiatrist confronted with a particularly difficult case.

To the memory of Ralph and Alice

Contents

7

List of Illustrations

Preface

IT IS WITH PIANO PLAYING that this book is concerned, and the history of piano playing begins with Mozart and Clementi. With Clementi, really, for even Mozart did not begin to concentrate on the piano until the middle 1770s. Like most musicians of his day, he had been trained on the harpsichord, clavichord and organ. But he was about the last of the great musicians of whom this can be said, and his lifetime saw the virtual disappearance of harpsichord and clavichord. From 1800 on, the piano became the most popular of instruments and the pianist the most popular of instrumentalists.

Yet, despite the spread of the piano as the favorite instrument of home and concert, there have been through the years very few studies of pianos and pianists. One exception in the last decade is the remarkable *Men, Women and Pianos* by Arthur Loesser. Another is Abram Chasins' *Speaking of Pianists*, which for the most part concentrates on the contemporary scene.

There are good reasons for the scarcity of studies about keyboard virtuosos, especially keyboard virtuosos of the past, for problem is heaped upon problem. Paleontologists who can reconstruct an entire skeleton on the basis of the fragment of one bone have an easier time of it. They at least have the fragment. But once a pianist in the days before recording removed his hands from the keys, the sound was gone forever. Obviously there can be no direct evidence of how Mozart sounded, or Liszt (though every once in a while up pops that tantalizing rumor about the existence of a Liszt cylinder).

Must we then say with Pascal that truth is such a subtle point that our tools are too blunt to touch it accurately? Not necessarily. Even if a Clementi, a Dreyschock, a Henselt, Chopin or Alkan was

inconsiderate enough to die before the development of the phonograph, a large amount of both physical and documentary evidence
survives to give us a reasonably accurate and sometimes even a quite
vivid idea of their playing. Biography, criticism, anecdotes, letters,
hearsay (when from a reliable source), the written music itself—all
play a part. We know, and have reconstructed, the instruments upon
which the great pianists of the past played. From their own music
we can deduce something about their physical characteristics and
hence their keyboard approach. For most of the great pianists of the
past were also composers who composed primarily for themselves. It
takes no great detective ability to look at Henselt's F minor Concerto, closely examine the left-hand extensions, and deduce that
Henselt had a remarkable stretch and probably a peculiar hand formation. Even so pure a composer as Mozart wrote for his own capabilities and was never so happy as when he could write to his father
boasting of the difficulties he had put into the piano part and how he
had "wowed" his audience. And when one reads through Chopin's
Là ci darem Variations, that remarkable Op. 2, considers its date, and
then takes another look at the complicated and daring piano figurations—figurations far in advance of anything conceived up to that
time—it becomes immediately apparent that (1) Chopin was a
genius so unprecedented as to be a sport (in the biological sense) and
(2) that his essential pianistic style had been consolidated at a very
early age. Even the fingerings in the published works of the pianist-
composers, not to mention their expression markings, can yield re-
vealing sidelights.

Often the pianists themselves have had quite a bit to say about
their keyboard philosophy. And there is the testimony of those who
heard them. This testimony can range from indiscriminate hero-
worship written by amateurs to detailed analyses by some of the best
musical minds from Mozart on. Not that the best musical minds are
infallible. Nobody has yet been born who does not have some kind of
parti pris, and sometimes it becomes necessary to discount the reli-
ability of a report, even when it comes from sources that approach
divinity. Clementi, for instance, could not have been nearly as bad
as Mozart told his sister Nannerl he was. Indeed, all the indications
are that Clementi was a much more brilliant virtuoso than Mozart.
And Mozart probaby knew it; hence, being all too human, his violent diatribe against his great colleague.

In short, evidence has to be carefully weighed, and a healthy amount of skepticism—cynicism, even—is mandatory. But the evidence is there, in massive doses. The more popular the virtuoso, the more was written about him—in *feuilletons*, in letters, in reviews, in articles of various kinds, in books, in unpublished manuscripts. On the whole, most of this information about any given artist builds to a fairly consistent body of opinion; and when one finds a particular report in very sharp variance with all the others, one automatically looks for the particular bit of prejudice on the part of the writer. Generally it can be found.

Of course, there is the problem of separating fact from myth. In the generations following any great pianist, a myth arises. The pupils of Liszt and Leschetizky, for example, spent years preaching and writing about their teachers. With each year, the figures of those two great men became taller and wider, with lightning playing around them. It has been no easy task to put them, and others, into true perspective.

But in the twentieth century the problem has at least been simplified through recordings. It comes as a surprise to many people, professionals included, to learn how many great pianists of the past made records. Many of those records, of course, are acoustic, i.e., pre-electrics made before 1925, and extremely difficult to locate today. A partial list of recorded pianists who were active in concert before the turn of the twentieth century would include Ansorge, Benoist, Buhlig, Busoni, Chaminade, Cortot, d'Albert, Davies, de Greef, de Lara, de Pachmann, Diémer, Dohnányi, Eibenschütz, Richard Epstein, Friedberg, Friedheim, Gabrilowitsch, Ganz, Godowsky, Goll, Grainger, Grieg, Grünfeld, Hambourg, Hofmann, Janotha, Koczalski, Kreutzer, Kwast-Hoddap, La Forge, Lamond, Leginska, Lévy, Georg Liebling, Marguerite Long, Matthay, Michailowski, Niemann, Paderewski, Pauer, Philipp, Planté, Pugno, Risler, Rosenthal, Saint-Saëns, Sapellnikoff, Sauer, Scharwenka, Selva, Sirota, Stavenhagen, Adela Verne, Vianna da Motta and Josef Weiss.

The chronological span of these pianists covers a good part of the nineteenth century. Even the playing of Brahms, who was born in 1833, can dimly be heard through the surface noise of an 1889 cylinder. Saint-Saëns, the first major pianist ever to record, was born in 1835. Chopin was only twenty-five years old at that time. De Pachmann, who recorded prolifically from the early 1900s until his death in 1933, was born in 1848. Pugno was born in 1852, Paderewski in

1860, Rosenthal, de Greef and Sauer in 1862, Rachmaninoff and Bauer in 1873, Lhevinne in 1874, Hofmann in 1876, and so on. Thus we have on records concrete illustrations of how nineteenth-century pianists went about their musical business. A few of these pianists continued to record well into the era of electrical reproduction. (Many of them also made piano rolls, but these are so untrustworthy that they are not considered in this book. Almost as much could be done to doctor a piano roll as can be done these days to magnetic tape. In addition, tempo, dynamics and pedalings are highly suspect.)

These recordings do not, of course, supply all of the answers, but in many cases they are unusually suggestive and articulate documents. Taken all together, they provide a compendium of romantic performance practice. It should be added that modern technology can drag information from those aged grooves that the makers never knew was there. Listeners exposed for the first time to even the earliest acoustics (such as the 1902 Eibenschütz discs) are simply amazed at the clarity of the recording.

These recordings certainly help round out the picture, and liberal use has been made of them in this book. So do the magazine and newspaper critics from the early 1800s on. So do the pianists themselves, in their letters, essays and frequent preachments. So do composers, writing to friends about pianists they have heard. So do members of the listening public when they give their impression of the artist on stage—untrained impressions, frequently, but often more graphic than those of their more professional brethren.

Another source for this book have been discussions with veteran musicians about pianists they have heard. Unfortunately, a certain amount of this information has been found to be entirely unreliable. Old men tend to live in the past and in the reflected glory of the great men they have known. This was as true in the nineteenth century (and in any century) as it is today. Some, indeed, have clutched so firmly to the past that they have actually succeeded in denting history. For the reminiscences of some old musicians have been taken as gospel, even when they are patently untrue and romanticized.

And so the task in this book has been to sift through an enormous amount of material, discarding that which is obviously false or unreliable, matching this bit of information to that in an effort to come as close as possible to the actual work of the great pianists. In the following pages the leading ones will be discussed—not biographically (except incidentally) but as keyboard specialists who had something unique to offer and whose playing made a mark not only on their own generation but in many cases helped shape the playing and the keyboard philosophy of the generation that followed.

Rather than clutter the text, it has been found practical to use the index for dates. In the index, next to the name of nearly every pianist found in this book, will be found birth and death dates. (Nearly every pianist, because concentrated research has failed to reveal the vital statistics of a few of the lesser artists who are discussed in passing.) It should be pointed out that the book does not pretend to be encyclopedic, and readers will find some names missing, especially names of contemporary pianists. It obviously would have been impossible to include everybody; and in any case contemporary pianism is a subject that could not be surveyed except in a book of its own. But it is hoped that no major figure has been omitted, and that this study will give an idea of the mainstream of piano playing from Mozart and Clementi to the present day.

· I ·

In the Beginning

OLD BACH HAD DIED in 1750, and with him had departed the learned contrapuntal style. Something new, around that time, was in the air, wafted from the French and Italian courts, espoused by a musical public that was just beginning to be formed, catered to by musicians (including the sons of Bach). It was the homophonic style, the *style galant*, or, as it was called in Italy, the *stile sueto*. It marked music's shift from the church to the salon, from fugue to sonata. It demanded a singing style, nuance and elaborate fioritura, politeness over force, fluffiness over deep content. It also demanded a new style of melody, a new kind of texture, a simplification of means. The audience to whom this music appealed was drawn from the top—from the cultivated clergy, the nobility, the richest and most ambitious of the bourgeoisie. ("Classical" music was not yet a democratic art.) This audience considered itself highly sophisticated. Indeed, it was, and also it was shallow. In music it demanded gaiety and grace. It did not want to think. Rather, it wanted to be charmed. Charles Burney, one of the first of the great music historians and a spokesman for his age, expressed the need when he called for music that offered "with clearness and propriety whatever is graceful, elegant and tender," rather than music expressive of "complicated misery and the tempestuous fury of unbridled passions."

Apparently the *style galant* arose more or less spontaneously in Europe early in the eighteenth century and was to run its course through the rococo works of Haydn and Mozart. Pergolesi was one of the early exponents of the break from the baroque; so was Sam-

19

martini; so were Stamitz, C. P. E. Bach and the early German school of song composers.

The piano was newly at hand, and it satisfied the demands of the *style galant*. Bartolommeo Cristofori, a harpsichord-maker from Padua, had invented the instrument in 1709. He constructed a device, in Florence, in which hammers activated strings. He called it a *gravicembalo col piano e forte*, the idea being that it could play soft and loud. The theory of such an instrument was not new. There had been hammer actions previously; and in one of his books Arnold Dolmetsch has described a Dutch pianoforte dating from 1610. But Cristofori was nevertheless the inventor of the piano, just as James Watt and not Heron of Alexandria was the inventor of the steam engine.

Cristofori's device captured the imagination of his contemporaries. Just two years after the pilot model was unveiled, a lengthy description appeared in the *Giornale dei letterati d'Italia*. This was translated into German in 1725, prompting Gottfried Silbermann in Germany to build a few (probably by 1730). At around that time, too, music was being composed for the gravicembalo. The first known examples are a series of sonatas by Lodovico Giustini in 1732.

Silbermann's instruments were known to Johann Sebastian Bach. It would appear that when Bach visited Dresden in 1736, he tried them out. All we know of the occasion is secondhand. Bach said something about the tone being pleasant, the treble too weak, the action too stiff. Silbermann, a man of temperament, took these criticisms personally and had some nasty things to say about Bach. Johann Friedrich Agricola, presumably writing from firsthand evidence, reports that Silbermann was "angry at Mr. Bach for a long time." Bach's word carried great weight. He was, after all, known in Germany as the greatest of organists, the most brilliant of clavierists, and a composer second only to the mighty Telemann.

A few years later, Silbermann improved his pianos along the lines Bach had suggested, thereby admitting that Bach had been right in the first place. He said as much to Agricola, who writes that when Bach had a chance to try out the improved model it "received . . . complete approval from him."

In the meantime, Frederick the Great, who collected everything and was himself a first-class musical amateur, started collecting Silbermann pianos. He had fifteen of them in 1747, the time of Bach's famous visit to Potsdam. (Henry Fowler Broadwood, the English piano manufacturer, saw them at Potsdam as late as 1850, "but in very bad repair.") The King was waiting for Bach when he arrived in the evening and immediately hustled him to the pianos, without even giving him time to change his traveling dress. He gave Bach a theme upon which to improvise. This Bach did so well "that not only His Majesty was pleased to show his satisfaction thereat, but also all those present were seized with astonishment." Presumably one of the people seized by astonishment was Bach's son Carl Philipp Emanuel, who was Frederick's accompanist for some twenty years.

But Johann Sebastian was not a pianist. He was a master of the clavichord and harpsichord, and he undoubtedly played the Silbermann pianos with a harpsichord touch. Admittedly Silbermann's instruments in 1747 were a long way from the instrument we know today, being light in action and feeble in carrying power. But they did have a wider dynamic variety than anything known up to then, and Bach was not the man to take full advantage of their potentialities. Bach's clavier style was, of course, based on the instruments he had studied as a youth. He played with bent fingers, directly over the keys. According to Bach's first biographer, Johann Nicolaus Forkel, "Bach is said to have played with so easy and so small a motion of the fingers that it was hardly perceptible. Only the first joints of the fingers were in motion; the hand retained, even in the most difficult passages, its rounded form; the fingers rose very little from the keys, hardly more than in a trill, and when one was employed the others remained quietly in position." This quietness extended to his position at the clavier. "Still less did the other parts of his body take any share in his playing, as happens with many whose hand is not light enough." As one could guess by looking at his keyboard music, Bach's own playing must have featured complete independence of hand and finger. This is corroborated by Forkel. "He rendered all his fingers, of both hands, equally strong and serviceable, so that he was able to execute not only chords and all running passages, but also single and double trills with equal ease and delicacy." Obviously he was a complete master on the instruments he had grown up with, and, of course, we can imagine his general musicianship. He once said to a friend that he believed he could play at sight anything ever written. But the piano came too late in his life —and also in the lives of Handel and Scarlatti. Harpsichord, clavichord, organ—these were the keyboard instruments of those three giants.

Having invented the piano, Italy proceeded to forget about it. The manufacture of the piano passed to other parts of Europe. By 1759 it was being advertised in France as "a harpsichord of new invention called *piano e forte*." Sébastien Érard was the first great piano-maker of France (he started in 1777), and he made the best instrument there until Ignaz Pleyel started to compete with him in 1807. In an article for *Early Music*, Virginia Pleasants states that the piano was played in Vienna as early as 1763 by an otherwise unknown Johann Baptist. In England, Johann Christian Bach was the first famous musician to give a public recital, though the piano had been known there previously and had even been played in public prior to Johann Christian's demonstration. The first mention of it in London seems to have been on May 15, 1767, at a benefit concert for a Miss Brickler at Covent Garden. She (said the advertisement) "will sing a favorite Song from JUDITH, accompanied by Mr. Didbin on a new instrument called a Piano Forte." Presumably Mr. Didbin was the famous Charles Didbin, very active in the musical theater of his day. Bach's solo took place at a benefit concert for Johann Christian Fischer, a well-known oboist and composer. It was given at The Thatched House on June 2, 1768. Bach played a four-and-one-half-octave instrument he had purchased from Johannes Zumpe (1735–1783), a Saxonian who had come to England in 1750 and had set up as a piano manufacturer. It was not until 1777 that the great Broadwood opened his plant in England.

Shortly after Johann Christian broke the ice in England, a popular pianist appeared on the scene. He was a German named Johann Samuel Schroeter, who made an immense success in London. But his was a short career. He was literally bought off by the father of the English girl he married. *His* daughter, said Papa, was not going to marry so vulgar a type as a professional musician, and a foreigner at that. So Papa made a gentleman of Schroeter by settling an annuity on him. Musicians were suspect in England as late as the Victorian period unless they were as rich and cultured as a Felix Mendelssohn. (Mr. Winterbourne in Henry James's *Daisy Miller* equates the Italian Mr. Giovanelli with a musician and other dreadful things. "He is not a gentleman," decides the young American. "He is a music-master, or a penny-a-liner, or a third-rate artist.")

In America, Thomas Jefferson, indefatigable violinist and music-lover, had a piano by 1771. By 1774, John Brent was making pianos in Philadelphia. By 1779, Vienna alone had more than three hundred piano teachers. So firmly was the piano entrenched as the century drew to a close that Haydn, in 1790, said he was no longer in the habit of playing the harpsichord, and he advised a friend to get a piano. Said the *Allgemeine musikalische Zeitung* in 1800: "Everybody plays [the piano], everybody learns music." The piano by then was well established. It had a five-octave normal range, and sixty-one keys (as against today's eighty-eight). Knee-action pedals were in general use, though the foot pedal, introduced in England, was beginning to make its way. Tone and action were light; the iron frame was still to come. With its wooden framework, the pre-1800 piano could not have had much resonance. Nor did it have a robust physique, and strings and hammers were forever breaking. Many of the early pianos had harpsichord-like stops. It took some time even for piano manufacturers to realize that dynamic changes had to be produced by the fingers and not by mechanical registrations. Not until about one hundred and fifty years after its invention did the instrument develop into the massive iron-and-wood piece of equipment we enjoy today.

Up to the early years of the nineteenth century, there were two types of piano that attracted the professional pianist—the Viennese piano and the English piano. Each had its adherents. The Viennese (or German) action, favored by Mozart, was light, with relatively little carrying power, and virtually no pressure was needed to depress the keys. Muzio Clementi, Mozart's great rival, helped develop the English piano, which was bigger, more heavily strung, more brilliant, not so easy to manipulate but much more capable of virtuoso effects. The differences between the two were summarized by a major pianist of a following generation, Johann Nepomuk Hummel:

The German piano [writes Hummel in his book, rather wonderfully named *A Complete Theoretical and Practical Course of Instruction in the Art of Playing the Piano Forte, Commencing with the Simplest Elementary Principles, and including every information requisite to the Most Finished Style of Performance*: so runs the title page of the English edition of 1827] may be played upon with ease by the weakest hand. It allows the performer to impart to his execution every possible degree of light and shade, speaks clearly and promptly, has a round, flute-like tone, which, in a large room, contrasts well with the accompanying orchestra, and does not impede rapidity of execution by requiring too great an effort.

The English piano, Hummel continues, also has much to offer. Among other things, it must be praised for its

durability and fullness of tone. Nevertheless this instrument does not admit of the same facility of execution as the German. The touch is much heavier, the keys sink much deeper, and consequently, the return of the hammer on the repetition of a note cannot take place so quickly. . . . As a counterpoise of this, however, through the fullness of tone in the English Piano-Forte, the melody receives a peculiar charm and harmonious sweetness.

Another important pianist of the 1820s, Friedrich Kalkbrenner, also has a few words to say about English and Viennese pianos in his *Méthode*:

The instruments of Vienna and London have produced two schools. The Viennese pianists are particularly distinguished for their precision, the clarity and rapidity of their execution. Thus the instruments manufactured in that city are extremely easy to play. . . . The use of the pedals in Germany is almost unknown. English pianos have a fuller sound and a heavier keyboard action. The players of that country have adopted a larger style and that beautiful way of singing that distinguishes them; and it is indispensable to use the large pedal in order to conceal the inherent dryness of the piano. Dussek, Field and J. B. Cramer, the chiefs of that school which was founded by Clementi, use the pedal when harmonies do not change. Dussek above all was responsible for that, for he used the pedal almost constantly when he played in public.

During the development of the piano, it took pianists time to forget about harpsichord or clavichord technique and concentrate on what the piano had to offer that was peculiarly its own. This involved a complete reorientation in fingering, in touch, in basic philosophy of sound. Not that the clavierists had failed to pay attention to fingering. Couperin's *Art de toucher le clavecin* (1717) goes into great detail on that subject, and he claimed to have instituted a new system—a claim that modern scholars disallow. It probably was

Johann Sebastian Bach. The pastel was made by his cousin, Gottlob
Friedrich Bach, in 1736. That was the year Bach tried out Silbermann's
pianos and found them wanting.

Johann Christian Bach, youngest son of Johann Sebastian, as painted by Gainsborough. Johann Christian gave the first public piano recital in England in 1768.

Carl Philipp Emanuel Bach, second son of Johann Sebastian. In his great *Versuch* he codified keyboard technique. Of him Mozart said, "He is the father, we are the children."

Carl Philipp Emanuel Bach,
Kapellmeister und Musikdirekter in Hamburg.

Aus Hochachtung gezeichnet und gestochen von A. Stöttrup.

J. S. Bach who worked out the basic principles of modern fingering. Up to his time, the thumb and little finger of the right hand had hardly been used. Right-hand scales were generally played with only the third and fourth fingers going up, the second and third coming down. Left-hand scales were run up with the thumb and forefinger. Bach seems to have been the first to allow the thumb to pass under the other fingers—at least, the first whose theories along that line attracted widespread attention. Domenico Scarlatti must have used a fairly modern type of fingering—it is hard to see how much of his music could otherwise be played—but he did not have gifted children to pass his work along as Carl Philipp Emanuel, Johann Christian and Wilhelm Friedemann did their father's. It should be pointed out that J. S. Bach still relied heavily on the old finger-over-finger technique. In the few examples of fingerings that he has left us (perhaps a hundred bars in all), he constantly passes the third finger of the right hand over the fourth. This inevitably would lead to a slight rhythmic imbalance, which scholars call "unequal rhythm." Nevertheless, Bach seems to have been the first to use his thumb extensively. He would derisively tell his children about hearing, in his youth, great players who used their thumb only when large stretches made it necessary. This he helped correct; and his principles were known in Germany as "Bach's fingering."

It remained for his son, Carl Philipp Emanuel, to write the definitive treatise. Part I of his monumental *Versuch über die wahre Art das Clavier zu spielen* (*Essay on the True Art of Playing Keyboard Instruments*) was issued in 1753. Part II came out in 1762. Bach aimed his books at harpsichord and clavichord players. "The more recent pianoforte, when it is sturdy and well built, has many fine qualities, although its touch must be carefully worked out, a task which is not without difficulties." Nevertheless, the *Versuch* was seized upon by piano players as a guide to fingerings, style and virtually anything that had to do with keyboard manipulation.

Carl Philipp Emanuel, the second son of Johann Sebastian, enjoyed a formidable reputation in his day. He was not only a skilled executant upon keyboard (and undoubtedly string) instruments, he was also an important composer in many forms of music. Naturally he contributed to the keyboard repertoire, and his series of clavier sonatas, written from 1742 to 1787, covers the period during which the piano began to elbow out the harpsichord. The consequent change in style is illustrated in C. P. E. Bach's sonatas, which progress from a type of writing illustrative purely of harpsichord technique to a style that encompasses the effects made possible by the new instrument. All of his music was regarded with great respect. Mozart said of him, "He is the father, we are the children." Beethoven greatly admired his keyboard music, and as late as 1809 was profuse in his endorsement. "Of Emanuel Bach's pianoforte works I have only a few things, yet a few by that artist serve not only for highest enjoyment but also for study." Beethoven took his own advice and the following year was asking his publisher for all the available music by C. P. E. Bach. And Clementi said of the *Versuch*, "Whatever I know of fingering and the new style, in short, whatever I understand of the pianoforte I learned from this book."

Unlike his father, Carl Philipp Emanuel had a good working knowledge of the piano. He had become thoroughly familiar with Silbermann's instruments while in the service of Frederick the Great. After leaving His Royal Highness (and presumably sick unto death of accompanying the royal flute; a story goes that one of the courtiers, after His Majesty had finished a solo, said, "What rhythm!"—to which Bach muttered, "What rhythms!"), he succeeded Telemann at Hamburg and made a big impression as a clavierist. A writer for a music magazine in 1770 described a concert in which Bach participated, "On this occasion various male and female amateurs were heard, besides our Mr. Bach, whose playing compelled the admiration of all, especially when he allowed us to observe his dexterity upon the magnificent-sounding pianoforte."

As a clavier player—the clavier was the generic name for any keyboard instrument, including the organ—Bach apparently was not the technician that his father, Handel or Scarlatti were. What appealed to his listeners was the expressiveness of his playing. Charles Burney, an experienced and reliable witness, was struck by the originality of his approach. "His performance today," Burney wrote in his *Present State of Music*, "convinced me of what I had suggested before from his works: that he is not only one of the greatest composers that ever existed, for keyed instruments, but the best player in point of expression; for others, perhaps, have had as rapid execution: however, he possesses every style; though he confines himself sharply to the expressive." In Bach's time there was a sharp cleavage between "expressive" and virtuoso players. It was felt that the master of one aspect could not also master the other.

Thus it was a very experienced, practical keyboard player who wrote the *Versuch*, a book that codifies virtually all that was known of the subject up to that time. Bach deals with fingerings, embellishments, performance practice, intervals, figured-bass realizations, accompaniment and improvisation. His fingerings for scales are astonishingly modern, with the thumb frequently turned under and only a few vestiges remaining of the 3-4-3-4 sequences. (He would not, however, permit the thumb or little finger on the black keys except if no other course were possible.) Bach recommended arched fingers and relaxed muscles and was quite specific about posture. The principles set forth in the *Versuch* were followed to the point of sheer plagiarism in successive How To manuals by such nonentities as Francis Linley (1790), James Hook (1788) and many others. But some important pianists and theorists were influenced by Carl Philipp Emanuel. When Dussek, in the 1799 edition of his *Instructions on the Art of Playing the Piano Forte or Harpsichord*, has as his cardinal dictum "Never displace the natural position of the hand," he is but following C. P. E. Bach's lead. Indeed, it is difficult to pick up *any* manual of keyboard practice before 1830 and not find echoes of the *Versuch*.

In addition to his remarks about technique, Bach's ideas about interpretation strongly influenced the playing of the entire classic period. He even has a lengthy paragraph on the tempo rubato, which may come as a surprise to those who consider rubato a romantic phenomenon. Bach was one of the first to describe it (although, of course, it was always used; music without rubato would be so inhumanly metronomic as to be unlistenable). As Bach's remarks about rubato were taken up by Mozart, and as rubato was to play such an important part in performance practices of the nineteenth century, Bach's historic statement deserves to be quoted in full:

On entering a fermata expressive of languidness, tenderness or sadness, it is customary to broaden slightly. This brings us to the tempo rubato. Its indication is simply the presence of more or fewer notes than are contained in the normal division of the bar. A whole bar, part of one, or several bars may be, so to speak, distorted in this manner. The most difficult but most important task is to give all notes of the same value exactly the same duration. [That is, do not distort note values: a quarter note remains a quarter note; an eighth, an eighth.] When the execution is such that one hand seems to play against the bar and the other strictly with it, it may be said that the performer is doing everything that can be required of him. It is only rarely that all parts are struck simultaneously. The beginning of a caesura which terminates in a tempo rubato may be drawn into manipulation, but the end, as in all endings of this tempo, must find all parts together over the bass. Slow notes and caressing or sad melodies are the best, and dissonant chords are better than consonant ones. Proper execution of this tempo demands great critical faculties and a high order of sensibility. He who possesses these will not find it difficult to fashion a performance whose complete freedom will show no trace of coercion, and he will be able to manipulate any kind of passage. However, practice alone will be of no help here, for without a fitting sensitivity, no amount of pains will succeed in contriving a correct rubato. As soon as the upper part begins slavishly to follow the bar, the essence of rubato is lost, for then all other parts must be played in time. Other instrumentalists and singers, when they are accompanied, can introduce the tempo much more easily than the solo clavierist. . . . *Most keyboard pieces contain rubato passages* [italics added].

Mozart's instructions about rubato, though much briefer, contain very much the same theory—the theory summarized in Bach's words, ". . . one hand seems to play against the bar and the other strictly with it." Mozart, naturally, had read C. P. E. Bach religiously, as had every other musician—and as most musicians today have not. It should be required reading in every music school. No better idea of performance practice in eighteenth-century music can be attained than from the *Versuch*. And something can be learned from C. P. E. Bach about that all-important word of the eighteenth century: taste.

Today, when we speak of a musician with taste, the general idea is that he does not intrude his own personality heavily on the music. But every age has its own notions of taste, and in the eighteenth century taste was precisely the opposite: the ability of the musician to intrude his own personality—his technique, his style, his musicianship—on what he was playing, whether or not it was music of his own composition. But there had to be limits, and the taste of a musician was judged accordingly. If he really created something of his own, based on the skeleton of the notes in front of him, he had good taste. If he exceeded the limits of his responsibilities, overindulging in stupid or vapid or uninventive display work, his taste was suspect.

Sensitive musicians of the eighteenth century, just as sensitive musicians do today, pondered deeply over the problem. This problem was all the more acute two hundred years ago, for the performer had much more leeway. There was leeway in how to realize a figured bass. There was even more leeway in the execution of the ornaments that played such an important part in baroque and rococo music. Indeed, the proper execution of these hundreds of ornaments poses one of the most irritating problems of modern musical scholarship. Signs and other indications for ornaments varied from country to country, and not only were they played differently from country to country but there is also good reason to believe that musicians from city to city had different ideas about how ornaments should be played. J. S. Bach himself wrote out some of his ornaments as a guide, and every instruction book up to the romantic period contained page after page describing and explaining ornaments. "Embellishments and their execution form a large part of good taste," wrote C. P. E. Bach.

In addition to the leeway granted by the notes themselves, the eighteenth century made it not only customary but mandatory for a performer to add his own ornaments and cadenzas. Today, for instance, a fermata over a note means a hold. In the eighteenth century it was an invitation for the performer to take off on his own. Dussek, in 1799, wrote, "It is an unmeasured pause or suspension," which is meant "to give the principal performer only an opportunity of dwelling upon that note over which it is marked, or to introduce voluntary graces, evolutions, agreeable to his taste and fancy." And C. P. E. Bach, in the foreword to his *Sechs Sonaten fürs Clavier mit veränderten Reprisen* (1760) has this to say:

Variation when passages are repeated is indispensable today. It is expected of every performer. The public demands that practically every idea be repeatedly altered, sometimes without investigating whether the structure of the piece or the skill of the performer permits such alteration. It is this embellishing alone, especially if it is coupled with a long and sometimes bizarrely ornamented cadenza, that often squeezes the bravos out of most listeners. How lamentably are those two adornments of performance misused! One no longer has the patience to play the written notes [even] for the first time. The absence of bravos is unbearable.

How well the performer extemporized on the ground plan determined his taste. But, as might have been expected, the egocentric little wheels of the virtuoso mind went wild when faced with such rich opportunities. C. P. E. Bach, like all other authorities, pleaded for restraint:

A prodigal use of embellishments must be avoided. Regard them as spices which may ruin the best dish, or geegaws which may deface the most perfect building. Notes of no great importance, and those sufficiently brilliant in themselves, should remain free of them, for embellishments serve only to increase the weight and import of notes, and to differentiate them from others. Otherwise I would commit the same error as orators who try to place an impressive accent on every word; everything would be alike and completely unclear.

Human nature being what it is, performers paid no attention to the pleas of such rational and tasteful musicians as C. P. E. Bach. The eighteenth-century freedom died hard, nor is it completely extinct. Throughout the early part of the nineteenth century, the virtuoso still remained lord, and very few instrumentalists played the notes exactly as written. Nor did singers, always more of a law unto themselves than other musical brigands, bother much with the printed note. Gluck had tried to stop this anarchy in his famous operatic reforms. "I did not think it my duty...to end the aria where its sense may not perhaps end in order to make it convenient for a singer desiring to show that he can vary a phrase capriciously in a number of ways." This, in deep disgust, from the preface to *Alcestis* (1767). But in 1816 the violinist-composer-conductor Louis Spohr complained about a soprano in Florence named Signora Georgi, who sang an aria from Rossini's *Tancredi* very well but who, at the recapitulation of the main theme, "embellished it so outrageously that the tune itself was unrecognizable." And, speaking of Italian orchestras, Spohr noted that "nuances of *piano* and *forte* are unknown to them. Even with this, however, one can make do. But each one [player] makes his own embellishments according to his own dictates, with the result that the sound resembles that of an orchestra tuning up rather than a coordinated performance." In 1819 Spohr heard the celebrated Alexander Boucher play the first violin in a Haydn quartet. Boucher "added so many inappropriate and tasteless embellishments that it was impossible for me to have any pleasure from it."

This was anarchy, but it seems to have been the mode of the day; and the chances are that were we to hear a Mozart symphony as it was played by an average orchestra in his own day, we would find it absolutely unrecognizable. It is interesting that C. P. E. Bach, alarmed by the irresponsibility of most performers, made a plea for composers to notate their music more accurately. (Yet Johann Adolph Scheibe in 1737 had attacked J. S. Bach for the very thing that C. P. E. was advocating: for writing his music too thoroughly and hence leaving no leeway for the performer. "Every ornament," mourned Scheibe, "every little grace, and everything that one thinks of as belonging to the method of playing, he expresses completely in notes.") Composers, said C. P. E., "act wisely who in notating their works include terms, in addition to tempo indications, which help clarify the meaning of a piece."

This was sadly needed. J. S. Bach's music, Scheibe notwithstanding, had virtually nothing in the way of tempo or dynamic markings, and long stretches ensue with no clue to the expression. All composers up to Beethoven were chary of markings. Beethoven, however, really made up for lost time, and some of his directions are so explicit as to be not only unheard of in their time but in all future times (almost). Instead of the previous curt *grave*, *andante* or *allegro*, he went in for markings like *allegro con brio ed appassionato*, or *un poco meno andante ciò è un poco più adagio come il tema*, or *Mit lebhaftigkeit und durchaus mit Empfindung und Ausdruck*. Beethoven, indeed, took a downright unreasonable view of performances of his music: he expected the notes to be played as written, with nothing added and nothing taken away. He once gave his pupil Carl Czerny a bad time for not following the music, blowing up but apologizing the next day. "You must forgive a composer who would rather have his work performed exactly as it was written, however beautifully you played it in other respects." Another Beethoven pupil, Ferdinand Ries, says that only twice did Beethoven allow him to add his own notes to a composition—to the Rondo of the *Pathétique* Sonata and the Rondo of the C major Concerto, where Beethoven let Ries play a few passages in double notes for added brilliance. Ries reports that Beethoven himself seldom added notes or even ornaments. It is interesting that the only other composer-pianist who expressed himself with equal vehemence on the necessity of fidelity to the printed note was Mozart.

Yet even Beethoven, when faced with the practical necessities of performance and publication, could bend his principles. He was worried about the length and difficulty of the *Hammerklavier* Sonata, and wrote to Ries, "Should the sonata not be suitable for London, I could send another one; or you could omit the Largo and begin straight away with the Fugue, which is the last movement; or you could use the first movement and then the Adagio, and then for the third movement the Scherzo—and omit entirely No. 4 with the Largo and Allegro Risoluto. Or you could take just the first movement and the Scherzo and let them form the whole sonata. I leave it to you to do what you think best."

By Beethoven's time there were pianists who, for the first time in history, started looking into works of composers other than themselves. In the middle half of the eighteenth century that almost never happened. Among other things, there were not too many professional pianists around. C. P. E. Bach and his brother Johann Christian were among the first to begin to play the piano in public. There were a few others, a surprising number of them women— Franziska von Auenbrugger, Caroline von Greiner, Barbara Ployer and Josephine Aurnhammer (Mozart had something to say about those two), the blind Therese von Paradis, Julie Candelle. There was very little literature for them. Not that it mattered much, for it was to be many years before a pianist played anything but his or her own compositions in public. When a Mozart, Clementi or Beethoven was the pianist, fortunate was the public. Otherwise pianists came and went, playing their own trumpery concertos and variations, waltzes, potpourris, battle pieces, Janizary music.

Nor was the institution of the public concert yet widespread. That did not come until much later. Public concerts probably started in England. During the early seventeenth century, Ben Jonson complained because he thought music and dancing at the drama attracted more attention, and more customers, than his plays. When the Puritans took over, music did not cease, as many believe. Church music suffered a decline, but secular music flourished in the taverns, and some of the "concerts" attracted good performers. The Banister concerts in London and those of the Tonkünstlersocietat in Vienna started in the same year, 1672. John Banister was an English violinist who got the epochal idea of charging admittance to concerts, for "a shilling a head, and call for what you please." His first advertisement ran in the London *Gazette* of December 30, 1672:

These are to give notice that at Mr. John Banister's house, now called the Musick-School, over against the George Tavern in White Friars, the present Monday, will be musick performed by excellent masters beginning precisely at four of the clock in the afternoon, and every afternoon in the future, precisely at the same hour.

Samuel Pepys describes a good deal of public musical activity in his diary; and in 1678 Thomas Britton started giving his famous concerts in the loft over his coal store. A contemporary said that "anybody that is willing to take a hearty Sweat may have the Pleasure of hearing many notable performers in the cheering Science of Musick." Handel played there on a Ruckers harpsichord and a small organ. So did his competitor, Pepusch. The famous Leipzig Gewandhaus concerts began in 1743, and the Berlin "Music Exercising Society" in 1749. In Paris there were the Concerts Spirituels, founded as early as 1725 by Anne-Hyacinth Philidor (a man, despite his feminine-sounding name). Audiences consisted largely of professionals and knowledgeable amateurs. It did not take long, however, before the middle class started moving in, all over Europe. Music was leaving the courts and churches. Interest was fed by the emergence of music magazines, music critics, advances in music printing and, above all, by the growing culture consciousness of the middle class, which decided, among other things, that it too wanted to go to concerts.

Early concerts were exhibitions. Emphasis was on the performer, and so great was the novelty that audiences looked on him almost as a freak. (The same may be true today, but at least we make the pretense of saying that the music is the important thing.) And it was unheard-of for a pianist, a violinist, or a singer to give a concert entirely on his own, unaided by other musicians. That was not to come until Liszt. On the whole, concerts until the 1830s followed a fairly regular format. The featured artist made only two or three appearances, playing a concerto, improvising, playing a solo, perhaps accompanying another performer. An overture or some other sort of orchestral piece would start things off. Orchestra in those days could mean anything from five instruments up to the burnished perfection of the great Mannheim ensemble. The chances are that in smaller cities the artist would have to play with a half-dozen or so musicians, often amateurs belonging to the town's music club, who played out of tune and were seldom together. The soloist, of course, played a composition of his own. It is virtually impossible to think of a pianist or a violinist before the 1850s who was not a composer. As a gesture toward a local compositional celebrity, the artist might play a concerto or a group of works not his own. Mozart in 1783 writes to his father giving the details of a program he gave in Vienna. It was typical:

(1) The new *Haffner* Symphony [which Mozart conducted from the clavier].
(2) Madame Lange sang the aria "Se il padre perdei" from my Munich opera [*Idomeneo*], accompanied by four [!] instruments.
(3) I played the third of my subscription concertos [in C, K. 415].
(4) Adamberger sang the scena [K. 369] which I composed for Countess Baumgarten.
(5) The short concertante symphonie from my last *Finalmusik* [K. 320].
(6) I played my Concerto in D major [K. 175] which is such a favorite here, and of which I sent you the rondo and variations.
(7) Mlle. Teiber sang the scena "Parto, m'affretto" out of my last Milan opera [*Lucio Silla*].
(8) I played alone a short fugue (because the Emperor was present) and then variations from an opera called *Die Philosophen*, which were encored. So I played variations on the air "Unser dummer Pöbel meint" from Gluck's *Pilgrimme von Mekka*. [Mozart doubtless improvised the fugue and variations.]
(9) Madame Lange sang my new rondo [K. 416].
(10) The last movement of the first symphony [i.e., a repeat of the finale of the *Haffner*].

In 1770 Mozart, on tour with his father in Italy, gave an exhibition (for it was an exhibition rather than a concert, even though it was "reviewed") at the Reale Accademia in Mantua. At the Accademia there were several professional musicians, and they prepared the program. First one of the boy's symphonies was played. Then he was soloist in a piano concerto that he had to read at sight from manuscript. Then he was supplied with a solo sonata which he not only had to read at sight but also supply with variations; and, that done, he had to transpose the work to another key. Then he had to compose an aria on the spot, to words given him, sing it himself and accompany himself on the clavier. Following this, the concertmaster of the orchestra gave Mozart a theme, and Mozart had to improvise a sonata from it. Then he had to improvise a strict fugue. Then he had to play the violin in a trio. Finally he conducted, from the cla-vier, one of his own symphonies. Mozart was fourteen years old at the time. A few years later he was to be instrumental in launch-ing the piano on its decisive career. He was the first of the great pianists.

It Should Flow Like Oil

AT THE AGE OF THREE he was picking at the harpsichord—not aimlessly, as most babies would, but carefully selecting thirds and other consonances. This amused him for hours at a time. At four he was studying little minuets. At five he was composing them. His ear was so accurate that it was bothered by quarter tones and so delicate that the close-up sound of a trumpet made him faint dead away. At six he was taken from Salzburg by his father, an eminent violinist, teacher, theoretician and all-around musician, on his first tour. Then tour followed tour. So was spent the childhood of Wolfgang Amadeus Mozart.

He did not give concerts as we understand the term. His father, a curious combination of knowledge and greed, merely put him (along with his sister Maria Anna, his elder by five years and also an accomplished clavierist) on exhibition as a prodigy. And what a prodigy! The child apparently could do everything without being taught. He could play string instruments, and improvise, and compose, and fluently play any keyboard instrument, and name any combination of notes on hearing them struck. Father Leopold was not bashful about exploiting his boy. He spread his fame throughout Europe. In the process he came close to breaking the child's spirit, and the constant traveling could not have been good for his health. Mozart grew up resenting his father, and—although the biographies and history books do not mention it—one of the reasons he was so eager to leave Salzburg for good was to escape parental domination. Of course, there was the Archbishop of Salzburg, whom Mozart cordially hated. But there was, more than anything else, the love-hate between Mozart and his father. When studied in the light of twen-

The six-year-old Mozart, painted by an unknown artist. The little man was already becoming a veteran of the concert stage.

The Mozart family in 1779. Wolfgang and his sister Nannerl are at the keyboard. Leopold Mozart holds the violin, and his wife, Anna Maria, gazes from the wall.

PAINTING BY NEPOMUK DE LA CROCE

NEW YORK PUBLIC LIBRARY

tieth-century psychiatry, the many letters that passed between father and son make chilling reading. Some day a competent psychiatrist versed in music will turn his attention to them.

As a child, Mozart played mostly the harpsichord, clavichord and organ. It was not until his trip to Paris in 1778, at the age of twenty-one, that he began to concentrate on the piano (although he surely had previously achieved a good working knowledge of it). He went to Mannhein in 1777; his mother had reported back to her husband that Wolfgang was making a big impression. "But he plays very differently than he does at Salzburg, because here they have pianofortes everywhere and he knows how to handle these so incomparably that nobody has ever heard the like; in one word, everybody who hears him says his equal is not to be found." From this year, 1777, Mozart concentrated on the piano, even though he retained his clavichord and continued to use it (along with the piano) in his own home. All of his post-1777 keyboard music was conceived for the piano—which means most of the sonatas and all of the concertos beginning with K. 414. (That is the consensus of most scholars, though A. Hyatt King, an eminent authority, thinks that Mozart had switched earlier, in 1774. King makes a very good case for his thesis.)

But, even before arriving in Paris, Mozart had been experimenting with the piano. En route, he and his mother dropped off in Augsburg, where he tried out some of Stein's pianos. Johann Andreas Stein had come up with several new concepts about the action of a piano, and they met with Mozart's full approval, as expressed in the famous letter to his father of October 17–18, 1777:

This time I shall begin at once with Stein's pianofortes. Before I had seen any of his make, Späth's claviers had always been my favorites. But now I prefer Stein's, for they damp ever so much better than the Regensburg instruments. When I strike hard, I can keep my finger on the note or raise it, but the sound ceases the moment I have produced it. In whatever way I touch the keys, the tone is always even. It never jars, it is never stronger or weaker or entirely absent; in a word, it is always even. . . . His instruments have this special advantage over the others that they are made with escape action. Only one maker in a hundred bothers about this. But without an escapement it is impossible to avoid jangling and vibration after the note is struck. When you touch the keys, the hammers fall back again the moment after they have struck the strings, whether you hold down the keys or release them. He [Stein] himself told me that when he has finished making one of these claviers, he sits down to it and tries all kinds of passages, runs and jumps, and he polishes and works away at it until it can do anything. For he labors only in the interest of music and not for his own profit; otherwise he would be finished almost immediately. He often says: "If I myself were not such a passionate lover of music and had not myself some slight skill on the clavier, I should long ago have lost patience with my work. But I do like an instrument which never lets the player down and which is durable." And his claviers really do last. He guarantees that the sounding-board will neither break nor split. When he has finished making one for a clavier, he places it in the open air, exposing it to rain, snow, the heat of the sun and all hell, in order that it may crack. Then he inserts wedges and glues them in to make the instrument very strong and firm. He is delighted when it cracks, for he can then be sure that nothing more can happen to it. Indeed, he often cuts into it himself and then glues it together and strengthens it in this way. He has finished making three pianofortes of this kind. . . . At four o'clock the Kapellmeister turned up and so later on did Herr Schmittbauer, organist at St. Ulrich, a nice, oily old gentleman. There I just played at sight a sonata by Beecke, which was rather hard and *miserabile al solitó* [miserable as usual]. Really I cannot describe the amazement of the Kapellmeister and the organist, who kept crossing themselves. Here and at Munich I have played all my six sonatas by heart several times. . . . The last one, in D [K. 284], sounds exquisite on Stein's pianoforte. The device too which you work with your knee is better on his than on other instruments. I have only to touch it and it works; and when you shift your knee the slightest bit, you do not feel the least reverberation.

If nothing else, this letter shows that Mozart knew the piano not only as a pianist. He was fascinated with its construction and knew a good deal about it. Also he evidently liked Stein the man as much as he liked Stein's pianos. The knee device to which he refers is the pedal. English pianos already had pedals where they are today, but it took some years before foot pedals became standard in Germany and Austria. Stein charged quite a bit for his pianos, and that is one reason Mozart did not get one. His father probably would not have allowed it. He answered Wolfgang's letter with, among other things, a comment that he was glad that Herr Stein's pianos were so good, "but indeed they are expensive." The piano that Mozart finally owned was made by Anton Walter of Vienna, around 1784. It had no pedals, but Walter built for Mozart a pedal attachment, operated by the foot and not the knee. Its range was around five octaves—F sharp below low C in the bass, to E in the octave above high C.

The piano developed in quantum leaps after Mozart's death, and the instrument favored by the romantics was much stronger, with a much wider range, than Mozart's five-octave toy. At least, nineteenth-century pianists, being anything but historically minded, would have considered it a toy. Today we think differently. Shortly after World War II, a few pianists—notably Paul Badura-Skoda, Jörg Demus and Virginia Pleasants—started collecting instruments of Mozart's and early Beethoven's day and even making records on them. But the big emphasis, the "authentic instrument" movement, did not flower until the 1970s.

Mozart's instrument is now called the fortepiano, presumably to distinguish it from today's grand pianoforte. It is beginning to become commonplace to hear music of the classic period played on authentic instruments. That means the fortepiano. It means violins with gut strings and a lower bridge, no chin rest and a bow of the period. It means valveless horns and winds. It means pitches about a half-tone lower.

It also means a reorientation on the part of those who have been brought up listening to music of the classic period being played on modern instruments. Hearing a Mozart concerto on a real eighteenth-century instrument, or a copy thereof, is a new aural experience. Textures sound thinner and clearer. The actual technique sounds more natural. The music suddenly has an elegance and proportion that no modern instruments can give. But, unfortunately, the movement has attracted some artists primarily interested in staking out a fashionable area. Not blessed with imagination or, sometimes, even professional techniques, they manage to make the music sound metronomic and dull.

From Mozart's letters there emerges a significant amount of detail about his keyboard approach. Unlike Beethoven, Mozart spelled out specifically what he thought about good and bad piano playing. And, again unlike Beethoven (whose deafness cut his playing short), Mozart continued as a virtuoso to his death in 1791 at the age of thirty-six. Mozart was as well known throughout Europe as a virtuoso as he was as a composer. Even if he was buried in a pauper's grave, it was not for lack of acclaim or lack of appreciation of his worth. Not only did such colleagues as Joseph Haydn acclaim him as the greatest musician in Europe; the connoisseurs, by and large, and also the public were well aware of that fact. Why Mozart failed to capitalize on it is another story. This aspect of Mozart's life has never been thoroughly investigated. Modern researchers suspect that Mozart made a great deal of money, but that he and his wife, Constanza, were poor money-managers and frittered it away. It is true that Mozart died in poverty. It is also true that in the months preceding his death he kept servants, a coach and horses, and sent Constanza to a spa.

As a pianist Mozart was not the fiery kind of virtuoso that his competitor Clementi was. Before the public, Clementi was pianist first, musician second. Mozart was musician first, pianist second. He insisted on naturalness—in playing, in interpretation, in posture at the keyboard. When he heard the daughter of one Hamm, in Augsburg (1777), he was greatly disturbed by the way she held her hand. "She undoubtedly must have a gift for music, as she has been studying only three years and yet can play several pieces really well. But I find it difficult to give you an idea of the impression she makes on me when she is playing. She seems to me so curiously affected. She stalks over the clavier with her long fingers in such an odd way. . . . She has made me laugh a great deal already at her expense." (That refrain in Mozart's letters, "laugh a great deal," or "I could have died laughing," comes up again and again, more and more unpleasantly each time. After a while, one cringes. Mozart could be impatient, arrogant and, to put it mildly, supercilious. Whenever he writes "I could have died laughing," something rather nasty is sure to follow. Even if he was Mozart, the greatest natural genius music has produced—or perhaps *because* he was Mozart?—he was always ready to "die laughing" at some unfortunate less gifted, instead of feeling compassion. He was not a good colleague, and seldom had a good word to say about a fellow musician.)

The Hamm girl was not the only one who excited Mozart's laughter in Augsburg. He reports home that he played his *Strassburg* Concerto (K. 218), "which went like oil. Everybody praised my beautiful, pure tone." Then he reminisces about Stein's eight-year-old daughter, Maria Anna. She was a prodigy who grew up to marry Johann Andreas Streicher, the piano-manufacturer; and she became a close friend of Beethoven. Mozart goes into great detail describing the child's playing:

Anyone who sees and hears her play and can keep from laughing must, like her father, be made of stone. [*Stein* in German means "stone."] For instead of sitting in the middle of the clavier, she sits right up opposite the treble, as it gives her more chance of flopping about and making grimaces. She rolls her eyes and smirks. When a passage is repeated, she plays it more slowly the second time. If it has to be played a third time, then she plays it even more slowly. When a passage is being played, the arm must be raised as high as possible, and according as the notes in the passage are stressed, the arm, not the fingers, must therefore do this, and that too, with great emphasis and clumsy manner. But the best joke of all is that when she comes to a passage that ought to flow like oil [this phrase, "flow like oil," occurs again and again in Mozart's letters] and which necessitates a change of finger, she does not bother her head about it, but when the moment arrives she just leaves out the notes, raises her hand and starts off again quite comfortably—a method by which she is much more likely to strike a wrong note.... She may succeed, for she has great talent for music. But she will not make progress by this method, for she will never acquire great rapidity, since she definitely does all she can to make her hands heavy. Further, she will never acquire the most essential, the most difficult and the chief requisite in music, which is rhythm, because from her earliest years she had done her utmost not to play in time. Herr Stein and I have discussed the point for two hours at least, and I have almost converted him, for now he asks my advice on everything. He used to be quite crazy about Beecke [Ignaz von Beecke (1733–1803), composer and clavierist]; but now he sees and hears that I am the better player; that I do not make grimaces and yet play with such expression that, as he himself confesses, no one up to the present has been able to get such good results out of his pianofortes. Everyone is amazed that I can always keep strict time. What these people cannot grasp is that in tempo rubato in an adagio, the left hand should go on playing in strict time. With them the left hand always followed suit. Count Wolfegg and several other passionate admirers of Beecke publicly admitted at a concert the other day that I had wiped the floor with him.

This letter is revelatory. From it we learn that Mozart sat quietly at the middle of the keyboard and played without making faces. We learn that he never changed tempo in repeated sections of a piece (though, the chances are, he made some kind of variation; for if he didn't, he was the only pianist of his age who didn't). We learn that he did not like the arm to be raised, and that he favored a light wrist with the fingers always in close contact with the keys.

From all this, one can see that Mozart's playing illustrated the classic ideal. It did not have extreme dynamics. Rather it was temperate, regulated, and had a legato that "flowed like oil." He prided himself on his tone and his technical accuracy; no "leaving out notes" for him. He could play fast when he wanted to. Above all, he had flawless rhythm. Judging from his remarks about the Stein girl's lack of rhythmic stability, it is easy to see the importance he attached to it. And he used rubato when playing slow movements. If what he says is to be taken at face value, he maintained the basic pulse in the left hand and varied it in the right, rather than lose the entire metric by allowing left hand and right hand to vary the pulse simultaneously. In actual practice, Mozart's stricture would be difficult to apply. What he probably did was make rhythmic displacements without ever losing the basic metrical pulse; and the chances are that he gave his left hand a little more leeway than he admitted. But in any case rhythm was always observed.

Mozart probably had a very precise and literal mind, and in his piano playing there must have been no room for evasion or taking the easy way out. He sends his sister some of his sonatas and enjoins her "to play them with plenty of expression, taste and fire, and to learn them by heart." But, above all, they must be played "with the proper precision." Speaking of Rosa Cannabich, one of his Mannheim pupils, to whom he was teaching one of his sonatas, he mentions that "if I were her regular teacher I would lock up all her music, cover the keys with a handkerchief and make her practice, first with the right hand and then with the left, nothing but scales, trills, mordents and so forth, very slowly at first, until each hand should be properly trained." Insecure training and faulty technique aroused his contempt, especially when encountered in the playing of an experienced musician. In 1778 he listened to the famous Abt Vogler reading through one of his, Mozart's, concertos. His remarks to his father were altogether blunt:

He took the first movement prestissimo, the Andante allegro, and the Rondo even more prestissimo. He generally played the bass quite differently from the way it was written, inventing now and then quite another harmony and melody. Nothing else is possible at such a tempo, for the eyes cannot see the music nor the hands perform it. Well, what good is it? That kind of sight-reading and shitting are all one to me. . . . Well, you may easily imagine that it was unendurable. At the same time I could not bring myself to say to him, *Far too quick!* Besides, it is much easier to play a thing quickly than slowly: in difficult passages you can leave out a few notes without anybody noticing it. But is that beautiful music? In rapid playing the right and left hands can be changed without anybody seeing or hearing it; but is that beautiful? And wherein consists the art of playing *prima vista?* In this: in playing the piece in the tempo in which it ought to be played, and in playing all the notes, appoggiaturas and so forth, exactly as they are written and with the appropriate expression and taste, so that you might suppose that the performer had composed it himself. Vogler's fingering, too, is wretched. His left thumb is just like that of the late Adlgasser [Anton Adlgasser (1729–1777), Salzburg composer and clavierist; Mozart succeeded him as court organist] and he does all the treble runs downward with thumb and first finger of his right hand.

Poor Vogler used the old pre–C. P. E. Bach style of fingering. Mozart had long discontinued it, if indeed he ever did use it. The chances are he didn't. Aside from Mozart's violent and even scatological attack on Vogler, the letter is interesting as still another indication of Mozart's sane approach to the keyboard. His idea when playing was to translate the notes exactly as written and, as he says, "with the appropriate expression and taste." And, of course, accuracy. Mozart could think of no greater compliment to pay his sister than to tell people that she played with greater precision than he: most interesting, if true. In any case there can be no doubt that Mozart was a disciplined pianist who took his musical responsibilities with the utmost pride and seriousness, who could play with unusual virtuosity when he wanted to, but was more on the lookout for musical values.

The word "taste" crops up in Mozart's letters even more frequently than "like oil." Taste is that eighteenth-century word, so difficult to pin down. Every musician who assaulted the muse did so in the name of "taste." But whatever it was, we can be assured that Mozart, with his patrician musical mind, had it to a greater degree than anybody in his period. He abhorred cheap effect, and his playing must have been a model of imaginative musicianship. His singing tone was admired by all who heard him, and his powers in improvisation left everybody speechless. Naturally, like all musicians of the day, he made considerable embellishments when he played his own (and other people's) music. This does not contradict Mozart's remarks in the Vogler letter about playing the notes exactly as they are written. Mozart would never have changed the harmonic or melodic sense, and he *would* have played the notes as they were set down. Then he would have amplified on them "with the appropriate expression and taste," to quote from the letter once more. No less was expected of any eighteenth-century virtuoso.

Mozart's sight-reading and improvisation naturally were a cause for comment among his fellow musicians. Wrote Ambrose Rieder, an Austrian composer, "I cannot describe my astonishment when I happened to be so fortunate as to hear the immortal Wolfgang Amadeus Mozart playing before a large company of people. Not only did he vary with great skill what he was playing, but he extemporized as well. I had never run across anything so great or so wonderful." Franz Niemetschek, Karl Ditters von Dittersdorf, Johann Friedrich Rochlitz and others who heard Mozart back up Rieder's remarks. The chances are that Mozart never played any of his compositions twice the same way. Indeed, we have his word for it. In 1783 he wrote home that whenever he played his D major Concerto (K. 175), "I always play what occurs to me at the moment." And, like many musicians of the time, he was reluctant to allow his manuscripts to be generally circulated for fear they would be copied, imitated and plagiarized. Once he sold his music to a publisher—and with Mozart that did not happen too often—the music was of course out of his control. But until that event for which he was paid, nobody was likely to get a close look at his scores. (Paganini, later on, would distribute the orchestral parts of his concertos only at the moment of performance and collect them immediately afterward. One shudders to think of what the accompaniments must have sounded like.)

The art of improvisation, or extemporization, has virtually vanished among serious musicians (in the twentieth century it popped up in jazz). Mozart must have been very good at it. Improvisation is the art of thinking and performing music simultaneously. Once music is notated, it ceases to be an improvisation. The better the quality of the musical mind, and the stronger the technique, naturally the better the improvisation. Beethoven was the first, in his *Emperor* Concerto, to write out a cadenza, for example; up to that time a soloist in a concerto was expected to improvise a cadenza on the spot. At every concert there was a section devoted to improvisations, in which soloists were presented with themes to work into a potpourri or subjects on which to create a fugue on the spot (*that* is hard). Naturally any pianist would have at his command a series of formulae to cover all contingencies. The diminished seventh chord, for example, lies naturally in the hand and is very easy to arpeggiate. Improvisers always have been able to make an enormous impression with it, sweeping grandly up and down the keyboard; the effect sounds infinitely more difficult than it actually is. Could it be that Mozart's piano fantasias in C (K. 394) and C minor (K. 396), with their rambling organization and cascades of diminished sevenths, are written-out improvisations? The chances are likely; and in addition those two pieces are so superior to anything written at the time that one can understand the excitement and awe of Mozart's contemporaries. Another indication that they may be written-out improvisations is in the nature of the pianistic style they employ—much more "pianistic" than almost anything in the concertos and sonatas. Which leads to the supposition that while playing his own music, Mozart would have used a much more lavish and virtuosolike technique than indicated by the printed notes that have come down to us. It is generally accepted that some of Mozart's manuscripts, such as the slow movement of the *Coronation* Concerto, exist only in skeletal form. What would one not give to have heard Mozart in his C minor or G major Concerto, playing with the impeccable clarity and rhythm, and the "taste," that were the despair of his competitors!

As it happened, the path that piano virtuosity was to take diverged from the Mozart ideal. Nobody disputed his greatness, but it was the playing of Clementi and Beethoven that was to prepare for the Liszts and Tausigs of the nineteenth century. Mozart's playing was, a few years after his death, considered beautiful but old-fashioned, correct but lacking in drama. New winds were sweeping Europe. It was drama and sheer virtuosity that the new school, with its bigger and more sonorous instruments, strove for. Carl Czerny claimed that Beethoven told him Mozart's touch was "neat and clean, but rather empty, flat and antiquated." In existence is a Beethoven conversation book in which Karl Holz asked the deaf titan about Mozart. This was in 1825. "Was Mozart a good piano player?" Holz wrote down on the pad. Beethoven must have sounded off at some length. Holz then wrote (apologetically, one feels), "Well, [the piano] was still in its cradle then."

Not only was the piano in its cradle. So were piano technique and concepts of phrasing. Now, Mozart was proud of his legato, his "oil-like" legato. (Legato is the binding together of consecutive notes, so that there is no audible break between them.) But what many twentieth-century pianists and even scholars do not realize is that in Mozart's day most passages were *not* played legato unless specifically marked. It was not until the beginning of the nineteenth century that, thanks to Clementi, Beethoven and John Cramer, legato playing as currently practiced came into being. Everything written after those three was then played legato unless otherwise marked. Every eighteenth-century musician, though, took pains to point out that legato playing occupied only a small part of the pianist's lexicon. C. P. E. Bach, in his *Versuch*, wrote that "notes which are neither staccato nor legato"—and those would be the larger part of any composition—"are held for half their value unless the word *Ten.* [*tenuto*] is placed over them." Friedrich Wilhelm Marpurg, one of the important theorists of the day, wrote in his *Anleitung zum Klavierspielen* (1765), "In contrast to legato and staccato there is the ordinary manner of playing, in which the finger is lifted from the key just before the following note is played. This ordinary manner of playing, since it is always taken for granted, is never marked." And Daniel Gottlob Türk, in his famous *Klavierschule* (1789), has this to say, "When playing notes in the ordinary manner, that is, neither staccato nor legato, the finger should be lifted shortly before the written value of the notes requires it."

Most eighteenth-century pianists—and there is no reason to suppose Mozart was any different—so played; and legato playing was the exception rather than the rule. Clementi was probably the first pianist who instituted the style that has since held good. He broke away completely from eighteenth-century notions of binding notes together only when specifically marked, and in 1803, when he had virtually finished playing in public, he wrote in his *Art of Playing the Piano Forte*, "The best rule is to keep down the keys of the instrument the FULL LENGTH of every note." The capitals are Clementi's. Obviously he had not come to this decision overnight. He was consciously trying to demolish the old style; and he did so. His keyboard style almost immediately swept Mozart's away (though the classic style lingered through Hummel and even pianists like Julius Epstein in the latter part of the nineteenth century).

As early as 1798—Mozart had been dead but seven years—Beethoven was immersed in the new style. He drew Czerny's attention to it. "And above all," Czerny writes in his reminiscences, "he drew my attention to the legato, which he himself mastered in so incomparable a manner, and which at that time all other pianists considered impracticable, as it was still the fashion (dating from Mozart's time) to play in an abrupt, clipped manner." *Sic transit....* Beethoven got his ideas from Clementi, a pianist Mozart simply abhorred. And for good reason. For Mozart, prince of pianists, had met Clementi in open battle in 1781 and may have been bested. Certainly the fury of his letters about the encounter attests to Clementi's strength. Mozart did not "die laughing" here. He was very much disturbed, and the match sent both musicians home with something to think about. But it was Clementi who was riding the wave of the future.

· III ·

Thirds, Sixths, and Octaves

MOZART RAN ACROSS Clementi under rather explosive conditions. The Italian-born English virtuoso, four years Mozart's senior, at that time was not too well known on the Continent. But his reputation had preceded his first European tour in 1780, and Emperor Joseph II arranged for a competition between the greatest Austrian pianist and the greatest pianist outside of Austria. Competitions were plentiful in the eighteenth century, and the early part of the nineteenth, too. Beethoven was in quite a few; and those two great rivals, Liszt and Thalberg, met face to face in the salon of the Princess Belgiojoso. Joseph II was anxious to hear Clementi and pit him against Mozart. The two pianists met early in January of 1781. Clementi told his pupil Ludwig Berger of his initial encounter with Mozart:

I had only been in Vienna a few days when I received an invitation to play before the Emperor on the pianoforte. On entering the music room I beheld an individual whose elegant attire led me to mistake him for an imperial *valet-de-chambre*. But we had no sooner entered into conversation than it turned on musical topics, and we soon recognized in each other, with sincere pleasure, brother artists—Mozart and Clementi.

It must have been quite an evening. Mozart, knowing the quality of the royal instruments, borrowed Countess Thun's piano, a Stein. This he used for his solos. For two-piano playing with Clementi, the Emperor asked Mozart to use the palace instrument; and, as Mozart later reported, it was out of tune and three of the keys were stuck. "That doesn't matter," grandly said His Majesty, with the air of a

51

manager telling his fighter that the boy in the opposite corner can't hurt us.

Clementi led off with an improvised prelude and his Sonata in B flat (Op. 47, No. 2). (Mozart, even though he sneered at Clementi's music, used the opening theme of this sonata in the *Magic Flute* Overture.) Then Clementi followed with one of his specialties, a toccata featuring thirds and other double notes. Now it was Mozart's turn. He too improvised a prelude, and followed with a set of variations. The Grand Duchess produced some sonatas of Paisiello ("wretchedly written out in his own hand," later complained Mozart), and both pianists read them off at sight, Mozart playing the allegros, Clementi the adagios and rondos. Both were asked to select a theme from one of these sonatas, developing it on two pianos. Presumably Mozart would have taken a theme and played it, Clementi noting the harmonies. Then Clementi would have accompanied Mozart on the second piano while Mozart developed his material. And vice versa. It probably ended with a grand two-piano splash, in which all the melodic fragments were woven together.

Victory was left undecided. Tradition says that Clementi won. But an onlooker named Giuseppe Antonio Bridi has left an account of the contest. Bridi says that the Emperor had bet the Grand Duchess that Mozart would excel—and won his bet. A few years later, the eminent composer Karl Ditters von Dittersdorf happened to be talking to Joseph II, and reported the following conversation in his autobiography:

EMPEROR: Have you heard Mozart play?
I: Three times already.
EMPEROR: How do you like him?
I: As any connoisseur must like him.
EMPEROR: Have you heard Clementi?
I: Yes, I have.
EMPEROR: Some people prefer him to Mozart, among them Greybig, *à la tête*. ["Greybig" was Franz Kreibach, violinist and conductor in Joseph's orchestra.] What is your opinion? Be honest.
I: Clementi's way of playing is art alone. Mozart's is art and taste.
EMPEROR: That's just what I said. . . .

After the competition, Clementi was very generous. He spoke with admiration of Mozart's singing touch and exquisite taste. Mo-

Muzio Clementi in 1794, at the height of his powers. Clementi, who shook Mozart with his unprecedented virtuosity, created the modern school of piano playing.

Clementi toward the end of his life, rich and venerated.

zart was less generous and dismissed his competitor with the kind of
hand wave that Wotan used to dispose of Hunding. His letter of
January 16, 1782, sums up his feeling about Clementi in four sen-
tences. "He is an excellent cembalo player, but that is all. He has
great facility with his right hand. His star passages are thirds. Apart
from that he has not a farthing's worth of feeling; he is a mere
mecanicus." And that was that.

Yet Mozart continued to brood about Clementi, and he unbur-
dened himself to his sister in 1783. He had just been looking over
several of Clementi's sonatas:

Every one who either hears them or plays them must feel that as compositions they are worthless. They contain no remarkable or striking passages
except sixths and octaves. And I implore my sister not to practice these
passages too much, so that she may not spoil her quiet, even touch, and
that her hand may not lose its natural lightness, flexibility and smooth
rapidity. For after all, what is to be gained by it? Supposing that you do play
sixths and octaves with the utmost velocity (which no one can accomplish,
not even Clementi) you only produce an atrocious chopping effect and
nothing else whatsoever. Clementi is a charlatan, like all Italians. He
writes *Presto* over a sonata or even *Prestissimo* and *Alla breve*, and plays it
himself *Allegro* in $\frac{4}{4}$ time. I know this is the case for I have heard him do so.
What he really does well are his passages in thirds; but he sweated over
them day and night in London. Apart from this he can do nothing, absolutely nothing; for he has not the slightest expression or taste, much less
feeling.

But Beethoven was to think differently, and also Brahms, not to
mention many twentieth-century scholars and pianists who have
been studying the Clementi sonatas with great respect. Mozart's
dislike can be traced to two causes. In Clementi he had, for the first
time, met a technician who was in many respects stronger than he.
(Certainly Clementi was the flashier of the two.) And, in addition,
almost everything that Clementi stood for in those days was abhor-
rent to Mozart, who, whatever else he might have been, was a pure
and noble musician. Clementi's showmanship, the extravagance and
technical brilliance of his piano music, his almost romantic modulations (not that Mozart was unadventurous in *his* modulations; but
Clementi's are decidedly romantic and unconventional, and lead
right into Beethoven), all added up to something offensive as far as

Mozart was concerned. In fairness to Mozart, it should be mentioned that Clementi the pianist of 1781 was a far cry from Clementi the pianist of 1790.

Mozart could not learn from Clementi, but Clementi could from Mozart. Most scholars believe that after the 1781 encounter Clementi discovered that there were other things beside technique and that a musician could be better employed than in a ceaseless attempt *pour épater la bourgeoisie*. In later years he studiously avoided mentioning Mozart's name. But Ludwig Berger asked him a quarter of a century later "whether in 1781 he had begun to treat the instrument in his present style. He answered 'no' and added that . . . he had subsequently achieved a more melodic and noble style of performance after listening attentively to famous singers, and also by means of the perfected mechanism of English pianos, the construction of which formerly stood in the way of a cantabile and legato style of playing." Clementi, it must be remembered, had worked only on the brilliant English pianos at the time of his encounter with Mozart. The latter's cantabile style on the more intimate Viennese pianos must have come as a revelation.

The object of Mozart's dislike was born in Rome on January 23, 1752, and developed into one of the most interesting and colorful musicians of the period. Even his childhood had a touch of the *outré* about it. He was adopted—"purchased" might be the better word—by Peter Beckford, a member of the wealthy and eccentric Beckford family. Peter, a member of Parliament, was a cousin of William Beckford, the author of *Vathek*. Somehow the Honorable Peter Beckford talked the Clementi family into letting him bring young Muzio—he was then fourteen—to England. Beckford was a collector and something of a musical connoisseur, and he detected genius in the boy. For several years Clementi remained quietly at the Beckford house in Wiltshire, studying. He did not waste his time. Later in life, in 1820, he told a French writer, J. Amadeé le Froid de Méreaux, something about his daily regimen when a young boy at the Beckford estate:

This is how his life was ordered: he devoted eight hours a day to the harpsichord; and if, because of social obligations which he fulfilled to please Sir Beckford, he was forced to reduce the length of his daily practice, he took note of the deficit and repaid it the following day. Sometimes he was obliged to work twelve or fourteen successive hours in order to remain abreast of the daily regimen he had imposed upon himself. It was the works of Sebastian and Emanuel Bach, of Handel and Scarlatti, that he practiced and studied continually. He did this from two different standpoints: that of finger technique and that of instrumental composition.

Thus, it was a highly trained, disciplined young musician who descended on London in 1773 and created a furor. His concerts at that time were on the harpsichord. Soon afterward he switched permanently to the piano. Except for several concert tours and visits to Europe to sell his pianos (he eventually became a piano manufacturer), Clementi spent all of his time in England. It was the English type of piano, with its resonant sound and carrying power, that helped shape Clementi's style. Until the emergence of Beethoven, Clementi far surpassed all of his contemporaries in dash, boldness, vigor and brilliance. Mozart's playing created great respect, especially among professionals; but Clementi's playing thrilled audiences as Mozart's never did. He has been called the founder of the modern piano school, the Columbus in the domain of piano playing and composition, the father of all technique. In all, he had about a thirty-year career and seldom played during the last twenty-five years of his life (he died in England in 1832). He did not have to play, for he was rich. An educated man, and one with a scientific bent, he started an association with the music-publishing and piano-manufacturing firm of Longman and Broderip in the early 1790s. Later the name was changed to Clementi and Company, and Clementi himself had much to do with the improvement of the action in the instrument he sponsored. In 1802 he went to Europe for several years, taking along with him some of his instruments and a young demonstrator named John Field. Field was his best pupil. The firm prospered.

Clementi's travels took him from Paris to St. Petersburg and Moscow. In Vienna he wanted to call on Beethoven, hoping to do business with the great man. But a certain protocol had to be observed. Who was the more important? Who should make the first step? So, though they knew each other by sight, Clementi and Beethoven did not at that time meet. Often Beethoven and his pupil, Ferdinand Ries, and Clementi and *his* pupil, Alexander Klengel, would dine at opposite tables in The Swan and pretend that neither existed. Naturally the pupils had to do what their masters did. It appears that

Beethoven's first inclination was to rush to Clementi, but his brother was the troublemaker and had told Beethoven that Clementi should visit *him*, not he Clementi. Clementi's friends told him the same: that he, Clementi, was more famous and in addition was the older man. That was in 1807. A few years later, Beethoven and Clementi did get together, with mutual satisfaction, and had some business dealings. Clementi arranged for exclusive rights to Beethoven's music for publication in England. When the negotiations were complete, Clementi wrote to his British partner, F. W. Collard, with some glee, "By a little management and without committing myself, I have at last made a conquest of the haughty beauty, Beethoven."

Clementi was reputed to be a miser. As Benoit-August Bertini, one of his pupils, dryly noted, "In his own home he was most abstemious, but he was very fond of good living in the homes of others." Unlike some musicians, he held on to everything and died a very rich man. He even survived a loss of forty thousand pounds when his factory burned down in 1807. Typical of his determination to amass money were his dealings with Field. When Beckford had brought Clementi to England, Beckford had paid all bills and had taken complete responsibility for Clementi's education. But when Clementi took Field as a pupil, the Irish boy's family had to pay a good sum. He worked in the factory and was called an apprentice. Clementi's avarice was the cause of some amused comment among musicians. Ludwig Spohr ran across Clementi in Russia, and noted in his diary:

In the evening I sometimes accompanied him to his large pianoforte warehouse, where Field was often obliged to play for hours, to display the instruments to the best advantage to the purchasers. . . . Even at that time, many anecdotes of the remarkable avarice of the rich Clementi were related, which had greatly increased in later years when I again met him in London. It was generally reported that Field was kept on very short allowance by his master and was obliged to pay with many privations for the good fortune of having his instruction. I myself experienced a little sample of Clementi's true Italian parsimony, for one day I found teacher and pupil with upturned sleeves engaged at the wash tub, washing their stockings and other linen. They did not suffer themselves to be disturbed, and Clementi advised me to do the same, as washing in St. Petersburg was not only very expensive, but the linen suffered from the method used in washing it.

Miser or not, Clementi was very popular among his colleagues and in his social life. He was, by all accounts, good-natured, well-read, a superb linguist, something of a classical scholar, absent-minded, somewhat careless of his dress, and altogether an attractive personality. He married a woman from Berlin in 1804, but she died in childbirth the following year. In 1811 Clementi found an English bride. He acquired property ("I am a young Italian but an old Englishman," he once said of himself), lived in the country, did much composing and became more English than the local squire. By the time of his death he was considered so much a native of England that he was buried in Westminster Abbey. A pleasant picture of Clementi as an old man is given by Ignaz Moscheles, one of the great pianists of the following generation. Moscheles describes Clementi in his old age, up with the birds, active and alert; and he impressed Moscheles as "one of the most vigorous old fellows of seventy that I ever saw." Once in a while he would sit at the piano with many excuses, saying that he had a stiff hand, the result of falling out of a sled in Russia. But, Moscheles notes, somewhat cattily, "there is a suspicion that his unwillingness is caused by his inability to follow the great progress the bravura style has made since that time." Yet the old man could rise to the occasion when he had to. At a testimonial dinner given for him when he was seventy-six, he was led to the piano. Moscheles was there. "The excitement was great," he writes, "the whole party eagerly listening. Clementi had not been heard for years. He extemporized on a theme from Handel and completely carried us away with his fine playing. His eyes gleamed with youthful fire. . . . What chiefly delighted his audience was the charm and freshness of his modulations in improvisation." Moscheles gives a charming account of a meeting between Clementi and Sir Walter Scott. This was in 1828, at a dinner party in honor of the singer Henrietta Sontag. After dinner Clementi got up and said, "Tonight I should also like to play." There were cheers, and Clementi extemporized "with the freshness of youth, and we listened with intense delight, for Clementi very rarely played before company. You should have seen the ecstasy of those two old men, Scott and Clementi; they shook each other by the hand, flirted in turn with Sontag without seeming jealous of one another."

Clementi always made a great impression with his improvisations, especially among the dilettantes. An anonymous writer in the London *Quarterly Musical Magazine and Review* (1820) describes the occasion on which he was present:

amongst many of the greatest musicians of the day when Clementi was prevailed upon to treat the company with a performance of this description. The inspiration which beamed in his eye, the bard-like enthusiasm with which he swept the keys, and the admirable effects which he produced, astonished and delighted everybody. Dussek was afterwards requested to play, and we remember with pleasure the modest and just reply which he made: "To attempt any thing in that same style would be presumption."

Moscheles, a fine, serious musician, once analyzed what Clementi had brought to the piano. The leading characteristics of the Clementi school, as Moscheles saw it, were "the cultivation of amazing powers of execution, overwrought sentimentality, and the production of the most piquant effects by the most rapid changes from the soft to the loud pedal, or by rhythms and modulations which, if not to be completely repudiated, should only be allowed on the rarest occasions." It was not a school that Moscheles particularly liked—he was of the Viennese school—but he realized that the Clementi style had caught the public fancy and was being taken up by all the younger virtuosos.

As happens to many long-lived creators, Clementi lived long enough to find himself an anachronism. Liszt was startling the world by the time Clementi died, and most musicians looking at the patriarch would be apt to forget his importance—especially as the piano of the 1830s had made inconceivable strides from what it had been in Clementi's heyday, around the turn of the century. At that time—even with all of the then unheard-of power and brilliance he brought to the instrument—the action even of the most rugged English piano was light. Fingers alone could manage it. Clementi had never found it necessary to raise his hands high, as Beethoven had done and as Liszt and all the young pianists were doing. Clementi favored a very quiet hand position, *pace* Moscheles, and from all accounts he never banged. Had he done so, anyway, the piano strings would have constantly been snapping. There is no report of Clementi leaving a trail of broken strings on his travels. On the contrary, he was the one who started the procedure of making his pupils practice with a coin on the back of their hands. The fingers alone should do the work, he would say, and if the coin fell off it was because of a faulty hand position. In the 1830s this was passé, though the coin idea did hang on to the twentieth century in some, one might say, quarters. Yet, quiet hand position and all, Clementi was an amazing virtuoso, and Friedrich Kalkbrenner, one of the great pre-romantic pianists, claimed that Clementi was the most vigorous pianist he had ever heard. Clementi's velocity, the clarity and evenness of his scales, the fullness of his tone, his technical strength (double notes; octave trills in one hand), the taste employed in slow movements—these were epochal, and left competing pianists of the 1780s and early 1790s gasping far behind.

In a way, too, Clementi's music was the first that really exploited the new instrument. Most of Haydn's keyboard works use clavichord and harpsichord rather than piano technique. There is no question that Mozart's concertos are infinitely superior as music to anything Clementi conceived, but there equally is no denying that Clementi wrote more effectively for the keyboard. His series of remarkable piano sonatas was started in 1773, and the pianistic layout in them is surprisingly modern. The music also carries many harmonic anticipations of Beethoven, and it was not for nothing that Beethoven had an extraordinarily high opinion of Clementi. According to Anton Schindler, Beethoven's first biographer, Beethoven assigned to Clementi "the very foremost rank." He considered Clementi's works excellent as practice studies, for the formation of taste, and as "truly beautiful" pieces for performance. In Beethoven's own words, "They who thoroughly study Clementi, at the same time make themselves acquainted with Mozart and other composers; but the converse is not the fact." He recommended Clementi's *School of Piano Playing* to students as late as 1826. "It will certainly produce good results." Beethoven was not the only admirer of Clementi. In her diary entry dated November 11, 1861, Clara Schumann writes that she had "an interesting conversation with Johannes [Brahms] about form. How the old masters had the freest form, while modern compositions move within the stiffest and most narrow limits. He himself emulates the older generation, and Clementi in particular ranks high, in his opinion, on account of his great, free form."

Clementi was a prolific composer, with over twenty symphonies, a hundred sonatas (sixty-four for piano) and a good deal of miscellaneous music. His *Gradus ad Parnassum* was finished in 1817. It originally consisted of a hundred studies covering every aspect of piano technique, and the modern art of piano playing rests on it. Not until the Chopin études was anything significant added. (The *Gradus* today, in most editions, has been edited down to thirty studies.) Clementi also was an important teacher. Among his pupils were Cramer, Kalkbrenner and Field—three of the heroes of the early 1800s. Moscheles worked with Clementi for a while, and so did Giacomo Meyerbeer, Alexander Klengel, Ludwig Berger and Charles Mayer, all important pianists. Meyerbeer was a strong virtuoso, but after the smashing success he made with his operas, he gave up the instrument for good.

In recent years, Clementi has been the object of some research, and his position in the world of music is beginning to be taken much more seriously than it was a generation ago. It is now realized that if Mozart was the first of the great *pianists*, Clementi was the first of the great *virtuosos* and, also, a composer of much more significance than has hitherto been granted him.

· IV ·

In Profile and on the Road

IT HAD TO COME. During the last quarter of the eighteenth century, with the institution of the public concert well on its way and with pianists beginning to capture international attention, the problem insistently asserted itself: how was the pianist to sit while playing before audiences in the concert halls? With his back to them? Facing them? The problem was new and had not previously arisen, for Mozart and Clementi had done nearly all of their playing in salons rather than concert halls. Jan Ladislav Dussek solved the problem once and for all time. He was the first to sit with his right side to the audience. This way two ends were accomplished. Dussek was able to exhibit his noble profile and the bow of the piano; and the raised lid of the instrument could act as a sounding board, throwing tone directly into the auditorium. Johann Wenzel Tomaschek, himself a pianist from Prague and a countryman of Dussek, later was to boast about Dussek's revolutionary achievement. Nobody can take *that* away from him, Tomaschek pointed out and added that all other pianists hastily followed suit, "although they may have no very interesting profiles to exhibit."

Dussek was also the first of the important touring virtuosos. Mozart, after his child prodigy days and his trip to Paris, was active only in Germany and Austria. Clementi, after two tours, stopped playing and settled down to selling his pianos. But the handsome Dussek—*le beau Dussek*, they called him after his first appearance in Paris—constantly was on the move, from France, to England, to Russia. He was a celebrity and a showman, and a good musician and great pianist to boot. By the age of twenty he was racing all over Europe, exhibiting his profile to ecstatic audiences. That was novel

Jan Ladislav Dussek, the first pianist to play with his profile to the audience. In his youth, the profile was considered worth looking at. In later life, *le beau Dussek* became enormously stout.

enough; also novel was his habit of sitting at the piano, spreading a silk handkerchief over his knees and rubbing his hands in his bran-filled coat pockets (those were pre-resin days).

He made an extraordinary impact on audiences and fellow musicians. Tomaschek may have been somewhat prejudiced in his favor, but his account of a Dussek concert in Prague in 1804 sounds honest:

After the few opening bars of his first solo, the public uttered one general *Ah!* There was, in fact, something magical about the way in which Dussek, with all his charming grace of manner, through his wonderful touch, extracted from the instrument delicious and at the same time emphatic tones. His fingers were like a company of ten singers endowed with equal executive powers and able to produce with the utmost perfection whatever their director could require.

Tomaschek was not alone with that kind of rave. François Joseph Fétis, in Paris, described Dussek's appearance as creating a furore. That was in 1808, and Fétis, one of the best critics in Europe, wrote that Dussek's playing eclipsed all that had ever been heard. "The broad and noble style of this artist, his method of *singing* on an instrument which possessed no sustained sounds, the neatness, delicacy and brilliance of his playing in short, procured him a triumph of which there had been no previous example." Another French critic pointed out Dussek's importance to Paris in 1808. Musically it was a bad time there, with charlatanism rather than art predominant. Daniel Steibelt was then the big piano hero in Paris. But "Dussek, one of the creators of the true style of pianoforte playing," swept all before him, including Steibelt and his cheap variations. "It was desirable that a man like Dussek come here and act as a reformer, and so bring the pianoforte back to its real greatness and its true sphere."

Dussek's "singing style" was universally admired, and his rival Kalkbrenner wrote with some reluctance (Kalkbrenner being the conceited man he was) that "no other pianist I ever heard more captivated his audiences." Felix Mendelssohn called him a prodigal, but noted that Dussek never made full use of his natural endowments. If that be true, and it probably is (for Dussek liked the good life rather than the discipline of practicing), Dussek even at half-strength must have been phenomenal.

He was the first pianist fully to investigate the resources of the pedals, and the first who, in his own printed music, actually indicated pedalings. He was also the first to play a six-octave piano in public. That was in London, in 1794, on Broadwood's newly designed instrument. Dussek's fingerings, too, were far in advance of his day, and he anticipated Chopin in his ideas about shifting fingers on the same key without actually striking it, so as to get a pure legato—or, as Dussek explained it, "to hold the vibration and to tie or bind one passage to another." Most of the music he composed is forgotten today, though occasionally a sonata is heard. But his music, while not all of a piece, contains passages of sheer prophetic genius. Figurations and harmonies à la Chopin, Schumann and even Brahms crop up here and there (the 1955 edition of *Grove's Dictionary of Music and Musicians* prints two fascinating examples, one of which is *echt*-Schumann, the other convincingly and idiomatically Brahms).

An idea of Dussek's impact can be obtained from the German critic Ludwig Rellstab, who in his memoirs wrote that Dussek was one of the first European piano celebrities. The favorite pianist in Berlin in 1807 was Friedrich Himmel, says Rellstab, "but far greater and emphatically so was Dussek, both as virtuoso and composer ... whose eminent technical resources afforded a much wider basis for varied development, and who, having accomplished a vast deal more for the elevation of the piano than most of his contemporaries, occupied a position in the musical life of Berlin which is vividly felt even now." Rellstab wrote this in 1850, thirty-eight years after Dussek's death. (Friedrich Himmel, incidentally, has a small place in history through his relations with Beethoven. He was born in 1765 and died in 1814, was the court *Kapellmeister* in Berlin and competed with Beethoven in 1796. Beethoven rudely broke into a Himmel improvisation, after the good *Kapellmeister* had been agitating the keys for some time, to ask when he was going to begin. Himmel, who had been thinking wonders of his performance, started up in a rage, and both musicians became very rude to each other. They subsequently made up. Several months later Himmel wrote Beethoven about the latest invention in Berlin—a lantern for the blind. Beethoven, a very gullible man, went all over Vienna telling everybody about this miracle. When the joke was pointed out he became furious and, characteristically, had no more to do with Himmel.)

Dussek was born in Čáslav, Bohemia, on February 12, 1760. He received a degree in theology in Prague, but he had been making music since he was a child and he decided to concentrate on the piano. It was in Amsterdam that he began his career, but he cut it short to go to Hamburg and study with C. P. E. Bach. From that point his life is a jaunt from country to country—Russia, Lithuania, France, Italy, England (where he remained for twelve years after his debut there in 1790), Germany. He married an English girl, a singer, and they opened a music shop that shortly came to grief. Dussek left his wife and fled to the Continent to escape his creditors. He never saw her again. A lovely story of a princess carrying him away seems to be a myth. But there was no myth about his friendship with Prince Louis Ferdinand of Prussia.

Ferdinand loved music to the point of fanaticism, and he surrounded himself with celebrated virtuosos. He appears to have been something more than an amateur; some of his compositions are thoroughly professional. Beethoven had enough respect for his pianistic ability to place him above Himmel (but we know what he thought of Himmel, so that it may be a small compliment after all), and was reported as saying that he did not consider Ferdinand "anything like a royal or princely performer, but a famous piano player." Between the Prince and Dussek was a close friendship. The violinist Spohr, who stayed at the royal castle in 1805, has described some of the activity that took place there:

Frequently at six o'clock in the morning, Dussek and I were awakened and conducted in dressing gown and slippers to the reception salon, where the Prince was already seated at the piano in yet lighter costume, the heat being then very great, and indeed generally in his shirt and drawers only. Now began the practice and rehearsal of the music that was intended to be played in the evening circles, and because of the zeal of the Prince this frequently lasted so long that in the meantime the salon was filled with bemedalled and bestarred officers.

Ferdinand died a year or so later on the battlefield of Saalfeld. Dussek never got over the loss of his friend. For him he composed a work called *Élégie harmonique*. Life never again was the same, although Dussek easily found new patrons. But in his last years he was no longer *le beau Dussek*. He grew so fat that he seldom got out of bed. To overcome his torpor he experimented with various stimulants and ended up an alcoholic. He died in St. Germain-en-Laye on March 20, 1812.

One of Dussek's biggest rivals after Clementi's retirement was a Clementi pupil, John Baptist Cramer. Though born in Germany in 1771, Glorious John—as he was to be called by worshipful Englishmen—had been brought to England by his parents when he was a year old. It is curious how London, up to the 1830s or so, attracted nearly all the leading European pianists: Clementi, Cramer, Hummel, Dussek, Field, Steibelt, Wölffl, Kalkbrenner. They all worked there, off and on, for many years, often simultaneously. Cramer turned out to be the most classic of the classicists. He was a prodigy, as all great pianists are, made his debut at the age of ten, worked for two years with Clementi, and started touring Europe shortly thereafter. His reputation was enormous, and it was a heightened reputation in that he did not make too many concert appearances, especially on the Continent, during the course of his long life. But the few times he did make the swing, he left behind him a trail of awed admirers. Where Dussek captivated by charm and incipient romanticism, Cramer never relaxed his stringent classicism. The purity and accuracy of his playing, and his clear and direct musical mind, were what impressed. Ries, Beethoven's pupil, quotes his master as saying that Cramer was the only pianist of his time. "All the rest count for nothing." Strong words indeed from the choosy Beethoven. Cramer and Beethoven had met once in competition, and the consensus was that while Beethoven had more power and energy, and was much the better improviser, Cramer's playing was more correct.

Cramer must have been an unusually deft player in his prime. He cultivated evenness of hands, an expressive touch and a superlegato. Technique meant little to him, though he apparently had more than enough to deal with his two favorite composers, Mozart and Bach. Cramer was one of the first pianists to feature on his programs, with a good deal of consistency, music not of his own composition. He himself was, of course, a prolific composer, and his studies are still part of any young pianist's growing up. The smoothness of Cramer's delivery astounded his colleagues, and Moscheles time and again refers to Cramer's fingers "gliding softly from key to key." Charles Salaman, a veteran British pianist, remembered Cramer from his youth as an almost immobile pianist. "It was a

John Baptist Cramer. Beethoven was more impressed by "Glorious John" than by any pianist of the time.

Johann Wenzel Tomaschek. His memoirs contain much information about pianists of the day.

pleasure to watch the easy grace with which John Cramer moved his hands, with bent fingers covering the keys." And Moscheles likened his Mozart to "breathings from the deep South."

It is from Moscheles that we get a pen portrait of Cramer. Moscheles, as a young virtuoso in London, had many dealings with his elder colleague. "Cramer," he wrote, "is exceedingly intellectual and entertaining: he has a sharp satiric vein and spares neither his own nor his neighbor's foibles. . . . He is one of the most inveterate snuff-takers. Good housekeepers maintain that after every visit of the great master, the floor must be cleaned of the snuff he has spilt; while I, as a piano player, cannot forgive him for disfiguring his aristocratic, long, thin fingers, with their beautifully shaped nails, by the use of it and often clogging the action of the keys." Cramer must have used the stuff by the barrel. "Those thin, well-shaped fingers are best suited for legato playing; they glide imperceptibly along from one key to the other, and whenever possible, avoid octave as well as staccato passages. Cramer sings on the piano in such a manner that he almost transforms a Mozart andante into a vocal piece. But I must resent the liberty he takes in introducing his own—and frequently trivial—embellishments." Moscheles' complaint raises the old question of "taste." By the time Moscheles heard Cramer, the latter's ideas about embellishment were old-fashioned. The romantic age was about to get under way.

Cramer lived long enough to be a legend to the romantics—as though Paderewski were still alive and could be persuaded to play once in a while. He died in 1858, and the younger pianists looked on him with a mixture of respect and (being young) amused tolerance. They poked fun, in a good-natured sort of way, at the venerable master. When Liszt was in London in 1841 he played a few duets with Cramer. Liszt was vastly tickled. He called himself the poisoned mushroom and then said deliciously, "and at my side I had my antidote of milk."

The following year Wilhelm von Lenz, that pushy young man and *soi-disant* pianist, heard Cramer in Paris. (After 1832 Cramer had left London to live and teach in Paris; he had played that 1841 duet with Liszt while visiting London.) Von Lenz remembered that he had listened to Cramer in 1829 and had been enraptured. He made an appointment with Cramer, that day in 1842, and waited tremblingly for the sanctified *venerabilis Beda* of pianists. What he found was a conservative old man who did not like what he saw around him. Von Lenz wanted to talk about the present, and Cramer wanted to talk about the past. After dinner, Cramer sat at the piano and played his first three Etudes. Von Lenz was appalled. "It was dry, wooden, harsh, with no *cantilena* in the third one, in D major. . . . The impression I received was painful, extremely painful. Was *that* Cramer? Had the great man lived so long, only to remain so far behind the times?"

But he had. He lived his old age wrapped in his mantle of Mozart and Bach, ostentatiously staying away from the young revolution-aries of the piano. Occasionally a youngster, such as von Lenz, would approach the patriarch. The old man would then inveigh against the modern school—the senseless bravura, the striving for sonority, what he called *la haute gymnastique musicale*. "That music is too strong for my poor eyes, for my senile fingers," he would say. "Formerly piano playing was mighty good [*fort bien*], now it's good and mighty [*bien fort*]."

Other popular pianists of the late eighteenth century were Joseph Gelinek (the Abbé Gelinek), Leopold Kozeluch, Daniel Steibelt and Josef Wölffl. Gelinek, a Bohemian pianist who had also studied for the priesthood and who had been ordained in 1786, is remembered largely because of his encounter with Beethoven. Until the rash young man from Bonn came along, Gelinek was the most popular pianist in Vienna and also a composer of variations that enjoyed a great vogue. Then Beethoven stormed into town. One day Gelinek told the father of the young Carl Czerny that he, Gelinek, was going to have a pianistic duel that night with an unknown pianist. "I'll fix him!" Next day the elder Czerny asked Gelinek how it had turned out. But let Carl Czerny tell the story:

Gelinek looked quite crestfallen and sad. "Yesterday was a day I'll re-member. That young fellow must be in league with the devil. I've never heard anybody play like that. I gave him a theme to improvise on, and I assure you that I've never heard anybody improvise so admirably. Then he played some of his own compositions, which are marvelous, really wonder-ful, and he manages difficulties and effects at the keyboard that one never dreamed of."

"I say, what's his name?" asked my father, with some astonishment.

"He is a small, ugly, swarthy fellow and seems to have a willful disposi-tion," answered Gelinek. "Prince Lichnowsky brought him from Germany to Vienna to let him study composition with Haydn, Albrechtsberger and Salieri, and his name is Beethoven."

Gelinek manufactured his popular variations like a counterfeiter molding coins. One was pretty much like the other, and all were worthless. Invariably there would be the theme, one variation in double notes, one with some left-hand arpeggios, one in chords, one syncopated, one in right-hand arpeggios, and none ever departing much from tonic-dominant. Beethoven became quite angry with him. Gelinek would listen to Beethoven play at the latter's home; or, if he were not invited inside, would stand outside Beethoven's window and eavesdrop, running home to make variations on the themes he had heard. In 1794 Beethoven fled to a building where Gelinek could not possibly hear him. In a letter to Eleonore von Breuning, he poured out his woes:

I have often observed that from time to time there was someone in Vienna who, when in the evening I had been improvising, usually spent the next day noting down and preening himself with many of my peculiarities. Now, as I foresaw that soon he would produce similar things, I resolved to forestall him. [This Beethoven did by publishing his set of Variations in G for Piano and Violin.] ... There was another reason: to embarrass the Viennese piano virtuosi. Many of them are my mortal enemies, so I wished to take my revenge in this manner, for I knew in advance that these variations would be submitted to them now and again, and that these gentlemen would give a poor account of themselves on these occasions.

Leopold Kozeluch was one of the competitors to whom Beethoven refers. Kozeluch was, like Dussek, a Bohemian, but nowhere near so good a pianist. Mozart said some nice things about him, and he could have succeeded Mozart at Salzburg. But Kozeluch was one of the most popular teachers in Vienna and had little to gain. Besides, he was a careful man and—in a way, to his everlasting credit—he knew his musical superiors. He wrote a friend that "the Archbishop's conduct toward Mozart deterred me more than anything; for if he could let such a man as that leave him, what treatment should I have been likely to meet with?" (Later Kozeluch's attitude toward Mozart changed and he had some petty things to say about his great colleague.)

Josef Wölffl, one of Beethoven's competitors. Everybody liked him — and he could stretch a tenth.

Daniel Steibelt, charlatan with perhaps a touch of genius. He played the piano while his wife shook her tambourines. Beethoven once played him under the table.

Josef Wölffl was a pianist of a different stripe and a rather important virtuoso. He had come to Vienna from Salzburg around 1795, under the patronage of Baron Raimund von Wetzlar. The baron promptly set him up against Beethoven. Wölffl had studied with Leopold Mozart and Michael Haydn, had made a big success in Warsaw as a pianist, composer and teacher, and was in addition a handsome six-footer with enormous hands. There seems to have been something pleasant and happy-go-lucky about Wölffl, who was always greatly liked as a human being. During one phase of his career, according to Fétis, he traveled with a singer named Ellmenreich, who doubled as a card sharp. From Ellmenreich, Wölffl learned the tricks of that interesting trade, and when their concerts did not make money there was always the gaming table. Ellmenreich was caught cheating in Brussels, got away, and fled to England with Wölffl. But word had gone ahead, and Wölffl was not received in society. Some of this story may be apocryphal, and *Grove's Dictionary* states that none of it is true, but there are enough passing references in gossip of the day to suggest that there may be more than a nugget of fact behind it. Our pianist's name, incidentally, has variously been spelled as Wölfl, Woelfl, Woelfft and other combinations.

He was considered an elegant bravura pianist; and he also had charm, wit, courtesy and good manners. A Viennese reviewer in the 1790s compared him with Beethoven, to the latter's disadvantage. "Wölffl has in his favor that, sound in musical learning and dignified in his compositions, he plays passages which are impossible with ease, precision and clarity (of course he is helped by the large structure of his hands), and that his interpretation is always, especially in adagios, so pleasing and insinuating that one cannot only admire it but also enjoy it." Wölffl, says this critic, also enjoyed an advantage over Beethoven because of his amiable bearing as against "the somewhat haughty pose" of Beethoven. When he wanted them, Wölffl had some sensational effects at his command, and in 1801 the *Journal des Débats* called him "one of the most astonishing pianists in Europe." And in his autobiography Tomaschek described Wölffl as "a piano player who is six feet tall, whose extraordinarily long fingers span a tenth without strain [we breed a bigger race in the twentieth century], and also, moreover, is so emaciated that everything about him rattles like a scarecrow; who executes difficulties which are impossibilities to other players, with the greatest ease and a small but neat touch without once disturbing the quiet posture of his body."

Wölffl was no great musical intellect, and he amiably gave the public what it wanted. Like the violinists of the day, who would entertain with barnyard sounds and imitations, Wölffl went in for this kind of titillation. In 1800 he gave a concert in Berlin with a "musical badinage" containing musical descriptions of "the quiet sea —the rise of a squall—lightning, thunder, a heavy storm which however subsides after some time—former condition of the sea— transition into a well-known song on which the player makes variations and improvisations." Somehow, one gets the idea that this effort is no *La Mer*. But at least Wölffl could be a quick thinker and resourceful musician. At Mayence a military band came playing down the street of the concert hall, right in the middle of a Wölffl improvisation. Wölffl immediately picked up the rhythm, modulated into the key of the band's melody, picked up all the themes, and improvised on the spot a concerto to band accompaniment.

A good deal can be guessed about a pianist's playing from the music he composes. Wölffl's most famous composition was the *Ne Plus Ultra* Sonata (or *Non Plus Ultra*, in many editions), and it is full of double thirds for both hands, full of left-hand arpeggios going up as much as two octaves (very advanced for the day), and considerable crossing-of-hands effects. Musically weak as it is, it must have nevertheless been a novel and exciting recital piece. Dussek went Wölffl one better by writing a sonata that he defiantly named *Plus Ultra*. Wölffl did not rise to the occasion, and it ended there.

The real charlatan of the late-eighteenth-century pianists was Daniel Steibelt. His obvious fakery has aroused the ire of later generations, summed up in Oscar Bie's comment late in the nineteenth century, "Bespattered with praise, he rushed through Europe with his trashy compositions, his battles, thunderstorms, bacchanals, which he played *ad libitum* while his wife struck the tambourines in concert with him." All of which is true, and Steibelt in many respects was a faker. But he also had a touch of genius which later commentators seem reluctant to admit. His personal characteristics were no help to his future reputation, either. His manners were uncouth, his vanity was colossal, his personal life distressing. He ran up debts, absconded, defrauded his publisher and, as the first edition of *Grove's Dictionary* puts it, on top of everything else "he seems to have been a victim of kleptomania." In Germany, his own country, he acted the foreigner and pretended not to know how to speak German. At his first concert in Berlin, his birthplace, the orchestra was so disgusted with his behavior that it would not take part in a second concert. And yet . . .

There is something intriguing about his life. He studied with no important teacher, but by 1787 was well established in Paris as a pianist and composer; and his operas were respectfully received. Of course, he had to mess up his life by selling some music, in slightly altered form, that he previously had sold to a different publisher. As a result he found it advisable to leave Paris in a hurry. A restless, roving man, he could never stay long in one place. Holland and England saw him in 1786 (in England he composed a wildly successful piece called the *Storm* Rondo). It was in England that he married a virtuoso on the tambourine, and from there on she appeared as an assisting artist on nearly all of his concerts, he playing the piano in bacchanals, so called, that he composed for her. Paris was his home in 1797. After his flight from that city, he turned up in Berlin, then in Prague, and in 1800 came to Vienna, where he had a competition with Beethoven and was played under the table. Back to Paris (things obviously had been smoothed over there), then London, then in 1810 to St. Petersburg, where he spent the rest of his life. Many of his operas were produced there. After 1814 he ceased playing the piano, though he did make an exception for the premiere of his Piano Concerto No. 8, on March 16, 1820. This concerto has a choral finale. Only one other in history has such a finale—the Busoni concerto.

Steibelt could not have been a great pianist, but he did add several things to the technical repertoire. He apparently knew more about the pedals than any pianist after Dussek and before Chopin. And he introduced the tremolo. In Europe he was known as The Tremolo Pianist, much as Thalberg later was to be known as Old Arpeggio. What storms he and his wife must have raised, he going up and down the keyboard all tremolando, she shaking her tambourines like mad! But that about ended it. Steibelt could only play fast. His inability to play a slow movement was universally discussed among musicians of his day. It is surprising that such a pioneer in pedal technique should not have been able to handle a slow movement. Steibelt knew his own weakness as well as anybody. Most of his sonatas have only two movements—allegro and rondo. Fast movements he played with a good deal of fire. But here again his equipment was not complete, and connoisseurs claimed that he had a weak left hand. Nevertheless his playing must have been strikingly original, with a good deal of stage projection, even if his fellow musicians scorned it. Generally they had good reason. Tomaschek has left a colorful account of Steibelt's 1800 appearance in Prague:

Steibelt, wrapped in his cloak, had only the orchestral interludes and *ritornellos* tried over, without himself touching the piano. The quartet that he played at the concert he rehearsed in his lodgings, and that behind closed doors. [This was not untypical behavior at the time. There was no such thing as copyright law. Steibelt was determined that nobody would steal or copy *his* precious effects.] The actual performance, like all concerts at that time, was to have taken place at seven o'clock; yet the artist, befogged by a rare conceit, was pleased not to meet the hour. After the nobility, which has a better understanding of the active rather than the passive side of waiting, had exhausted itself in French in all kinds of indignation, and the orchestra was ready to go home with its job undone, the long-yearned-for virtuoso finally came, one hour after the appointed time. He arrived nearly out of breath, distributed the parts and gave the signal for the overture. . . . At the end of the concert he improvised on the well-known theme . . . *Pace caro mio sposo*, in a manner degrading to the artist, for he did nothing but repeat the theme in C major a number of times *vibrando* [tremolando] into the midst of which he squeezed a few little runs with his right hand, and after a few minutes he concluded the entire *fantasie*. This *fantasie*, as he called this cling-clang, and certain of his moral blemishes startled the nobility. . . . As a pianist he has a neat and yet rather firm touch. His right hand was excellent in its cultivation. . . . On the other hand, the development of his left hand stood in no harmonious relationship whatever to his right; clumsy, almost imbecile, it hobbled along. . . . He had with him an Englishwoman whom he introduced as his wife and who played the tambourine, accompanying him with it, with him at the piano. . . . The new combination of such diverse instruments so electrified the gentlefolk that they could hardly see their fill of the Englishwoman's pretty arm. Likewise the wish to manipulate this instrument stirred in all the ladies, and so it came that Steibelt's girl friend was gladly persuaded to give instruction in it. . . . Thus it happened that Steibelt remained in Prague for several months and gradually sold a large wagonload of tambourines.

Yet those who look at Steibelt's piano music may be in for a surprise. The charlatan composed a good deal of impossible junk, but he also was capable of extraordinary flights of imagination. Some of his piano pieces are beautifully laid out for the instrument and are full of romantic touches. His Études (Op. 78) are not easy, and No. 3 in A has anticipations of Mendelssohn, while No. 20 in G minor is a most effective double-note study. No copy of his Piano Concerto No. 8 seems to be available, but that choral finale certainly is intriguing. It dates from 1820, and the Beethoven Ninth was not done until 1824, though the *Choral Fantasy* (which uses piano, orchestra and chorus) does go back to 1808. Steibelt was a rascal, but he was not without ideas, and he is one of the most interesting of the turn-of-the-century pianists.

String-Snapper, Hands on High

IN MANY THINGS, Beethoven was ahead of his time, and so was his piano playing. It had unprecedented power, personality and emotional appeal. In many respects he can be considered the first romantic pianist: the one who broke all of the laws in the name of expression (for in the nineteenth century the word "expression" was to take the place of the eighteenth-century "taste"); the one who thought orchestrally and achieved orchestral effects on the piano. In that he was alone in his day, and his like was not to be seen until the maturity of Franz Liszt.

But it was piano playing that raises a few questions. Why, for instance, is Beethoven's own piano music so relatively conservative, not to say often old-fashioned, in its layout? Clementi, Dussek, even Steibelt added more to piano technique on the printed page than almost anything to be found in the Beethoven sonatas, incomparably greater musically as the latter are. One answer would be, of course, that with Beethoven the idea counted more than its execution. His sonatas are not necessarily conceived in terms of the piano *per se*, but in terms of idea expressed in form. Some of his piano writing can be frightfully difficult, but it is not "pianistic." There is a great difference. (Much the same can be said about Beethoven's contemporary, Franz Schubert; but where Beethoven was a brilliant pianist himself, Schubert was not, although he could get around the piano well enough.)

Another answer might lie in the fact that Beethoven was, in many respects, a self-taught pianist. His instructors, when he was a child, were not professional pianists. Professionals, when they teach, generally instill into their pupils the proper regard and respect (not to say reverence) for their instrument, and in ninety-nine cases out of a hundred the instrument ends up being more important than the music. Quite the reverse was the case with Beethoven, who turned out to be a musician first, a pianist second. His tenor-singing father, who wanted to put him on display as a second Mozart, might have been aghast had he been musician enough to know where the child's training was leading. Around 1781, Beethoven's teacher was Christian Gottlob Neefe, court organist at Bonn, and he was the best Beethoven ever had. Neefe turned out to be not only a sympathetic mentor but a friend, and in 1793 Beethoven was writing to him, "I thank you for the counsel which you gave me so often in the progress of my divine art. If I ever become a great man, yours shall be a share of the credit."

Instead of starting Beethoven with flashy "technical" music, Neefe put Beethoven on the *Well-Tempered Clavier* and also instructed him in organ, theory and composition. Beethoven made giant strides, and Neefe hastened to let the world know what he had developed. In his news letter of March, 1783, he wrote about his twelve-year-old pupil, "He plays the clavier very skillfully, with power, and (to put it in a nutshell) he plays chiefly the *Well-Tempered Clavier* of Sebastian Bach, which Herr Neefe put into his hands. Whoever knows this collection of preludes and fugues in all the keys, which might almost be called the *ne plus ultra* of our art, will know what this means." Young Beethoven in addition was a formidable improviser and sight reader, and at twelve he was cembalist and violinist in the Bonn orchestra. It was this kind of training that led to such feats of pure musicianship as playing the rehearsal of his C major Concerto in B major because the piano was a half-tone out of tune.

It was in 1792 that the short, homely Beethoven exploded over Vienna. His playing—and it was as a pianist, not as a composer, that he made his initial impact—was overwhelming. And it was overwhelming not so much because Beethoven was a great virtuoso (which he probably wasn't) but because he had an oceanlike surge and depth that made all other playing sound like the trickle of a rivulet. Certainly Vienna had heard pianists who had a more polished delivery—Mozart, Clementi, Wölffl and Cramer, to mention but four. Beethoven's playing probably was rough in comparison. But a pianist with Beethoven's elemental force and conception was entirely unknown up to that time: a shellburst among the bows and arrows of his contemporaries. The well-known story of his playing for Mozart, and of Mozart saying, "Keep an eye on this young man. He will make a great splash in the world," is said to be apocryphal. But, then again, nobody has really proved it never took place. Anyway, all Vienna realized it was up against something new, something elemental, a primal, impolite force that, with unparalleled harmonic daring and disrespect for the niceties, would swarm all over the piano with complete confidence and freedom, storming the most distant keys, swinging through the most abstruse modulations.

His originality was hailed from the very beginning. Carl Ludwig Junker in 1791 pointed out that Beethoven's playing "differs greatly from the usual method of treating the piano, that it seems as if he had struck out an entirely new path for himself." The critic commented on Beethoven's "fiery expression." Everybody was struck by Beethoven's fiery expression. When Tomaschek first heard Beethoven, he was so disheartened by the young pianist's splendor that he could not touch the piano for several days. (Then, reasonably, he decided to return to practicing with ever-increased industry, Beethoven's sound always in his inner ear.)

Where Beethoven especially shone was in his improvisations. His improvisations, indeed, were better than his performances of published pieces, for after coming to Vienna Beethoven had little time, or inclination, to practice. How much Beethoven prepared his improvisations we do not know. Most pianists did prepare, knowing full well that sooner or later they would be called upon to supply an improvisation on "Batti, batti" or a similar well-known tune. And all pianists had at their command a thorough supply of passagework by the yard, which they could snip off and use for any possible contingency. But when Beethoven improvised, prepared passagework or no, it was evident to his hearers that after a while he was on his own, idea pouring after idea. Then he would get carried away, pound the piano, and the strings of the delicate Viennese instruments would pop, or hammers would break. No piano was safe with Beethoven. Czerny says that Beethoven's bearing, while playing, was "masterfully quiet," but that does not quite jibe with the impression of most others who saw him in action. A quiet player does not snap strings and break hammers. Almost every pianist of the day kept his hands close to the keys, but there is plenty of evidence that Beethoven was a most lively figure at the keyboard, just as he was on the podium. Ignaz von Seyfried told Spohr that once, at a public concert, Beethoven got into a rage about something and, at the first chords of his solo, broke half a dozen strings. And Anton Reicha relates that one evening, when Beethoven was playing a Mozart concerto at court, "He asked me to turn pages for him. But I was mostly occupied in wrenching the strings of the pianoforte which snapped, while the hammers stuck among the broken strings. Beethoven insisted on finishing the concerto, and so back and forth I leaped, jerking out a string, disentangling a hammer, turning a page, and I worked harder than Beethoven." (This would have been about 1795 or 1796. Beethoven for the most part played only his own music in public, and only two exceptions are known. On March 31, 1795, he played a Mozart concerto at a benefit concert for Mozart's widow, and he repeated it on January 8, 1796. At home, of course, he would play or read through a variety of music by other composers.) Beethoven broke more pianos than anybody in Vienna. Czerny, who hailed Beethoven's "titanic execution," apologizes for his messiness by saying that he demanded far too much from the pianos then being made. Which is very true; and which also is a polite way of saying that Beethoven banged the hell out of the piano.

It is impossible to describe a Beethoven improvisation, though the opening of the *Choral Fantasy* is supposed to give an idea. J. B. Cramer told his pupils that nobody could say he had ever heard improvisation had he not heard Beethoven. Carl Czerny said that Beethoven's improvisations were so brilliant and amazing that often the eyes of his listeners filled with tears, while some members of the audience would sob loudly, "for apart from the beauty and originality of his ideas, and his ingenious manner of expressing them, there was something magical about his playing." Czerny describes the hands that caused such magic; he says that they were densely covered with hair; that the fingers, especially at the tips, were very broad; that the stretch was not large, hardly capable of a tenth. Those hands may have wrenched tears from many eyes, but to some conservatives Beethoven's harmonies were uncontrolled. Tomaschek, who so admired Beethoven's playing in 1798, never could get used to his "frequent daring deviations from one motive to another. . . . Evils of this nature frequently weaken his greatest compositions." But to Ignaz von Seyfried, Beethoven's improvisations were "a cataract, elemental, a force of nature." Woe be to the pianist who crossed Beethoven in competition when the latter was in a combative mood. The insufferable Steibelt once felt the full force of Beethoven's fury.

Steibelt had come to Vienna in 1800, fresh from his glories in Paris (and his precipitate retreat therefrom). Beethoven's friends were worried that the visitor would be too much for him, especially as Steibelt was not particularly bashful about advertising his own virtues. He beat his drum much louder than his wife the tambourine. Naturally Steibelt did not take the trouble to visit Beethoven. That would have been beneath his dignity. They finally met at the house of Count Fries, where Beethoven played the piano part in his new Trio in B flat. Steibelt listened with condescension and apparently gave Beethoven a few compliments of a not-bad-old-boy variety, one great composer to another. Then Steibelt sat down to play *his* music, making a great effect with his specialty, the tremolo passages, at that time something quite new. Beethoven listened but could not be induced to play a solo. A week later the two met once more at Fries's house. This time Steibelt had prepared a brilliant fantasy for piano and strings, the theme coming from the Beethoven trio he had heard the previous week. Steibelt's admirers were in raptures. Now the issue was joined, and Beethoven *had* to show his strength. He walked to the piano, grasped the cello part of the Steibelt work *en route*, put it upside down on the piano and insultingly drummed out a theme with one finger. Then he improvised, and—angry, excited, on his mettle—how he must have improvised! Before Beethoven had finished, Steibelt stole from the room. He never again would meet Beethoven and made it a condition before going anywhere in Vienna that Beethoven not be invited.

In that he produced new effects, broke all the rules, used an extraordinarily wide dynamic palette, and was highly expressive in his playing, Beethoven was the direct link to the romantic pianists. Unlike the disciplined Mozart or Cramer, he played as he felt, unclassically, wrong notes and all. The chances are that he never, even at his best, was an accurate pianist, and his work at times must have been distressingly sloppy, even before deafness set in. He "played like a composer." The hero-worshiping Schindler was forced to admit that his performances left much to be desired "on the score of pure execution." But, Schindler hastens to add, "all music performed by his hands appeared to undergo a new creation. These wonderful effects were, in a great degree, produced by his uniform legato style, which was one of the most remarkable peculiarities of his playing." Nobody seemed to mind Beethoven's technical roughness except purists like Moscheles. But Moscheles, who complained of the lack of precision and clarity in Beethoven's playing, did not hear him until 1814, by which time Beethoven's hearing was all but gone. And enough evidence of Beethoven's playing until 1805, when deafness caused him to curtail the number of his professional appearances, is available to reconstruct his style with fair certainty.

At the beginning he had a good enough technique. Czerny points out that nobody equalled Beethoven in the rapidity of his scales, double trills, skips and such like matters—not even Hummel. Schindler discusses Beethoven's combinations of distant intervals and keys, heightened by idiosyncrasies of rhythm and staccatos, and set off by a smooth legato. "Unlike Steibelt, Dussek and some of their contemporaries in their effort to *draw* out the tone, Beethoven would often throw it out in detached notes, thus producing the effect of a fountain gushing forth and darting its spray on all sides, well contrasting with the melodious episodes which he still preserved." Nobody ever referred to Beethoven's "singing style," a description often applied to other pianists. He was far too dynamic. He also made far greater use of the pedal than was customary. Czerny says that in 1803 (when Beethoven could still hear, and was in practice) he held the pedal through *the entire slow movement* of his C minor Concerto. Granted that Beethoven was using a light Viennese piano, in which the sustaining tones quickly dissipated, this still sounds like an incredible statement. Could Beethoven have forgotten his pianistic ABCs under the stress of public performance and left his foot on the pedal? But we do know he was lavish in the use of it, as witness his own pedal markings at the opening of the D minor Sonata (Op. 31, No. 2). Czerny says that Beethoven used the pedal "far more than is indicated in his works." (How could Artur Schnabel ever have written, in the preface to his edition of the Beethoven sonatas: ". . . the fact being that the pedal is very seldom used in the classic piano literature as a means of coloring"?)

One of the most fascinating sections in the Schindler biography concerns Ferdinand Ries's observations on how Beethoven played his own music. Ries was a piano student of Beethoven's from 1801 to 1804, later settling in London. Whether or not Ries himself was a

ENGRAVING BY JOHANN NEIDL,
BASED ON A LOST PORTRAIT BY G. STEINHAUSER

The young Beethoven, about 1801. At this time Beethoven was easily as well known as a pianist as he was as a composer.

Beethoven in 1814. At this period the playing days of the deaf musician were over. Nevertheless, he rejoiced in the noble Broadwood piano he received four years later.

ENGRAVING BY BLASIUS HÖFEL,
AFTER L. LÉTRONNE

good pianist—he had a high reputation, as any Beethoven pupil would, but von Lenz called him a woodchopper and most experts agreed—he at any rate was a trained observer. And he has some fascinating things to say about Beethoven's style at the piano:

In general he played his own compositions in a very capricious manner, but he nevertheless kept strictly accurate time, occasionally, but very seldom, accelerating the tempo. On the other hand, in the performance of a crescendo passage he would introduce a ritard [so much for present-day purists], which produced a beautiful and highly striking effect. Sometimes, in the performance of specific passages, he would infuse into them an exquisite but altogether inimitable expression. He seldom introduced notes or ornaments not set down in the composition.

To which Schindler adds that all the pieces he himself heard Beethoven play were, with hardly any exceptions, thoroughly free and flexible. "He adopted a tempo rubato in the proper sense of the term, according as subject and situation might demand, without the slightest approach to caricature." Schindler likens it to "the most distinct and intelligible declamation."

Schindler goes into a detailed analysis of how Beethoven played the E major and G major Sonatas (Op. 14, Nos. 1 and 2). The Schindler biography is not hard to come by, but most pianists today seem unaware of this very important analysis and its implications. The section is long, but deserves to be quoted substantially in full, for it raises more questions than it answers and, if Schindler is accurate (and there is no reason why he should be distrusted), the difference between Beethoven's own conception of his music and how we today approach it in the name of "fidelity" becomes apparent.

I will now, as far as verbal description may permit, endeavor to convey an idea of the manner in which Beethoven himself used to play the two sonatas contained in Op. 14. His wonderful performance of these two compositions was a sort of musical declamation, in which the two principles [the contrasting principles of sonata design] were as distinctly separated as the two parts of a dialogue when recited by the flexible voice of a good speaker.

He commenced the opening allegro with vigor and spirit, relaxing these qualities in the sixth bar, and in the following passage:

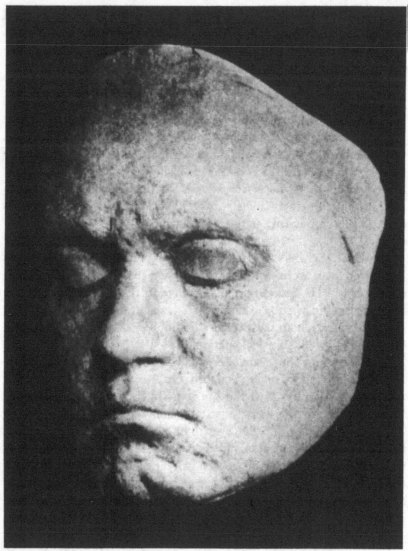

Life mask of Beethoven, made by Franz Klein in 1812.

Here a slight *ritardando* made preparation for gently introducing the entreating principle. The performance of the phrase,

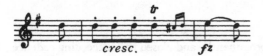

was exquisitely shaded; and to the following bars,

Beethoven's manner of holding down particular notes, combined with a kind of soft, gliding touch, imparted such a vivid coloring, that the hearer could fancy he actually beheld the lover in his living form, and heard him apostrophizing his obdurate mistress. In the following groups of semiquavers,

he strongly accented the fourth note of each group, and gave a joyous expression to the whole passage; and, at the succeeding chromatic run, he resumed the original tempo, and continued it until he arrived at this phrase,

which he gave in *tempo andantino*, beautifully accenting the bass, and the third notes of the upper part of the harmony, as I have marked them in the last two bars of the above example, thereby rendering distinct to the ear the separation of the two principles. On arriving at the ninth bar,

cresc.

he made the bass stand out prominently, and closed the succeeding cadence on the dominant in the original tempo, which he maintained without deviation to the end of the first part [*i.e.*, to the double bar].

In the second part, Beethoven introduced the phrase in A flat major by a *ritardando* of the two preceding bars. He attacked this phrase vigorously, thus diffusing a glow of color over the picture. He gave a charming expression to the following phrase in the treble by strongly accenting and holding down longer than the prescribed time the first note in each bar,

while the bass was played with gradually increasing softness, and with a sort of creeping motion of the hand.

The passage next in succession was touched off brilliantly; and in its closing bars the *decrescendo* was accompanied by a *ritardando*. The following phrase was started in andante tempo,

pp

At the fifth bar, there was a slight *accelerando*, and an increase of tone. At the sixth bar, the original tempo was resumed. Throughout the remainder of the first movement, Beethoven observed the same tempo as that which he had taken in the opening bars.

Various as were the tempi which Beethoven introduced in this movement, yet they were all beautifully prepared, and, if I may so express myself, the colors were delicately blended with one another. There were none of those abrupt changes which the composer frequently admitted in some of his other works with the view of giving a loftier flight to the declamation. Those who truly enter into the spirit of this fine movement will find it advisable not to repeat the first part: by this allowable abridgment, the gratification of the hearer will be unquestionably increased, while it may possibly be diminished by frequent repetitions of the same phrases. . . .

With regard to the second Sonata in E major (Op. 14), the subject of which is similar to that of the first, I shall confine myself to the description of Beethoven's manner of performing a few passages. In the eighth bar of the first *allegro* movement,

as well as in the ninth bar, he retarded the tempo, touching the keys more forte, and holding down the fifth note, as marked above. By these means he imparted to the passage an indescribable earnestness and dignity of character.

In the tenth bar,

the original tempo was resumed, the powerful expression still being maintained. The eleventh bar was *diminuendo* and somewhat lingering. The twelfth and thirteenth bars were played in the same manner as the two foregoing.

On the introduction of the middle movement [i.e., second subject of first movement],

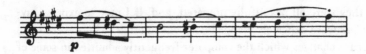

the dialogue became sentimental. The prevailing tempo was *andante*, but not regularly maintained; for every time that either principle was introduced, a little pause was made on the first note, thus,

At the following phrase,

a joyous character was expressed. The original tempo was taken, and not changed until the close of the first part.

The second part, from this passage,

forward was characterized by an increased breadth of rhythm, and augmented power of tone, which, however, was further on shaded into an exquisitely delicate *pianissimo*; so that the apparent meaning of the dialogue became more perceptible without any over-strained effort of imagination.

The second movement *allegretto* was, as performed by Beethoven, more like an *allegro furioso*; and until he arrived at the single chord,

on which he made a very long pause, he kept up the same tempo.

In the *maggiore*, the tempo was taken more moderately, and played by Beethoven in a beautifully expressive style. He added not a single note; but he gave to many an accentuation which would not have suggested itself to any other player. On the subject of accentuation, I may state, as a general remark, that Beethoven gave prominent force to all appoggiaturas, particularly the minor second, even in running passages; and, in slow movements, his transition to the principal note was as delicately managed as it could have been by the voice of a singer.

In the rondo of the sonata to which I am here referring, Beethoven maintained the tempo as marked until he arrived at the bars introducing the first and third pauses. These bars he made *ritardando*.

The two sonatas in Op. 14; the first sonata (F minor) in Op. 2; the first sonata (C minor), Op. 10; the *Sonate pathétique* (C minor), Op. 13; the *Sonata quasi Fantasia* in C sharp minor, Op. 27, and some others, all are pictures of feeling; and, in every movement, *Beethoven varied the tempo according as the feelings changed* [italics added].

Well! Schindler's remarks indicate something that could have been guessed without them: that Beethoven was no metronome. But there is only one thing wrong with playing those sonatas that way in the year 1990. The pianist who tried it would be laughed off the stage as an incompetent, a stylistic idiot who knew nothing about the Beethoven style, and as a bungler who was incapable of adhering to a basic tempo. Ries's remark about Beethoven keeping "strictly accurate time" must be taken relatively. By the standards of Beethoven's own day, the metrical pulse was strict; by present-day standards it would be intolerable. Twentieth-century pianists know as much about Beethoven's pianistic style as he knew about ours. We would consider his performances sheer anarchism if he returned today, while he would listen to current Beethoven specialists and consider them dry, unmusical and anything but expressive.

Free as Beethoven was in his playing, he tried hard to train his pupils according to classical ideals. Do as I say, don't do as I do. "Place the hands over the keyboard in such a position that the fingers need not be raised more than necessary. That is the only method by which the player can learn to *generate* tone." He did follow Clementi by insisting on legato playing, terming the old-fashioned Mozart style "finger-dancing" or "manual air-sawing." One pupil Beethoven did not take was his nephew Carl. He turned him over to Czerny, but kept close watch on his progress. Beethoven was constantly telling Czerny how to teach his nephew. Carl, he said, should first be taught to concentrate on fingering; then rhythm; then the notes "with tolerable correctness." And, Beethoven insisted, "do not stop his playing on account of minor little mistakes, but only point them out at the end of a piece."

Beethoven even wrote out a series of suggested exercises for the boy. In his early years Beethoven constantly recommended C. P. E. Bach's piano-instruction books; later he turned to Clementi. But at all times he was particular about correct hand position, about students working on scales in all the keys; and especially the use of the thumb. As he grew older he, like many people, grew more conservative (though not in his own music!). He told Tomaschek in 1814 that "it has been known that the greatest piano players were the greatest composers; but how did they play? Not like the pianists of today, who only run up and down the keyboard with long-practiced passagework, *putsch, putsch, putsch!* What does that mean? When the true piano virtuosos played," continued Beethoven, warming up, "it was something integrated, something whole. One could regard it as a work written in good continuity. That is real piano playing. The rest is nothing." Thus spoke the master of form.

Then who were the pianists Beethoven admired? For the Steibelts and Voglers of the world he had nothing but contempt. Mozart he considered old-fashioned, and he had some slighting things to say about Moscheles. His opinion of Cramer, however, was very high, and he had great respect for Clementi. Several women pianists interested him: whether because they were pianists or because they were women is hard to say. Unfortunately he did not, in his letters, write much about other musicians and performers, as Mozart had done. But he did, in 1817, write to Marie Pachler-Koschak in more than extravagant terms. "I am delighted that you are sparing us another day. We will make a great deal more music. Surely you will play for me the Sonatas in F major and C minor [probably Op. 54, and the *Pathétique*], won't you? I have not found anybody who performs my compositions as well as you do, and I am not excluding the great pianists, who often have merely mechanical ability or affectation. You are the true fosterer of my spiritual children."

Marie Bigot de Morogues was another lady whom Beethoven held in high regard. She may have been good. When Haydn first heard her, he folded her in his arms and is reported to have said, "My dear child, that music is not mine; it is yours." And Beethoven, hearing her, was impelled to say, after she played one of his sonatas, "That is not exactly the reading I should have given, but go on. If it is not exactly myself, it is something better." Marie in 1814 had played the *Appassionata* Sonata from manuscript. A woman who could do that could do anything. It is very likely that Beethoven had a crush on Marie. A letter to her, written in 1807, makes clumsy advances—at least, so it might indicate to a suspicious mind:

MY DEAR AND MUCH ADMIRED MARIE!

The weather is so divinely beautiful—and who knows what it will be like tomorrow?—So I propose to fetch you about noon today and take you for a drive.—As Bigot [Marie's husband] has presumably gone out already, we cannot take him with us, of course—but for that reason to abandon my plan altogether, why, Bigot himself would surely not want this—Only the morning is now the most lovely part of the day—why not seize the moment, seeing that it flies so quickly?—

It so happened that Bigot had a suspicious mind, and Beethoven had to write several long letters to Herr and Frau Bigot, apologizing and making all kinds of lame excuses for his proposal to gather his rosebuds. He put on a wounded air. "How can our kind Marie put such an evil construction on my actions?" Beethoven was not cut out to be a Don Juan.

Marie Bigot was not the only woman who specialized in Beethoven's music. So did Dorothea von Ertmann, to whom Beethoven dedicated the most subtle of his sonatas—the A major (Op. 101). Beethoven was constantly calling upon her to help him in his concerts. The relationship between them was close; she had studied with him since 1803, and was always available when he needed a pianist. Clementi called her a great master. She was married to an army officer, Baron Stephan von Ertmann, and Beethoven was never anything but polite to *her*.

Piano problems constantly plagued Beethoven. For most of his life he used Viennese pianos, at first with a five-plus octave range, then —starting with the *Waldstein* Sonata—a six-octave instrument. But he was never happy with them and kept asking the manufacturers for a more rugged, sonorous product. He wrote the piano manufacturer Johann Streicher a bitter letter as early as 1796. "There is no doubt that as far as the manner of playing it is concerned, the pianoforte is still the least studied and least developed of all instruments: often one thinks that one is merely listening to a harp. And I am delighted, my dear fellow, that you are one of the few who realize and perceive that, providing one can feel the music, one can also make the pianoforte sing. I hope that the time will come when the harp and the pianoforte will be treated as entirely different instruments." The day did not come soon enough for Beethoven to take advantage of it. In 1818 John Broadwood sent Beethoven a magnificent grand piano, with a range of over six octaves—a sonorous giant, as unharplike as any piano at that time could be. Beethoven was ecstatic, and kept the instrument the rest of his life.

Some scholars in recent years, however, have come to doubt Beethoven's attachment to the Broadwood. In 1970 William S. Newman wrote an article for the *Journal of the American Musicological Society* stating that Beethoven never lost his allegiance to the Viennese type of instrument with which he had grown up; that he had a lifelong association with the Stein and Streicher piano firms. But, as Newman is forced to point out, Beethoven never liked *any* instrument of his day. None of them gave him the sonority and range he was looking for, and as late as 1826, the year before he died, he said that the piano "is and remains an inadequate instrument." It also must be pointed out that Beethoven was pretty deaf by 1810, and in 1818, when he received his Broadwood, his hearing was about gone. The deaf, frustrated composer would sit before his instrument with a wild look on his face, banging out wrong notes that he could not hear. And soon his beloved Broadwood became a tangle of wires. At his best, Beethoven could never keep a piano in decent condition. Ries said that he seldom laid his hand upon anything without breaking it, and he had the habit, just fine for a piano, of emptying the inkwell in it. Toward the end of Beethoven's life he was visited by an instrument-maker named Johann Andreas Stumpff, who was taken directly to the Broadwood. Stumpff recollected the scene in horror. "Quite a sight confronted me," he later wrote, cut to the quick. "The upper registers were mute, and the broken strings in a tangle, like a thorn bush whipped by a storm." Yet Beethoven could once in a while coax music out of it, deaf as he was, battered as the instrument was. When Friedrich Wieck visited him, Wieck—who was the father and teacher of Clara Schumann and knew what he was talking about—said that Beethoven played "in a flowing, genial manner, for the most part orchestrally, and was still quite adept in the passing over of the right and left hands (a few times he missed the mark), weaving in the clearest and most charming melodies." But these moments were atypical. For a picture of the pity and the terror of the old Beethoven, one turns to Sir John Russell's account of the pianist who had once been the *enfant terrible* of Vienna, the great interpretive artist who had brought tears to the eyes of his listeners:

The moment he is seated at the piano he is evidently unconscious that there is anything else in existence. . . . The muscles of his face swell and its veins stand out; the wild eye rolls doubly wild; the mouth quivers; and Beethoven looks like a wizard overpowered by the demons he has called up. . . . And, considering how very deaf he is, it seems impossible that he should hear all he plays. Accordingly, when playing softly, he does not bring out a single note. He hears it himself in his "mind's ear," while his eye, and the almost imperceptible motion of his fingers, shows that he is following out the strain in his own soul through all its dying gradations. The instrument is actually as dumb as the musician is deaf. . . .

· VI ·

In the Interim

THE LAST TWO DECADES of the eighteenth century saw the birth of a number of important pianists who can be considered a bridge between classicism and romanticism. Johann Nepomuk Hummel, indeed, anticipated the last two decades by two years; he was born in 1778. John Field came along in 1782, Friedrich Kalkbrenner in 1785, Carl Maria von Weber in 1786, Carl Czerny in 1791 and Ignaz Moscheles in 1794. By the time of their maturity, they were gazing upon a very complex age; one that was altering all notions of life as it had been known up to then. When they were born, it was to eighteenth-century ideas about society and music. At their death the Industrial Revolution was well under way; and the romantic pianists, much to their resentment and bewilderment, had taken over. The bridge pianists had learned to play on small, rather unresonant pianos (for even as between the brilliant English instruments and the quieter Viennese ones, the difference was only a matter of degree as compared to the piano of the 1830s) and had been brought up on the economical finger motions of Clementi and Cramer. Most of these pianists, and they were good ones, did anticipate some of the romantic formulae. But they never adopted romanticism, and they looked on it with great suspicion. They lived unhappily between two worlds.

Everything was in flux; everything moving fast. Now the train, rather than the stagecoach, was beginning to speed virtuosos from city to city. Formerly a piano manufacturer made twenty or so instruments a year. By 1802, thanks to improvements in technique and thanks to the steam engine, Broadwood was turning out over four hundred a year, and by 1825 his number was fifteen hundred.

96

Prices went down, too. And pitch went up. Mozart's "A" was probably around 412 cycles per second, almost a half-tone below ours. As piano frames strengthened and could take more tension, pitch rose to the more brilliant A-435 demanded by the virtuosos. Heavier hammers and strings were being used, and Érard patented a double-escapement device that gave pianists a new ideal of instrumental rapidity and responsiveness. In the 1820s metal frames were being developed all over Europe. Broadwood had introduced steel tension bars in 1823, and Babcock in Boston had developed the single-casting frame in 1825. The demand for pianos, pianists and piano music was impressive. London in 1750 had twelve music shops. In 1824 there were 150.

Just as C. P. E. Bach had codified clavier technique as it was known in the 1750s, so the bridge pianists from Clementi onward tried to codify piano technique. Glorious confusion and disagreement resulted, but that is the rule in piano technique to this very day. Clementi, in his *Introduction to the Art of Playing on the Pianoforte*, commanded the student to hold the hand and arm in a horizontal position. Franz Hünten, a well-known pianist and composer of the 1820s and thereafter, agreed with Clementi, and wrote in his *Nouvelle méthode* that the player's arms "should be horizontal to the keys." But Hummel and Henri Bertini (Bertini's *Méthode* was in use for many years, and he himself was one of the popular pianists of the time) wanted hands and wrists "turned rather outward." Dussek wanted the pianist seated toward the left of the keyboard, to favor the left hand. Most authorities wanted the pianist in the middle. But Kalkbrenner favored the right of middle. Clementi said that the palm and hand should be stationary, with only the fingers moving. Dussek said that the hands should "lean toward the thumb." Hummel wanted the fingers to lean outside, so as to give the thumb more liberty on the black keys. Kalkbrenner said that the secret of playing octaves was a loose wrist, but Moscheles recommended a tight wrist.

To help young pianists along, various devices were invented. John Baptist Logier came forth with the much-discussed chiroplast in 1814. This was a weird mechanism, made of brass and wood, that was clamped to the keyboard and "assured" the student of a correct hand and arm position. This nonsense actually achieved a wide Continental vogue, and who knows how many talents it may have destroyed. Kalkbrenner modified the chiroplast to the *guide-mains* and told the world that it determined "positively" the correct height of the piano seat, by making the arms perfectly horizontal to the keyboard. "With the *guide-mains* it is impossible to contract bad habits." Then Henri Herz sprang the dactylion on a breathless world. Here the fingers were inserted into suspended springs. Later came the chirogymnaste, the manumoneon, the pocket hand exerciser, the technicon and goodness knows what else. All promised perfection with the minimum of work. In the meantime the good teachers, undisturbed, continued teaching the good old way. The pianistic blood lines of the century were being drawn up. Among Clementi's pupils were Moscheles and Field. Moscheles taught Mendelssohn. Hummel's teachings lived on in Hiller, Benedict, Henselt, Thalberg and Ernst Pauer. Beethoven taught Czerny, who taught Liszt, Leschetizky and, among many others, the estimable pianist and teacher, Theodor Kullak. Liszt and Leschetizky taught everybody.

One thing that did not change until a few decades later was the make-up of the public concert. As before, the pianist appeared on a program in which an orchestra—so called, even though it could number as few as four players—shared the program, along with a violinist, singer or harpist. Until about the late 1830s, a section devoted to the pianist's improvisation was mandatory. The quality of the music was generally dreadful. Pianists, for instance, thought nothing of making up a concerto out of three separate movements by other composers. Thus Ludwig Schunke on one occasion played a concerto in which the first movement was the first movement of the Ries C minor Concerto, the second movement a part of Beethoven's *Emperor*, the third the *Hungarian Rondo* by Pixis. The works of those we consider the great composers—Bach, Mozart, Haydn, Beethoven—were seldom played in public, at least up to the 1790s. But suddenly pianists started appearing who began investigating the work of the masters. Cramer had been one of the few to bring Bach and Mozart to public attention. Another was the now-forgotten Alexandre Pierre François Boëly (1785–1858), who concentrated on Bach as early as 1810 and who himself composed some music that technically is on a par with Clementi's in exploiting the resources of the piano. Clementi himself played some Bach in public and a good deal of Bach privately. Still another Bach player was Joseph Lipavsky. Czerny rated him high as pianist and sight reader. Maria Szymanowska toured Europe, was called the "female Field," was much admired by Goethe (he apparently fell in love with her and wrote some poems for her), and occasionally would play Beethoven.

Goethe placed her as a pianist above Hummel, though he was one of the few who did. ("Those who do so," dryly wrote Mendelssohn, "think more of her pretty face than her not pretty playing.")

If there was one important composer who was played, it was Beethoven. Certainly the musicians who came into Beethoven's orbit spread the gospel. Ries, in London, played a good deal of Beethoven. Cipriani Potter, the esteemed British pianist who had visited Beethoven in 1818, introduced to England the C major, C minor and G major Concertos in 1824 and 1825; and another Englishman, Charles Neate, who had been associated with Beethoven for eight months in 1815, gave the first English performance of the *Emperor*. Moscheles, in the Beethoven circle, played some of the sonatas while the composer was still alive.

But despite these few, standards were very low. That was what so distressed Robert Schumann when he started the *Neue Zeitschrift für Musik* in 1834. "At the piano nothing was heard but Herz and Hünten; and yet but a few years had passed since Beethoven, Weber and Schubert lived among us." Schumann was substantially right, though he was making the situation a little worse than it actually was, as enthusiastic young men on the side of the angels are entitled to do. His observations are backed up by Wilhelm von Lenz, who had come to Paris from Riga in 1828 with a crush on the music of Weber. To his surprise he found that few musicians knew anything about his beloved Carl Maria:

And what, indeed, did one find at that time in the piano repertoire? The bland master-joiner Hummel; Herz; Kalkbrenner and Moscheles; nothing plastic, dramatic or expressive for the piano. Beethoven was not yet understood; of his thirty-two sonatas, three were played—the A flat major Sonata with variations (Op. 26), the C sharp minor *quasi Fantasia* [*Moonlight*], and the Sonata in F minor, which a publisher's fancy—not Beethoven's—christened *Appassionata*. The last five sonatas passed for the monstrous abortions of a German idealist who did not know how to write for the piano. People understood only Hummel & Co.; Mozart was too old-fashioned and did not write such passages as Herz, Kalkbrenner, Moscheles—to say nothing of the lesser lights.

And Spohr, writing about Paris in 1820, takes a dim view of the culture there. "One seldom or never hears in the musical *réunions* here an earnest, well-digested piece of music, such as a quartet or quintet of the great masters. Everyone produces his show piece; you hear nothing but *airs variés, rondos favoris,* nocturnes and the like trifles, and from the singers romances and little duets."

Nor were there, until much later, many concert halls in which serious musicians could play. Generally the big virtuosos played in salons or engaged an opera house, theater or ballroom. As late as the 1830s, Berlioz, Fétis and Castel-Blaze were deploring the lack of concert halls in Paris. At the turn of the century the only hall in Paris available to touring musicians was the Salle of the Conservatoire. In Vienna a riding school was pressed into service. University halls and hotel rooms could and did serve for concerts. Germany had to wait until 1781 for the Leipzig Gewandhaus. The Odeon in Munich was not opened until 1828. Spohr in 1819 pointed out that Berlin did not have one suitable concert hall. In London the Argyll Rooms and Hanover Square Rooms were used, both small (800 seating capacity at most) and neither originally designed for concert purposes. Naturally there was no such thing as a box office. Tickets generally were on subscription, and one had to find out who was sponsoring the event.

Nevertheless the pianists kept coming and coming, especially from the atelier of Carl Czerny, one of the greatest pianists who never played in public. It is true that Czerny did make occasional appearances as a young man, but he was revolted by travel and the strain of public performance. So he stayed home in Vienna and taught and composed. He wanted to do nothing else. He never married, nor had he brothers, sisters or near relations. Instead, he had cats. There were always from seven to nine of them around the house, many in the process of having litters. Czerny spent a great deal of time trying to locate good homes for his kittens. When he died in 1857, he left his considerable fortune to the Vienna Conservatory and to some charities. He was an incredibly prolific composer, with over a thousand published opus numbers to his credit and an enormous amount of material in manuscript. A skullcap on his head, he would work on four or five compositions simultaneously, running from one to the other as the ink dried enough for him to turn the pages, meanwhile carrying on an animated conversation with anybody who happened to be in the room. Not all of the music is bad, and in the 1940s Vladimir Horowitz unearthed a set of variations named *La Ricordanza* that is highly effective and has more than routine interest to recommend it. Another work that probably has not been played in public since 1850, but is well worth looking at, is the *Sonate d'Étude* (Op. 268). It is a brilliant work, surprisingly romantic, and its figurations call for the utmost virtuosity. On the less stimulating side are the hundreds and hundreds of exercises that pianists since the 1830s have had to struggle through. But that does not lessen their pedagogic worth.

Czerny was born in Vienna in 1791. He was brought to Beethoven's attention and worked with him from 1800 to 1803. The great man gave the boy a recommendation in 1805, "I, the undersigned, am glad to bear testimony to young Carl Czerny having made the most extraordinary progress on the pianoforte, far beyond what might be expected at the age of fourteen. I consider him deserving of all possible assistance, not only because of what I have already referred to, but because of his astonishing memory." Czerny's father had come to Vienna from Bohemia and had set up as a music teacher. He himself first taught Carl, who could play at three, compose at seven, and by ten could handle anything in the standard repertoire. Another Bohemian-around-town was one Wenzel Krumpholz, a friend and admirer of Beethoven. It was Krumpholz who introduced young Carl to Beethoven in the winter of 1799–1800. Carl played the *Pathétique* Sonata, and Beethoven is reported to have said, "The boy has talent. I accept him as a pupil and will teach him myself. Send him to me once a week." Carl left Beethoven in 1803 but remained in close contact, playing much of Beethoven's music, including the first Viennese performance of the *Emperor* Concerto on February 12, 1812.

It is as a teacher that Czerny is of paramount importance. Franz Liszt was the most famous of his pupils, but there were also Döhler, Kullak, Jaëll, Leschetizky, Belleville—all important artists of the next generation. Many of them taught. While Liszt never was a systematic teacher, Leschetizky certainly was, and he got a good deal from Czerny, whose methods were not too dissimilar. "Practical empiricism" was the way Kullak described Czerny's teaching. Instead of having preconceived notions about piano technique, as Hummel did, Czerny decided that in actual practice there could be no such thing as a method applicable to all. That even extended to fingerings, he said, for hands differ in shape, size and formation. Every piece of music, then, had to be applied specifically to the case at hand. In some of his instruction books, Czerny could be as didactic as the next theorist. ("The thumb must never be placed on the black keys. Never strike two or more keys one after the other with the same finger. In runs the little finger must never be placed on the black keys.") But in actual operation he seems to have been entirely flexible. The full story of Czerny's place in the history of piano playing, through his pupils Liszt and Leschetizky, remains to be told. Was the instruction of both those two great teachers a reflection of Czerny (as Leschetizky's would appear to be)? If so, Czerny was the fountainhead of modern piano playing. And as he had studied with Beethoven, it seems reasonable to assume that Liszt and Leschetizky, and through them *their* pupils, were closer to the Beethoven way of playing Beethoven than modern pianists, even though the modernists, with their scholarship and textual accuracy, deride the romantic notions of the L & L school of Beethoven playing.

Like Cramer and several other of the older virtuosos, Czerny outlived his time. When Chopin visited Vienna, he looked up the master and even played together with him on two pianos. "He is a good fellow but nothing more," Chopin wrote home. As usual, Chopin was witty and a trifle malicious. "He has arranged another overture for eight pianos and sixteen pianists, and seems quite happy about it." They said a fond good-by to each other, and Chopin reflected that "Czerny was warmer than any of his compositions."

Another fine pianist who did not play much in public, although for other reasons, was none other than Carl Maria von Weber. His reasons make good sense: he was too busy composing, conducting, staging his operas and writing reviews about how bad Beethoven's music was. But he had been a prodigy and, despite inferior training, seems to have developed considerable powers as a virtuoso. He had to work everything out himself, and he carefully listened to all the great pianists of the day. His own piano music of the decade between 1810 and 1820 is considerably in advance of anything written in Europe at the time, Hummel and Moscheles included. More than anybody else in that decade he explored the potentiality of the piano and was thoroughly cognizant of what could be done with it. He had imagination. Correct but dry pianists like Hummel bothered him, and he told a friend that Hummel had not made a study of the nature of the piano. This in 1815, about one of the recognized masters! But the proof is in the writing, and the following year Weber came out with the great Sonata in A flat, which was full of original ideas and in addition contained far more technical expertise than

Carl Czerny in 1833. He studied with Beethoven, composed thousands of teaching pieces, and had among his pupils Liszt and Leschetitzky.

Carl Maria von Weber, a pianist considerably in advance of his day.

anything Beethoven had written for the instrument. Weber also composed a good deal of inferior salon music, but even much of that is effective and brilliant—and, for its day, impossibly difficult.

Weber had hands as big as Wölffl's, and his stretch was such that he could play left-hand chords like A flat, E flat, A flat and C (from the A flat Sonata); or F, C, F, A, or C, G, B flat, E (both in the fourth variation of his Variations on an Original Theme, Op. 9). The man must have been able to stretch a twelfth at least. His piano music is full of awkward stretches, of difficult jumps and brilliant running passages. It was piano music loved by the romantics, and throughout the entire nineteenth century one was never far from the *Concertstück*, the *Invitation to the Dance*, the A flat Sonata or the *Polacca brillante*. Von Lenz says that he introduced Liszt to Weber in 1828, and his remarks about Liszt's reactions—if true; von Lenz was inclined to exuberance, and his claims must be taken with caution—make fascinating reading. Von Lenz says, among other things, that Liszt could not tear himself away from the *Invitation*, playing it through again and again, playing the second part of the minor section in octaves, and experimenting with various reinforcements. Whether or not von Lenz was the moving force, a few years later Liszt was talking in extravagant terms about Weber, and told a pupil, Valérie Boissier, that he considered Weber's music as superior to other music "as the gigantic nature of the New World and the virgin forests of America are to the belted, box-treed, enclosed gardens of Europe." Did Liszt *really* speak like that? But he was reading Byron, Rousseau and Lamartine in those days. . . .

Quite forgotten today is Johann Peter Pixis, and yet he was a very important pianist, composer and teacher. Not one of his many compositions has survived, but in his heyday not many concerts were given in which the name of Pixis did not figure. He was born in Mannheim, was resident in Munich, Stuttgart and Paris, and after 1845 settled in Baden-Baden. An idea of his popularity can be gauged by the fact that on the great occasion when the Princess Belgiojoso decided to round up the six greatest European pianists for one of her famous soirées, the great men selected were Liszt, Chopin, Herz, Czerny, Thalberg—and Pixis. Each composed a variation on an air from a Bellini opera, and it was published under the title of *Hexameron*. Liszt frequently played the work in public. Spohr referred to Pixis' playing as "false, yet fiery," whatever that means. False notes or false art?

Not too much about Pixis has come down to us, though we know that the unfortunate man had a colossal nose that was the target of many jokes. Heine called poor Pixis' nose "one of the curiosities of the musical world." Nose or not, Pixis got around, and he liked 'em young. When Chopin looked Pixis up, he wrote home in glee, "Just imagine! He has with him a very pretty girl of sixteen whom, he says, he is going to marry. I met her at his house when I visited Stuttgart." Chopin goes on to say that Pixis was not at home, that he and the girl were chatting away when the great lover entered, peering suspiciously about. "At last the old chap was pacified, took me by the arm and led me into the room. In his excitement he did not know what to do with me, for he was afraid that if I were offended, I should make better use of his absence another time. Finally he accompanied me downstairs, and seeing the smile which I could not suppress, at the idea of any one thinking me capable of such a thing, he asked the porter how long I had been there. That functionary must have satisfied him, for ever since Pixis has not been able to say enough to his friends about my talents." Chopin was amused. "What do you think of it? I a dangerous *séducteur*."

From Ireland to Bohemia

THE FOUR MOST IMPORTANT pianists immediately prior to the arrival of the romantics were John Field from Dublin, Johann Nepomuk Hummel from Pressburg in Bohemia, Friedrich Kalkbrenner from a point between Cassel and Berlin (he was born in a stagecoach) and Ignaz Moscheles from Prague. Of these, Field was the most poetic and the one who came closest to the Chopin style. Hummel was the classicist. Kalkbrenner was the virtuoso with the most superficial brilliance. Moscheles was the bravura pianist who developed into a classicist and was the best musician of the four.

As a personality Field is the most interesting of this group even if his art remained unfulfilled. He was born in Dublin on July 26, 1782, the son of a violinist at the Theatre Royal. His first teacher was his father, and then he worked with one Tommaso Giordani. At the age of six he was giving concerts. Having soaked up all that Dublin could give him, he was sent to the great pianist of the day— Clementi. Not for nothing: Clementi did not work that way. Field's father had to pay Clementi a hundred guineas for the privilege of having his son accepted as an apprentice. Clementi gave Field some lessons and also promptly put him to work in his piano salon, demonstrating the Clementi instrument. Hence the "apprenticeship." Naturally Field learned a good deal from Clementi, and also from Dussek, who was in London at the time. Field was a surly, morose boy who all his life suffered from an inferiority complex. The menial treatment he received from Clementi did not help his confidence. Clementi kept him on short rations and bad clothing. Spohr in his autobiography commented on Clementi's treatment of the poor boy. In the warehouse "Field had to play for hours to display the instruments to the best advantage of the purchasers. I still have in recollection the figure of this pale, overgrown youth. . . . When Field, who had outgrown his clothes, placed himself at the piano, stretched out his arms over the keyboard so that the sleeves shrunk up nearly to his elbows, his whole figure appeared awkward and stiff in the highest degree." Yes, they laughed when he sat down at the piano. But as soon as he touched the keys there was technical perfection and what Spohr refers to as "dreamy melancholy." Perhaps already the nocturnes he was to create were germinating in the young man's head. He worked hard, was a dogged pianist, and would slave over a difficult passage hundreds of times in succession until he got it the way he wanted it. After a while, Field became compulsive about practice. He would place a box of counters before him and remove one after every exercise, not stopping until the box was empty.

No wonder he grew up a secretive, uncommunicative person. But he developed into a powerful pianist; and he was one of the type who expressed at the keyboard the visions and hopes he could not hope to expect from life. In 1802 Clementi took him to Paris, and let him give a few concerts. Field made an overwhelming impression. Among other things, he played Handel and some Bach fugues "with such precision and inimitable taste" (wrote a critic) "as to call forth from a Parisian audience the most enthusiastic applause." Field had undoubtedly derived his taste in Bach from Cramer, who generally had some of the old master's music on his programs. (It is one more piece of evidence to gnaw away at the myth that Bach was forgotten after his death until Mendelssohn revived the St. Matthew Passion in 1829. Anyone who does any browsing through French, German and English magazines and books of the early nineteenth century and before sees constant references to Bach, who is invariably referred to with the greatest respect.) After Paris came Vienna and then Russia, where Field got the nerve to break away from his teacher. When Clementi returned to St. Petersburg in 1806, he found Field a big success as pianist, composer and teacher. And this despite Field's growing indolence, bad manners and dipsomania. In 1808 Field married a French actress. They were separated five years later. In 1814 he published the first three of his nocturnes. The year 1822 saw Field making a move to Moscow, where his love affairs became the *scandale* of the city, and where he dissipated wildly, lost his fortune and became Falstaffian in appearance. Bitter and ill, he revisited London and Paris in 1832, and his playing still managed to make an impression. But Franz Liszt, who often wrote reviews for French magazines, was rather disturbed and had some perceptive things to say. Liszt pointed out that Field's concert in Paris was not only handicapped by an inferior piano, but that he had no showmanship at all. To the glittering Franz, the greatest showman of them all, Field's grayness of demeanor was as flat as a glass of champagne the next morning. Liszt commented on the almost complete immobility of Field's hands—the coins that Clementi had put on them had done their work—"and his inexpressive look aroused no curiosity. . . . His calmness bordered on apathy and nothing could trouble him less than the impression he might produce upon his audience." Liszt's summation was that Field's playing was "melodious dreaming." A British critic in 1838 wrote a retrospective account that upholds Liszt's description. Field, he said, was immobile at the piano. "His fingers alone played, without unnecessary movement of hand or arm, each finger striking the key with such mechanical power and nicety that he was enabled to produce the loudest as well as the softest tones, the shortest [i.e., fastest] as well as the longest notes, without the slightest visible effort."

On his return to the West, Field made the rounds, renewing acquaintances and listening to the younger virtuosos, none of whom impressed him very much. He heard Chopin and dismissed him as "a sickroom talent." He played in Italy, took sick in Naples, left the hospital in poverty, was bailed out by a Russian family, made his way to Vienna (where he stayed with Czerny), returned to Russia and died in Moscow on January 11, 1837. The following colloquy is attributed to Field on his deathbed:

"Are you a Protestant?" asked the priest.

"No."

"Perhaps you are a Catholic?"

"Never mind."

"Then you are a Calvinist."

"No, I am not a Calvinist. I am a Clavecinist."

It was in Russia that he had made his biggest successes. His first public performance there took place in St. Petersburg in 1804, and Count Orloff immediately offered him the post of court pianist. Field refused. *La cour n'est pas pour moi, et je ne sais pas lui faire la cour.* ("The court is not for me, and I do not know how to pay court to it.") In Moscow he amply made up for his early privations. He was by far the most successful and highly priced musician there.

When he gave lessons he demanded champagne, which he would sip while instructing the aristocracy. "Instruct" may not be the best word. He is said to have been a poor teacher who hated every minute of it. He never bothered to trouble himself or his pupils by explaining such things as shading and phrasing. He merely concentrated on fingering, which took up all of the lesson. If, however, he did come across a talented pupil, he would illustrate at the piano. At least then the pupil might have learned something. He would instruct his pupils never to use the pedals, saying that it was the task of the fingers to solve pianistic problems. But he did see to it that his pupils had good music. He prescribed Bach, Handel, Haydn and Mozart. No Beethoven, though. Beethoven he referred to as "*le torchon allemand*"—"the German dishrag."

He was not a pleasant man, and his eccentricities were the talk of Russia. When he arrived there he was entranced with the skins used for winter coats, and he immediately purchased a bearskin for a cloak. So fond of it was he that he often wore it while playing in public. More than once it saved him from freezing to death. A Russian amateur once noted in her diary, under the date of April 21, 1827, "Yesterday a concert was given.... Field was the only one missed. He was so drunk that if measures had not been taken in time he would have died of cold." Naturally when Field returned to England he made himself obnoxious by talking too much, bragging too much, drinking too much. Moscheles describes him at a party:

> His legato playing delights me, but his compositions are not all to my taste. Nothing can afford a more glaring contrast than a Field nocturne and Field's manners, which are often of a cynical order. There was a big commotion among the ladies yesterday when he drew from his pocket a miniature portrait of his wife and loudly proclaimed that she had been his pupil, and that he had only married her because she never paid for her lessons and he knew she never would. He also bragged of going to sleep while giving lessons to the ladies of St. Petersburg, adding that they would often awake him by asking, "What does one pay twenty rubles an hour for, if you go to sleep?"

Moscheles did not especially admire Field's playing, which he thought lacking in spirit, accent, shading and depth. But Moscheles heard Field many years after his best days. The decades of being spoiled and idolized in Russia, plus the alcohol and undoubted lack of practice, had taken their toll—as Liszt had pointed out elsewhere in his review. Most pianists and critics had more respect for Field in his prime. Such was his reputation that Chopin, who in 1831 had just come to Paris to set himself up, could think of no better comparison to describe his own success than "Finished artists take lessons from me and couple my name with that of Field." Clementi called Field his favorite pupil. "He has correct and irreproachable execution; he also has something impossible to describe but which is felt, and which nobody has ever been able to imitate." Field undoubtedly brought the singing, legato style to its highest peak in the pre-romantic days. The English pianist Charles Salaman called Field "a really great player . . . romantic and poetic, as if interpreting some beautiful dream, while in the singing quality of his touch, the infinite grace and delicacy of his execution, his emotional expression, he was unrivaled in his day." Glinka described Field's approach poetically. "His fingers, like great drops of rain, poured over the keys as pearls on velvet." (That "pearls on velvet" cliché is to be encountered from 1800 to the present day and has not yet run its course.)

It is clear that Field anticipated Chopin in many directions. As is well known, his series of eighteen nocturnes, with their arpeggiated left-hand figurations and Bellini-like melodies, directly inspired the Chopin nocturnes. (Field was jealous of Chopin, and especially of the popularity of the Chopin nocturnes against the neglect of his own.) As a pianist Field, again like Chopin, featured tone and delicate dynamics. There is no doubt that Field anticipated Chopin's type of fingering, with changes on a single key to achieve a perfect legato. Field also carried Dussek's pedal experiments one step further. It is true that he did tell his pupils not to pedal, that the fingers should do the work. But every teacher tells that to his pupils, the idea being that they shouldn't walk before they can crawl. There always comes a time when the pedal has to be used, and Field was recognized as a master of delicate pedal effects. Of course he was still a transitional, Clementi-trained pianist, complete with coins on the backs of his hands and a classic approach. Yet he triumphed over his training to become, with Dussek, the first of the piano-poets, and as such was a much more significant innovator than the flashy Kalkbrenner or the arch-classicist Hummel.

Or even Anne Caroline de Belleville, so popular in her day. She was one of Czerny's best pupils, and Beethoven was greatly inter-

ENGRAVING BY C. MAYER

John Field, who was sold into "slavery" to Clementi, drank himself to death in Russia, but developed a piano style that was the precursor of Chopin's.

Friedrich Kalkbrenner, the *soi-disant grand seigneur* who volunteered to make a pianist of Chopin in three years. His playing, however, did have remarkable clarity and precision.

ested in her. By 1830 she was being compared to Clara Wieck. Robert Schumann (in this case scarcely a disinterested observer, for Clara was to be his wife) admitted that Belleville had a better technique than his Clara. Nevertheless Clara was superior, said Schumann, for "Anne is a poetess; Clara is poetry itself." Chopin heard her in Warsaw. "There is also a certain Mlle. Belleville here, a Frenchwoman, who plays the piano very well, most lightly and elegantly." And, ten years later, in 1840, he addressed a most respectful letter to her:

As for the little waltz which I had the pleasure of writing for you, I beg you to keep it for yourself. I do not wish it to be published [it was, as Op. 70, No. 2]. But I would like to hear it played by you, dear Madam, and to attend one of your elegant *réunions*, at which you so marvelously interpret such great masters as Mozart, Beethoven and Hummel, the masters of all of us. The Hummel Adagio, which I heard you play a few years ago in Paris at M. Érard's, still sounds in my ears; and I assure you that, in spite of the great concerts here, there is little piano music which could make me forget the pleasure of having heard you that evening.

Chopin was not in the habit of issuing idle compliments to other pianists. Belleville must have been good. She married the famous British violinist Antonio James Oury in 1831, and they concertized together. After 1846 she devoted herself to composition and published 180 pieces, nearly all of them pretty bad drawing-room music.

It is interesting to note Chopin's complete acceptance of Hummel as one of the great classic masters. Few musicians of the 1830s would have argued otherwise. If ever a composer was assured of immortality it was Hummel. Born on November 14, 1778, Hummel came by his classicism fairly. He was a pupil of Haydn and Mozart, and the latter was so taken with the boy that in 1785 he received him into his house in the Grosse Schulenstrasse and kept him for two years. At ten the boy was taken by his father on a four-year tour of Europe. Then Hummel was taken to London, where Haydn taught him for a while in 1793. These lessons were resumed briefly, two years later in Vienna. About ten years after that, Hummel succeeded Haydn—from 1804 to 1811—as *Kapellmeister* to Prince Eszterházy. (He was fired for neglecting his duties.) Hummel did a certain amount of touring as a concert pianist, but for the most part concentrated on teaching and conducting. And, of course, composition. From 1811 to 1816 he was in Vienna; from 1816 to 1820 at Stuttgart; and from 1820 to his death on October 17, 1837, he was *Kapellmeister* at Weimar.

He used the Viennese piano, and his playing was remarkable for its clarity, evenness and steady rhythm. Hummel must have been a pianist close to the style of Cramer, and Moscheles indicates as much. For when Hummel revisited England in 1830, he not only lacked the strength and resilience of youth to plunge into the London concert life, but also (says Moscheles), "England, proud of Cramer, discovered that his legato was equal to Hummel's, and preferred native to foreign talent. Hummel, possibly annoyed at seeing this view adopted by many of the newspapers, refused when asked by Cramer to play a duet with him at his concerts, and this refusal created an unpleasant feeling against him." But in Vienna, where Hummel was an important resident, he created a sensation, and his playing split the city into two camps. "Never before," writes Czerny, "had I heard such novel and dazzling difficulties, such clarity and elegance in performance, or such intimate and tender expression, or even such good taste in improvisation." Czerny rushed to take lessons from him. Naturally his playing was set up against Beethoven's. Hummel's admirers called Beethoven's playing noisy, unnatural, overpedaled, dirty, confused. Beethoven's clique said that Hummel's playing lacked imagination, was "as monotonous as a hurdy-gurdy, that the position of his fingers reminded them of spiders." Both sides may have been right, to a point, though in 1811 Beethoven's playing must have been altogether erratic. Hummel and Beethoven had an uneasy off-and-on friendship that foundered when Beethoven tore up Hummel's four-hand arrangement of the *Fidelio* Overture and gave the assignment to Moscheles. They were reconciled on Beethoven's deathbed, and Hummel was one of the pallbearers at the funeral.

In person Hummel was anything but elegant. He was coarse, ungainly, slovenly, and his face was pitted by smallpox. Czerny called him "a very striking young man, with an unpleasant, common-looking face that constantly twitched." Czerny also comments on his "utterly tasteless clothing. He wore valuable diamond rings on almost all his fingers." In later life he grew monstrously stout, and a place had to be cut into his dining room table, both at home and at court. When he played he puffed, blew and perspired.

But he was a refined musician and, aside from Beethoven, the

Johann Nepomuk Hummel: coarse, slovenly, ungainly, but one of the greatest of the classic pianists. He carried the Viennese school to its height.

Death mask of Hummel.

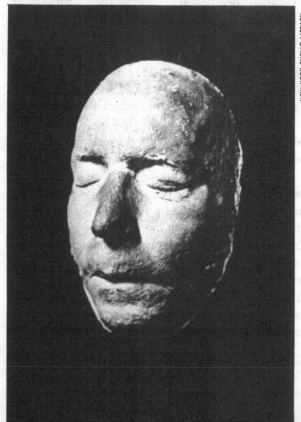

greatest improviser of his age. Many even thought him superior to Beethoven, in that he was more disciplined. Spohr flatly calls him the greatest improviser of them all, and gives an example of his powers:

I especially remember with great pleasure one evening when he improvised in so splendid a manner as I never since heard him, whether in public or private. The company was about to break up when some ladies, who thought it too early, entreated Hummel to play a few more waltzes for them. Obliging and gallant as he was to the ladies, he seated himself at the piano and played the desired waltzes, to which the young folks in the adjoining room began to dance. I and some other artists, attracted by his playing, grouped ourselves around the piano with our hats already in our hands, and listened attentively. Hummel no sooner observed this than he converted his playing into a free improvisation-fantasy, but one that constantly preserved the waltz rhythm, so that the dancers were not disturbed. He then took from me and the others who had played their own compositions during the evening a few easily combined themes and figures, which he wove into his waltzes and varied them at every recurrence with a constantly increasing richness and piquancy of expression. Indeed, he even made them serve at length as fugue themes, and let loose all his science in counterpoint without disturbing the waltzers in their pleasure. Then he returned to the *galant* style and in conclusion passed into bravura such as even from him seldom has been heard. In this finale the themes taken up were all constantly heard, so that the whole rounded off and ended in real artistic style.

The Rhadamanthus of English music criticism, Henry Fothergill Chorley, also had occasion to hear Hummel improvise, and was enraptured:

By none who have heard Hummel's improvisation can it ever be forgotten. It was graceful, spontaneous, fantastic. The admirable self-control of his style as a player (displayed in a measurement and management of tempo unequalled by any contemporary or successor that I have heard), so far from leading him to hamper his fancy or humor, enabled him to give both the fullest scope—inasmuch as he felt that he could never ramble away into a chaos, under pretext of a flight across Dream-land. The subjects he originated in improvisation were the freshest, brightest, most various conceivable: his treatment of them could be either strict or freakish, as the moment pleased;—or he would take the commonest tune, and so grace, and enhance, and alter it, as to present it in the liveliest forms of a new pleasure. I remember once to have heard Hummel thus treat the popular airs in Auber's "Massaniello" [sic] for an hour and a half, throwing off a Neapolitan *fantasia* with a felicity in which his unimpeachable beauty of tone and execution were animated by the bright spirit of the south, as he wrought together the Chapel Hymn, and the Fisherman's [sic] Chorus, and the *Tarantella*, and *Massaniello's* air by the side of the sleeping Fenella.

Hummel was the climax of the Vienna school. He carried on — and just about ended—the Mozart style of piano playing. Only Hummel was much more brilliant than Mozart and a more powerful technician. He had an easy, natural way of playing, and from Clementi he adopted octaves and double notes. Naturally, considering his teaching, his fingers were close to the keys. This eminently correct pianist was too classic to have much passion, and Tomaschek summed it up in 1816 when he heard Hummel in Prague. "Hummel's touch was more feminine than virile and reminded me for the most part of Wölffl's playing. . . . [Hummel] played very nicely, never losing strict tempo, a virtue that is not practiced much in these times." In line with his classic approach, Hummel used the pedal very sparingly. In his book, *The Complete Theoretical and Practical Course of Instructions on the Art of Playing the Pianoforte*, he wrote that playing with the foot constantly on the pedal "is a cloak to an impure and indistinct method of playing." He recommends the pedal primarily for slow movements, and even there only "where the harmony changes at distant intervals." All other pedal effects "are of no value, either to the performer or to the instrument."

His many instruction books were taken as gospel. Today it is hard to conceive the weight those books carried in the first half of the nineteenth century. In them Hummel systematized technique, introducing every known problem: he and Czerny ruled the roost for a century in that respect. And it was Hummel who was instrumental in confusing future generations about the trill as practiced in classic times. Up through Beethoven, a trill was started from above, in almost all cases. But in his *Complete Theoretical and Practical Course*, Hummel decided around 1825 that a new age deserved new ideas:

With regard to the trill, we have hitherto followed the ancient masters, and always begun it with the subsidiary note above. . . . But as each instrument has its peculiarities as to touch and position of the hand, so likewise has the pianoforte; and no reason exists why the same rules which were given for the management of the voice must also be observed for the pianoforte, without admitting of alteration or improvement. Two principal reasons determine me to lay down the rule: "that in general every trill should begin with the note itself, over which it [the trill symbol] stands, and not with the subsidiary note above, unless the contrary be expressly indicated."

So Hummel was the villain. The reasons he gives are: because the main trilled note ought to be the more strongly impressed on the ear than the subsidiary note; and because on the piano it is generally more convenient to begin with the principal note. All of which makes sense, but Hummel, who should have known better, ignored the harmonic reason for the classic trill, and that is the glint of dissonance given by the upper partial, a semitone or tone above the main note. Anyway, he was the one who set off the later nineteenth century—and, until recent years, the twentieth—to a misunderstanding of one of the important points of execution in classic music.

He was a highly regarded composer in his day—overrated then, underrated now. By far his most popular work was the celebrated Septet, of which Czerny reported that when it was first heard in Vienna (around 1820) it created such a sensation by virtue of its novelty and brilliance that men would stop each other in the streets to talk about it as they would some great national event. Even today the Septet remains a remarkable work. Hummel may have been a classicist, but his music verges on romanticism and contains some remarkable anticipations of Chopin. The openings of the Hummel A minor and Chopin E minor Concertos are too close to be coincidental; and the B minor Concerto has a type of brilliant, florid figuration—and exceedingly pianistic it is, too—that must have influenced the Polish composer. It also is hard to escape the notion that Chopin was very familiar with Hummel's now-forgotten Op. 67, composed in 1815—a set of twenty-four tiny preludes in all major and minor keys, starting with C major. The two men knew each other; they had met in Warsaw in 1828, and later Chopin visited Hummel in Vienna.

For many years Hummel was only a name in the history books. His music totally disappeared except for a single piano piece, the Rondo in E flat. But, thanks to the romantic revival of the 1970s, it is possible to hear a surprising amount of Hummel's music today.

Most of it is on records; he is still not often played in the concert hall, though there are sporadic performances of the A minor and B minor Piano Concertos and the Trumpet Concerto. On records it is possible to hear not only the above works but also a good deal of chamber music, including the once-famous (and still lovely) Septet, all of his piano sonatas and some of his religious music.

Even a few recordings of music by Friedrich Kalkbrenner have resulted from the romantic revival. It is doubtful, though, if a single piece by Kalkbrenner has been heard this century in a major concert hall. Gone is his great war horse, the *Effusio musica*, with its diminished sevenths, prestissimo octaves and crimson passage work, with which Kalkbrenner used to titillate the salons of Paris and London. Gone are his operas, sonatas and piano concertos, and it is just as well.

In a way, Kalkbrenner was to England and France what Hummel was to Germany and Austria—a close-to-the-keys pianist of the old school who represented the classicism of Cramer. But Kalkbrenner was a more superficial musician, in addition to being a *bourgeois gentilhomme* of colossal vanity. He not only preferred himself to all other pianists, but he had rubbed so much against English and French nobility that he conceived of himself as a grand seigneur and was only too happy to forget his common origin. Kalkbrenner could never resist name-dropping. He would talk with familiarity about the nobility in an effort to make everybody believe he was on intimate terms with great lords and ladies. "You know," this popinjay would say, "that Louis Philippe has asked me to accept a peerage. I thanked him but I thought it better to refuse, not being a politician and feeling it necessary to preserve my independence." After a while this developed into monomania. Sometimes he was caught with his G string down, as when he "improvised" before Professor Adolph Marx of Berlin. A few days later Marx received a bundle of new music from Paris, and among the pieces was Kalkbrenner's *Effusio musica*, the supposed improvisation. Then there gleefully made the rounds of Europe the story of Kalkbrenner's son, trained to be a prodigy. Kalkbrenner went around bragging of his son's ability in extemporization, and the King of France decided to test the eight-year-old boy. The child started playing, stopped after a few moments and turned a beseeching face toward Kalkbrenner. "Papa, I have forgotten..."

A man with such foibles was fair game, and everybody poked fun at him. Mendelssohn, Chopin, Liszt and Hiller once got together to tease him. They dressed as beggars and waylaid him in an elegant café, greeting him loudly, making a ruckus and terribly mortifying poor Kalkbrenner. The sharp Heinrich Heine has left to posterity a thumbnail sketch, "[Kalkbrenner] was admired for his faultless manners, for his polish and sweetness, and for his general air of something turned out by a confectioner, almost but not quite concealing Berlinisms of the lowest order." When Kalkbrenner gave a concert in Paris in 1843, Heine reported, "On his lips there still gleamed that embalmed smile which we recently noticed on those of an Egyptian pharaoh, when his mummy was unwrapped at the museum here." Clara Schumann's description is even more amusing. She went to a concert at which a Kalkbrenner work was being played and noticed Kalkbrenner in the first row, "smiling sweetly, and highly satisfied with himself and his creation. He always looks as if he were saying, 'Oh, God, I and all mankind must thank Thee that Thou hast created a mind like mine.'"

But he could play the piano and did from the age of five, when he played a concerto in public. He had come from Germany to the Paris Conservatoire and had graduated at the age of thirteen. For ten years he lived in London as a fashionable pianist and teacher and, in 1824, settled in Paris until his death in 1849. As a member of the Pleyel piano firm, and as a busy teacher and successful pianist, he died a rich man.

His playing might have been emotionally and dynamically limited, but there could be no denying the polish, elegance and accuracy of his performances. All qualified observers, and that includes some of the best musicians of the day, commented on his neat, limpid execution and his pure style. "Polished as a billiard ball," said Ernst Pauer. "Undisturbed, unexcited, with a gracious smile, he controlled his obedient fingers as a captain a company of well-drilled soldiers." That the style may also have been tedious, as Louis Moreau Gottschalk pointed out, did not detract from the pure pianistic flow. The best description of Kalkbrenner in action is supplied by Charles Hallé, who almost became his pupil in 1836:

He took me into his sitting room, where there was the most beautiful grand piano, and I played him his own *Effusio musica*. He made several remarks about the tempo and said several times "very good," "first-rate," until I got to the part where both hands had scales in octaves during several passages; when I had finished them he stopped me, and asked why I played the octaves with my arms and not from my wrists? "You are quite out of breath," he said (which was the case); *he* could play scales in octaves for an hour without the least fatigue; and why had God given us wrists? He was sure, if the Almighty played the piano, He would play from the wrist! He made several other remarks. He said I held my fingers rather too high, must hold them closer to the keys, especially in legato passages, to make them more finished and obtain altogether a rounder and more ringing tone. . . . He then played part of the piece I had played, to make it clear to me. After this he began another, and altogether played for me more than half an hour. You can imagine my delight. It was the first time I had ever heard a celebrated musician, and this half-hour has been of the greatest use to me. In Kalkbrenner's playing there reigns a clearness, a distinctness and a neatness that are astonishing. In octave scales he has an immense facility and precision, especially in the left hand; then he has a special mode of handling the piano, particularly in melodious passages, which made a great impression, but which I cannot describe to you; the reason of it lies mostly in that he keeps his fingers so closely over the keys.

A few months later Hallé heard Chopin play and that was the end of Kalkbrenner. The amusing thing is that Chopin himself, on his arrival in Paris, had—like Hallé—been swept off his feet by Kalkbrenner. Chopin was a hick boy from a provincial European capital, newly arrived in the pianistic center of the world. He managed to get an introduction to Kalkbrenner ("the first pianist of Europe"), heard him, and then wrote home a hysterical letter. "You would not believe how curious I was about Herz, Liszt, Hiller, etc. They are all zero beside Kalkbrenner. . . . It is hard to describe to you his calm, his enchanting touch, his incomparable evenness and the mastery that is displayed in every note. He is a giant, walking over Herz and Czerny and all." Chopin played for Kalkbrenner and received a few compliments. He was told he had Cramer's method and Field's touch (this pleased Chopin), but that he had no real schooling, and that he, Kalkbrenner, was the only one who could teach him, for "after his death, when he finally stops playing, there will be no representative of the great pianoforte school." Kalkbrenner ended up offering to take Chopin in hand for three years. Had he done so he would have destroyed the most original piano talent of the century. Fortunately reason prevailed and Chopin dropped the idea, especially after Mendelssohn assured him that he played better any day than Kalkbrenner at his best. Anyway, Mendelssohn did not like Kalkbrenner and his opportunism. He dryly described one occasion when Kalkbrenner "came in and played various new compositions. The man is become quite romantic, steals themes, ideas and similar trifles from Hiller, writes pieces in F sharp minor [a "romantic" key], practices every day for several hours and is, as he always was, a knowing fellow."

Like all other successful pianists, Kalkbrenner wrote a *Méthode*. It was posthumously published in the 1850s. Some of the Kalkbrenner's remarks about interpretation are of interest as indicating how pianists of the day went about their business. Kalkbrenner recommends that rising passages be played crescendo, descending passages diminuendo. The longest note in a measure should be the loudest. All endings of melodic phrases should have a ritard (this seems to have been Beethoven's way, too). When a passage is repeated it should always sound different: if loud the first time, it should be low the second.

In short, exactly the kind of instructions that the better teachers today tell their pupils *not* to follow—and what everybody was doing in the early part of the nineteenth century and, indeed, throughout most of the century.

The true man of the transition was Ignaz Moscheles, a sensitive musician, a gentleman, as noble and respected a figure as music has to show. Field was an eccentric who did not play much in public, while Kalkbrenner and Hummel formed their style early and did not change. But there are three distinct styles in Moscheles' life. He started as a bravura pianist, though it was bravura in the Clementi tradition: a very quiet hand position; no excess motion; finger and hand muscles rather than wrist and arm; very sparing use of the pedal. (As late as 1830 Moscheles was writing, "All effects now, it seems, must be produced by the feet—what is the use of people having hands? It is just as if a good rider wanted forever to use spurs." The true classicist speaking!) But within those limitations he managed to excite his public with the unheard-of precision of his repeated notes—he was the first pianist to feature them—as well as with the accuracy of his wide skips and fast-moving chords. He made a European reputation when he stormed the Continent with his *Alexander's March*, a flashy set of variations, composed in 1815, that showed off his whole bag of tricks. But with his four-hand Sonata in E flat he emerged as a fine musician as well as a virtuoso. He was a flexible enough artist to take advantage of the developments in piano manufacture, and he himself states that one reason for his growth as an artist was the inspiration he received in 1830 from the new Érard piano, "a very violoncello." Finally there were his last years, reflective and scholarly, when he was not nearly so well liked by the public—or by his colleagues, for that matter. Liszt's opinion of the old Moscheles was widely held. Moscheles, said Liszt, played superbly between the ages of thirty and forty, but as he grew older he became too old-womanish and set in his ways.

The trouble, as Moscheles himself realized, was that he was caught between two schools and could do nothing about it. No man can fully escape his training, and Moscheles' training under Dionys Weber (1766–1842; a Bohemian composer and teacher) was of the old school. As Moscheles grew older and studied the work of Chopin and Liszt, he realized, as Hummel and Kalkbrenner did not, that something was lacking in his own playing. And he did try to do something about it. His remarkably frank memoirs quite take the reader into the author's confidence. Around 1838, pondering the new music, patiently studying it and trying to make sense of it, he admitted his failure with touching humility:

I play all the new music of the four modern heroes, Thalberg, Chopin, Henselt and Liszt, and find their chief effects lie in passages requiring a large grasp and stretch of finger, such as the peculiar build of their hands enables them to execute. I grasp less, but then I am not of a grasping school. With all my admiration for Beethoven, I cannot forget Mozart, Cramer and Hummel. Have they not written much that is noble, with which I have been familiar from early years? Just now the new manner finds more favor, and I endeavor to pursue the middle course between the two schools, by never shrinking from any difficulty, never despising the new effects, and withal retaining the best elements of the old traditions.

But Moscheles never combined the two schools. He never stopped trying, however, and was broad-minded enough to admit that there could be valid things undreamed-of in his philosophy. The first time

Ignaz Moscheles, the true man of the transition. Around 1815, when this lithograph was made, he was a young bravura pianist.

Moscheles in 1859, toward the end of his career. He was one of the first to play Beethoven sonatas in public, was the teacher of Mendelssohn, and was loved as one of the purest musicians of the first half of the nineteenth century.

he read through the Chopin études he admitted their originality but, he added, "my thoughts, however, and through them my fingers, stumble at certain hard, inartistic, and to me inconceivable modulations. On the whole I find his music often too sweet, not manly enough, and hardly the work of a profound musician. . . . Practice them as I will, I can never do them smoothly." But the day came when he heard Chopin play, and he was big enough to change his mind on the spot. "Now for the first time I understand his music. . . . The hard, inartistic modulations, so like those of a dilettante—which I can never manage when playing Chopin's music—cease to shock me, for he glides over them almost imperceptibly with his elfish fingers. . . . Enough; he is perfectly unique in the world of pianoforte players." Then, good musician that he was, Moscheles swung over to Schumann, and he was one of the very few before 1850. "The proper ground for finger gymnastics is to be found in Thalberg's latest compositions, but for *Geist* [soul] give me Schumann. The romanticism of his works is so completely new, his genius so great, that to weigh correctly the peculiar qualities and weaknesses of this new school I must go deeper and deeper into the study of his works."

It was this open-mindedness and sweetness of nature that made his contemporaries love, admire and respect him. And what a tradition his long life represented! Born in Prague on May 30, 1794, he settled first in Vienna (where, in 1816, he was Hummel's big competitor; and he was also on very good terms with Beethoven). In 1824 he taught the fourteen-year-old Mendelssohn, and between student and teacher grew a lifelong friendship. Then Paris; then, in 1826, London. He made London his headquarters, but made frequent tours of Europe. When Mendelssohn asked him to join the newly founded Leipzig Conservatory, Moscheles was happy to accept. For twenty years he taught in Leipzig, loved by all, taking his best students into his home and helping their careers. He also was a prolific composer, though his music is now forgotten. The last piece to hold on was his G minor Piano Concerto. It disappeared from the active repertoire around 1900, thirty years after his death.

He was a very important pianist, both as a performer and as a symbol. Among other things, he was the first touring virtuoso to make a consistent effort to bring the best music to the people, and to act as a moral force. Moscheles anticipated the romantics in his attitude that in living the life of a musician he was fulfilling a holy mission. The fact that he was a gentleman, a friend of the Roth-schilds, Prince Albert and assorted European nobility, an artist who demanded his right in society—all this helped put the profession in a respectable light. It was he who flattened out the road over which later artists tramped.

Musically his tastes were high. One of the original Beethovenists, he had memorized the *Pathétique* Sonata at the age of ten and, at private concerts later in life, would introduce fellow musicians to Op. 109 and Op. 111. This was dangerous music, largely unknown. Some of his listeners were bored, some were moved, and some were "scared by the extravagances of the master, and do not recover their equanimity until I favor them with the more intelligible D minor Sonata." As conductor of the Philharmonic Society in London, he led the first performance there of Beethoven's *Missa Solemnis* in 1832 and later conducted the Ninth Symphony several times.

Moscheles and Mendelssohn had one of the beautiful relation-ships in music. When Mendelssohn was first put in Moscheles' hands, the older man was ecstatic. "Felix, a boy of fifteen," he wrote, "is a phenomenon. What are all the prodigies as compared with him? Gifted children, but nothing else." Moscheles, of course, was correct in his estimate, and with great pleasure watched the development of the wonder boy. Through their lives they remained in close professional association, and in letter after letter Mendels-sohn tells of the joys of making music with Moscheles. In London, in 1829, they played Mendelssohn's Two-Piano Concerto in E, and the composer wrote home that he had a wonderful time. "I had no end of fun. You cannot imagine how we coquetted; how the one constantly imitated the other; and how sweet we were. . . ."

Moscheles was one of the first of the serious pianist-musicians. He was the precursor of the Clara Schumanns and Hans von Bülows: a virtuoso who transcended virtuosity and was guided only by the nobility of his art. For a time, he was in eclipse, and the thundering young virtuosos of the 1840s and 1850s outraced him. He was the Schnabel of his day, and he was born too early. But he never grew bitter, and he accepted growing old with grace, serenity and humor. He practiced his piano and watched life go by:

The influx of pianists is as great as ever. I confess I am annoyed when such birds of passage come picking sentimentally at my Érard, or boldly smashing a chord or two. They show no curiosity to hear how I would play the poor thing. In fact, to them I am simply dead. They do not see that music is still to me as my own life blood, and while they are burying me, I am quietly feeding on the toccatas and fugues of old Bach; and the moderns, too, furnish an occasional meal. . . .

· VIII ·

Romanticism and Its Rules

THE ROMANTIC PIANISTS all decided to be born at much the same time—Mendelssohn in 1809, Chopin in 1810, Liszt in 1811, Thalberg in 1812, Henselt in 1814. In recent years musicologists have done an immense amount of work in baroque and pre-baroque music and to a large extent have disdainfully ignored the nineteenth century. Thus, while musicians by now are beginning to understand eighteenth-century performance values and have learned not to approach Bach or Mozart with the nineteenth or twentieth century in mind, they have not (for the most part) learned that nineteenth-century music, too, must not be approached with a twentieth-century mind. In many respects the nineteenth century, and especially its first half, is as little understood today as Bach ornamentation was fifty years ago.

Certain facts must be reconsidered. By the time of the romantic upheaval, starting around 1830 in Paris, the piano—with a few later modifications, such as Steinway's cross-stringing innovation in the 1850s—was substantially the instrument we know today. And it occupied a place in most European homes which we today find hard to visualize. It was not only the favorite instrument of the romantic musicians; it was a social instrument. Young ladies were required to play it, sing to it, be on familiar terms with it. It was the piano, too, that disseminated music in a manner analogous to the phonograph of the twentieth century. As soon as a composer wrote a symphony, or a piece of chamber music, or even an opera, it was immediately made available in reduction for one or more pianos, or for piano duet. That is how music was spread in those days. It was the only way for

127

the professionals, and the public too, to become familiar with music old and new. Young Charles Hallé and Stephen Heller, madly making music together in Paris, first became familiar with Schubert's Symphony in C through its publication as a piano duet. "But the same," writes Heller, "was the case with all the great compositions for orchestra, or orchestra with chorus, arranged in a similar form. How often we must have played Beethoven's symphonies it is impossible to tell; and how we enjoyed them! All the more as the opportunities of hearing them performed by the orchestra were then most rare, the Concerts du Conservatoire bringing forward only two or three during a season, so that certain of them, for instance Nos. 4, 7 and 9, were heard perhaps once in three or four years."

Since so many people played the piano, they wanted to hear pianists. And hear pianists they did. Pianists sprang up from every corner in Europe, all of them hastening to Paris to make their headquarters there. (But it is surprising how few French-born pianists of importance there were at the time.) Came the virtuosos like Liszt and Thalberg, the thumpers like Leopold de Meyer, the poets like Chopin, the salonists like Herz, the eccentrics like Alkan, the shy ones like Heller and Henselt, the extroverted ones like Litolff and Rubinstein, the scholarly ones like Clara Schumann and Hans von Bülow, the showmen like Dreyschock. They were off and running, and the pattern was set. As early as 1818 Tomaschek wrote words as true then as they are now about the touring virtuoso, "Never settled in one place, always touring, always busy preparing programs for concerts, they never have time to study anything new. As a result their programs are mostly repetitions of earlier programs, except that the pieces may be presented in different order."

Almost to a man and woman, though, the virtuosos were spiritual descendants of Paganini, in that he was the first to serve as the archetype of the flamboyant matinee-idol virtuosos, the ur-virtuoso, the law that transcends law. Paganini, in league with the Prince of Darkness, a devil himself (or so they thought), was the one who almost physically transferred himself from stage to audience, wrapping his listeners in the aura of virtuosity transcendent. Pianists looked, listened and tried to copy (Liszt and Schumann even wrote piano pieces based on the Paganini caprices). Nor was there any longer the close-to-the-keys fingering and phrasing of a Kalkbrenner or Hummel. Pianists strolled out, the lords of creation, and lifted their hands high, with crashing sonorities and extravagant body movements to match. Technique passed from finger and hand to wrist and arm (and frequently the entire torso). Power and showmanship elbowed the classic proprieties into oblivion. Who wanted to hear Moscheles when Liszt was putting on an act that the great Rachel herself could not match? Out came the bags of tricks—Thalberg with his imitation of three hands, Liszt with the cascade of his *Grand Galop Chromatique*, Dreyschock with his octaves. Piano playing became an orgy, and the serious old-time musicians clucked about it like a flock of hens in a coop around which prowled hungry foxes. The virtuoso was king. After Liszt's performance in Berlin in 1842, he was transported by a carriage drawn by six white horses, escorted by thirty carriages-and-four and followed by hundreds of private coaches. "Even the court had ridden into town to take a look. . . . Not *like* a king but *as* a king did he depart, surrounded by the shouting crowd."

Naturally, with the emphasis on the virtuoso, the institution of the solo concert was not long in coming into being. Who was the first hero to walk on stage and look an audience in the eye, in all his pianistic nudity, unaided by supporting musicians? Moscheles in his memoirs puts forth a claim, but it is not valid. In 1837 he did announce a performance of piano music, and many of his colleagues called this a dubious venture. But Moscheles went ahead, "taking the precaution to interweave a little local music with the instrumental, so as to relieve the monotony which people warned him against." This introduction of vocal music disallows Moscheles' claim. Liszt seems to have the honor. In 1839, while in Rome, he started exhibiting himself without any supporting cast. He describes this in a letter, dated June 4, 1839, to the Princess Belgiojoso:

. . . these tiresome *musical soliloquies* (I do not know what other name to give these inventions of mine) with which I contrive to gratify the Romans, and which I am quite capable of importing to Paris, so unbounded does my impudence become! Imagine that, wearied with warfare, not being able to put together a program that would have common sense, I have ventured to give a series of concerts all by myself, affecting the Louis XIV style, and saying cavalierly to the public, *"le concert, c'est moi."* For the curiosity of the thing, I copy a program of my soliloquies for you:

1. Overture to *William Tell*, performed by M. Liszt.
2. Fantasy on reminiscences of *I Puritani*, composed and performed by the above-named.

3. Studies and Fragments, composed and performed by same.
4. Improvisations on a given theme—still by same.

Note that Liszt called these epoch-making programs "soliloquies." The term "recital" had not yet come into being, although the word had been in use as a description of vocal and instrumental solo performances. Danneley's *Dictionary of Music* (1825) has the following entry under *recital*: "From the French verb *réciter*, the generic name for whatever is sung by a single voice or performed upon by a single instrument." But certainly the term was not in general use. The credit for its adoption seems to go to T. Frederick Beale, who had founded a London instrument firm with the celebrated J. B. Cramer. In 1840 Beale secured for Liszt a performance in the Hanover Square Rooms, and on May 1 the newspaper *John Bull* carried an advertisement headed "LISZT'S PIANOFORTE RECITALS." This would appear to be the first public use of the word, and people were confused. "What does he mean? How can one *recite* upon the piano?" But by 1841 Liszt had established the tradition of the unassisted piano recital, bringing it to Paris, as he had promised Belgiojoso. Heine reports on the novelty, "Liszt has already given two concerts in which, contrary to custom, he played alone without the assistance of other musicians."

But it must not be thought that all pianists immediately fell in line or that recitals soon became the solemn affairs they now are. It took time for such a new institution to stabilize itself. At the beginning everything was done on an informal basis. At his precedent-breaking "recital" in London, Liszt, after playing a piece or two on the program, "would leave the platform and, descending into the body of the room, where the benches were so arranged as to allow free locomotion, would move about among his auditors and converse with his friends, with the gracious condescension of a prince, until he felt disposed to return to the piano." Audiences would babble, laugh, smoke, eat, come and go during the course of the music. Only a few great artists were eccentric enough to demand quiet and respect from their listeners. But in a way one can sympathize with the audience. Programs were very long, especially when given by an orchestra, and very few listeners could maintain undivided attention. Moscheles complains about the length of programs in 1830: "It is a mistake to give at every Philharmonic concert [in London] two symphonies, two overtures, besides two grand instrumental and four vocal pieces. I can never enjoy more than half." Up to 1830 the composers most likely to be played on these marathon programs were Paër, Pixis, Winter, Mayr, Weigl, Hummel, Reicha, Onslow, Gyrowetz or Spohr. Occasionally Beethoven, Weber, Haydn and Mozart showed up, with increasing frequency after 1830.

The audience too had changed, and patronage was beginning to be a thing of the past. Conservatories were springing up all over the place: Paris (1795), Milan (1808), Naples (1808), Prague (1811), Vienna (1817), London (1822), Brussels (1832), Leipzig (1843), Munich (1846). And private music schools proliferated. All of these started grinding out graduates, who in turn started grinding out performances all over Europe. Audiences—democratic, middle-class audiences—started paying for the privilege of going to concerts. But, on the whole, standards were low and very few orchestras were on a permanent basis. If an orchestra had to be assembled for a concert it normally would be a pickup group from the opera house, augmented by whatever amateurs were on hand. Until the middle of the century, orchestras outside of a few major cities were on a disastrously low level. Moscheles, playing concertos in Liverpool in 1825, had to content himself with an orchestra consisting of a double string quartet and "four halting wind instruments." In York, in 1833, "the flute was the sole support of the harmonies." Even in Vienna there was no decent orchestra—none that could compare with those of Paris, London or Leipzig—until the 1840s. In Rome, Spohr conducted an orchestra, and although it contained the best musicians locally available it was "nevertheless the worst that had yet accompanied me in Italy. The ignorance, want of taste, and stupid arrogance of these people beggars all description."

Spohr knew whereof he spoke. A distinguished violinist and composer, it was also he who had started the vogue of the conductor as we understand him today. By 1840 these great men were fairly common. Previously the "conductor" led from the keyboard, or with his violin bow; or perhaps there was, in addition, a musician designated as time-beater. In that case the audience was lucky if it heard the music over the time-beater's noise, for he rapped a tightly rolled bundle of music against a stand. At the Berlin Opera around 1800, Bernard Anselm Weber used a roll of leather stuffed with calf's hair. He would pound so vigorously that the hair would fly about. It is true that in 1794 Guillaume Alexis Paris had been directing opera in Hamburg with a foot-long baton. His innovation did not catch on until Spohr popularized it. That was in 1820. He faced the London Philharmonic, drew from his pocket his secret weapon—a sliver of wood—and gave the signal to begin. "Quite alarmed at such a novel procedure, some of the directors would have protested against it, but when I besought them to grant me at least one trial, they became pacified." Whereupon history was made. Not many years after that, the tiny, bushy-eyebrowed Cipriani Potter, a friend of Beethoven and an important English pianist, stared an orchestra down without a baton, making energetic motions with his two bare hands, thus anticipating Leopold Stokowski by three generations or so. From Spohr on, pianists and all other soloists began to work very closely with conductors. Anyway, nearly all conductors in those days—Berlioz and Wagner were the two early exceptions—were practicing virtuosos themselves.

By the 1860s, European audiences were becoming sophisticated, and programs began to be very much along the lines of programs today. But in the early period of romanticism there was chaos. The greatest instrumentalists—even the angelic Clara Schumann—catered to the low tastes of their listeners. Whether or not they wanted to, they had to. As Liszt said, they were the servants of the public. Of course not all of the instrumentalists were as naïve as the organist who undertook to play six million notes on the piano in less than twelve hours (he played without stopping for eight hours and twenty minutes, winning his bet), but some were not too far removed. Flooding the concert halls were variations on national airs; salon music with sentimental titles (*Plaisir d'amour, Rêve d'une bergerette*), homages to this, that and the other; fire pieces (*The Burning of Mariazell*); geographical pieces (*Souvenir de Paris*); and, above all, operatic paraphrases and potpourris. If there was one type of piece that was ever-present in piano recitals to 1850 or so, it was the operatic paraphrase or variations on a theme from a popular opera. (Audiences loved to see famous pianists play together, and sponsors of concerts would simultaneously light such flares as Liszt, Herz, Thalberg, Moscheles, and watch them incinerate several pianos in some kind of operatic fantasy, which the great pianists would alter to suit themselves.)

Until midway in the century, pianists were brought up on a "serious" repertoire that has long since been forgotten. Anton Rubinstein, as a student in the 1830s, had a repertoire consisting of

Hummel, Herz, Moscheles, Kalkbrenner, Diabelli and Clementi. No Bach, Mozart, Beethoven, Schubert. (As late as 1865 Gottschalk was reprimanded by a critic in Virginia City for playing his *Last Hope* and similar advanced, abstruse compositions. Gottschalk was compared unfavorably with a violinist whose imitations of birds and quadrupeds were inimitable. *That* kind of music, wrote the critic, could be felt and understood without any need of being a musician; everybody understands it. Europe, at least, was more advanced, although the great Clement, who introduced Beethoven's Violin Concerto, edified his audiences with barnyard imitations on the fiddle, and also played it upside down.) Mendelssohn was disgusted with the musical life in Munich in 1830. "Even the best pianists had no idea that Mozart and Haydn had also composed for the piano. They had just the faintest notion of Beethoven, and considered the music of Kalkbrenner, Field and Hummel more classic and scholarly."

Yet it was Mendelssohn who, in his famous 1829 revival of Bach's *St. Matthew Passion*, did not hesitate to chop, cut, alter and modernize it. This was considered most logical, for the music was thus "rendered practical for the abilities of the performers." Everybody got into the act. When the estimable Cipriani Potter played the Mozart D minor Piano Concerto in England, he recomposed the orchestral part and filled out the piano solo. Wagner, in his autobiography, contentedly tells how he improved Gluck's *Iphigenie in Aulis*, linking passages together, interpolating, composing connecting links, introducing his own recitatives, "and throughout the rest of the work I revised the whole instrumentation more or less thoroughly." Yet Mendelssohn and Wagner were two of the greatest, most scrupulous musicians of the century.

We may laugh, but it is hard to put ourselves in their place. They had a different viewpoint on music, one conditioned by romanticism and the dreams thereof. The ego was all-important, and the world was seen almost solipsistically. *I* am the artist; *I* am the performer; *my* inner world is what I shall describe. Rousseau had earlier expressed the new yearning for personalized expression, "I am different from other men. If I am not better, at least I am different." Music to the romantics was not the not-to-be-tampered-with force it is today. It was part of the Mystery, and it had a Meaning or Meanings, an Idea or Ideas, that were bound up with Nature, the Soul, Life. Music expressed states of mind and feelings, and it had to have a program, explicit or implicit. There was hardly a musician in the nineteenth century, and that includes such intellectual stalwarts as Clara and Robert Schumann, Joseph Joachim and Hans von Bülow, who did not see in any specific piece of music a message far outstripping the written note. How they used to read things into music! Carl Tausig, Liszt's favorite pupil, had a ready explanation for the Chopin *Barcarolle*. "This tells of two persons, of a love scene in a secret gondola; we might call this *mise-en-scène* symbolic of lovers' meetings in general. . . . In this modulation into C sharp major (marked *dolce sfogato*) one recognizes a kiss and an embrace—that is plain enough." And so on, at great length and in greater detail. (What would have happened had Chopin named his Op. 60 differently? Rest assured that whatever the title it would have suggested a "plain enough" story to Tausig.) Even simple things like the Mendelssohn *Songs without Words* were not exempt, and the Reverend H. R. Haweis has supplied, in *My Musical Life*, a fearsome three-page analysis of one of them, abounding in words like "soul," "spirit," "Paradise," "joy," "triumph" and "glory."

Liszt told Vladimir de Pachmann all about Chopin's F minor Fantasy, claiming that the program of the work had come from Chopin himself. It runs something like this: Chopin had been playing the piano and was in a depressed mood. A low knocking on his door suggested the first two bars of the Fantasy, and the third and fourth bars suggested his invitation to enter. The doors swing open and admit George Sand, Camille Pleyel, Liszt and others. They take up positions around Chopin, who plays agitated triplets. Sand, with whom he has quarreled, falls on her knees and begs forgiveness. At the final march the visitors go out, leaving Chopin to complete his work.

It is bad enough when fatuous or sentimental writers disgorge such nonsense, but what to do when the composers themselves follow suit? Schumann was always doing it. After he had finished *In der Nacht* from the *Fantasiestücke*, he found to his delight that it contained the story of Hero and Leander. "Of course you know it, how Leander swam every night through the sea to his love. . . . When I am playing *In der Nacht* I cannot get rid of the idea. First he throws himself into the sea; she calls him; he answers; he battles with the waves and reaches land in safety. Then the cantilena, when they lie clasped in one another's arms, until they have to part again, and he cannot tear himself away, until night wraps everything in darkness once more. Do tell me if the music suggests the same thing to you." Of course the doting Clara, to whom this letter was addressed, undoubtedly said yes. Hero and Leander figured in quite a few nineteenth-century minds, and in many contexts. Joachim, for instance, was convinced that the finale of the Brahms F major Symphony represented those two lovers, and that the second motive in C major represented the swimmer breasting the waves. (But Clara Schumann called the symphony *A Forest Idyll* and sketched out a complete program for it.)

When a piece of music came supplied with a romantic title, analysts went wild. Alexander Oulibischeff, the Beethoven authority of the 1850s, found in the first movement of the *Moonlight* Sonata (which, of course, Beethoven did not so name; it was published as *Sonata quasi Fantasia*, Op. 27, No. 2) the moving plaint of a love that knows no realization and feeds on itself like a flame lacking fuel. "As the melody sounds more brokenly, the moon discovers her pale, corpselike face and veils itself again in a moment behind the gloomy clouds hastening past." Oulibischeff objected strenuously to Liszt's quiet definition of the second movement as "a flower between two abysms." Oulibischeff found this description "inapt." (The literary interpreters defended their interpretations with the vigor of a schoolman defending a knotty theological position.) Adolph Marx, one of the founders of the famous Stern Conservatory in Berlin, found the first movement of the *Moonlight* "a soft song of renouncing love.... Life, too, glides downward with ghostly calm into depths wherein no balm is found for these pains." The pianist Louis Köhler found the movement to contain a churchyard, weeping willows, pale moonlight and funeral urns; while the Beethoven savant Ernest von Elferlein heard measured sighs "escaping from the tormented heart." Peter Cornelius thought bigger. To him the first movement was "a majestic Gothic cathedral... a blessed spirit-world."

Hans von Bülow had one of the finest musical minds of the nineteenth century, but that did not prevent him from playing the romantic game of reading things into music. In the 1880s he gave a Beethoven recital in Boston, playing the A major Sonata (Op. 101), the *Hammerklavier*, the *Diabelli* Variations and the *Rondo a Capriccioso*. Eager to help his audience, he placed on his program an explanation of each of the thirty-three variations:

Theme. I. Alla marcia. II. Burial dance. III. Dialogue. IV: Joined by a third interlocutor. V. Joined by a fourth one. VI. Didactic shakes [trills]. VII. Positive assertion. VIII. Soft compliance. IX. Boxing. X. Runaways. XI. Deliberation. XII. Determination. XIII. Mocking Bird. XIV. Nocturnal procession. XV. Trifling. XVI. Gymnastic exercises of the left hand. XVII. Ditto of the right. XVIII. Interview. XIX. Racing. XX. Dreams. XXI. Antithesis. XXII. Mozart sends his Leporello. XXIII. Petulancy of the virtuoso. XXIV. Act of Devotion. XXV. On tiptoe. XXVI. Invitation to dancing. XXVII. Stumbling a dance. XXVIII: "Galop infernal." XXIX. Fit of melancholy (minor). XXX. Expanding gloominess (minor). XXXI. Between Bach and Chopin. XXXII. Revival (Fugue, E flat). XXXIII. Good bye (Minuet and Coda).

But this is nothing compared to von Bülow's exegesis of Chopin's twenty-four Préludes. It is one of the greatest pieces of nineteenth-century fiction. First von Bülow gives each of the Préludes a title:

1. Reunion
2. Presentiment of Death
3. Thou Art So Like a Flower
4. Suffocation
5. Uncertainty
6. Tolling Bells
7. The Polish Dancer
8. Desperation
9. Vision
10. The Night Moth
11. The Dragon Fly
12. The Duel
13. Loss
14. Fear
15. Raindrops
16. Hades
17. A Scene on the Place de Nôtre-Dame de Paris
18. Suicide
19. Heartfelt Happiness
20. Funeral March
21. Sunday
22. Impatience

Then von Bülow supplied a complete program for each Prélude. These interpretations were endorsed by Wilhelm von Lenz and a pupil of Liszt named Madame de Kalergis, both of whom said that the annotations "reflect the composer's feelings and intention with the utmost accuracy." Thus, the E minor Prélude, we have it on such impeccable authority, pictures

one of the paroxysms to which Chopin was subject on account of his weak chest. In the left hand we hear his heavy breathing, and in the right hand the tones of suffering wrung from his breast. At the twelfth measure he seeks relief by turning on the other side; but his oppression increases momentarily. At the stretto he groans, his pulse redoubles its beat, he is near death; but toward the end he breathes more quietly (the chords must be breathed rather than played). His heart-throbs grow slower and fainter; at the chord resting on B flat (third measure from the end) they suddenly cease for a moment. Four eighth-notes must be counted to every half note, so that these beats, though not audible, may yet be felt. The final chord shows that he sleeps.

Or take this about No. 10 in C sharp minor:

A night moth is flying around the room—there! it has suddenly hidden itself (the sustained G sharp); only its wings twitch a little. In a moment it takes flight anew and again settles down in darkness—its wings flutter (trill in the left hand). This happens several times, but at the last, just as the wings begin to quiver again, the busybody who lives in the room aims a stroke at the poor insect. It twitches once . . . and dies.

It takes about as long to read this program as to play the piece itself. But the most unforgettable of von Bülow's fancies—though all of the twenty-four are masterpieces—pertains to No. 9 in E major. This is surrealistic:

Here Chopin has the conviction that he has lost his power of expression. With the determination to discover whether his brain can still originate ideas, he strikes his head with a hammer (here the sixteenths and thirty-seconds are to be carried out in exact time, indicating a double stroke of the hammer). In the third and fourth measures one can hear the blood trickle (trills in the left hand). He is desperate at finding no inspiration (fifth measure); he strikes again with the hammer and with greater force (thirty-second notes twice in succession during the crescendo). In the key of A flat he finds his powers again. Appeased, he seeks his former key and closes contentedly.

If pressed to the wall, von Bülow might have admitted that his interpretations could have been a little extravagant and that he was supplying them as an emotional prop against which his students could lean. These hints suggest the expression and emotion of the Préludes, he might say, and are not to be taken too literally. But that this inanity could have come from what was conceded to be the sharpest musical mind of the time passes belief.

With an esthetic background that could in a straight-faced manner accept "interpretations" like these, how could there be much attention to scholarship? And, not unexpectedly, there wasn't. In line with the ideals of nineteenth-century romanticism, it was the personality that was important, and it followed that the personality was more important than the music. There was precedent to back up such a concept. The 1830s, after all, were not too far removed from the classic period, when it was the obligation of the performer to show his taste by embellishing or improvising or improving the notes before him. Nobody thought twice about such a procedure in the eighteenth century, and nobody thought twice about it in the nineteenth. Liszt thought nothing—and he was applauded for the action—of making up a piano sonata using the theme and variations of Beethoven's A flat Sonata (Op. 26) for the first movement, and ending with the finale of the *Moonlight*. Von Bülow studied the Weber *Concertstück* "with some added effects," and in concerts he would often join the Liszt Twelfth Rhapsody with the latter part of the Second. There was nothing particularly unusual about this, and von Bülow described what he was doing in a letter to his teacher, who happened to be none other than Liszt himself. Liszt, who could never keep his hands off other people's music, never cared too much what others did to *his* music. Alexander Siloti once brought in the Hungarian Rhapsody No. 14 to Liszt, "telling him that I had dared make some alterations in it, and even to omit certain passages, and that I wanted his opinion." After Siloti played, Liszt gave his entire approval.

When Liszt edited the piano music of Schubert he took great satisfaction in letting the world know that he had gone beyond the call of duty. Such was his love for Schubert that he edited the music wholesale, and he proudly stated that "several passages and the whole of the C major Fantasia I have rewritten in modern piano form, and I flatter myself that Schubert would not be displeased with it." That old argument, still prevalent: "If Bach were alive today. . ." Von Lenz subscribed to that school of thought, and when Tausig made his spectacular transcription of the *Invitation to the Dance*, von Lenz was more than willing to ride along, explaining that if the piece was going to be played to an audience of a few thousand people, "of course it must don ball attire and appear in the full panoply of the modern, Olympian concert grand, an instrument that reaches far beyond the possibilities of the piano known to Weber." Note the matter-of-fact "of course," and note it also in Mendelssohn's letter to his sister of November 14, 1840. Of the arpeggio sections of Bach's *Chromatic Fantasy and Fugue*, Mendelssohn writes, "I take the liberty of playing them with all possible crescendos, and pianos, and fortissimos, pedal of course, and to double the octaves in the bass." Of course. One took certain things for granted, just as (later in the century) Teresa Carreño played the ending of the Grieg Concerto in octaves rather than arpeggios—for the self-evident and unchallenged reason that she had good octaves. Nobody complained except the composer, a little bit. And when Henselt, who had a marvelous technique, approached Chopin's *Black Key* Étude, he added octaves to the right hand (what a feat!), extended some chords in the left hand (his left-hand extensions were famous) and added a few bars of his own.

These kinds of goings-on were not confined to the piano. The better musicians, while accepting the artists' monomania as part of the current style, and also accepting the artists' right to make a certain number of changes and additions to the music, did deplore the excesses as loudly as Spohr fulminating against Madame Georgi. Singers, for instance, always have been less interested in the printed note than most other musicians. Singers, indeed, tend to pay as much attention to the printed note as an African Bushman to mosquitoes. The first time Adelina Patti sang for Rossini it was at one of his famous soirées, and he himself accompanied her in *Una voce poco fa* from *Il Barbiere di Siviglia*. When she finished, Rossini coldly asked her who had composed the aria she had just sung. Saint-Saëns saw Rossini the following day, and he was still burned up. Saint-Saëns reports him as saying, "I know well enough that my arias *ought* to be embroidered somewhat. They were designed for that. But in the recitatives, not to leave a note as I wrote it—that is too much." And Chopin, writing from Paris about the tenor Rubini, was interested in what he did to the music. "He produces his tones authentically and not in falsetto, and sometimes sings roulades for two hours altogether (but sometimes embroiders too much and makes his voice purposely tremble); also he continually trills; which, however, brings him more applause than anything else." Singers, like instrumentalists, took fantastic liberties in the name of the highest authorities. The great Manuel Garcia, the most important voice teacher of the early nineteenth century, instructed his pupils that "a musical idea, to be rendered interesting, should be varied, wholly or in part, every time it is repeated. Pieces whose beauty depends on recurrence of the theme—as rondos, variations, polonaises, airs, and cavatinas with a second part—are particularly adapted to receive changes. These changes should be introduced more abundantly, and with ever-heightening variety and accent. The exposition of the opening theme alone should be preserved in its simplicity."

Piano teachers were telling much the same things to their pupils. If so strict a pedagogue as Czerny allowed a liberal use of ritards and interpolations, one can imagine what the romantics did. Czerny, in his *Klavierschule*, allows ritards practically everywhere—at the return of the principal subject; when a phrase is to be separated from the melody; on strongly accented long notes; at a transition to a different tempo; after a pause; at the diminuendo of a quick passage; in a crescendo passage; at the introduction or end of an important passage; in passages "where the composer or performer gives free rein to his fancy" (which could mean anywhere); when the composer writes *expressive*; at the end of a trill or cadence. And what is one to make of a give-and-take passage like the following: "Every composition must be played in the tempo prescribed by the composer and adhered to by the executant. But in almost every line of music there are certain notes and passages where a little ritardando or accelerando is necessary, to beautify the reading and to augment the interest." Which may be an invitation to rubato, but which also is a passport to anarchy. It can safely be stated that only within the last eighty years has there been such a thing as the concept of a basic metrical pulse and a sobriety in the use of such expressive devices as the ritard, accelerando, rubato and dynamic extremes—not to mention fidelity to the printed note. As late as 1905 Theodor Leschetizky made a piano roll of Chopin's D flat Nocturne. Leschetizky was the most popular, respected and productive teacher after Liszt, and he produced some of the greatest pianists of the twentieth century. And how does Leschetizky play the nocturne? Leaving interpretive considerations aside, he introduces new harmonies, a new cadenza or two, and does quite a bit of rewriting. By present standards it is intolerable. But in 1905 nobody gave it a second thought. Old recordings of Francis Planté (born in 1839), Vladimir de Pachmann (1848) and Paderewski (1860), not to mention those of later artists like Lamond, d'Albert, Grünfeld and Friedheim, confirm the statement. By present standards their playing tends to be capricious, rhythmically unsteady, unscholarly and egocentric. But we blame them for the very things for which they were praised in the nineteenth century. When listening to pianists born before 1875, or trying to visualize how they played, it is necessary for us in the latter half of the twentieth century to change our entire concept about the very nature of music. For they ordered things differently in those days. Franz List would have thought Artur Schnabel's Beethoven and Schubert as sapless, arid and unimaginative as Schnabel would have considered Liszt's Beethoven and Schubert eccentric, willful and extravagant. Who is to say who is correct? Both were, according to the standards of their old age.

But every generation sees a shift in emphasis, and it seems clear, judging from the testimony of their recordings, that the pianists born around and after 1850 brought a set of values to their playing significantly different from the playing of their immediate predecessors. This is especially true of the pianists born after 1870.

Around the turn of the century, Saint-Saëns wrote an article about Liszt. He ended with the comment that the memory of having heard the greatest of all pianists consoled him for no longer being young. Nobody who heard Liszt is alive today. But a dwindling band of elderly listeners in the late 1980s have heard some of the last generation of romantic giants—Rachmaninoff, Hofmann, Lhevinne, Godowsky, Rosenthal, Friedman, Moiseiwitsch and the others. The memory of their playing remains a consolation. It is also a consolation that others can share. For we have concrete illustrations of their playing that those who heard Liszt, Tausig, Anton Rubinstein and so forth back to Mozart did not have, and that, of course, is the phonograph record.

These late-romantic pianists, one can see from their records, avoided the excesses of early romanticism and carried the art of romantic pianism to its peak, setting the all-time standards of romantic performance practice. By and large they concentrated on their "own" music, which means the music from Chopin, Schumann and Liszt to the end of the century. It was not an adventurous repertory. They seldom played Bach except in transcription. Haydn and Mozart did not interest them. Of Beethoven most of them played only the "name" sonatas. They seemed frightened of Debussy, playing only the shorter and more popular pieces. If they lived long enough, they took Rachmaninoff into their repertoire.

They were all individualists. On the surface they had little in common. Certainly it would be hard to link such disparate approaches to the keyboard as, say, the red-hot Friedman and the cool, poised, classic Hofmann. Or the aristocratic, authoritative, bronze-sounding Rachmaninoff and the mercurial, miniaturist de Pachmann. Or the warm-hearted Moiseiwitsch and the unruffled, superperfect Godowsky. But listening carefully to the records made by the late-romantic pianists reveals that no matter how different they were as artists they all also had many things in common, sharing a series of pianistic and musical conventions that today have been largely forgotten.

Take, for instance, sound—pure sound. Those who heard the last romantic pianists keep insisting that they never made an ugly sound, and their records back that contention. Sound was one of the romantic ideals. Singers, violinists, pianists, all were expected to produce beautiful sounds. In those days there was none of the current nonsense about the piano being a percussion instrument. They knew how to link sounds in the most melting of legatos, how to project a melody and make it sing like a cello solo. They could get massive sonorities without ever banging, and they had tonal mixtures that astonish and ravish young pianists coming to their records for the first time.

Another thing that the late-nineteenth-century pianists had in common was fluctuation of tempo. Contrary to popular belief, they used very little rubato. When they did use it, it was with taste and restraint. German pianists, curiously, adopted a much more pronounced rubato than the Slavic ones. But all late-romantic pianists constantly modified the basic tempo (in many ways similar to Schindler's description of Beethoven's playing), using ritards to announce second subjects or contrasting sections, accelerandos to supply a *frisson* of excitement, all handled in a way that never lost the basic meter, broke the line or threw the architecture out of skew. The best romantic pianists—and this point cannot be overemphasized—were *not* self-indulgent. Their playing, by and large, had few of the eccentricities, textual changes or misreadings, insane virtuosity or abuses in taste so commonly believed to be an integral part of romanticism. They were musical aristocrats whose apparently free playing was under strict rhythmic and emotional control. They also had techniques better than almost anything to be heard today. A rash-sounding statement; but listen to the Lhevinne recording of the *Blue Danube*, the Moiseiwitsch of Liszt's *La Leggierezza*, the Hofmann of Liszt's *Venezia e Napoli*, the Rachmaninoff of Schumann's *Carnaval*, and the listener is faced with an order of technique that has largely vanished from the earth.

With fluctuation of tempo was joined a knowledge of how to move the bass lines of a piece. The late-romantic pianists all linked up adjacent bass notes (especially in slow movements) for a touch of color and harmonic interest, and they had a canny knowledge of how to balance a melodic line against the bass. Of course, they brought out the inner voices so carefully notated by the composers and so carefully ignored today.

Nor was this merely a romantic trait. A good deal of music by Beethoven and Mozart contains inner voices, real or implied. Judging from the markings in music published during Haydn's and Mozart's day, there is every reason to believe that the performers of the time were employing devices (tempo fluctuation, left-hand melodic lines) commonly believed to have originated in the 1830s. We still have so much to learn about performance practice of the past. But at least we have, thanks to the records of musicians born in the previous century, concrete examples of how the romantics went about their musical business.

· IX ·

Tubercular, Romantic, Poetic

IT WAS CHOPIN who properly set romantic pianism on its rails and gave it the impetus that still shows no signs of deceleration. He did this all by himself, evolving from nowhere the most beautiful and original piano style of the century. He was the very first of the new pianists, the one who snapped for all time the thongs of classicism. The basic elements of his style of playing, his innovations in fingering and pedaling, were not to be substantially altered until Debussy and Prokofieff appeared. Once Chopin's Études were published, there was little more to add.

He was a slight, refined-looking man, not much over a hundred pounds in weight, with a prominent nose, brown eyes (say some; others say blue-green), a pale complexion and beautiful hands. He was a snob and a social butterfly, to whom moving in the best circles meant everything. He was fastidious in his toilet, dressed in the height of fashion (even foppishly so), kept a carriage, had a precise mind and precise manners, could be witty, was a fine mimic, was ultra-conservative in his esthetic tastes. He made a good deal of money and spent it lavishly, always complaining that he did not have more. "You think I am making a fortune? Carriages and white gloves cost more, and without them one would not be in good taste." Good taste meant very much to him. It certainly meant more to him than the romantic movement that was sweeping Europe. That he avoided as much as he could. He even disliked the word "romanticism." Delacroix was perhaps his closest friend, but he did not understand, or even like, the paintings of Delacroix.

That went for music, too. He was on good terms with all the musicians of his day, but did not like their music. He abhorred the

144

scores of Berlioz; considered Liszt's music vapid and empty; told his friend Stephen Heller that Schumann's *Carnaval* was not music at all; ignored the work of Mendelssohn. He had no interest in Schubert, and Beethoven disturbed him. The behemoth of Bonn, with his turbulence and titanic hammer strokes, frightened him. The only two great composers who meant anything to him were Bach and Mozart. Those he adored. He also adored the operas of Bellini. Chopin was a romantic who hated romanticism.

This is the paradox. It was Chopin who, of all the early romantics, has turned out the most popular. Virtually everything he composed has remained in the repertoire, and a piano recital without some Chopin on it is still the exception. Mendelssohn, the god of his day, has faded; very little of Liszt's fantastic output has remained in the repertoire (though there are signs of revival); and of Schumann's large amount of piano music, only a dozen works, at most, are played with any regularity. But Chopin's popularity shows no signs of diminishing.

In his day he was a revolutionary. To many his music was exotic, inexplicable, perhaps insane. Critics like Rellstab in Germany, Chorley and Davison in England, dismissed much of Chopin's music as eccentricities full of earsplitting dissonance. (And, indeed, a near-atonal piece like the A minor Prélude is hard going even today.) Ignaz Moscheles was not the only professional who found Chopin's music impossible to comprehend. Liszt himself, romantic of romantics, referred to Chopin's "bold dissonance and strange harmonies," and in his biography of Chopin was to write of him as "one of those original beings . . . adrift from all bondage." The only one who really understood him from the beginning was Schumann, who introduced him to Germany with the review of the *Variations on Là ci darem la mano* (Op. 2) that contained the famous phrase, "Hats off, gentlemen! A genius!" Chopin repaid Schumann by feeling embarrassed with that extravagant review (many more were to follow), complaining to his friends about it, and crying that Schumann was making him look like a fool. (It may be, though, that the review which so amused and embarrassed Chopin was written by Friedrich Wieck in 1831 in *Caecilia*. Schumann's and Wieck's reviews are strikingly similar, often even in phraseology.)

But about his piano playing there was no disagreement. What an artist he must have been! Heller spoke of Chopin's slim hands—how they would "suddenly expand and cover a third of the keyboard. It was like the opening of the mouth of a serpent about to swallow a rabbit whole." (Over a hundred years later, Alfred Cortot was to write a prose poem on Chopin's hands, ". . . with a skin through the pores of which everything ignoble has evaporated.") Mendelssohn, a notoriously picky man, was charmed by Chopin's playing. It continued to enchant him, even though it represented everything he disliked, and he wrote to his sister Fanny, after hearing him a few times, "I am persuaded that if you, and Father, had heard him play some of his better pieces as he played them to me, you would say the same. There is something entirely original in his piano playing and it is at the same time so masterly that he may be called a perfect virtuoso." Mendelssohn considered Chopin "one of the very first of all. He produces new effects, like Paganini on his violin, and accomplishes things nobody could formerly have thought practicable." Of course Mendelssohn, being Mendelssohn, had to enter a demurrer about Chopin's extravagance in tempo and rhythm. A more sympathetic listener was Schumann, always responsive to the new, who has left us a lovely description of Chopin himself playing the *Aeolian Harp* Étude (Op. 25, No. 1). "It would be a mistake to suppose that he allowed us to hear every note in it. It was rather an undulation of the A flat major chord, brought out more loudly here and there with the pedal, but exquisitely entangled in the harmony. We followed a wondrous melody on the sustained tones, while in the middle a tenor voice broke clearly from the chords and joined the principal melody. . . ."

The man who was capable of these effects had developed them by himself. Certainly his teacher in Warsaw, Joseph Elsner, could not have given them to him. Elsner was a good teacher but a musician of the old school who panted to have his student write sonatas and other classical compositions. No musician of that background could have given the young Chopin an insight into the new school. As yet, indeed, there *was* no new school, though certain pieces by Field, Spohr, Hummel and Weber contained seeds of romanticism. As a composer, Chopin was helped by those four men, and by several others. As a pianist he was helped by nobody, and it was he who created the new school. He came to Paris in 1831, aged twenty-one, a fully formed musician and, aside from Liszt, the greatest pianist in Europe. He may have been a provincial when he came to Paris, but he already knew his worth and he knew his mission. And even though his experience with Kalkbrenner had rattled him for a few months—that crush on Kalkbrenner's playing is one of the most ludicrous incidents in the history of music—he almost immediately recovered. His own good sense, and the supplementary advice of Mendelssohn, Elsner and his own family, kept him from accepting Kalkbrenner's incredible proposal of three years of study. Chopin weighed the pros and cons:

In Germany I could not have learned the piano from anyone; for though there were persons who felt that I still lack something, no one knew what; and I also could not see the beam in my own eye which still prevents me from looking higher. Three years are a long time; too long; even Kalkbrenner admits that, now that he has examined more closely: which should convince you that a genuine virtuoso knows no jealousy. But I would be willing to stick to it for three years if that will only enable me to take a big step forward in what I have undertaken. I understand enough not to become a copy of Kalkbrenner. Nothing will interfere with my perhaps overbold but not ignoble desire to create a new world for myself.

The fact is that in 1831 nobody in Europe could have taught Chopin a thing or could have succeeded in anything but destroying his natural talent. He had come out of Warsaw as fully developed, to all intents and purposes, as he ever would be. By that time the two piano concertos were written, many of the Études had been composed, and Chopin was never substantially to add to his technique either as pianist or composer (of course there was an emotional deepening and broadening as he grew older).

Where in heaven's name could he have developed these incredible conceptions? It is true that he had been a prodigy, but what great pianist has not been a *Wunderkind*? Chopin's development was precocious but not unusual among the great musicians. As a child he would cry when he heard music. As a five-year-old he had learned all that his eldest sister could teach him. At sixteen he was the pride of the Warsaw Conservatory. All doors were open to the young genius—those of Prince Czartorski, Count Potocki, Prince Sapieha, Prince Czerwertynski, Viceroy Zajaczek, Prince Lubecki, Prince Radziwill, General Sowinski. Those wonderful, jagged Polish names! From those houses he got his impeccable manners and his taste for the good life. At eighteen he had triumphed in Vienna. At twenty he left Poland, arriving in Paris by way of Vienna and Stuttgart. Paris had always been his goal. "When shall I get there?" he wrote in his diary. "In how many years? Fifty?"

The point is that up to his arrival in Paris he had been exposed to very few of the new concepts sweeping Europe. From John Field he had absorbed a few things, and also from Hummel. But his style and his harmonic structure, his way of treating the instrument, his use of functional ornamentation (unlike so much of the music of Liszt and the other virtuosos, nearly all of Chopin's bravura passages—and all, in his maturity—have a melodic rather than a purely bravura function), his amazing harmonies and modulations, the piquancy of his rubato, his use of folk elements in the mazurkas and polonaises—all these he had developed on his own by the time he was twenty-one. He was one of the fantastic geniuses in history.

Liszt and Chopin became acquainted shortly after the Pole arrived in Paris. Liszt was then, and remained—Liszt: the thunderer, the matinee idol, the actor with the long locks, the lady-killer, the Paganini of the keyboard. Chopin envied him his strength with the intense feeling that only the physical weakling can have for the strong man. Even as a youth Chopin admired strength, and he once wrote about a Herr Lehmann, otherwise unknown to history, "I envied him his fingers. I broke my roll with two hands; he crushed his into a wafer with one." That was in 1828, and the eighteen-year-old Chopin, all set to conquer the world at the keyboard, knew that he would have to do it by finesse rather than power. When he played in Vienna he was prepared for the critical remarks about his lack of sonority. It is true that his success was enormous, but, as Chopin wrote, "It is being said everywhere that I played too softly, or, rather, too delicately for people used to the piano-pounding of the artists here." In Warsaw, where he played the premiere of his F minor concerto, those who could hear him were ravished; "on the other hand the gallery complained that I played too softly." This lack of sonority was the single defect in Chopin's equipment—if it was a defect. In Paris he confined his playing almost exclusively to the salons, where everybody could hear him without difficulty.

But that does not mean he did not wish he had more power. What he wanted to do and what he could do were two different things. He once listened to a young pianist play his *Polonaise militaire*, and the young man broke a string. He apologized in confusion. "Young man," said Chopin, "if I had your strength and played that polonaise as it

An 1838 drawing of Chopin by his good friend Delacroix. This was the sketch for Delacroix' well-known painting.

Luigi Calamatta's drawing of Chopin (1840) gives a good idea of the dandified, yet sensitive, Polish-born composer.

Chopin in 1849, a few months before his death of consumption. The Idzikowski-Sydow *Portret Fryderyka Chopina* calls this a photograph, not a daguerreotype, as has commonly been believed.

Chopin's death mask, molded by Auguste Clésinger. Clésinger was the son-in-law of George Sand, with whom Chopin had an affair for many years.

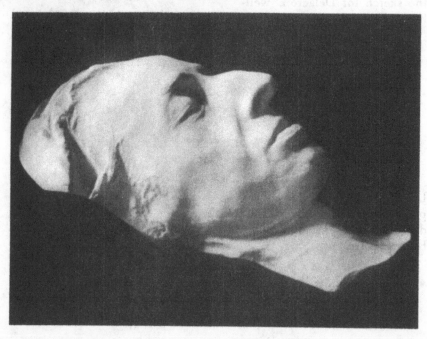

should be played, there would not be a string left in the instrument by the time I got through." On another occasion he wrote to Heller, "Liszt is playing my études, and transporting me outside of my respectable thoughts. I should like to steal from him the way to play my own études." The relationship between Chopin and Liszt was love-hate. They respected and even admired each other, and certainly Liszt owed much to Chopin, but there was always a tinge of jealousy and spite on Chopin's part. Their uneasy friendship lasted, off and on, for many years. Chopin lived for some time at 38, Rue de la Chausée d'Antin, and Liszt at the Hôtel de France on the Rue Lafitte, only a few blocks away. They saw a great deal of each other. Liszt could afford to be generous toward his frail colleague. He once decided to write a review about a Chopin concert for the *Gazette musicale*. Chopin was told by the critic Ernest Legouvé that a Liszt review was very important; that Liszt "will create a fine kingdom for you." Chopin gave a sour smile. "Yes," he said, "within his own empire." In a letter to Jules Fontana, Chopin twisted the knife. Liszt, he said, "will live to be a deputy or perhaps even a king, in Abyssinia or the Congo; but as for the themes of his compositions, they will repose in the newspapers." If Josef Novakowski's anecdote is true, there was one occasion when Chopin stood directly up to Liszt instead of muttering about him or quietly stewing. Novakowski tells of a soirée in 1843, when Liszt played a Chopin nocturne and added all kinds of fancy embellishments. Chopin told Liszt to play the music as written or not play it at all. "Play it yourself," said Liszt, piqued. Chopin did. Whereupon Liszt embraced Chopin and apologized. "Works like yours should not be meddled with." A romantic invention, or the truth? The story just might be true.

Most biographies state that Chopin had little to do with Liszt after 1843. The ostensible cause of the rupture, again according to the biographies, was that Liszt made free with a young lady in Chopin's rooms. The story sounds apocryphal. Chopin was not that much of a prude, dandy though he was. Anyway, his letters as late as 1848, the year before his death, refer to "my friend Liszt." In 1852 Liszt brought out a biography of Chopin, probably written in whole (and most certainly in part) by his mistress, the Princess Carolyne Sayn-Wittgenstein. Liszt had doubts about its style and organization, for he sent the manuscript to Sainte-Beuve. The eminent critic told Liszt, as tactfully as possible, that the whole thing was a mess and would have to be rewritten. What a pity that Liszt did not take his advice! He knew Chopin better than most people, and could have given us so much. Instead, the infuriating biography of Chopin that appears under his name is a smug, purple-prosed, wretchedly written essay on things like national music, and Chopin plays a very small part in it. The Princess was not only one of the worst writers in the history of prose; she was also a very stupid woman.

Because Chopin detested public appearances he seldom appeared outside the salons. As his frame began to weaken from the oncoming tuberculosis, his physical strength became such that he could not play a forte. He compensated by using a pianissimo with infinite degrees of shading (he must have had extraordinary control—more, perhaps, than any pianist who ever lived) and so delicate was his approach that when he came near a normal forte it sounded thunderous. Toward the end, though, his playing must have been wraithlike, with tiny tones dissolving faintly into the air. Thalberg once came out of a Chopin recital and shouted all the way home. "I need some noise because I've hard nothing but pianissimo all evening," he explained.

Was there ever anything to compare with those salons in which Chopin played? Paris in the 1830s was the intellectual capital of the world, and everybody who was anybody in the world of music, letters, art or science would attend one of the big soirées. Chopin might share the program with the cellist Auguste Franchomme, or the contralto Maria Malibran, or the tenor Adolphe Nourrit. If Liszt were around there would be four-hand music, Liszt playing the treble, Chopin the bass (he always insisted on taking the *secondo* part; nobody was going to drown *him* out). Or there might be some two-piano playing, with Mendelssohn or Moscheles at the second piano. Games would be played. Heine might improvise a story to Chopin's accompaniment. Chopin might sit at the piano to imitate the way Liszt played, and not to be outdone Liszt would return the compliment. Grouped around the piano might be George Sand, the Countess Marie d'Agoult (she, mother of two children, who ran away with Liszt and had a child who married Liszt's pupil, the pianist-conductor Hans von Bülow, *that* child, Cosima, later running away from von Bülow to live with, and eventually marry, Wagner), Balzac, Delacroix, Lamartine, Gautier, Rossini (when he went out; normally people came to *his* house), Viardot-Garica, Eugène Sue, Meyerbeer.

It was Liszt who had brought Chopin and George Sand together. She was tiny (under five feet), dark, big-eyed and cigar-smoking, a feminist, a successful novelist, and her love affairs were the talk of Paris. After separating from her husband she had been the mistress of Jules Sandeau, Prosper Mérimée, Alfred de Musset, Michel de Bourges, Pietro Pagello and, possibly, Liszt. With Chopin she entered into a long relationship, though it appears pretty certain that after an initial year of rapture their relationship was platonic. When it did break up, though, it was with permanent scars for both.

Chopin's pianistic style was so original, and so thoroughly discussed and analyzed by his contemporaries, that it is fairly easy to reconstruct. Two things must be considered—his altogether novel rubato and his classic bent. His playing was dynamically restricted, because of his lack of strength, but within its framework it had everything—a completely supple and responsive technique, imaginative pedal effects (he always used a Pleyel instrument; thought the Érard "too insistent"), incredible nuance of touch and tone, and a revolutionary way of fingering. Hallé heard Chopin in 1836 and said that in listening to him all powers of analysis were lost. "You did not for a moment think of how perfect was his execution of this or that difficulty; you listened, as it were, to the improvisation of a poem." One of the things about Chopin's playing that especially excited Hallé, and all others, was his rubato, which nobody in his day could duplicate and which was so misunderstood.

Chopin got his rubato with his milk. It was a Polish characteristic, and he transported it into everything he played. To ears not accustomed to those delicate rhythmic displacements, the meter sounded awry. Chopin in 1842 was giving a lesson to Wilhelm von Lenz when Meyerbeer walked in. The tiny Mazurka in C (Op. 33, No. 3) was being played, and von Lenz tells what happened:

Meyerbeer had seated himself; Chopin let me play on.

"That is two-four time," said Meyerbeer.

For reply, Chopin made me repeat, and kept time by beating loudly on the instrument with his pencil; his eyes glowed.

"Two-four," Meyerbeer repeated quietly.

I never but once saw Chopin angry; it was at this time! A delicate flush colored his pale cheeks, and he looked very handsome.

"It is three-four," he said *loudly*, he, who always spoke so softly.

"Give it me for a ballet in my opera"—*l'Africaine*, then kept a secret—"I will show you, *then*."

"It is *three*-four," almost screamed Chopin, and played it himself. He played it several times, and stamped time with his foot—he was beside himself! It was of no use; Meyerbeer insisted it was two-four, and they parted in ill humor.

Somehow this little scene, as described by von Lenz, has the ring of truth. And it is backed by a reliable Hallé, who was on good terms with Chopin for some thirteen years:

A remarkable feature of his playing was the entire freedom with which he treated the rhythm, but which appeared so natural that for years it had never struck me. It must have been in 1845 or 1846 that I once ventured to observe to him that most of his mazurkas (those dainty jewels) when played by himself appeared to be written not in ¾ but in ⁴⁄₄ time, the result of his dwelling so much longer on the first note of the bar. He denied it strenuously, until I made him play one of them and counted audibly four in the bar, which fitted perfectly. Then he laughed and explained that it was the national character of the dance which created the oddity. The more remarkable fact was that you received the impression of a ¾ rhythm whilst listening to common time. Of course this was not the case with every mazurka, but with many. I understood later how ill-advised I had been to make that observation to him and how well disposed towards me he must have been to have taken it with such good humor, for a similar remark made by Meyerbeer, perhaps in a somewhat supercilious manner, on another occasion, led to a serious quarrel, and I believe Chopin never forgave him.

What all this means is that Chopin's rubato differed—in the mazurkas, at least—from all others in that it was broader, thanks to his Polish heritage, and hence that much more puzzling to his contemporaries. And he probably used far less rubato while playing his non-national music. But it seems sure that his rubato was always controlled, never capricious. When Salaman heard Chopin in 1848, he specifically mentions that "in spite of all I had heard of Chopin's tempo rubato, I still recollect noting how precise he was in the matter of time, accent and rhythm, even when playing most passionately, fancifully and rhapsodically." Both Liszt and von Lenz testify to the control that Chopin brought to his rubato. So does Hallé.

Liszt described it as "a tempo agitated, broken, interrupted, a movement flexible, yet at the same time abrupt and languishing. . . . All his compositions should be played with this accented and measured swaying and balancing." The key word here is "measured." In matters of exact, measured rhythm Chopin was, as his pupil Mikuli, said, inexorable, and he always had a metronome on the piano. Rubato should never be an invitation to license. The secret as Chopin practiced it is that the feeling of individual note values was always preserved, whatever the temporary rhythmic displacement; the rhythm would fluctuate but never the underlying metrical pulse. Thus a quarter note remained a quarter, a dotted eighth a dotted eighth. (How many pianists distort by making eighth into quarters!) Hallé and Meyerbeer notwithstanding, Chopin's rubato must have been metrically precise. They had trouble counting because of the unusual and unprecedented freedom Chopin employed; his approach was too novel for anybody trained in the old school. Indeed, Chopin's rubato, except for its broader quality, was probably not unlike Mozart's. Mozart had written that in an adagio tempo rubato the left hand should go on playing in strict time. Von Lenz, who could not have known of Mozart's letter, quotes Chopin as saying, "The left hand is the conductor, it must not waver or lose ground; do with the right hand what you will and can. Supposing that a piece lasts a given number of minutes; it may take just so long to perform the whole, but in the details deviations may occur." Liszt's famous definition says much the same thing, but allegorically, "Do you see those trees? The wind plays in the leaves, life unfolds and develops beneath them, but the tree remains the same—that is the Chopin rubato!" In short, vary as much as is necessary, but never lose the basic meter.

One can but guess, and the guess here is that where many nineteenth-century pianists went wild in the name of rubato, Chopin never did, for his classic streak was too strong. Chopin and classicism may sound incompatible, but of all the romantics he was at once the most revolutionary and the most classic—classic in that for the most part (exceptions are the two sonatas and the two concertos) his forms are perfectly matched to content, his workmanship jeweled and precise. There is little padding, no superfluous passagework. Bach was always an inspiration to Chopin; and before a concert he would shut himself up and play from the *Well-Tempered Clavier*. The year he died he spent much time with Delacroix, and the great painter recounts in his journal one afternoon he spent with Chopin. "During the day he talked music with me and that gave him new animation. I asked him what establishes logic in music. He made me feel what counterpoint and harmony are; how the fugue is like pure logic in music, and that to know fugue deeply is to be acquainted with the element of all reason and all consistency in music." Imagine our little romantic Chopin talking like a *Kapell-meister*! And yet the classic element was always there. His Préludes in all the major and minor keys were inspired, at least in key concept, by the *Well-Tempered Clavier* (and is not Chopin's first Prélude, in C, a compliment to Bach's first Prelude, also in C? Play both at a slow tempo; the resemblances are too striking to be coincidental). The Études start out with a major-minor key relationship which, however, does peter out after a while.

In addition to Bach, Chopin's great love was Mozart. The Trio in E (K. 542) figured repeatedly on his programs. He achieved little identity with Beethoven, though once in a while he would play the A flat sonata (Op. 26). He told Hallé that the E flat sonata (Op. 31, No. 3) was "very vulgar." But Mendelssohn's *Songs without Words* are not vulgar, and he did not like them either. No; Chopin had a mighty pull only toward Bach and Mozart. He studied them thoroughly, and their ideals of workmanship figured in his own music and piano playing.

Delicate as his playing was, it never seemed to miss fire when heard in a small room. As Moscheles said, his pianissimos required only a mere breath; "he requires no powerful forte to produce the required contrasts. The consequence is that one never misses the orchestral effects that the German school demands of a pianoforte player." Naturally Chopin's perfect technique provided absolute lucidity, but that is not what most impressed his contemporaries. What struck them were his freedom, poetry and nuance. When he played the climax of his *Barcarolle* he had to use a pianissimo instead of fortissimo as marked; "but with such wonderful nuances," exclaims Hallé, "that one remained in doubt if this new reading were not preferable to the accustomed one." This kind of nuance and color was helped by a perfect legato. One reliable observer of Chopin's last years was Alfred Hipkins of the Broadwood firm. He not only heard Chopin in London in 1848; he was Chopin's piano-tuner (as well as being a fine pianist himself, a historian and a pioneer in harpsichord research). Chopin played in such homes as that of Mrs. Adelaide Sartoris at 99 Eaton Place, which had about 150 seats, just the right size for the sick and fragile pianist. In 1848 he was near death, and an observer said he was so emaciated "he looked transparent."

Hipkins has left a record of Chopin's super-pianissimos and singing legato touch. He says that Chopin used plenty of pedal, especially in left-hand arpeggio passages, "which swelled or diminished like waves in an ocean of sound. He kept his elbows close to his sides and played only with finger touch—no weight from the arms. He used a simple, natural position of the hands... adopting the easiest fingering, although it might be against the rules, that came to him. He changed his fingers on a key as often as an organ player." Chopin never hesitated to use the thumb on the black keys, a practice frowned upon by the classicists of the Czerny-Hummel school, or to pass the thumb under the fifth finger, or to slide a finger from black key to white key, or even from white key to white key.

But Hipkins' statement that Chopin played only from the fingers must not be taken to indicate that Chopin always played so. At that stage in his last illness, his motions necessarily had to be extremely economical, and his weakness would not have permitted any heavy shoulder or arm movements. Chopin himself is on record as saying that the upper arm must be used. It is only fair to state, however, that Chopin was the least flamboyant physically of all the great pianists, and the French pedagogue Marmontel went as far as to say that in equality of fingers and perfect independence of hands, Chopin stemmed from the school of Clementi. There is more than a grain of truth in the statement.

Disliking public performance as much as he did, and further handicapped by his illness, Chopin made surprisingly few public appearances in his life. His reputation as a pianist rests upon about thirty concerts. He did not have to play much, for he derived a thoroughly satisfactory income from teaching; and he also made quite a bit from his music. Primarily he was a busy society teacher ("I have to give a lesson to young Mme. Rothschild, then to a lady from Marseilles, then to an Englishwoman, then to a Swedish one..."), and he apparently had only one pupil of genius. That was Karl Filtsch, the delicate blond genius from Hungary who died of consumption at the age of fifteen. "The blade was too keen for the scabbard," Moscheles sorrowfully told Sir George Grove. It was Filtsch of whom Liszt said, "when the little one goes on the road, I shall shut up shop." A youth named Paul Gunsberg who, like Filtsch, died very young, was also considered one of Chopin's few really brilliantly talented students. Otherwise the list of Chopin's pupils was a social register—Princess Marcelline Czartoryska, Princess C. de Spuzzo, the Countess d'Apponyi, Princess Elisabeth Czernicheff, Baroness Bronicka and so on. The list could be extended to cover several pages. As a teacher, Chopin was *very* fashionable. In addition to little Filtsch, there were a few good artists who came out of Chopin's atelier. Some of them went on to useful careers in music, though none appears to have been of outstanding skill as a soloist. Georges Mathias became a prominent teacher at the Paris Conservatoire; Carl Mikuli (whose editions of Chopin were standards for many years) went on to teach at Lemberg; and Gustave Schumann (no relation to the composer) established a good reputation as a teacher in Berlin. Adolph Gutmann made a big career out of being a pupil and friend of Chopin, but nobody seemed to think seriously of him as a pianist. He was a man of considerable size, with big hands, and Chopin admired him because of his strength. Von Lenz describes him as "a rough fellow at the piano, but with robust health and a herculean frame. . . . I heard him at Chopin's; he played like a porter. . . . Chopin took so much trouble to try and carve a toothpick out of this log!" Chopin dedicated to Gutmann the Scherzo in C sharp minor.

As a teacher Chopin was strictly business—both financially and artistically. He was punctual ("with me, things go by the clock") and he started at 8 A.M., ushering the student into his studio, which contained two pianos—a Pleyel grand and a small cottage piano on which Chopin accompanied. The lesson cost twenty francs, and the student was expected to leave the money on the mantelpiece. Chopin, fashion plate that he was, always dressed impeccably for his lessons: hair curled, shoes polished, clothes elegant. Lessons were supposed to last an hour but sometimes ran over.

His pupil Mikuli is the authority for the statement that Chopin started all his pupils with Clementi. Then came Cramer, Moscheles, and Clementi again with the *Gradus ad Parnassum*. Bach, Handel and Scarlatti were also used. For advanced pupils Chopin was surprisingly catholic, whatever his private feelings about contemporary composition might have been. In the repertoire of his students were pieces by Mozart, Dussek, Field, Hummel, Ries, Beethoven (up to Op. 57), Weber, Moscheles, Heller, Hiller, even Schumann, Liszt and Thalberg—and, of course, Chopin. While teaching, Chopin did much illustrating and explaining at the second piano. He could be cutting. Pupils disagreed about how effective a teacher he was. One said that "his only method was to play like an angel and then tell me to do likewise. . . . The hopeless part of it was . . . each time he played, his interpretation was entirely different." But another pupil testifies that Chopin was patient and tolerant. Mme. Rubio, one of his assistants, said on the contrary that he was often irritable; and Mikuli bears this out by saying that some of Chopin's princesses and countesses walked away in tears. Mathias once saw him break a chair in rage. All of which indicates that Chopin approached his pupils differently, and that each saw him through a particular set of circumstances. The same would be true of any teacher who ever lived. Teachers are always patient and tolerant with their talented pupils, irritated by the stupid ones.

Chopin intended to bring out a book on teaching, and left some preliminary notes. These are of great importance—not so much for what they actually say as for what they indicate about Chopin's own method. Following are some of Chopin's own strictures (not in his own words unless set off in quotation marks):

Everything depends on good fingering.

Kalkbrenner's method of playing from the wrist only is wrong. Forearm and upper arm should be used in addition to the wrist, hand and fingers.

Suppleness is of extreme importance. (During Chopin's first lessons with a pupil his most-used words were "Easily . . . easily.")

Do not use a flat hand. Ease of movement is impossible if the fingers are outstretched.

Kalkbrenner was also wrong in advising his pupils to read a newspaper while practicing technical exercises. No! said Chopin. Practicing demands intensity and concentration. It is not purely mechanical.

Avoid muscular fatigue. Chopin feared the *abrutissement* of his pupils—the stupor brought on by overpractice. He recommended no more than three hours daily.

The correct use of the pedal remains a study for life.

Concentrate on legato. Hear great singers. "If you want to play the long cantilena in my Scherzo [in B flat minor], go hear Pasta or Rubini." (Chopin adored good singing all his life, was a friend of Bellini, and in his nocturnes tried to capture a Bellinian type of melody over a John Field bass. The legato style of the great singers had a decided influence on Chopin's playing.)

Fingers are unequal in strength. Special exercises should be developed to make the best of each finger. Chopin derided teachers and schools of playing that aimed at the myth of equal finger strength. "Flying in the face of nature, it has become customary to attempt to acquire equality of strength in the fingers. It is more desirable that the student acquire the ability to produce a finely graded quality of sound, or so it seems to me. The ability to play everything at a level tone is not our object. There are as many different sounds as there are fingers."

All this may not be revelatory today, but in the 1840s it was prophetic—far in advance of its time, and a sharp break from traditional teaching. Here Chopin was the first modernist, just as he was the first modern pianist. It is too bad that he never got beyond a few penciled pages of his *méthode*. Fortunately the picture as it stands is quite complete, and the figure of Chopin clearly emerges: that marvelously controlled, original, poetic, nuanced classic-romantic pianist and musician, whose physical resources may have been small but whose spirit and conception were epical. More so, even, than Liszt, though Liszt was the greatest pianist, the greatest showman, one of the most important composers and the most renowned teacher of the nineteenth century.

· X ·

Thunder, Lightning,
Mesmerism, Sex

WHEN LISZT PLAYED the piano, ladies flung their jewels on the stage instead of bouquets. They shrieked in ecstasy and sometimes fainted. Those who remained mobile made a mad rush to the stage to gaze upon the features of the divine man. They fought over the green gloves he had purposely left on the piano. One lady fished out the stub of a cigar that Liszt had smoked. She carried it in her bosom to the day she died. Other ladies came away with priceless relics in the form of broken strings from the piano he had played. These *disjecta membra* were mounted in frames and worshiped. Liszt did not give mere concerts; they were saturnalia. The bemused Heine once asked a medical man whose specialty was women to explain the nature of the hysteria that Liszt created. The physician, wrote Heine, "spoke of magnetism, galvanism and electricity; of contagion in a sultry hall filled with innumerable wax lights and some hundred perfumed and perspiring people; of histrionic epilepsy; of the phenomenon of tickling; of musical cantharides; and other unmentionable matters." Heine tells of a concert he attended at which two Hungarian countesses, contending for Liszt's snuffbox, threw each other on the ground and fought until they were exhausted.

Liszt himself well knew the impact he was making and was not averse to adding a little drama of his own. He could scare the daylights out of his audience. An Englishman named Henry Reeves heard Liszt in Paris, and has left us a description of the great man in one of his more florid moments:

I saw Liszt's countenance assume that agony of expression, mingled with radiant smiles of joy, which I never saw on any other human face except in

161

the paintings of Our Saviour by some of the early masters; his hands rushed over the keys, the floor on which I sat shook like a wire, and the whole audience were wrapped in sound, when the hand and frame of the artist gave way. He fainted in the arms of the friend who was turning over the pages for him, and we bore him out in a fit of hysterics. The effect of this scene was really dreadful. The whole room sat breathless with fear, till Hiller came forward and announced that Liszt was already restored to consciousness and was comparatively well again. As I handed Madame de Circourt to her carriage, we both trembled like poplar leaves, and I tremble scarcely less as I write this.

Some unkind critics—oh, the perfidy of man!—actually suggested that Liszt paid to have his ladies faint and fight. But with his profile—and reputation—he had ladies swooning all his life. They went wild over him when he was young and dazzlingly handsome; and they went wild over him when he was an old man in a cassock, with great wens on his noble face. He was a proud man, and never did he let anybody forget that he was Franz Liszt. In 1875, eleven years before his death, he gave a concert in Leipzig. It was reported by a correspondent for the *Musical Record* in London:

Precisely at eleven o'clock a silver head of hair and a well-known countenance above a cassock-girt figure moved majestically down the room, and received with Caesar-like condescension the applause of the surrounding crowd. After having remained standing long enough to allow all the opera glasses a sufficient survey of his fine head, Liszt . . . began an extempore fantasia. After a few bars of prelude he took the theme from Wagner's *Kaisermarsch* and by degrees worked himself up into a storm of rain-like runs, hail-like trills, lightning arpeggios and thunder chords, until at last the hair fell over his forehead, and as he tossed it back the figure at the piano recalled the well-known inspired look of the pictures of our youth.

He was an egomaniac and could never bear to have anybody's eyes off him. In concerto appearance he would, during the tuttis, talk, gesticulate, beat time, stamp the floor, wiggle around so that the medals and decorations he loved to wear would clink and clank. Often he would have three pianos on stage, using them as his fancy dictated. Seldom would one of those pianos emerge without broken strings and hammers; and in 1840 a British critic bitterly noted that Liszt had been presented with a silver breakfast service "for doing that which would cause every young student to receive a severe reprimand—viz., thumping and partially destroying two very fine pianofortes." No wonder the shrewd old Friedrich Wieck, comparing Liszt to Thalberg, said that Liszt played with inspired affectation, Thalberg with inspired vacuity.

Liszt had these mannerisms almost from the beginning. Not at the beginning, though. Unlike Chopin, he took some time developing as a pianist and as a personality. Of course he had amazing talent to start with, but it was a talent that had been poorly trained and was threatening to dissolve into nothing. His only important teacher was Carl Czerny, and when that fine pedagogue heard Liszt in 1819 (Liszt was then eight years old) he was appalled. Many years later Czerny gave his impression of the young Liszt:

He was a pale, delicate-looking child and while playing swayed in the chair as if drunk, so that I often thought he would fall to the floor. Moreover his playing was completely irregular, careless and confused, and he had so litle knowledge of correct fingering that he threw his fingers all over the keyboard in an altogether arbitrary fashion. Nevertheless, I was amazed by the talent with which nature had equipped him. I gave him a few things to sight-read, which he did, purely by instinct, but for that very reason in a manner that revealed that Nature herself had here created a pianist.... Never before had I so eager, talented or industrious a student. Since I knew from numerous experiences that geniuses whose mental gifts are ahead of their physical strength tend to neglect solid technique, it seemed necessary above all to use the first months to regulate and strengthen his mechanical dexterity in such a way that he could not possibly slide into bad habits in later years.... Since I made him learn each piece very rapidly, he finally became such a great sight reader that he was publicly capable of sight-reading even compositions of considerable difficulty; and so perfectly as though he had been studying them for a long time. Likewise I tried to equip him with skill in improvising by frequently giving him themes to improvise on.

It was Czerny who introduced Liszt to Beethoven. That seems to have been in 1823, and the legend is that Beethoven attended a Liszt concert and kissed the boy on the forehead. Liszt in later life claimed the story was true, but present-day scholars are inclined to doubt it. Beethoven was quite deaf at the time, and he almost never attended a public concert. He probably did meet Liszt privately, at which time Liszt would have received the Kiss. It was just around that time that Liszt left Vienna. Czerny says that Liszt's father took the boy away too soon, "just at the critical time," and suggests that the elder Liszt was interested primarily in exploiting his child and making money. When Czerny heard Liszt in Paris, sixteen years later, he found his former pupil's playing "rather wild and confused in every respect, the enormous bravura notwithstanding." There spoke the classicist, but few at that time would have agreed with him.

Liszt worked like a maniac after leaving his teacher. In the days of his teens he was a rather mild, romantic young man without the flamboyance that later characterized him. He was polite, anything but arrogant, and in 1828 he impressed Charles Salaman as "a charmingly simple boy, natural and unaffected." He also was obsessed with the ambition to be a learned man, to make up for his inadequate schooling. By hard work he pulled himself up by his bootstraps. "For this fortnight," he wrote to a friend in 1832, "my mind and my fingers have worked like two damned ones. Homer, the Bible, Plato, Locke, Byron, Lamartine, Chateaubriand, Beethoven, Bach, Hummel, Mozart, Weber, are all around me. I study them, I devour them with fury; furthermore I practice exercises for four or five hours (thirds, sixths, octaves, and tremolos, repeated notes, cadences, etc.). Ah, unless I go mad, you will find an artist in me." How much of this five-foot shelf Liszt actually digested may be questionable, but his memory was good and he was able to pass as a cultured man—although how much the practice of tremolos and repeated notes can lead to artistry is something that may well make many musicians wonder. Liszt's parenthetical insert is, in a way, an unconscious giveaway. Already he was practicing at being the showman, not the artist. Fortunately he had enough genius to be able to make the best of both worlds, and when he wanted to he could play the classics as well as anybody in Europe. But basically he was a romantic. Before his liaison with the Countess d'Agoult, who put the final buff of social polish on him, he was a bohemian, and he affected—like all the romantic young men of Europe—a Byronic manner. The awe-struck Hallé has left us a memorable pen portrait of Liszt as he was in 1836:

He is tall and very thin, his face very small and pale, his forehead remarkably high and beautiful; he wears his perfectly lank hair so long that it

The young Liszt, about 1830, in the pencil drawing by Ingres. He was as good-looking as the drawing suggests.

Magnetism? Galvanism? Electricity? Liszt's recitals sent the ladies into a bacchanalian frenzy. This anonymous caricature of the 1840s records a phenomenon widely noted when Liszt played.

spreads over his shoulders, which looks very odd, for when he gets a bit excited and gesticulates, it falls right over his face and one sees nothing of his nose. He is very negligent in his attire, his coat looks as if it had just been thrown on, he wears no cravat, only a narrow white collar. This curious figure is in perpetual motion: now he stamps with his feet, now waves his arms in the air, now he does this, now that.

Liszt, the son of a humble Hungarian official in the service of Prince Eszterházy, was a king during a long life that extended from 1811 to 1886. With his combination of genius and charisma, he did not have to search for success. Success, as Berlioz perhaps enviously commented, pursued him. He became the most famous man in Europe, and more than anybody else he was responsible for social equality of the artist. For that alone he was a hero among the young people of Europe. The great Viennese critic Eduard Hanslick rightly called him "one of the most extraordinary men of his time, one of the most remarkable and most attractive incarnations of the modern spirit." He moved loftily among royalty. Indeed, he had mocked royalty, letting them know who their superior was. He insulted Louis Philippe by refusing to play before him. When Frederick Wilhelm IV of Prussia gave him diamonds, he threw them into the wings. Ludwig I of Bavaria was not invited to his concerts, for Liszt and Ludwig were rivals for the affections of Lola Montez. Because court etiquette forbade a personal invitation to Isabella II of Spain, he would not play for her. His remark to Nicholas I of Russia, who had talked while he played, was quoted all over Europe. Liszt had risen and said, "Music herself should be silent when Nicholas speaks." Liszt had created his own kingdom and expected to be worshiped accordingly. He did not even kiss the ladies' hands. They kissed his. Like a king, he never took a cent from his pupils. At his classes—so unforgettably described by the bright Amy Fay in her once-popular *Music Study in Germany*—the students would gather and restlessly wait, talking in whispers. Around 4 P.M. everybody would begin to murmur, "*Der Meister kommt.*"

Der Meister walks into the room. All stand and respectfully bow toward him. The ladies kiss his hand. Liszt grandly tells all to be seated. Normally he is never spoken to unless he speaks first. He looks over the pile of music on the piano. (It was not a good instrument; every hopeful in Europe had pounded it into a discordant mess.) A piece interests him. The pianist who has prepared it comes forward at the royal summons. He plays. Liszt listens and comments. Sometimes he impatiently sweeps the miserable wretch from the piano and plays the piece as it should be played (producing from the battered piano, his pupil Siloti has said, "music such as no one could form any idea of without hearing it"). All the young girls in the class start swooning. *Der Meister* smiles deprecatingly, but he is pleased.

Only one musician ever topped the impact Liszt made on audiences. That was Paganini, upon whom Liszt modeled a good number of his concert habits. Liszt always took from the best sources. Paganini had made his Paris debut at the Opéra on March 9, 1831, and Liszt had been in the audience (along with Gautier, Janin, Sand, Delacroix, de Musset, Rossini, Auber, Heine and every violinist in Paris). Liszt was swept off his feet. For the first time he saw a consummate showman in action (and one of the supreme virtuosos in history). Paganini turned out to be one of the decisive influences in his life, for Liszt consciously set out to outdo Paganini: to create on the piano the equivalent effects Paganini had created on the violin.

The other great influence was Chopin, whom Liszt first heard in the following year, 1832. From Chopin, Liszt learned that the piano could be a means of delicate expression as well as a bravura instrument. Paganini had opened the door to transcendental bravura; Chopin opened it to poetry, style, finesse. And so Liszt put everything together. He developed a technique that *was* the equivalent of what Paganini could do on the violin (his transcriptions of six Paganini caprices carried bravura piano technique to unheard-of heights), and he also modified virtuosity rampant to take in the color and poetry Chopin had introduced. More than any pianist who ever lived, Liszt combined technique, showmanship and poetry. And while it has been the fashion in recent years to look down on Liszt the musician, we are slowly beginning to realize that behind the flamboyance—and, sometimes, actual fakery—was one of the startling creative minds of the century. Liszt was a dazzlingly equipped musician, and when he played at his best he could add his profound musicianship to all his other attributes. No wonder some of his competitors thought that it was unfair for one man to have such a concentration of pianistic and musical genius.

And in addition he had at least one attribute that the dour, satanic Italian violinist lacked, and one that the diminutive Chopin wished he had. In his youth, Liszt—slim, blond, aristocratic, volatile— was breathtakingly good-looking, and physically he was made of iron. His entrance on stage was enough to turn all the ladies' heads. Liszt reciprocated, and all Europe was agog over his love affairs. More or less in chronological order, there were Caroline de Saint-Criq, the Countess Adèle Laprunarède, Marie d'Agoult, Marie Duplessis (the Lady of the Camellias, Marguerite Gautier, immortalized by Dumas and through him by Verdi in *La Traviata*), Lola Montez, Marie Pleyel, Maria Pawlowna (the Grand Duchess of Saxony)—but why go on? His last permanent liaison was with the Polish-born, cigar-smoking Princess Carolyne Sayn-Wittgenstein. She met Liszt in Kiev and left her husband and her thirty thousand serfs to live with him. In 1856 she and Liszt decided to get married, but the ceremony had to be cancelled because of a Church ruling. The Princess Carolyne was Liszt's constant companion and outlived him by a year, having lived long enough to finish the twenty-fourth and last volume of her *Causes intérieures de la faiblesse extérieure de l'Eglise*. She was a religious fanatic who concentrated on theological books, among them the eight-volume *Petits entretiens practiques à l'usage des femmes du grand monde pour la durée d'une retraite spirituelle*. What could Liszt have seen in her? During this liaison he consoled himself with, among others, the so-called Countess Olga Janina; the jealous and fiery Cossack who met the old wizard in 1870, had an affair with him, threatened him with a revolver, and said she would commit suicide without his love. (She didn't. Nor was she either a countess or a Cossack.)

Not only women admired him. Liszt at the piano made incoherent stammerers of all who came in contact with him—even when they did not especially like him or his playing. It is true that when Mendelssohn first heard him in 1825, his impression was negative, probably with good reason. The fourteen-year-old Liszt was still musically unformed, and Mendelssohn, two years older, at that time probably was the better pianist. But by 1840 Mendelssohn, whose soul revolted at what Liszt stood for, was forced to admit that Liszt "plays the piano with more technique than all the others . . . a degree of velocity and complete finger independence, and a thoroughly musical feeling which can scarcely be equaled. In a word, I have heard no performer whose musical perceptions so extend to the very tips of his fingers." Mendelssohn and Liszt could never have been close friends; Mendelssohn was too prissy, too bourgeois, too classic in his orientation. Emotionally, esthetically and socially they were miles apart. Mendelssohn was a pianist of the Moscheles school; fleet-fingered, playing from the wrists, never seeking a thunderous sonority. A refined, elegant pianist, he was never a virtuoso, nor did he ever try to be. Anton Strelezki, a Liszt pupil, once wrote about a party at which Liszt and Mendelssohn were present. Mendelssohn played Liszt's Fourth Rhapsody "abominably," says Strelezki. Knowing he was making a mess of it, Mendelssohn modulated into his own Capriccio in F sharp minor, which he played brilliantly. Then he asked Liszt to play. Liszt played the same Capriccio, and Mendelssohn admitted that he had been beaten at the keyboard. He took Liszt's right arm, examined it thoroughly, and said that since Liszt had proved the superior pianist the only way to vindication would be a boxing match. But having taken a close look at Liszt's physical equipment he would abandon that position. So everything passed over smoothly. But, Liszt said some years later, "Mendelssohn forgave but he never forgot."

When the good, gray Moscheles first heard the seventeen-year-old Liszt, he was overcome. "As to his playing, it surpasses in power and mastery of difficulties everything I have ever heard." Years later, when both were older, he still could not understand how Liszt, with all the "tossing about of his hands," could accomplish the most perilous jumps with scarcely a mishap. When Hallé first heard Liszt it was with the feeling that Tomaschek had experienced on first hearing Beethoven. Poor Hallé sat speechless "in a stupor of amazement," and then went home "with a feeling of thorough dejection. Such marvels of executive skill and power I could never have imagined."

He was a giant [continues Hallé], and Rubinstein spoke the truth when, at the time his own triumphs were greatest, he said that, in comparison with Liszt, all other pianists were children. . . . Liszt was all sunshine and dazzling splendor, subjugating his hearers with a power that none could withstand. For him there were no difficulties of execution, the most incredible seeming child's play under his fingers. One of the transcendent merits of his playing was the crystal-like clearness which never failed him for a moment, even in the most complicated and, for anybody else, impossible passages; it was as if he had photographed them in the minutest detail upon the ear of his listener. The power he drew from his instrument was such as I have never heard since, but never harsh, never suggesting "thumping." His daring was as extraordinary as his talent. At an orchestral concert given by him and conducted by Berlioz, the *Marche au supplice*, from the latter's *Symphonie fantastique,* that most gorgeously orchestrated piece, was performed, at the conclusion of which Liszt sat down and played his own arrangement, for the piano alone, of the same movement, with an effect even surpassing that of the full orchestra, and creating an indescribable *furore.*

And so it went. Clara Wieck was in despair because "Liszt played at sight what we toil over and at the end get nowhere with." Like Hallé, she was overwhelmed when she first heard him in 1838. "I sobbed aloud, it overcame me so. Beside Liszt, other virtuosos appear so small, even Thalberg." Robert Schumann felt much the same way. "I have never found any artist except Paganini to possess in so high a degree as Liszt the power of subjecting, elevating and leading the public." Schumann's only regret was that Liszt could have used his genius to better musical purpose. Von Lenz summed up the general feeling by saying that when Liszt appeared, all other pianists disappeared.

For Chopin may have been the one who liberated piano technique once and for all, but it was Liszt who spread the results through Europe. Chopin might well have been the better pianist of the two, but he lacked the strength, the power, the flair and the sex appeal to drive audiences to sheer madness. As far as Europe was concerned, it was Liszt who had freed the piano. Up to his time all pianists, with the exception of Beethoven, had played with their hands as close to the keys as possible. Liszt threw all that overboard. He was the first to *orchestrate* on the piano, and it was no accident that some of the most popular pieces in his early repertoire were his arrangements of symphonies by Beethoven and Berlioz. Liszt came on stage, shook his mane, lifted his hands high and came crashing down on the keys. Strings snapped, great volumes of tone filled the air, and a new world of pianistic color and excitement was discovered as the king of virtuosos swept up and down the keyboard.

No competition could exist before this kind of tonal cataclysm. Liszt's biggest rival of the 1830s was Sigismond Thalberg, the Swiss-born virtuoso who really must have been extraordinary in his way. Thalberg first appeared in Paris in 1836 while Liszt was away with his countess (he had been gone from Paris for eighteen months.) Paris immediately divided itself into the Thalbergians and the Lisztians. Liszt heard the news of a contender for the crown. Nostrils dilated, he rushed back to Paris, only to find Thalberg gone. And so Liszt gave two soirées at the Érard salon, both of which were reviewed by Berlioz in the *Gazette musicale*. According to Berlioz, Liszt had grown artistically, to a point where his playing was hard to recognize. Previously, Berlioz said, it had been exaggerated, rhythmically unsettled and overornamented; now it had stature and musicianship. One of the pieces that Liszt played as a challenge to the absent Thalberg was Beethoven's *Hammerklavier* Sonata. Until then, Berlioz wrote, the *Hammerklavier* had been "the Sphinx' enigma of almost every pianist. Liszt, another Oedipus, has solved it in a manner that, if the composer could have heard it in his grave, would have sent a thrill of joy and pride over him. Not a note was left out, not one added (I followed, score in hand), no inflection was effaced, no change of tempo permitted. . . . Liszt, in thus making comprehensible a work not yet comprehended, has proved that he is the pianist of the future."

For Berlioz and the four hundred or so connoisseurs who crowded into Érard's, Liszt played nothing but the best. For his public appearances he chose different material. It was not until 1837 that he and Thalberg met face to face, and for these occasions he chose the other material. Prior to the meeting, Liszt had written a review of Thalberg's music and said it was trash. The review appeared in the January 8, 1837, issue of the *Gazette musicale*. Liszt flatly called the Thalbergian output mediocre, pretentiously empty, supremely monotonous, boring. "If this judgment appears severe . . ." That "appears" is lovely. In a letter to Sand, Liszt said that he had become impatient to hear Thalberg's complete works, which everybody was raving about, "so I shut myself in for a whole afternoon to study them conscientiously." Liszt could have his moments of wit. So could Thalberg. The story was going around Paris that Liszt made a call on Thalberg suggesting a joint concert on two pianos. Thalberg politely turned him down. "No," he said, "I do not like to be accompanied."

Thus there was some bad blood between Liszt and Thalberg. The latter returned to Paris in 1837 and appeared on the afternoon of March 12 at the Conservatoire, playing his *Fantasia on God Save the King* and his *Moses Fantasia*. The following Sundy, Liszt took over the opera house, hurling back at Thalberg his (Liszt's) *Niobe Fantasia* and the Weber *Concertstück*. So far it was a standoff, with Liszt

Liszt in 1859. He was forty-eight years old and still the most Byronic, dynamic and overpowering figure in music at the time.

The still defiant old eagle and his pupil Bernhard Stavenhagen, about 1885.
Liszt was still actively teaching, and he even made sporadic public
appearances.

showing the greater daring by renting the opera house. When the Princess Belgiojoso (herself a fair amateur pianist) invited both pianists to play in her salon on March 31, at a benefit for the Italian refugees, she scored the social coup of the decade. The *Gazette musicale* announced the program on March 26. "The greatest interest will be without question the simultaneous appearance of two talents whose rivalry at this time agitates the musical world, and is like the indecisive balance between Rome and Carthage. MM. Listz [*sic*] and Thalberg will take turns at the piano." The French always had trouble spelling Liszt's name, which often as not appeared as Litz, Lits or Listz. Tickets were priced at forty francs, and everybody in Paris who could be there was there. Quite a few musicians participated on the program—Massart, Urhan, Lee, Dorus, Brod, Pierret, Matthieux, Géraldy and the female artists Taccani and Puget. But they might have been playing or singing in a vacuum for all anybody cared. All eyes and ears were on Liszt, who played his *Niobe,* and Thalberg, who played his *Moses.* It was decided that Thalberg was the best pianist in the world. And Liszt? He was the *only* one.

As Liszt grew older, he became more complicated, and he constantly grew as a musician. He remained a complicated man—a mixture of genius, vanity, generosity, lust, religion, snobbery, democracy, literary desires and visions: part Byron, part Casanova, part Mephistopheles, part St. Francis. He spent his life restlessly looking for something, torn between the demands of art, religion and the flesh; and it was typical that he enter a type of holy order that did not interfere with any of his major preoccupations. In 1865 he became a priest and received the tonsure in Rome. The priestly duties of the Abbé Liszt were not demanding. He received four of the seven degrees of priesthood, which meant that he could not celebrate mass or hear confession. At first he had rooms in the Vatican. Naturally. Then he lived at the Villa d'Este for four months of the year, spending the rest of the time in Rome, Weimar and Budapest.

His career as a pianist did not occupy the major part of his life. At the height of his fame, in 1847, he stopped concertizing and never again appeared in public as a paid artist. That does not mean he stopped playing in public. Almost to the day he died he made appearances. Flattery and public adulation were as necessary to him as the air he breathed. But these appearances were generally at charity concerts. He spent more and more time teaching, and he concentrated on his duties as musical director of the Weimar court, which he made the headquarters of the Music of the Future. Most of this revolved around Wagner. Weimar was a shrine to which flocked all the gifted musicians of the world—pianists, composers, violinists, singers, conductors. All of them came under the surveillance of Liszt. How did he ever find time for his own work? Yet he did. Throughout his life, Liszt was incredibly busy, and his output was stupendous. Consider his music alone—his original piano pieces, his symphonic poems, his various choral and orchestral pieces, his transcriptions, arrangements, concertos, his editions of the various composers. A glance at Humphrey Searle's catalogue in *Grove's Dictionary* makes one quite giddy. One wonders where Liszt found the opportunity merely to notate so much music, much less compose it. Then there was his teaching schedule, and his own playing, and his reviewing, and his incredible correspondence. Toward the end he finally had to cut down on his work load. But as early as 1862 he took out advertisements in several musical journals to announce that he had to forbid the forwarding of scores and other musical documents. Every musician in Europe had been sending him music to play, conduct or promote. By 1881 he started to get tired. "My dislike of letters," he wrote, "has become immense. How can I answer more than two thousand a year without losing my reason?"

When it came to the craft of music there seemed nothing he could not do. His work as a conductor has not received much attention, but Wagner wrote that when Liszt conducted *Tannhäuser* he "was astonished to recognize my second self on this occasion. What I felt in the creation of this music, Liszt felt in conducting it." Liszt could do tricks so awesome that in a well-regulated society he would instantly have been burned at the stake for sorcery. He could hear a complicated piece of music for the first time and immediately play it back without recourse to the printed note. Percy Goetschius, the American composer and theorist, was floored when he played his own sonata for Liszt, who then sat down and, without looking at the manuscript, demonstrated how a certain passage could be improved.

Beyond any doubt Liszt was one of the two greatest sight-readers who ever lived (the other was Camille Saint-Saëns), and all musicians of the nineteenth century testified to his miraculous powers. Mendelssohn once, at Érard's, showed Liszt the manuscript of his G minor Piano Concerto. Mendelssohn said it was hardly legible, but Liszt rattled it off at sight "in the most perfect manner, better than anybody else could play it." Ferdinand Hiller, to whom Mendelssohn told the story, was not surprised, "having long known from experience that Liszt played most things best the first time, because they gave him enough to do. The second time he always had to add something for his own satisfaction." Grieg's account of how Liszt read the A minor Piano Concerto at sight is well known. But another Grieg experience is less familiar. It concerned his first meeting with Liszt in 1868. He had brought one of his violin sonatas. Grieg, incidentally, was no mean pianist himself.

Now you must bear in mind [Grieg wrote] that in the first place he had never seen nor heard the sonata, and in the second that it was a sonata with a violin part, now above, now below, independent of the piano part. And what does Liszt do? He plays the whole thing, root and branch, violin and piano, nay, more, for he played fuller, more broadly. The violin part got its due right in the middle of the piano part. He was literally all over the whole piano at once, without missing a note, and how he played! With grandeur, beauty, genius, unique comprehension. I think I laughed—laughed like a child.

Liszt was just as good with an orchestral score. An American composer named Otis B. Boise visited him at Weimar in 1876, bearing a full score. Liszt asked him to play it. Boise is rather amusing on the subject:

There has never been an occasion in my career when my pianistic calibre seemed to me so small, as when I for that moment contemplated exhibiting it for the first time to that great master; and I also felt that my innocent composition would suffer in his esteem through its shortcomings. He evidently noticed my worry and relieved me at once by saying, "I think after all I should obtain a better idea of details if I play it myself." Accordingly he seated himself, glanced at the instrumental scheme, turned the successive pages to the end, tracing my themes and procedures, and then, with this flash negative in his mind, began the most astoundingly coherent rendering of an orchestral score that I had heard and such as I never since heard from another musician. Those who have attempted such tasks know that the ten fingers being inadequate to the performance of all the details, it is necessary to cull such essentials from the mass of voices as well as clear the line of development. Liszt did this simultaneously. No features of the workmanship, contrapuntal or instrumental, escaped his notice, and he made running comments without interrupting his progress.

That remark of Hiller's about Liszt playing best when reading a work for the first time is interesting, and very true. The fact appears to be that things at the piano came too easily for Liszt, and he was bored unless he could keep up his interest by adding to the music. He never could keep his hands off music or play things as written, even if he was a good boy when he played the *Hammerklavier* for Berlioz. In later years he reproached himself for those liberties (as Chopin said, "Liszt must have his hand in everything"), but that did not stop him. In his prime, around 1840 to 1850, his interpretations of the classics must have been unrecognizable, and Salaman gently scolded him. "He was rarely content with the simple work of art; he must elaborate it and 'arrange' it, often indeed to extravagance. . . . Magnificent as was Liszt's playing, the works of such great masters as Beethoven, Weber and Hummel needed no such embellishments as the pianist introduced." When he played sonatas with Joachim, the German violinist found the collaboration a thrill only if the music was new. Then Liszt played it as written. Otherwise at the second or third performance Liszt would transpose simple passages to octaves or thirds or convert ordinary trills into sixths. He would indulge in such tricks even in Beethoven's *Kreutzer* Sonata. The Russian composer Alexander Borodin, who visited Liszt in 1883, adds another bit of testimony along the same line. Borodin admired the technical command of the seventy-two-year-old pianist, but "having played some piece, he will sometimes begin to add things of his own, and gradually under his hands will emerge not the same piece but an improvisation on it." This could be hard on other pianists, for such was Liszt's authority that even good musicians believed his interpretations were definitive. When other pianists played the same piece, they were reproached for not making an equal effect. To protect themselves, they would imitate Liszt in making the music more "effective."

Thus, if Liszt played today as he did in his more irresponsible moments (and it would strongly appear that irresponsibility was his norm), he would have responsible musicians and critics frothing at the mouth. His mechanical equipment, however, would probably hold up against even that of today's brilliant virtuosos. All are agreed that difficulties did not exist for him, and that wrong notes—which came often during performances in his later years—were sheer carelessness and not the result of insufficient technique. Wrong notes never bothered him. Amy Fay, the young American who wrote so enchantingly about the European musical scene of the 1870s, tells of Liszt playing before a very distinguished audience:

He was rolling up the piano in arpeggios in a very grand manner indeed, when he struck a semi-tone short of the high note which he had intended to end. I caught my breath and wondered whether he was going to leave us like that, in mid-air, as it were, the harmony unresolved, or whether he would be reduced to the humiliation of correcting himself like ordinary mortals, and taking the right chord. A half smile came over his face, as much as to say—"Don't fancy that *this* little thing disturbs me"—and he instantly went meandering down the piano in harmony with the false note he had struck, and then rolled deliberately up in a second grand sweep, *this* time striking true. I never saw a more delicious piece of cleverness. It was so quick-witted and so exactly characteristic of Liszt. Instead of giving you a chance to say, "He has made a mistake," he forced you to say, "He has shown how to get out of a mistake."

However, the Liszt legend is overpowering, and one sometimes wonders if he were as good a technician as his contemporaries thought. That he was the best in his day there can be no doubt; but technique has gone a long way since then. Unfortunately we can never know. Arthur Friedheim, who worshiped Liszt and was one of his important pupils, says that Rosenthal and Godowsky exceeded Liszt in certain "specialized" kinds of technique; and the eminent pedagogue Rudolf Breithaupt called many pianists Liszt's technical superiors. But neither of them could have heard Liszt in his prime, when he was in practice. The chances are that in the last thirty years of his life Liszt never practiced at all.

Breithaupt, incidentally, writes that Liszt had a large hand, with the stretch of a twelfth. This is highly unlikely, though there has been much conflicting testimony about the size of Liszt's hand. William Mason, an early pupil, said that Liszt's stretch was in no way remarkable. Amy Fay described Liszt's hands as "very narrow, with long and slender fingers that look as if they had twice as many joints as other people." But the question would seem to be settled by another pupil, Carl Lachmund. Lachmund, who studied with Liszt at Weimar from 1882 to 1884, wrote an unpublished book called "Living with Liszt," and was present at an occasion when Liszt played the slow movement of the *Hammerklavier*:

At the last chord, which is reiterated four times slowly, I was watching his hands, which he usually held in unconventional disregard of rules. It struck me that he could barely cover the tenth in each hand sufficiently to play the chord quietly, without breaking it.

The chord is F sharp, C sharp and A sharp in the left hand, A sharp, F sharp and C sharp in the right hand. Lachmund quotes Liszt as saying, "The public credits me with having a very large hand, but you see I can just stretch this tenth to play it quietly."

As for Liszt's repertoire, he played everything. Once he had gone through something, he never forgot it. Amy Fay, in the 1870s, gives a delicious account of Liszt being reminded of a silly but difficult piece by Herz he had last played forty years previously. Liszt sat down and rattled it off. In private, before friends and pupils, he played music by the best composers. His public concerts during the 1839–1847 tours also had some surprising (for the period) things in them. Liszt seems to have had the entire repertoire at his fingertips. In public he was, of course, constantly playing his own showpieces. But he also played many masterpieces from Bach to his own time. In the first volume of his biography of Liszt, Alan Walker has appended Liszt's concert repertoire. It contains such things as Bach's *Goldberg* Variations, many Beethoven sonatas (including the last five), much Chopin, some Schubert, Weber and Schumann, concertos by Beethoven, Mendelssohn, Chopin, Weber and Bach (the Concerto for Three Pianos) and, of course, a great deal of his own music. He never forgot, however, that he was, as he put it, "the servant of the public"; he knew what they wanted, and he gave it to them. Hallé tells a story that is not very much to Liszt's credit:

The programme of one of his concerts given in the Salle du Conservatoire contained the *Kreutzer* Sonata, to be played by Liszt and Massart, a celebrated and much-esteemed violinist, professor at the Conservatoire. Massart was just commencing the first bar of the introduction when a voice from the audience called out "*Robert le Diable!*" At that time Liszt had composed a very brilliant fantasia on themes from that opera, and played it always with immense success. The call was taken up by other voices, and in a moment the cries "*Robert le Diable! Robert le Diable!*" drowned the tones of the violin. Liszt rose, bowed, and said: "Je suis toujours l'humble serviteur du public, mais est-ce-qu'on désire la fantaisie avant ou après la sonate?" Renewed cries of "*Robert! Robert!*" were the answer, upon which Liszt turned half around to poor Massart and dismissed him with a wave of the hand, without a syllable of excuse or regret. He did play the fantasia magnificently, rousing the public to a frenzy of enthusiasm; then called Massart out of his retreat and we had the *Kreutzer,* which somehow no longer seemed in its right place.

As Liszt retired from the arena, and as he grew older, there was less of this kind of egocentricity, though he was never entirely without it.

Liszt himself was no theorist of technique and must have played without thinking twice about how he accomplished his effects. It seems clear, though, that he employed a weight technique, playing with loose shoulders and a fairly high position of hands and fingers, with hands slightly outturned so that they naturally covered the E major scale (Amy Fay is quite specific about this). He probably worked out his own style fairly late, for in 1831 he was telling his pupil Valerie Boissier not to play from the arms and shoulders. Of course, Liszt had not been too far removed from Czerny at that time, nor had he yet heard Chopin, whose free and original playing proved such an influence. Liszt was the technical son of Beethoven and the spiritual father of Anton Rubinstein, in that he did not concentrate on pinpoint accuracy, where every note and scale has to be in exact place. The effect, the sonority, the excitement and *diablerie* and boldness of attack, the orchestration on the piano and the exploitation of the instrument—those were the important things. Which is not to imply that Liszt could not play with poetry and dignity when he wanted to. But he stands primarily for something elemental, as contrasted with the disciplined, often bloodless classical style. He was the greatest bravura pianist of all time. Bravura, it should be noted, transcends technique. Many—indeed, most—pianists have technique, but only a few can put that technique to use for exciting, breathtaking, daring deeds. That is bravura, and it demands a certain type of mind, plus a discipline of its own.

Liszt and his pupils sparked the bravura school of the nineteenth century, to the great distress of the musically virtuous. All the young pianists took Liszt as their model, just as the youngsters of the 1940s tried to play like Vladimir Horowitz. The academicians became worried. In a passage that could have been written today, Louis Köhler, a highly respected pianist and composer who himself had studied with Liszt, bewailed in 1874 (in the *Neue Zeitschrift für Musik*) the attitudes and training of the new school of virtuosos. They all sound the same, said Köhler; they play with no soul and with machinelike precision; they all want to "sport with the prodigious" and play like Liszt; they even copy his mannerisms, with their hair falling into their eyes. Liszt, says Köhler, could get away with it. But his followers, "with their unnatural and unsuitable forcing of the tone, the senseless accelerando and ritardando, the constant rubato, which leaves one uncertain whether it is the player or the hearer whose head is turned," Köhler could not abide. Yet he would have had trouble finding an important pianist who was not of the Liszt school. Liszt had taught all his life, from the 1820s, and had produced such notables as Hans von Bülow, William Mason, Carl Tausig, Rafael Joseffy, Sophie Menter—the list seems endless. James Huneker's list of Liszt pupils, in his biography, runs on for many pages and is far from complete.

Of course the good-natured Liszt took literally thousands of pupils who were not really pupils. They were auditors who might have played for him once or twice, and then went home to hang out shingles advertising themselves as Liszt pupils. Anybody could get a letter of introduction to the amiable old gentleman, and he received them all. Siloti disgustedly says that anybody who wanted to could come to Liszt's Weimar classes (Tuesday, Thursday and Saturday, from 4 to 6 P.M.) and sit in on Liszt's lessons without paying a cent. Liszt had so many pupils at Weimar that the citizens had to be protected, and anybody heard practicing with open windows was fined three marks. But mixed among the hangers-on was a group of titans who went on to careers that lasted well into the twentieth century. The last eight years of Liszt's life saw him supervising the pianistics of Eugene d'Albert, Moriz Rosenthal, Alfred Reisenauer, Carl Pohlig, Alexander Siloti, Arthur Friedheim, Adele aus der Ohe, Emil and George Liebling, Conrad Ansorge, Bernhard Stavenhagen, Frederic Lamond and Vianna da Motta. Da Motta was the last survivor of this noted band; he was a brilliant pianist who spent most of his life in his native Portugal and died in 1948 at the age of eighty, a few months after the death of Lamond.

As a teacher Liszt had no system or *méthode*. After 1845 he took only advanced pupils and did not concentrate on technique. "Wash your dirty linen at home." Mostly it was a matter of coaching. Liszt was unpredictable. Sometimes he was severely academic; at other times complacent and easygoing. When a pupil proved stupid, and many were (it was von Bülow who said that at the best pianist's house one could hear the worst playing), Liszt could be violent and cutting. At times he would profusely illustrate for his class, and at other times days would go by before he touched the piano. But his best pupils managed to come away with much from the man who had been kissed by Beethoven, who had been Chopin's friend and Thalberg's competitor, whose great career virtually spanned the century. Liszt lived to be a venerated symbol, and well he deserved to be. He had fought the good fight. And with all of his youthful miscalculations and showmanship, with all of his vanity and tinkering with the music of other men, he ended up finally as the pianist who preached the gospel of Chopin, Beethoven, Schumann, Wagner; the representative of the Music of the Future; the one who had helped almost every young progressive composer in Europe; the Liszt whose own music leads into Wagner (he had invented the "Tristan" chord before *Tristan*), Richard Strauss and the French impressionists (in the curious, non-virtuoso last pieces like *Nuages gris*); and, above all, the Liszt whose piano playing was an inspiration to every instrumentalist in the world.

Old Arpeggio, Other Salonists, and the American Penetration

LISZT'S BIGGEST RIVAL could not have been more different as a pianist and as a human being. Where Liszt swarmed all over the keyboard with wild gesticulations, Sigismond Thalberg sat erect and prim, creating his effects with a minimum of gesture. But he too had his pianistic secrets. What he did was develop a trick in which listeners would swear that the playing could not possibly be accomplished with only two hands. Thalberg's specialty was to bring out the melody with both thumbs, in the middle register of the piano, and surround that melody with arpeggios from top to bottom of the keyboard. It sounded as though he had three hands. He had gotten the idea from the harpist Parish Alvers. It is not a difficult trick, and it sounds (and looks) much harder than it is, but it was new in the 1830s and it caused a sensation. Thalberg was promptly named Old Arpeggio. Audiences were entranced and would rise up from their seats to see how Thalberg did it.

Thalberg was an unusually finished, disciplined technician, and he claimed to be the illegitimate son of Count Moritz von Dietrichstein and the Baroness von Wetzlar. He grew up to be a courtly, aristocratic man, and everybody believed his story to be true. But it wasn't. His father was a merchant from Hamburg named Thalberg and his mother a woman named Stein. As a child, however, he came under Dietrichstein's wing, and the Count saw to it that he was sent to the best schools. His talent showed up early, and he studied with Hummel and Moscheles, making his Vienna debut in 1829. Handsome, aristocratic, talented, he immediately gathered unto himself a following. Like Liszt, he was extremely popular with the ladies, though in a more genteel, languishing way. His concerts never developed into the weird affairs that Liszt's ladies could make of them. Yet Schumann wrote that "if anybody were to criticize Thalberg, all the girls in Germany, France, and the other European countries would rise up in arms."

He worked hard at his piano playing. Vincent Wallace, the Irish composer, once heard him practice two bars of his *Don Pasquale Fantasy* all night. Often he would get up at three in the morning to practice. And he did develop a flawless mechanism, with incredibly even scales, birdlike trills and precise chords. It was his pride to execute the most fabulous technical maneuvers without bodily motion. "His whole bearing as he sits at the piano," wrote Moscheles, "is soldier-like. His lips are tightly compressed and his coat closely buttoned. He told me he had acquired this attitude of self-control by smoking a Turkish pipe while practicing his exercises; the length of the tube was so calculated as to keep him erect and motionless." Naturally Thalberg would have none of the febrile attack à la Liszt. A melody should be played, he once wrote, "without forcibly striking the keys but playing them closely and nervously, *pressing* them with energy and vigor.... When the melody is of a tender and graceful character, the notes should be kneaded, the keys being pressed as though with a boneless hand and fingers of velvet." All very vague, this pressing and kneading, but Thalberg managed to get the effects he wanted, and Liszt is said to have admiringly remarked that "Thalberg is the only man who can play the violin on the piano."

Professional pianists being professional-minded and responsive to craft, Thalberg's colleagues found a good deal to admire in his disciplined approach, and they also felt virtuous in playing him off against the eccentric Liszt. Sweet old Salaman in 1901 remembered his playing very well:

Nothing seemed difficult to him; like Liszt he could play the apparently impossible, but unlike Liszt he never indulged in any affectation or extravagance of manner in achieving his mechanical triumphs. His strength and flexibility of wrist and fingers were amazing, but he always tempered his strength with delicacy. His loudest fortissimos were never noisy. His own compositions, which he chiefly played in public, enabled him best to display his astonishing virtuosity, but to be assured that Thalberg was a really great player was to hear him interpret Beethoven, which he did finely, classically, and without any attempt to embellish the work of the master.

The last part of this comment is a dig against Liszt. Thalberg's style was, its bravura notwithstanding, allied to the classical school, and it is not surprising to find a classical-oriented pianist like Clara Schumann raving about Thalberg's exquisite touch and the clarity of his execution. But Clara, being the sensitive musician she was, did point out that the "higher poetry" was beyond him. Hallé also said that his playing was beautiful but cold; and in addition, said Hallé, it was always the same. "It was said of him with reason that he would play with the same care and finish if roused out of the deepest sleep in the middle of the night." Yet the bell-like clarity of his delivery entranced all pianists, and Hans von Bülow's reference to Thalberg's "exquisitely poetical and thoroughly finished execution" was typical.

Mendelssohn, a classicist who found many of Liszt's mannerisms offensive, decided that Thalberg, with his composure "and within his more restricted sphere, is more perfect as a real virtuoso." In a letter from Leipzig, dated March 30, 1840, Mendelssohn compared Liszt and Thalberg, and it is a fascinating, important (coming from one of the sharpest musical minds of the time) and very clear analysis:

A fantasia by Thalberg (especially that on [Rossini's] *Donna del Lago*) is an accumulation of the finest and most exquisite effects, a crescendo of difficulties and embellishments that is astonishing. Everything is so calculated and so polished, and shows such assurance, skill and superlative effects. At the same time the man has incredibly powerful hands and such practiced, light fingers that he is unique.

Liszt, on the other hand, possesses a certain suppleness and differentiation in his fingering, as well as a thoroughly musical feeling that cannot be equaled. In a word, I have known of no performer whose musical perceptions so extend to the very tips of his fingers and emanate directly from them as Liszt's do. With his directness, his stupendous technique and experience, he could far have surpassed the rest, were not a man's own thoughts in connection with all this the main thing. And these, so far, at least, seem to have been denied him by nature, so that in this respect most of the great virtuosi equal, or even excel him. But that he, together with

Sigismond Thalberg in 1835, two years before his great battle with Liszt. The blood of nobility was in his veins, and he looked the part.

The young Sigismond Thalberg. Born a year after Liszt, he was considered by many an equal talent.

Thalberg toward the end of his concert career. He was still called "Old Arpeggio," and audiences would go wild trying to figure out how he achieved his three-hand effects.

Thalberg, *alone* represent the highest class of pianists of the present day, seems to me indisputable.

Even Schumann, although one would have expected him to find Thalberg's music repulsive—had he not attacked Herz and Hünten?—found much to admire. But Chopin's witty and devastating character sketch, from Vienna in 1830, tells us everything in a capsule. "As for Thalberg, he plays excellently, but he is not my man. Younger than I, pleases the ladies, makes potpourris from *la Muette* [Auber's opera *La Muette de Portici*], gets his soft passages by the pedal, not the hand, takes tenths as easily as I take octaves—has diamond shirt studs—does not admire Moscheles."

Thalberg was well liked as a human being. One admirer gave him a fine estate, another a magnificent mansion in Vienna. He was a well-groomed man with impeccable manners. Was not his, after all, blue blood? In 1843 he married one of the daughters of the great basso Lablache. By 1863 he had made all the money he could ever spend, and he retired as a wine-grower in Italy, where he died in 1871. When Thalberg stopped playing, he really stopped. He did not even have a piano in his home.

His tours took him all over Europe, and he was one of the first of the great artists to play in the United States. In 1856 he made his debut in New York and set a new standard. His recital in Boston led the critic of the *Post* to literary heights unsurpassed before or since:

Rarely has the omni-ambient aether pervading the purlieus of the palatial metropolis vibrated resonant to more majestic music, to more soothing strains, than sought the cerulean empyrean vault, "as the bee flieth," on Saturday morn from the digitals of the gifted Sigismond.

This is enough to make the opticals pop. On the strength of notices like these, Thalberg was kept busy. From 1856 to the winter of 1858 he played fifty-six concerts in New York alone, sometimes giving three a day. Naturally he played his own music almost exclusively (generally he would make two appearances on any given program, playing once before and once after intermission, and seldom giving more than four pieces). Richard Hoffman, the English-born American pianist, claimed that Thalberg's American repertoire consisted of about twelve of his operatic fantasias. But that is not accurate. A search of newspapers of the day reveals that he did play the *Moonlight* Sonata, a few pieces by Mendelssohn and even the first movement of Beethoven's C minor Concerto. Hoffman, however, was substantially correct. People came to hear the three hands, and Thalberg obliged. On one memorable occasion Thalberg played several two-piano compositions with the American idol, Louis Moreau Gottschalk. One piece was a fantasy on themes from *Il Trovatore*, and Hoffman says it created a good deal of excitement. "A remarkable double trill, which Thalberg played in the middle of the piano, while Gottschalk was flying all over the keyboard in the *Anvil Chorus*, produced the most prodigious volume of tone I ever heard."

Thalberg must have composed fifty or sixty fantasias on opera themes. The music is not very good, mostly because it is lacking in harmonic imagination. But it is effective, highly pianistic and often very difficult, and it captured the imagination of the day to the extent of being widely imitated. All of Thalberg's fantasias follow much the same form, and the *Grande Fantaisie sur des motifs de l'opéra Don Pasquale de Donizetti* is typical. It contains a rather quiet five-page introduction. This leads into a cantabile section where the going gets a little rougher, with broken right-hand arpeggios and left-hand octaves. Then comes the specialty: a theme in the tenor surrounded with arpeggiated chords above and below, and also some difficult trill work. There follows a section of *leggierissimo* octaves that pass from right to left hand, the theme still singing out in the tenor range. The writing here is very ingenious. More octaves ensue, followed by chromatic passagework with filigree scales. The climax approaches, heralded by rapid, broken-up arpeggiated figurations in the right hand, these figurations incorporating the melody. Now we are near the end, and the melody goes back to the tenor, hemmed in by brilliant chromatic passagework, double thirds and sixths, a rapid chord build-up and, finally, a slam-bang downward arpeggio. Musically the piece has little to offer, but it is exciting in its pianism, and as played by Thalberg it must have caused his audiences' hair to curl. Nobody but Liszt, in those days, could write a flashier example of virtuosity for the sake of virtuosity.

Toward the end of his career, Thalberg stopped composing. Wilhelm Kuhe, a Czech-born teacher resident in London, asked him why. "Alas!" said Thalberg. "My imitators have made me impossible." His music, though, was doomed to a short life. Today it is forgotten, and he himself is a shadowy figure. Liszt moved with the times, constantly growing, while Thalberg was content to be the virtuoso with his little bag of dated tricks.

Thalberg had been preceded in America by four international figures: the New Orleans-born Louis Moreau Gottschalk, the Austrian-born Henri [Heinrich] Herz, the German-born Leopold de Meyer (or von Meyer), and the Austrian-born Alfred Jaëll. De Meyer was the first; he came to the United States in 1845. Herz came the following year. Herz was at least an elegant salon pianist and a witty, urbane human being. De Meyer seems to have been a faker. The Lion Pianist, as he was called because of his leonine mane and his assault on the keyboard, was born in Baden in 1816, studied in Vienna under Franz Schubert (not *the* Franz Schubert) and started touring Europe. He was a clown, a precursor of Vladimir de Pachmann. He would sit at the piano, then decide he did not like its location, and would have it pushed around, meanwhile making speeches to the audience. Sometimes he played only with his thumbs, sometimes with his fists and elbows. Audiences loved it. Naturally he played only his own music, fantasias on this and that. Pauer's *Dictionary of Pianists* refers to de Meyer in one of the great lines in the language, "As a performer he was demonstrative to a degree that the risible muscles of the audience were frequently called into activity." His warhorse was the *Marche Marocaine*, a virtuoso work that had nothing Moroccan about it. Its original title was *Air guerrier des Turques*. Berlioz, for some reason, liked de Meyer, and orchestrated two of his pieces—the *Marche marocaine* and the *Marche d'Isly*. He said that de Meyer's music had "a charming originality."

In appearance he was short and fat, and he ran around bragging about it. He would tell everybody that he was the only one of the great pianists who was fat. This, he said, enabled him to bear the immense amount of physical exertion and nervous excitement that he put into his work. Apparently at least one part of his description held water. While pummeling the piano he went about it with such exertion that perspiration ran from him in torrents. His repertoire consisted mostly of operatic paraphrases, variations on *Yankee Doodle* in honor of America, and his audience stunner, the *Marche Marocaine*.

Herz, who was brought to Paris from Vienna and took first prize at the Conservatoire when he was fifteen, was a man of different stamp and must have been an elegant pianist in his way. He was the king of the salon and was immensely popular, though his great contemporaries took turns poking good-natured fun at him. Herz did not care, and it is doubtful if he took himself too seriously. As Schumann wrote, "What more does he want than to amuse and become rich?" Rich he did become. His empty, graceful salon pieces—an incalculable number of variations, rondos, marches, nocturnes, sonatas, potpourris, paraphrases, concertos, *morceaux*—were consistent best sellers. He also interested himself in a piano firm and built a concert hall. In his otherwise unoccupied moments he took more pupils than he could handle. How he taught! In 1828, when Charles Salaman wanted to study with Herz, the only hour he could spare was five o'clock—in the morning. The French magazine *Le Corsaire* poked fun at Herz ten years later:

M. Henri Herz, No. 38, Rue de la Victoire, is quite an eccentric professor. His lesson generally lasts half an hour—ten minutes for arranging the large curls and the cravat of M. Henri Herz; ten minutes more to draw his watch—his showpiece from Bréguet—out of his fob, which he hooks with ceremony on the piano; the last ten minutes for the instruction and advice which M. Henri Herz, No. 38, Rue de la Victoire, invariably gives while arranging his curls. . . . He rises at five o'clock in the morning, and goes to bed at midnight, and as long as the day lasts he gives lessons on the piano. He gives them at midnight, just as well as six o'clock in the morning—while drinking, while walking, while reposing, while, in fact, doing anything. It sometimes happens that he wakes in the night and asks his *valet de chambre* if there is a pupil in the anteroom.

Before Chopin and Liszt came on the scene, Herz and Kalkbrenner were the two big pianists in Paris. With his rapidity of finger technique and attractive, shallow tone, Herz was able to compete very successfully with Kalkbrenner. Mendelssohn looked at both of them with a mixture of amusement and amazement. Kalkbrenner, he wrote in 1832, had become a romantic:

He is playing his dream, some sort of new piano concerto where he makes his conversion to romanticism quite evident. He says, first, that it starts with indefinite dreams. Later comes despair, after that a confession

of love, then finally a military march. No sooner did Henri Herz hear of
this than he quickly composed a romantic piano concerto, and he too has
given some kind of explanation. First there is a dialogue between a shepherd and a shepherdess, then a thunderstorm, later a prayer with evening
bells, and a military march at the end.

Herz reminded Mendelssohn of rope dancers and acrobats. But it
all added up to money. So did his trip to the Western Hemisphere.
Between 1845 and 1851 Herz toured the United States (he played in
California in 1849), Mexico and the West Indies. But de Meyer had
been the first pianist of importance—or, at least, of international
reputation—to come to America, making his debut in New York on
November 7, 1845 (having preceded it with a great publicity cam-
paign). He and his agent, one G. C. Reitheimer, had prepared a
biographical notice, a caricature, many copies of his portrait and
even publicity about his two Érard grand pianos. The memoir had
drawings of de Meyer playing before Louis Philippe and Queen Vic-
toria (but a correspondent for the London *Musical World* was unkind
enough to point out that de Meyer had never played at the French or
English courts). The concert took place at the Broadway Tabernacle, and Reitheimer had trouble filling the hall. So he hired a group
of carriages to drive up and give the appearance of great activity. De
Meyer made out pretty well on his tours, though the caliber of his
programs bruised some lofty American spirits, such as the correspondent of the Boston *Musical Gazette*, who could discover little
music in the recital from beginning to end. The only *real* music the
critic could recall and approvingly cite were the variations on *Hail
Columbia, Yankee Doodle* and *William Tell.*

Herz, who toward the end of his long life wrote an amusing little
book called *Mes Voyages en Amérique,* made his American debut in
New York on October 29, 1846. The *New York Tribune*'s review of
the concert appeared two days later, and among other things had this
to say:

We should rather compare his execution to the most delicate flowerwork
which the frost fairies draw upon the window-pane in their frolicsome
hours of winter moonlight. His harmonies and combinations are so symmet-
rical and his fingering is so rapid and precise, that one would think a bird
had escaped from his fingers and went undulating and swinging through
the air.

After which glorious prose it is a little disconcerting to read the next sentence, "But we must confess that we were not excited by his playing."

One of the first things Herz did was to acquire a pushy young man named Bernard Ullmann as press agent. Ullmann presented himself and talked his way into a job. This kind of work was something new to Herz. He asked Ullmann what his duties would be. "Nothing," said Ullmann, "and everything. Try me. I will take care of the announcements of your concerts. I will have your programs printed, I will see to it that everything is in order in the hall where you will give the concert, I will bring you to the attention of the newspaper editors. The papers are the nerves of artistic success, just as money is the nerves of war." Herz agreed, and it turned out that Ullmann earned his keep.

Herz's book goes on to give his impressions of America, its leading citizens and its institutions. He reads the Declaration of Independence ("*Quand, dans le cours des évenements, il devient indispensable pour un peuple de dissoudre les liens qui l'attachent à un autre peuple...*") and is struck by it. He meets Phineas T. Barnum, who offers him second billing in concerts with Jenny Lind. Herz refuses. He notes with interest some of Ullmann's ideas. One of them was to give a concert lighted by a thousand candles—no more, no less. "This," writes Herz, "excited such a curiosity in the Americans... that in less than a day the hall was sold out." Herz plays the concert. At the end of the first piece a loud voice fills the hall, "But there are not a thousand candles!" The man had counted and decided there were eight short.

Ullmann kept dreaming up "bizarre and impossible things to excite the ardor of the music-lover." One such vision was a political concert. On the program would be a *Hommage à Washington* (soloists, chorus, five orchestras, 1,800 singers), a *Concerto de la Constitution* (composed and played by Herz), a speech on the genius of the American people, a *Grande marche triomphal* (to be arranged by Herz for forty pianos), *Le Capitole* (a *choeur apothéosiaque*, to be composed by Herz), and a grand finale, *Hail Columbia*, played by all the military bands of Philadelphia and surrounding environs. Ullmann, it must be conceded, thought big. But here Herz put his foot down. He wrote a piece for eight instead of forty pianos. Ullmann objected. "Your refusal shows you do not understand the American character." Herz stood firm, and the concert was a great success. In

(*Above left*) The Lion Pianist in his old age. This is the only known photograph of Leopold de Meyer.

(*Above right*) Caricature of de Meyer at the time of his controversy with Henri Herz. Note the pianist's left knee, occupied in hitting the keys.

Henri Herz, the idol of the salons, at the age of nineteen. In 1845, thirteen years later, he came to America and tangled with Leopold de Meyer.

the South he listened to Negro music (*"le banjoo est une sorte de guitare"*) and was one of the first trained musicians to pay any attention to it.

It was inevitable that Herz and de Meyer cross paths, and some lively *affaires* resulted. In Baltimore the two were appearing on successive days. De Meyer played first and did not bother to have his Érards removed from the hall. Herz raised a fuss and there was a subsequent *scandale*, much to the enjoyment of Americans along the Eastern seaboard. Both pianists appealed to the public through letters in the *Baltimore Sun*, the *Advertiser* and other papers. De Meyer started the ball rolling:

TO THE PUBLIC

The undersigned is particularly indisposed to appear before the public of Baltimore, from whom he has received the kindest indulgence, upon a subject of private rather than of a public nature. Yet he feels it due to himself to make a simple statement of facts. ... The citizens of Baltimore are aware, that the undersigned gave a concert in this city, at Calvert Hall, on Wednesday evening, and as usual left his pianos in the building, which he was informed yesterday morning were so disposed as to leave no possible inconvenience to Mons. Herz, who was announced to give a concert, in the same place, last evening. It was, therefore, much to the surprise of the undersigned, that he received a note from the servant of Mr. Herz last evening, shortly before 6 o'clock, when the rain was pouring down in torrents, of which the following is a translated copy:—*The two pianos of Meyer, have to be taken away immediately or they will be thrown into the yard of the hall.* B. ULLMANN.

Upon the receipt of this abrupt and offensive note, Mr. Meyer... requested his friend, Mr. G. Reitheimer, to call immediately on Mr. Herz at Calvert Hall, and attend to the business. He there met Mr. Herz, and suggested, in consequence of the state of the weather, that the pianos should remain, alluding at the same time to the impertinent note of Mr. Ullmann. Mr. Herz observed that he should not interfere in the matter, and that whatever had been done by his servant, was by his approval. Mr. Reitheimer at once proceeded to remove the pianos, though it was with considerable risk, and with some injury to one of them.

Then de Meyer went on to charge Herz with further unethical conduct, suggesting that during his (de Meyer's) absence from Philadelphia, Herz had announced a concert in New York with eight pianos. "At that time Mr. Meyer had one of his superb Erard pianos in that city . . . which, with a most vague and strange idea of the proprieties of life, Mr. Herz actually possessed himself of, and procured to be removed to the Tabernacle for his purposes." It grieved de Meyer, he said, to have to acquaint the good people of Baltimore with this fact.

Herz and Ullmann did not take this lying down. They also took out an advertisement, and, like de Meyer, addressed it

TO THE PUBLIC

In an address to the public in this morning's *Sun*, M. Leopold de Meyer has sought to provoke M. Henri Herz into a newspaper controversy, and has endeavored to give point to his address by calling the undersigned M. Herz's servant, and by using other impertinencies of language which it would not be becoming to notice. At the risk of giving M. de Meyer a consequence which he does not merit . . . the undersigned contents himself with saying that the publication, in every essential particular, is entirely false.

Ullmann went on to give particulars. He said that the stage of Calvert Hall was too small to take both artists' pianos at the same time; that de Meyer should have removed his; that he did not do so; that he, Ullmann, had stated to one of de Meyer's associates, a Mr. Burke at 9 A.M., that he would require the removal of the large piano only and that the smaller one could remain; that de Meyer took no steps to remove either of them. As for the second charge, Ullmann claimed that de Meyer had, in the presence of witnesses, offered Herz the use of the Érard. Then Ullmann really got mad:

These are the plain facts, and the public can judge of them. M. de Meyer's difficulties heretofore, with Thalberg, with Sivori, and with every other artist who appears, as he supposes, to stand in his way; his unblushing method of reaching the public through the press, as disclosed in the late trial between Burchardt and himself, for the price of the puff, and now this attempt to embroil Mr. Herz in controversy with him, will sufficiently convince the public that he relies on other means for giving himself consequence than professional science.

The letter was signed with an indignant flourish: *Bernard Ull-mann, A.M., Doctor of Philosophy and Élève of the Imperial Polytech-nic Institute of Vienna.* Servant, indeed. (*Was* there any such thing as the Imperial Polytechnic Institute of Vienna? And if so, did it pro-duce "*élèves*"?) Ullmann's reference to Burchardt concerns a lawsuit that was brought against the Lion Pianist. It seemed that de Meyer had employed one C. B. Burchardt to translate a flattering notice from German to English, and Burchardt was to see to it that it got published in an American paper. This Burchardt did and charged twenty-five dollars. But the Lion Pianist roared that the price was highway robbery and paid him only ten dollars. Burchardt brought suit, and the case was reported in the *New York Evening Post* of November 11, 1846. The jury found for Burchardt and awarded him fifteen dollars.

De Meyer hit right back, rather wittily:

TO HENRI HERZ

A publication of the *Patriot* of yesterday evening, under the name of an individual who, instead of your *servant*, should, as it seems, have been styled your *savant*, demands a passing notice. . . . I now declare it to be untrue that I ever gave my consent that you should use one of my grand pianos at your concert. . . . In reference to the statement of your *savant* that Mr. Burke received any communication relative to the pianos at 9 o'clock, it was either an inexcusable mistake or a willfull misrepresentation. . . . And now, Sir, a parting word. Concealed as you choose to be under the shelter of your *savant* that you may avoid the necessity of an excuse "to the public," for your discourtesy, unworthy of a true artist, I take occasion to invite the attention of the public to the correspondence of Signor Rapetti in the New York press of the 9th and 10th inst., for a full exhibition of those traits of your character which are calculated, unhappily, at once to excite pity and contempt. The unwise, and not to say most unjust insinuation of your *savant* against the character of the American press as a mercenary instru-mentality, I leave to be adjusted between him and a profession which I deemed beyond reproach.

More mudslinging. Since Ullmann had led the ghost of Bur-chardt, de Meyer trumped it with the specter of Rapetti. Michel Rapetti was a violinist and conductor who had an orchestra in New

York, and Herz engaged him for his first concert. Then, for one reason or another, Herz abandoned him and engaged George Loder for his next three concerts. Whereupon, grievously hurt, Rapetti went TO THE PUBLIC, taking out letters in the *New York Herald* and the *New York Daily Tribune*, claiming that Loder had put pressure on Herz and that the pianist down deep in his soul preferred him, Rapetti.

Herz finally went back home to become professor of piano at the Paris Conservatoire. He also had made enough money in America to keep his piano factory alive, and his instrument prospered after winning first prize at the Exposition Universelle of 1855. He died in 1888. De Meyer, after returning to Europe, decided to honor America once more, and returned in 1868. He was considered old-fashioned by then, a quaint relic. "More extravagant than ever," said *Dwight's Journal of Music*. Ullmann, still rankling, wrote a report in *Dwight's* to the effect that Steinway had paid de Meyer fifteen thousand dollars to demonstrate their instruments. Not much was heard of de Meyer after the 1860s. He died in 1883.

A few years after Herz and de Meyer were having at each other, a really good pianist came to America. This was Alfred Jaëll, who had studied with Moscheles and developed into a very popular virtuoso. He was a short, stout man ("our good, fat Jaëll" is the way von Bülow referred to him in one of his letters) whose tone was exceptionally sweet and penetrating. He made his debut in New York on November 15, 1851, and was ecstatically received—so ecstatically, indeed, that he did not return to Europe until 1854. On his first concert, at Tripler Hall, he was supported by the Italian Opera Company and "the powerful orchestra of the Astor-place Opera House" (so ran the advertisements). Jaëll played the *Sonnambula Fantasy* of Thalberg, Gottschalk's *Le Bananier* (a graceful tribute, that) and several drawing-room pieces of his own. (The program ended with *Bird on the Tree*, "warbling the lesson composed by his mistress, composed and executed by Miska Hauser." Hauser was a violinist then active in New York.) A heavy storm on the night of the debut led to a poor house. Jaëll could well have been gratified with his reviews, however. Wrote the *New York Times*, "The labored effects and startling descents upon the keys, which grated the sensitive ear of the listener to de Meyer, are as much avoided as the tameness and torpidity of Henri Herz." The *Times* then went on to praise Jaëll mightily. For Jaëll's second concert, on November 22, something special was offered. Announced the advertisements: "Mr. ALFRED JAELL will also have the honor to introduce before the American public a MUSICAL WONDER, ADELINE [sic] PATTI, only seven years of age."

Dwight's Journal of Music in Boston has a review, in the issue of January 22, 1853, that gives a good idea of what America thought of Jaëll:

Alfred Jaëll is now, we suppose, generally acknowledged to be the foremost pianist who has visited this country. Evident to any one who hears him play, in whatever music, is the brilliance of his touch, the limpid purity and consummate finish of his passages, the well-conceived, clear, elegant rendering of the whole piece.... No matter how terrifically swift and torturous and crowded the fantasia, or how learned, closely written, fraught with meaning the sonata, trio, or concerto, he performs it so that not a note or expressive feature of the work is lost or marred, as if it were child's play for him, and as if he never dreamed of knowing any difficulties.

Jaëll (who was married to Marie Trautmann, a good pianist and an eminent teacher who wrote several important books about the physiology of playing) did considerable touring and helped raise standards in America. So did the English-born Richard Hoffman, who studied with Moscheles, Liszt, Döhler and others, and came to America in 1847. He settled in New York as pianist, teacher and composer, played with the Philharmonic almost every year from 1848 to 1892, and became a fixture in New York's musical life.

There were others who contributed. From Germany came Henry C. Timm, William Scharfenberg and Daniel Schlesinger, all of whom settled in New York. Timm and Scharfenberg were instrumental in founding the New York Philharmonic in 1842. Schlesinger, reputedly the most brilliant of the three, died young. Maurice Strakosch, who came to the United States from Poland via the Vienna Conservatory, gave a few concerts around 1850 before drifting off into the impresario business. Robert Goldbeck came from Germany and from Henry Litolff's teaching to settle in Chicago and St. Louis. John Ernst Perabo was said to have played the entire *Well-Tempered Clavier* from memory at the age of nine. He came to America from Wiesbaden at the age of seven, but was sent to Hamburg in 1858, and then to Leipzig, where he studied with Moscheles and Reinecke. On his return to New York in 1865 he started playing—of all things—Schubert; and in a series of matinees went through all the Schubert piano music known at that time.

August Hyllested, born in Stockholm of Danish parents, studied with Liszt for three years, came to America and associated himself with the Chicago Musical College and the University of Wisconsin. The Philadelphia-born Charles H. Jarvis was one of the first American pianists *not* to study overseas. He helped mold American tastes by giving twenty-four historical programs. Among his accomplishments was an active repertoire of three hundred pieces and a working knowledge of seven hundred others.

Even more important in the American pianistic and musical scene was William Mason, who went abroad to study with Alexander Dreyschock and Liszt. When he came home in 1854, it was with a set of ideals and accomplishments that no American musician could match. He promptly started introducing Beethoven, Chopin and Schumann to his bemused audiences, followed Liszt's lead in giving recitals without assisting artists, and concentrated primarily on the best music. In that, during the 1850s, he was unique in America and, with the exception of von Bülow and Clara Schumann, in Europe, too.

One of Mason's friends and associates was the British-born Sebastian Bach Mills, who *had* to be a musician with that name. Mills came to America in 1859, after his studies with Moscheles and Liszt, and immediately established himself as one of the best pianists. Mills never became an American citizen, but he played so often in the United States that most Americans thought he was one. He introduced several major works to America, including the premiere of Beethoven's *Emperor* Concerto in 1865. Carl Wolfsohn, from Germany, settled in Philadelphia, where he concentrated on Beethoven and chamber music. He played the thirty-two sonatas in 1863 (repeating them in New York and still later in Chicago). Then he played a Chopin cycle, then a Schumann one. In 1873 he settled permanently in Chicago, where among his pupils was the great Fannie Bloomfield. Wolfsohn, who had attended Anton Rubinstein's historical series of seven concerts, did the Russian virtuoso one better in 1877, giving eighteen evenings of historical concerts. The Boston-born Carlyle Petersilea made the European trek to study with Moscheles and Liszt. Returning to Boston, he started a series of Schumann soirées, played the Beethoven cycle and taught at the New England Conservatory. Otto Bendix, one of Petersilea's col-

leagues at the New England Conservatory, came there as an experienced recitalist who had studied with Kullak and Liszt. And Louis
Maas was still another Liszt pupil who taught at the New England
Conservatory, which must have had an exceptionally strong faculty
during the last quarter of the nineteenth century.

All of these fine and sincere musicians quietly started to raise
American standards of piano playing, and of music making in general. But there was one celebrity who for a while attracted more
attention than all of them put together—the curious and pathetic
Blind Tom, a Negro slave from Georgia who was owned by a man
named Perry H. Oliver. Blind Tom, who was born around 1850 and
was a mental defective, was exhibited as "the greatest musical prodigy since Mozart." It would seem that he had absolute pitch and the
ability to play back, after a fashion, anything he heard. Much interest in the blind, half-witted child was created by a long article that
appeared in 1862 in the *Atlantic Monthly*. The writer, a woman, said
that Blind Tom was incredibly gifted: that he could play back any
piece, no matter how complicated, on hearing it only once. The good
lady, who obviously knew nothing about music, makes mistake after
mistake in the article, but there were few in America at the time
who could point them out. And her description of one of Blind Tom's
appearances shrivels the soul. The boy would sit at the piano with
great blubbery lips, would be begged to play by Mr. Oliver, would be
bribed by cakes and candy. "The concert was a mixture of music,
whining, coaxing." At the end of each piece Blind Tom, without
waiting for the audience, would applaud himself violently. "Some
beautiful caged spirit, one could not but know, struggled for breath
under that brutal form and idiotic brain." But America was as naïve
as the writer, and Blind Tom was successfully exhibited, even at the
White House. A book on him—clearly written by a press agent—
was published and helped promote the Blind Tom myth. It contained
such passages as: "As an additional proof of his remarkable powers of
imitation, he gives recitations in Greek, Latin, German, French, as
well as imitations of the Scotch bagpipe, the hurdy-gurdy, the
Scotch fiddler, the American stump orator, comic speaker, and, in
short, any sound he may hear."

Then *Dwight's Journal of Music* began to start questioning Blind
Tom's accomplishments. Qualified observers wrote in and made it
clear that the boy could not do a fiftieth of the things credited to
him. As a matter of fact, he could not do anything except play back a

few tunes he knew. He was taken to England in 1866, where his sponsors managed to wangle guarded testimonials from Moscheles and Hallé. If these two admirable musicians are accurately quoted, they confirm that at least Blind Tom had absolute pitch. After a few years Blind Tom dropped from the scene and nothing was heard of him. He died in Hoboken on June 13, 1908.

· XII ·

More Salonists, and the
Revolutionary in Octaves

SALON PIANISTS THROVE in the early romantic period, and then died away never to return. The closest equivalent today would be the so-called "cocktail pianist." Salon pianists got their name as indicated: by playing in salons rather than concert halls, or, if they did take a fling at concerts, achieving most success in the salon. They concentrated on a very light repertoire, tickling their listeners with the lowest forms of musical trash.

Of course there were pianists who strode midway between salon and concert. In England there was William Sterndale Bennett, friend of Mendelssohn and Schumann, composer of graceful piano music. Theodore Döhler, the Austrian-born prodigy who studied with Czerny, attracted much attention, though Mendelssohn did not like him. "I am surprised to hear of Döhler's being lionized. His playing only interested me the first time; afterward he seemed to me very cold and calculating and rather dull." Heine was amusing on the subject of Döhler. "Some say he is among the last of the second-class pianists, others say that he is the first among the third-class pianists. As a matter of fact he plays prettily, nicely, and neatly. His performance is most charming, evincing astonishing dexterity of finger, but giving no evidence of power or spirit. Delicate weakness, elegant impotence, interesting pallor." None of the salon pianists from Herz on had much power. That might have startled the countesses and duchesses who loved to hear them play. Their approach was uniformly facile, light-fingered, elegant and empty. They filled a need as paid entertainers to a wealthy and frivolous society.

Stephen Heller could have been one of the best of the salonists, but he shrank from playing in public. He wrote charming piano pieces that in their day were rated by many musicians above Chopin's. They are not nearly that good, of course, but some of them deserve revival. The English-born Henry Litolff was good enough to be compared with Liszt by von Bülow. Litolff studied with Moscheles, was well received as a pianist, composed prolifically, was much married, and started the famous *Collection Litolff*, a cheap and accurate edition of the best music. Only one of his pieces has remained in the repertoire—the Scherzo from his *Concerto Symphonique No. 4*, for piano and orchestra. It is a piece that Saint-Saëns must have known very well, for the entire piano layout and melodic format is very close to the work of the later French composer. In its way the Scherzo is a brilliant, effective and melodious piece, and if it is typical of Litolff's work, his music still has something to offer.

The age had its eccentrics. Mortier de Fontaine went all over Europe with one piece, Beethoven's *Hammerklavier* Sonata, and from all accounts he played it very badly. The Lion of Poland, on the other hand, had a big repertoire and he played all of it badly. The Lion of Poland was Antoine de Kontski, and audiences shuddered under his impact. Apparently he could not play two correct notes in succession, and he never played under a fortissimo. Critics were appalled. "From battle, murder, sudden death, and from the Lion of Poland's piano playing, Good Lord, deliver us," wrote one.

Hundreds of forgotten pianists, once popular, made their careers and vanished. Jacob Rosenhain was supposed to be one of the best, but he soon concentrated on composition to the total neglect of his piano. Another fine artist in her day was Marie Pleyel, the wife of the piano manufacturer. Her maiden name was Marie Moke. She was one of Moscheles' best pupils, had also studied with Herz and Kalkbrenner, and was greatly admired by Liszt, Mendelssohn and Schumann. Berlioz had been in love with her; it was she who caused his precipitate rush back to Paris (loaded with poison and revolvers) from the Villa Medici in Rome. He had learned she was unfaithful to him, and he was going to do away with her, and then himself. In 1848 she became head of the piano department of the Brussels Conservatoire. She probably was a superior musician, and Liszt admired her teaching as much as her playing. Fétis went all out. "I have heard all the celebrated pianists from Hallmandel and Clementi up to the famous ones of today [*ca.* 1870] but I say that none of them has given me, as has Mme. Pleyel, the feeling of perfection." And the extravagant Marmontel wrote that her playing had the clarity of

Marie Pleyel, one of the most admired pianists of the 1830s. Berlioz was in love with her, but she married the prominent French piano manufacturer.

The hero of octaves. Alexander Dreyschock, the Horowitz of his day. One of his specialties was to play Chopin's *Revolutionary* Étude with left-hand octaves instead of single notes.

Kalkbrenner, the sensibility of Chopin, the spiritual elegance of Herz and the dashing quality of Liszt. If true, this would have made her the greatest player in history.

The trouble with Marmontel, a professor at the Paris Conservatoire, was that he rated *everybody* almost as highly in his book *Les pianistes célèbres*. By coincidence, many of his subjects also happened to have been his pupils. His book is littered with names that have made absolutely no impact on history; and yet they did have big careers in their day. Here are some of the pianists over whom Marmontel gushes: Émile Prudent, Amédée de Méroux, Madame Farrenc, Pierre Zimmerman, Camille Stamaty, Louis Adam, Madame de Mongeroult, Lefébure-Wély, Alexandre-Édouard Goria, Louis Lacombe, Jules [Julius] Schulhoff, Aglaé Massart, Henri Ravina, Édouard Wolff, Félix le Couppey, Georges Mathias, Eraim-Miriam Delaborde, Jules Cohen, Caroline Montigny-Rémaury, Auguste-Emanuel Vancorbeil. Some of these became highly rated teachers, composers and conductors, but none ever set the world on fire as a pianist. Nor did Léopoldine Blahetka, the idol of Vienna in the 1820s. "Young, pretty and a pianist," was how Chopin described her. He also said that she "thumped frightfully."

For a while, though, Alexander Dreyschock did set the world on fire. He came storming out of Bohemia, where he had studied with Tomaschek, and from 1838 proceeded to startle audiences with his prodigies of execution. In a way he was the Vladimir Horowitz of his day—the hero of titanic technical stunts, the master of thirds, sixths and octaves. He is one of the freak piano technicians of history. When old Cramer heard him, he collapsed in astonishment. "The man has no left hand; they are both right hands." Dreyschock indeed did have a marvelous left hand and composed various pieces for the left hand alone, such as his *Fantasy on God Save the King*. He played loud, and he played fast, and he may not have had a refined musical mind, but he certainly knew how to excite an audience, as von Bülow discovered on coming to Vienna. Dreyschock was always popular there, and von Bülow could not compete with him. So he called Dreyschock an "*homme-machine*, the personification of absence of genius, with the exterior of a clown," and defended his own failure by calling his competitor's success "a got-up furore." But that was not true. Dreyschock was a spectacular technician, and Theodor Kullak, who was a trained observer and knew what he was talking about, said that Dreyschock's technique was better than Liszt's.

In certain respects it probably was. Europe started talking about the new trinity, of which Liszt was the father, Thalberg the son, and Dreyschock the holy ghost. He was also probably a better musician than he was given credit for. His stunts were what most people remembered and judged him by, and his real contributions to the art of piano playing were ignored. As Hanslick ponderously put it, Dreyschock "completed the succession of those virtuosi whose bravura was capable of attracting and fascinating a numerous public which admired technical magic and was happiest in astonishment."

An American pupil, one Nathan Richardson, has described Dreyschock's dogged monomania. Dreyschock would practice sixteen hours a day with the left hand alone, and got to the point where he could play octaves as fast, and as smoothly, as single-note passages. He was proud of his octaves and would thunder them out. Heine once said that when Dreyschock played in Munich and the wind was right, you could hear him in Paris. Heine reviewed Dreyschock's debut in Paris, and he carried the analogy a little further. "He makes a hell of a racket. One does not seem to hear one pianist Dreyschock but *drei Schock* [three-score] of pianists. Since on the evening of his concert the wind was blowing south by west, perhaps you heard the tremendous sounds in Augsburg. At such a distance their effect must be agreeable. Here, however, in this Department of the Seine, one may easily burst an eardrum when the piano-pounder thumps away. Go hang yourself, Franz Liszt! You are but an ordinary god in comparison with this god of thunder!"

But it was not all thunder. He *could* play with great beauty when he wanted to, and Mendelssohn said as much. "He plays some pieces so admirably that you fancy yourself in the presence of a great artist, but immediately afterwards something so poorly that you change your mind." Clara Schumann, who hated display pianism, saw only the worst of him. Dreyschock, she said, had a great deal of execution but no mind, "and he renders things in a horrible way."

The chances are that after a while Dreyschock did lose most of whatever sensitivity he had, and began to look on music only as a means to show off his technique. His most celebrated stunt was what he did with Chopin's *Revolutionary* Étude. It all started when he overheard Tomaschek talking about the advance of piano playing. "I should not be surprised," said Tomaschek, pointing to the Étude, "if one of these days a pianist appears who could play all these single left-hand passages in octaves." The entire left-hand part of the *Revo-*

lutionary Étude consists of fast extended arpeggios. Dreyschock took the suggestion seriously. For six weeks he worked twelve hours a day until he had overcome the problems. If he really played those octaves in tempo it was a hair-raising—one might claim impossible—feat. Yet many competent observers say that he did play the piece in tempo, and he put it on every one of his programs.

His programs were restricted, and he may have had the smallest repertoire of any of the great pianists. Moscheles comments on his left-hand *tours de force*, but says that Dreyschock could play only twelve pieces. While Moscheles was not accurate in this statement —perhaps he only heard Dreyshock play twelve pieces—his remarks about Dreyschock's inability to read music well can be taken at face value. "You shall hear the story," he writes. "He was trying over with me some 'Scale Pieces' and played the pupil's part, but was so often at fault in the rhythm that Clara ran up to her mamma, calling out (luckily in English, which Dreyschock probably did not understand), 'Mamma, hasn't Mr. D. learned the scales?' You may imagine my horror at the 'enfant terrible.' "

Wilhelm Kuhe, who heard Dreyschock play the be-octaved *Revolutionary* in Vienna, tells how Liszt practiced a little one-upmanship. Liszt came to Vienna in 1847 and played, among other things, Chopin's F minor Étude (Op. 25, No. 2). Then he played the first bar in octaves, slowly. Then faster, then still faster, just the first bar. Then he played the entire Étude with right-hand octaves in Chopin's correct tempo. The Viennese public got the point.

One anecdote about Dreyschock is lovely. It was told by Richard Mansfield, whose mother was in the Viennese court. At Dreyschock's first court appearance he played before the Emperor in a very hot room, with closed windows. Dreyschock began to perspire. The Emperor listened intently and watched him even more closely. When the pianist got up and faced the Emperor, he was afraid to wipe his face. The Emperor approached. "My dear Dreyschock, I have heard Moscheles play." Dreyschock bowed. "I have heard Thalberg." Dreyschock bowed lower. "I have heard Liszt." Dreyschock bowed very low indeed. "I have heard all the great players. But I never, never, never saw anybody perspire as you do."

Two Sensitive Ones

TWO VIRTUOSOS, ALMOST EXACT contemporaries, who held exceptional reputations but who do not seem to fit anywhere in the main line of piano playing were Charles Henri Valentin Morhange, better known as Alkan (1813–1888), and Adolf Henselt (1814–1889). One reason is that neither played much in public. Alkan was a misanthrope and an eccentric, while Henselt was too nervous. But both seemed to have awed their contemporaries. In a way Alkan was the Charles Ives of his time—seldom in the public eye, a recluse, the composer of some amazing and virtually unplayable music. He has not lacked admirers in the present century. Busoni, who called Alkan's pieces "the greatest achievement in piano music after Liszt," was fascinated with the man, and as late as the 1930s Egon Petri included in his recitals a set of Alkan études that lasted half a program.

Not too much is known about Alkan. Marmontel, in his *Pianistes célèbres*, peppers his account of the man with words like "*mystère . . . énigme.*" He was born and died in Paris, was brought up to be an orthodox Jew, was admitted to the Conservatoire at the age of six, won first prize in piano and harmony at the age of thirteen, started giving concerts at fourteen, was a well-known virtuoso at seventeen. At that time he had not developed the curious streak that sent him indoors, and he was a member of a literary circle that included Victor Hugo, Lamennais and Sand. Chopin and Liszt were his close friends, and Chopin appeared as a guest artist on his concert appearances, such as the one on March 3, 1838, in the salon of M. Pope. It was a very long program, and the ninth selection was "excerpts from Beethoven's Symphony in A, played on two pianos by MM.

Alkan, Chopin, Gutmann and Zimmerman." Pierre Zimmerman, head of the piano department of the Conservatoire from 1820 to 1848, had been Alkan's teacher. Chopin thought enough of Alkan to remember him on his deathbed. Albert Grzymala ministered to Chopin in his last hours, and in a letter to the banker Léo said that Chopin had asked him "to destroy many pieces not worthy of me." Burn them, Chopin ordered, "with the exception of the beginning of the *Méthode*: this I leave to Alkan and Reber. Let them have some use from it." Napoléon-Henri Reber was a minor composer of the day.

But soon, at the age of 25, Alkan left the concert life, dropped his pupils, and concentrated on teaching and composition. After 1845 he gave no concerts for twenty-five years. He taught a good deal and was nearly as fashionable a teacher as his friend Chopin. Seldom did he leave his apartment. Once in a while he would emerge to play at fashionable gatherings, at which he was heard (in the words of Isidor Philipp) by "*des dames très parfumées et froufrouantes*." A hypochondriac, he purchased and cooked his own food. Only close friends could get to see him. Friedrich Niecks, a scholar of the piano and pianists, tried to see Alkan once in 1880. The concierge said that M. Alkan was not in. When, then, would he be at home? "Never!" In 1873, for some reason, he came out of seclusion and started giving what he called *petits concerts*. According to legend, his death was as unusual as his life. The old man was attempting to reach for a Hebrew religious book on top of a large shelf when the entire bookcase turned over and crushed him to death. Roland Smith, in his short Alkan biography, thinks the story is apocryphal. But if it cannot be proved, it cannot be disproved either.

His music started appearing in 1838, and the usually gentle Schumann, writing about *Trois Morceaux dans le genre pathétique* (Op. 15) tore into the work, calling it "false, unnatural art... inward emptiness... outward nothingness." There must have been something very strong in the music to have so riled Schumann. Liszt reviewed the *Trois Morceaux* too, but was more generous. Of course, he was a close friend. The later music of Alkan was studiously ignored by critics and pianists. What could be said of the Concerto in G sharp minor, the first movement of which alone contains 1,343 measures, more than the entire *Hammerklavier*? Small reason that Alkan was called the Berlioz of the piano. In all, seventy-six of his works were published with opus numbers. There also were quite a few published without opus numbers and a good deal more in manuscript. Some of this music is little more than of a genre salon nature. But part of it is imaginative, original and defiantly unorthodox. A few pianists, starting with Raymond Lewenthal and Roland Smith, have played and recorded a good deal of Alkan's music, but unfortunately there seems no evidence of any great public interest.

Those who heard him play in his prime called him an exciting virtuoso, especially imaginative in his use of pedal effects. And, if he could play his own music as written, he must have been a formidable technician. Indeed, Liszt told the pianist Frits Hartvigson that Alkan had the finest technique he had ever encountered. In attempting to reconstruct Alkan's style, Smith writes that he must have been "a unique pianist combining all the finest attributes of the French school—its equality of touch, clarity, lucidity and rhythmic severity with the intellectual penetration of a Busoni." Smith's remarks are backed up by a pianist-composer named Francesco Berger, who wrote a piece about Alkan in 1918. Berger had gone to one of Alkan's *petits concerts* to hear him play Bach, Mendelssohn and his own music. He knew some of Alkan's wild music and was prepared for anything, but got a pleasant surprise. The playing was "masterly ... free from any kind of extravagance ... firmness, repose and sobriety in rhythm and dynamics ... clearness of phrasing and the richness of delicate shading ... avoidance of the abuse of tempo rubato." Berger concluded that Alkan's "legato element" may be said to have been the predominant characteristic of his playing.

The other shy pianist, Adolf Henselt, was no misanthrope. He was merely terrified of the public, and it was a pathological terror. Once he was recognized in a café, and the band gave him an ovation. The horrified, suddenly galvanized Henselt blindly raced through the crowd and escaped through the kitchen. When playing with an orchestra, he would hide in the wings until the opening tutti was over, rush out and literally pounce on the piano. On one occasion he forgot to put aside the cigar he was nervously chomping—this was in Russia—and played the concerto cigar in mouth, smoking away, much to the amusement of the Czar. The mere thought of giving a concert made him physically ill. He gave very few throughout his career—far fewer than any of the great pianists, including Alkan— and in the last thirty-three years of his life apparently gave no more than three. (At least, that is what several reference books say.) He was offered fabulous sums to appear but turned down all offers. He just could not control his fingers when he knew people were listening. William Mason, who admired Henselt, has a story to tell about his nerves:

An anecdote of Adolf Henselt, also related to me by Dreyschock, is entertaining as well as suggestive, especially to piano-forte players, who are constantly troubled with nervousness when playing before an audience. Henselt, whose home was in St. Petersburg, was in the habit of spending a few weeks every summer with a relative who lived in Dresden. Dreyschock, passing through that city, called on him one morning, and upon going up the staircase to his room, heard the most lovely tones of the piano-forte imaginable.

He was so fascinated that he sat down at the top of the landing and listened for a long time. Henselt was playing repeatedly the same composition and his playing was specially characterized by a warm, emotional touch and a delicious legato, causing the tones to melt, as it were, one into the other, and this, too, without any confusion or lack of clearness. Henselt was full of sentiment but he detested "sentimentality." Finally, for lack of time, Dreyschock was obliged to announce himself, although, as he said, he could have listened for hours. He entered the room and after the usual friendly greeting said, "What were you playing just as I came up the stairs?" Henselt replied that he was composing a piece and was playing it over to himself. Dreyschock expressed his admiration of the composition, and begged Henselt to play it again, but alas! his performance was stiff, inaccurate, and even clumsy, and all of the exquisite poetry and unconsciousness of his style completely disappeared. Dreyschock said that it was quite impossible to describe the difference; and this was simply the result of diffidence and nervousness, which, as it appeared, were entirely out of the player's power to control.

All this may have come about because at his debut, according to Alice Diehl, he had a memory lapse, left the stage and refused to return. He had been born in Bavaria and had studied with Hummel. Hummel thought him a young anarchist, and Henselt thought Hummel was an old fogy. When Henselt finally got enough nerve to appear in public he made an overwhelming impression. "Liszt, Chopin and Henselt are continents; Tausig, Rubinstein and Bülow are countries." Thus Wilhelm von Lenz. Liszt appears to have been amazed. "Find out the secret of Henselt's hands," he told his pupils. "I could have had velvet paws like that if I had wanted to." Schu-

Adolf Henselt, considered by many the peer of Liszt. He was, however, too nervous to play in public.

mann wrote rave reviews, referring to Henselt as a mighty pianist who eclipsed everybody, "who possesses the most equally developed hands, of iron strength and endurance, and capable of softness, grace and singing quality." Henselt must have been able to draw a very penetrating tone from the piano. One of his pupils, Bettina Walker, tried to describe his touch, said it was hopeless to try, an absurd task, and then went on for a few hundred well-chosen words in which "crystalline," "sea," "pearl," "chalice," and "flower" figure prominently. Pupils, of course, have a tendency to fall in love with their teachers, and their remarks are not to be taken too seriously. But Walker's remarks are echoed by too many good musicians for them to be unfounded.

The technical feature that Henselt had to an unprecedented degree was his amazing extensions. His hands were not particularly large; they were thick, fleshy, and had short fingers. But he worked so diligently on his extensions that he got to the point where his left-hand stretch could take in C-E-G-C-F and his right hand B-E-A-C-E. "Leather! Just look how it is stretched," he would say, displaying his palms. Such was the strength of his hands that he could get thunderous orchestral effects from his fingers alone, where Liszt had to work from the arms. Years and years of compulsive practice had brought him to the point where his fingers were absolutely independent, and musicians were entranced when he played Bach, bringing out the counterpoint with amazing clarity.

He may have been the most compulsive practicer in history—more, even, than Dreyschock, more than Godowsky. One reason for this concentration was that he was not a natural pianist, as Liszt was. He had to slave. By 1832 he got into the habit of working at the piano for ten hours a day, and he never let up. Even at the intermissions of his concerts, or on trains, or in stage coaches, he would have a dummy keyboard on his knees. This kind of compulsive practice *could* not have meant much, if anything; it was merely relief from tension, a kind of withdrawal, atonement for sin. One does not know whether to laugh or cry at von Lenz's description of Henselt at home:

Such a study of Bach as Henselt made, every day of his life, has never before been heard of. He played the fugues most diligently on a piano so muffled with feather quills that the only sound heard was the dry beat of the hammers against the muffled strings; it was like the bones of a skeleton rattled by the wind! In this manner the great artist spared his ears and his nerves, for he reads, at the same time, on the music rack, a very thick, good book—the Bible—truly the most appropriate companion for Bach. After he has played Bach and the Bible quite through, he begins over again. The few people whom Henselt allows to approach him in those late, hallowed evening hours, he requests to continue their conversaton—that does not disturb him in the least.

"At home" to Henselt was St. Petersburg. He had gone there in 1838 and immediately been named court pianist, much to the despair of Charles Mayer. Mayer, a pianist with a good European reputation, had studied with Field in Russia and settled in St. Petersburg. There he had played and taught—and had not once been asked to play at court. It was the only thing he wanted in life. Poor Mayer, broken-hearted, left St. Petersburg and went to Dresden to die. Henselt replaced him as the pianistic celebrity, taught plentifully (including the royal family) and gave a series of matinees at court where, before a small audience, he could play at his best. He did not like audiences, but a small one, mostly of friends, was preferable to a big one.

Henselt was a textbook German, relentless to the point of savagery as a teacher (he obviously detested teaching), and he was equally arrogant in his musical *obiter dicta*. Certain modernistic things in music he never understood, and the dissonant chord that opens the last movement of the Beethoven Ninth he referred to as "a monster." To illustrate this chord he would turn his back to the piano, sit on the keys and say, "It sounds something like this." His teaching sessions were on the spectacular side. Students would enter all atremble to be greeted by a Henselt dressed in a white suit, wearing a red fez, clutching a fly-swatter in his hands. "Begin!" The pupil would begin and soon hit a wrong note. "*Falsch!* Play it again!" So went the lesson. "*Falsch! Falsch!*" In the meantime he was striding around the room, swatting flies. If he were completely uninterested in the pupil, he would stop trying to decimate the fly population of Russia, bring in his dogs and play with them. Small wonder that he never turned out an important pupil. Students who did interest him received fairer treatment, including much illustration at the second piano; but Henselt was notoriously short-tempered and few seemed to interest him. Those few came away with their spirit broken. He worked them to death, and assured them that they had no talent. There was a saying in pianistic circles: "Henselt kills."

He composed. His F minor Piano Concerto, once in the active repertoire, disappeared around the turn of the century. Anton Rubinstein once heard Henselt play the concerto. "I was amazed at his dexterity at the piano," Rubinstein is reported having said, "especially in the way of stretches, wide-spread chords and incredible jumps around the keyboard. However, I noticed that his stretching was lost on the general public. Only the pianists present realized what resounding feats he was accomplishing. I procured the concerto and his etudes, but after working on them for a few days I realized it was a waste of time, for they were based on an abnormal formation of the hand. In this respect Henselt, like Paganini, was a freak."

Only one piece of Henselt's has survived—the Etude in F sharp major, named *Si oiseau j'étais*. Once in a while this charming, innocent *morceau* turns up in recital. Otherwise there is nothing. When he died in 1889, three years after Liszt, he was the last but one of the great romantic pianists of the 1830s (Clara Schumann outlived him by seven years), the last link with Hummel, Thalberg, Chopin, Schumann and Mendelssohn and the other great men who had inaugurated a marvelous epoch in music.

· XIV ·

The First American

TO EUROPEANS OF THE 1840s, America was a country of steam engines, wild Indians and white barbarians. When in 1842 Pierre Zimmerman received an application from the thirteen-year-old Louis Moreau Gottschalk, he would not even let the boy audition for entrance into the Paris Conservatoire. For this he had good reason. Nobody, he said, who had passed his first thirteen years in the savage atmosphere of America could become a piano virtuoso. He advised the boy to go home and become a mechanic. Moreau, instead, ended up studying with Charles Hallé and then with Camille Stamaty. The prodigy from Louisiana turned out to be a major talent. Three years after arriving in Paris, he made his debut and was instantly accepted as one of Europe's great pianists. The novelty of his birth did not hurt. An exotic from romantic, far-off Louisiana! with good looks and perfect manners! with extraordinary skill at the piano! with endorsements from Chopin, Berlioz and Kalkbrenner! Perhaps the New World was growing up? *La France Musicale* was amazed, especially when Gottschalk started writing his piano pieces. "An American composer, *bon Dieu!*" This was in 1848, and *La France Musicale* helpfully assisted its readers in the pronunciation of Gottschalk's name. "Close the lips, advance the tongue, appear a little like whistling, and you will have the key."

Gottschalk was born in New Orleans in 1829. His father had come from London; his mother had been born in New Orleans, of French descent. Moreau developed as all prodigies do, and by twelve had learned all that any teacher in New Orleans could give him. His family, fairly well-to-do, sent him to Paris. It seems that he did not get very much from Hallé's teaching, and the association did not last

217

very long. Stamaty was more stimulating; and one of the stimuli he provided was a seven-year-old boy who was studying with him. That youngster was Saint-Saëns (six and a half years younger than Gottschalk, he outlived him by over fifty years), who must have given the provincial Moreau something to think about. When Stamaty finally brought Gottschalk forward, at the Pleyel salon on April 2, 1845, word had gotten around, and a distinguished audience, including Chopin and Kalkbrenner, was present. Gottschalk played Chopin's E minor Concerto and operatic transcriptions by Liszt and Thalberg. Chopin went backstage and is reported to have said, "Give me your hand, my child. I predict you will become the king of pianists." The chances are that the story is not apocryphal. Léon Escudier, the important French critic, was at the concert and later wrote in *Mes Souvenirs* that Chopin took Gottschalk in his arms and said, "Fine, fine, my boy." Kalkbrenner, who did not go backstage, received Gottschalk the morning after the concert. He had nice things to say but complained about his repertoire. "You and Stamaty should have chosen *my* music. It is classical, and besides, everybody likes it."

Chopin may have been almost right in his prediction. Gottschalk might have become the king of pianists—or, at least, one high in the nobility—had he wanted to. But a combination of many things— indolence, lack of discipline, extracurricular pleasures—kept him from the heights. Certainly his career started as auspiciously as that of any pianist. Shortly after his debut he became the vogue, and so did his music. For he started composing piano pieces based on Negro and Latin-American melodies, and those pieces hit Europe with an impact hard to realize today, when Gottschalk and his music are pretty well forgotten. "Who does not know *Bamboula?*" rhetorically asked *La France Musicale*. All the journals referred to Gottschalk as "the celebrated pianist," which meant that he had arrived. He was spoken of in the same breath with Liszt, Thalberg, Herz, Chopin. Chopin especially. There was a slight resemblance between the two men to begin with. Both were slim, aristocratic-looking, rather short. Both composed exotic national music—Chopin with his mazurkas, Gottschalk with his plantation tunes. And both were extraordinary pianists. In later years Gottschalk was to refer to himself, matter-of-factly, as "one of the old Chopinists." Marmontel brought Chopin into the picture while discussing Gottschalk's platform presence. "His distinguished and modest nature made him very sympathetic; his expressive playing, his Chopin-like sonorities, were seductive." Marmontel was enchanted with Gottschalk's compositons, *"un parfum spécial."* In addition, Marmontel made a strong comparison between Gottschalk and Chopin, citing the "dreamful and melancholy" look of each. In Gottschalk's playing, said the French professor, were many Chopinesque features—"certain melodic contours, certain undulations...." And Gottschalk's "work as a composer approached Chopin's. As a virtuoso he must be placed between Liszt and Thalberg. He obtained special sonorities. His playing, by turns nervous and of extreme delicacy, astonished and charmed." And Adolph Adam wrote, "... all the grace of Chopin with more decided character."

It is no cause for surprise that Gottschalk's music excited such wonderment. A good deal of his output is bad (though all of it has a period charm), but his nationalistic pieces are prophetic. Gottschalk was not only America's first important pianist; he was also the first national composer. His works on native (and Latin-American) folk elements are amazing, and pieces like the last movement of Milhaud's *Scaramouche* (composed in 1939) or his *Saudades do Brasil* (1920–1921) are not really too different in conception from Gottschalk's *El Gibaro* or *Le Bananier.* Gottschalk uses spicy tango and rumba rhythms of real complexity, and the music is beautifully laid out for the piano. Nowhere near so good as these excursions into nationalism are Gottschalk's two most popular pieces—*The Dying Poet* and *The Last Hope.* Both of these drawing-room *morceaux,* embarrassingly sentimental, enjoyed a phenomenal vogue in America for many years. We can smile at those; but the nationalism of Gottschalk is not easy to dismiss.

Triumph followed triumph for Gottschalk. Pleyel called him the successor of Chopin, Berlioz described him as the poet of the piano, and Thalberg was entranced. Gottschalk fraternized with kings, queens and assorted royalty, moved in the best circles, and had a most satisfactory number of love affairs. During the 1850–51 season Gottschalk gave more than seventy-five concerts in Paris alone. Not only that, but some of the leading pianists—Alexandre Goria, Alfred Jaëll, Josef Wieniawski, Emile Prudent—started taking his music into their repertoire and making it extraordinarily popular. As Berlioz wrote, "Everybody in Europe is now acquainted with *Bamboula, Le Bananier, Le Mancenillies, La Savane* and twenty other ingenious

America's idol, Louis Moreau Gottschalk. From 1845 to 1853 he was one of the European stars. This lithograph was made in 1853, the year he returned to the United States.

About ten years later, with mustache and medals. For important concerts Gottschalk wore his medals while playing.

fantasias." Critics hearing this music became hysterical and referred to Gottschalk's "chants of the New World, chants which bring tears to our eyes, so much do they breathe of sadness and simplicity. One transports us to forests . . . another represents faithfully the indolent Creole swinging in his hammock . . . and what shall we say of the third? Does it not seem to be overwhelmed by that solemn silence and that solitude which one feels traversing those vast prairies at the foot of the Rocky Mountains?" Charles Schriwanek, who wrote this outburst for the *Gazette de Lausanne*, had probably never been west of Paris.

Gottschalk toured Western Europe and spent some time in Spain. He had been invited there by the Queen, and his career almost came to an abrupt end when a jealous courtier slammed a carriage door on his hand. So many reviews were written about his playing that his name became a household word. In those days Gottschalk still played music by other composers (later he was to concentrate almost exclusively on his own), including the Beethoven *Appassionata* (one of his big numbers) and works by Bach, Liszt, Thalberg and Chopin. He was a natural pianist who never had to practice much (when he left Stamaty at the age of seventeen he never took another lesson and never felt he needed one), was blessed with a facile technique and a special ability in repeated notes and rapid figurations. He used considerable pedal, and he exploited the upper reaches of the piano (this, too, is found in much of his music; he liked the silvery sound of rapid quasi-glissando patterns in the high treble). His tone was clear and penetrating, without much sonority; he was not an "orchestral" pianist like Liszt and was more the salon type. Critics kept referring to his "silvery sound" and his "fingers of steel." He seems to have had a good ear for delicate color effects, and his playing had charm and rhythmic vitality. Altogether he was an original, skillful and exciting pianist, able to compete on equal terms with any of the great European figures. Berlioz took his work very seriously:

Gottschalk is one of the very small number who possess all the different elements of a consummate pianist, all the faculties which surround him with an irresistible prestige and give him a sovereign power. He is an accomplished musician; he knows just how fancy can be indulged in expression. He knows the limits beyond which any freedom taken with the rhythm produces only confusion and disorder, and upon these limits he never encroaches. There is an exquisite grace in his manner of phrasing sweet melodies and scattering the light passages from the top of the key-board. The boldness, brilliancy, and originality of his play at once dazzle and astonish. . . .

Having conquered Europe, Gottschalk went home to America. His first concert was given in New York, at Niblo's Saloon, on February 11, 1853, although he had made a private appearance several weeks previously. The New York critics went wild. One of them assured the public that it was useless any longer to speak of Beethoven. Gottschalk, fresh from having his head turned in Europe, was out to impress his countrymen, and he must have given them a real show. New York had certainly never heard anything like it, for Gottschalk was a much better pianist than Herz or de Meyer or even Jaëll ever aspired to be. The astonished *New York Herald* called Gottschalk's performance "more like that of an orchestra than of a single instrument. . . . You wonder that you never knew before that the piano was capable of such power. He sweeps his hands as high as his head and his fingers come down upon the reverberating keys like so many sledge hammers, but with unerring precision. . . . He combines the sublimity and grandeur of Thalberg with the beauty and finish of Liszt." William Henry Fry was the *Tribune* critic in those years, and the review presumably was written by him. Fry had spent some time in Paris in the 1840s and had heard Liszt and Thalberg.

Naturally the elegant, suave Gottschalk became the rage in American society and was overwhelmed with attention. His love affairs, especially with the actress Ada Clare, were the talk of the United States. The great Barnum himself came around, hat in hand, and offered Gottschalk a three-year tour at twenty thousand dollars a year, guaranteed, over expenses. Gottschalk, on the advice of his father, turned it down. They probably felt that he could make more on his own. They were mistaken, although Gottschalk's reception at first indicated a much higher income than what Barnum had offered.

Gottschalk did not get a bad review until he played in Boston and ran foul of the dour, prim, uncompromising John Sullivan Dwight, the Boston-born minister-critic. In 1852 Dwight established his *Journal of Music*, the most important music magazine in America until it was discontinued in 1881. Not entirely naïve about music, as most American critics at that time were, Dwight was a ferocious fighter for the things he considered right; and what he considered musically right was anything in the Germanic tradition. When he heard Gottschalk he conceded the pianist's fine execution and touch ("the most clear and crisp and beautiful that we have ever known"). Then came the knockout. "But what is the execution without some thought and meaning in the combinations to be executed?" The rest of the review was a diatribe against Gottschalk's repertoire, which contained nothing but his own music, and its superficiality. Dwight's advice to Gottschalk: play some *real* music. Dwight was right. By that time Gottschalk was spoiled and pampered and could not take criticism. Between him and Dwight there grew an undying hatred. Neither could or would understand the other. Dwight regarded himself as the defender of a great tradition. (In addition, he was a Unitarian and an abolitionist, and he hated Southerners. Gottschalk was a Southerner: a liberal one, to be sure, but Dwight did not know that.) Gottschalk despised Dwight and thought him a pompous fool. The fact that Dwight fell into a trap that Gottschalk had prepared did not increase the pianist's respect for him. At a Boston concert Gottschalk, without telling anybody, played a Beethoven bagatelle instead of the piece listed on the program, one of his own works. No Boston critic, Dwight included, noticed the change.

With one interregnum, Gottschalk's life in America was one of tour after tour. In 1857 he concertized in the West Indies with the fourteen-year-old wonder child, Adelina Patti, and he liked Cuba so much that he surrendered completely to the tropical lassitude, remaining there five years. The quality of his playing must have dropped off considerably even before he went to Cuba, and when he played music other than his own he was apt to lay himself open to knowledgeable criticism. Thalberg, in the meantime, had come to America and taken the edge off Gottschalk's novelty. And Thalberg was in better pianistic condition than the hedonistic, pampered Gottschalk. It is true that Gottschalk did have a repertoire in America that contained a few pieces not by himself. These included the Weber *Concertstück* and the two Weber concertos, the Henselt F minor Concerto and *Si oiseau j'étais*, some Chopin including the B flat minor Scherzo, Schumann's Andante and Variations for two pianos, Beethoven's *Pathétique* Sonata and a few others. These he trotted out on special occasions. In New York he played the Henselt in 1857 and had the bad luck to run into a critic who obviously had studied the work and hence knew what he was talking about. It is an interesting review (written by the New York correspondent of the *Philadelphia Musical Journal* in the issue of January 28, 1857), for it demonstrates Gottschalk's irresponsibility:

Mr. Gottschalk *attempted* to play the first part of Henselt's Concerto, Op. 16. We say "attempted," not because he substituted for the difficult runs of the middle part his usual easy ones, leaving out entirely those for the left hand, nor because he dropped a good many notes; but because, in spite of these abbreviations and simplifications, the remaining difficulties of the piece appeared to be so immense to him, that he could not afford to show the least expression, nor any thing of an artistic-like conception or treatment.

In common with all pianists of the day, Gottschalk made changes in all music he played, though generally not on the piratical scale on which he dealt with the Henselt. Richard Hoffman says that Gottschalk loved to play Weber's *Concertstück,* "rather a strange choice, as it was physically impossible for him to execute the octave glissando passages as marked, from a habit of biting his nails to such an extent that his fingers were almost devoid of them, and a glissando under these circumstances was out of the question. He substituted an octave passage, played from the wrist with alternate hands, very cleverly, to be sure, but missing a good deal of the desired effect. He was so persistent in this habit of biting his nails that I have known the keys to be covered with blood when he had finished playing."

The rest of Gottschalk's life can be briefly told. Between 1862 and 1864 he gave more than fifteen hundred concerts, traveling on trains and coaches, getting mixed up in the Civil War as an innocent by-stander (although his father, who had died in 1857, was a slave owner, Gottschalk freed them; he was a liberal, an abolitionist, and his sympathies were with the North), playing for all kinds of audiences. The year 1865 saw the restless Gottschalk on the West Coast, playing in mining towns, roughing it, exerting his charm on San Francisco. There he had an affair with a young lady that blew up into a scandal, and Gottschalk just made it to a ship ahead of the vigilantes. From there he continued to Peru, played his way to Buenos Aires, made a great impression on Emperor Dom Pedro II and started to organize music festivals in Brazil. He died there in 1869 at the age of forty. Some said the cause of his death was cholera; others, peritonitis; some said that he had been assassinated by a jealous husband. Modern scholarship inclines toward peritonitis resulting from a ruptured appendix. His body was sent back to America and buried in Greenwood Cemetery, in Brooklyn.

Through the years he kept up a diary written in French, which was posthumously translated and published by his sisters in 1881 under the title of *Notes of a Pianist*. It is a remarkable book, and few better impressions of Civil War America have ever been written. The *Notes* are far from being entirely devoted to music. They are filled with observations on American life and manners from the viewpoint of a remarkably urbane, witty, civilized man. Gottschalk had the eye of a reporter and no mean literary style. It is hard to resist quoting extensively from a book that contains such observations as:

St. Louis is the capital of Missouri and contains about two hundred thousand inhabitants. It is a dull, tiresome town. . . . I was introduced to an old German musician, with uncombed hair, bushy beard, in constitution like a bear, in disposition the amenity of a boar at bay to a pack of hounds. I know this type; it is found everywhere. It should be time that many great unknown musicians should be convinced that a negligent toilet is the *maladroit* imitation of the surly and misanthropic behavior of the great symphonist of Bonn. . . . Besides, soap is not incompatible with genius; and it is now proved that the daily use of a comb does not exercise any injurious influence on the lobes of the brain.

* * *

They fear that the Confederacy, on taking the offensive, have a design of marching on Washington. . . . A bad business for me, who ought to give a concert there in two days. I very well understand how to fill the hall; but it is dangerous. It would be to announce that I would play my piece called *L'Union*, and my variations on *Dixie's Land*. In the first I would intercalate *Yankee Doodle* and *Hail Columbia*. The second is a Southern Negro air, of which the Confederates, since the commencement of the war, have made a national air. It is to the music of *Dixie's Land* that the forces of Beauregard invariably charge the soldiers of the North. At the point at which men's minds are now—the hall would be full of partisans of both sections, who would certainly come to blows. But I should make three or four thousand dollars. It is true that in the tumult I might be the first one choked.

* * *

President Lincoln is the type of American of the West. His character answers but little to the idea which they have of a nation's ruler. Tall, thin, his back bent, his chest hollow, his arms excessively long, his crane-like legs, his enormous feet, that long frame whose disproportionate joints give him the appearance of a grapevine covered with clothes, make of him something grotesque and strange, which would strike us in a disagreeable manner if the height of his forehead, the expression of goodness and something of honesty in the countenance, did not attract and cause his exterior to be forgotten.

* * *

I am convinced that some savant will one day discover that time is a fluid which expands or contracts according as it is exposed to such or such moral atmospheres. No one will ever make me believe, for instance, that [Sunday in] Elmira is composed of twelve such hours as the other days of the week.

* * *

The devil take the poets who dare to sing of the pleasures of an artist's life.

* * *

Infamous concert [at Adrian, Michigan]. Seventy-eight dollars!! The people say that they prefer "a good Negro show." They are furious at the price of admission—one dollar. . . . One dollar admission! it is the universal theme. Everybody talks about it, and, singularly, it is with animosity, as if the fact of putting on the bills one dollar was sufficient to take the price of admission out of their pocket.

* * *

New Jersey is the poorest place to give concerts in the world, except Central Africa.

* * *

Arrived at half-past eight at the hotel, took in a hurry a cup of bad tea, and away to business. One herring for dinner! nine hours on the train! and, in spite of everything, five hundred persons who have paid that you may give to them two hours of poesy, of passion, and of inspiration. I confess to you secretly that they certainly will be cheated this evening.

* * *

I met a Bloomer. The Bloomers are the disciples of a sect founded by Mrs. Bloomer, the champion of women's rights. We have many female lawyers and doctors in the United States. I do not believe in women who assert their rights. I shall be converted when I meet one who is young and pretty.

* * *

I am daily astonished at the rapidity with which the taste for music is developed and is developing in the United States. At the time of my return from Europe I was constantly deploring the want of public interest for pieces purely sentimental [i.e., musical]; the public listened with indifference; to interest it, it became necessary to strike it with astonishment; grand movements, *tours de force*, and noise had alone the privilege in piano music, not of pleasing, but of making it patient with it. I was the *first* American pianist, not by any artistic worth, but in chronological order. Before me there were no piano concerts except in particular cases, that is to say, when a very great name arriving from Europe placed itself by its celebrity before the public, which, willing or unwilling, through curiosity or fashion rather than from taste, made it a duty to go and see the lion. Now, piano concerts are chronic, they have even become epidemic: like all good things, they are abused. . . . I cannot help feeling a pride in having contributed within the modest limits of my powers in extending through our country the knowledge of music.

In his way, Gottschalk did help raise standards in American music and performance. Before he returned to America in 1854 piano recitals were likely to fall into the class of the entertainments given by a man named Wolowski, who played on two pianos at the same time and announced that he could play four hundred notes in one measure (he did not say how long the measure was; and, in any case, nobody got excited because it was generally agreed that the notes could not be counted). The fifteen years following Gottschalk's return made an enormous difference. Gottschalk himself helped glamorize music, while Gustav Satter, William Mason, Henry Timm and others—more serious and better musicians than Gottschalk—did the bread-and-butter work. This glamorization that Gottschalk brought somehow captured the imagination of Americans, and Amy Fay, hearing of his death while she was in Germany, expressed the sense of loss by writing, "If anything more is in the papers about him you must send it to me, for the infatuation that I and 99,999 other American girls once felt for him, still lingers in my breast."

During his last years in America, Gottschalk must have felt that life was passing him by. Once in a while he was tempted to return to Paris, where he was still talked about, and where his music was still selling well. He was asked back several times and refused. Privately he must have known that he was a relic, and that he would have had no chance against the younger pianists—the Tausigs and Rubinsteins and von Bülows. Publicly he gave another reason—bashfulness. "It was painful for me to return to Paris, first theatre of my great success, and confess that I had not succeeded in my own country, America, which at this epoch was the Eldorado, the dream of artists, and which from the exaggerated accounts of the money which Jenny Lind had made there [but they were not so exaggerated] rendered my ill success more striking."

The times were changing, as he himself had noted in his diary, but he did not change with them, and instead of breaking free from pure exhibitionism and turning his attention to the best of music, he was content to tickle his audiences and titillate them with his salon pieces and his little tricks. He was one of the last of the pianists—in the line of Herz, Kalkbrenner and Thalberg—celebrated only for his execution, not for the strength of his interpretations or the probity of his musicianship; one of the last pianists who played only his own music: a representative of a school just about dead. As early as his return from Cuba in 1862 some critics started poking fun at his restricted repertoire. The *Musical Review and World* pointed out, apropos of Gottschalk, that "some twenty-five years ago a concert player could amuse his audience for several years with six fantasias of his own make, and become famous on the strength of them. This has fortunately changed, although, to judge from some features of the compositions of Mr. Gottschalk, and the complacent consistency with which he adheres to them, we should think he is not aware of the change." Gottschalk pretended to be unperturbed. But what went through his head as he killed himself grubbing for a few dollars, this erstwhile dandy and idol of the Paris salons, the inheritor of Thalberg's mantle, the hailed successor of Chopin? He, who could have become a great pianist, would shrug his shoulders. "What will it matter a thousand years from now?" he wrote in his diary, and then sat down to play *The Dying Poet* for the million-and-first time.

XV

The Virtuous

THERE WERE THALBERG, Dreyschock, Gottschalk, Herz and the other virtuosos—showmen all, thunderers, salonists, matinee idols, tinklers in their several ways. They were counterbalanced by another group of great pianists, the virtuous ones—musicians who dedicated themselves to the best in music, to the holy names, to the ideals of art. At first they formed a little, though important, minority group, but they eventually grew bigger and bigger and took over the field. Music, rather than stunts, began to be the thing. Interpreters started coming along who took the word "interpret" seriously, confining themselves to the music of the masters. A new species began to appear—the performing musician who was not necessarily a composer. These, aided as they were by real concert halls rather than salons, helped the concert as an institution come into being. By the 1860s the battle put up by this new breed was virtually won, and concert programs began to appear pretty much as they appear today. Also, the piano primacy was beginning to pass from Paris, and many of the pianists who led the fight were German. Felix Mendelssohn was one. Mendelssohn, the most correct of the romantic players, was not primarily a concert pianist, and most of his public appearances were as soloist with orchestra in his own music. But he must have been a perfect instrumentalist and, as a prodigy, was on the level of a Mozart or a Saint-Saëns. He started playing the piano at the age of four and was composing at eight, by which time he had memorized all the Beethoven symphonies and could play them on the piano. He may have even been superior creatively to Mozart as a young man, for Mendelssohn at sixteen had already written the Octet and was to follow it up the following year with the *Midsummer*

Night's Dream Overture. Mozart at the same age had nothing comparable to show. (It is interesting, too, that Mendelssohn, like Mozart,
had a talented sister. Fanny Mendelssohn was a brilliant pianist.)

The young Mendelssohn aroused his teacher, Moscheles, to
frenzy upon frenzy of admiration. Moscheles found the fifteen-year-
old boy already a finished artist. He had lessons every second day.
"The slightest hint from me and he guesses at my conception." Naturally, being the musician he was, Mendelssohn was one of the
greatest improvisers of musical history, probably superior even to
Hummel. Reports of his improvisations, incidentally, give a good idea
of the state of musical scholarship in the first half of the nineteenth
century; and it must be remembered that the period showed no finer
and more honest musical mind than Mendelssohn's. For example,
Hiller described Mendelssohn at sixteen improvising on themes from
Handel's *Judas Maccabaeus*, "I hardly knew which was more wonderful—the skillful counterpoint, the flow and continuity of the
thoughts, or the fire, expression and extraordinary execution which
characterized his playing. He must have been very full of Handel at
this time, for the figures which he used were thoroughly Handelian,
and the power and clarity of his passages in thirds, sixths and octaves were really grand." One can legitimately question how "thoroughly Handelian" were improvisations that contained grand thirds,
sixths and octaves, but the early nineteenth century was the last
period in the world to raise those questions. Was not Mendelssohn,
after all, the great scholar and historian who had revived Bach's *St.
Matthew Passion*? Salaman throws further light on Mendelssohn's
playing, and on what was considered appropriate Bach style at the
time:

I recall an interesting incident at a morning concert given in June, 1844,
in honor of that gifted and most pathetic of famous violinists, Heinrich
Ernst. Bach's triple Concerto in D minor was played by Moscheles, Thalberg and Mendelssohn—what a trio of giants! and each performer was to
play an impromptu cadence [cadenza]. Moscheles, a famous improvisatore,
led off with a fine cadence. Thalberg followed with perhaps even more
brilliant effect. Then Mendelssohn, who had been leaning listlessly over
the back of his chair while the others were playing, quietly began his cadence, taking up the threads from the subject of the Concerto; then, suddenly rousing himself, he wound up with a wonderful shower of octaves,

H. Kiehe

Felix Mendelssohn. "His fingers *sang* as they rippled over the keyboard."

Death mask of Mendelssohn. He was one of the most polished and natural of pianists.

indescribable in effect, and never to be forgotten. The audience was so excited that the applause at the end was all for Mendelssohn.

Mendelssohn's playing must have been free, spirited, amazingly pure and accurate, with a spare use of pedal. Not being a professional virtuoso he could, and did, appear at charity or benefit concerts playing Beethoven, Handel and Bach. He may have been the only pianist of his day, Clara Schumann included, who did not play operatic paraphrases or salon music. That, apparently, did not interfere with his success. Quite a few musicians whose testimony is to be relied upon speak of Mendelssohn's powers to excite an audience. His technique was up to anything and was especially adapted for running passages; and his touch, writes Salaman, "was exquisitely delicate . . . his fingers *sang* as they rippled over the keyboard." All were agreed that no pianist ever approached Mendelssohn in his own G minor Concerto, and an English musician named John Edmund Cox wrote bemusedly about Mendelssohn's combination of lightness and strength. "Whilst in all the delicate nuances his fingers seemed to be like feathers, in those of more forcible and impetuous character there was a grasp and an *élan* which almost took away one's breath. Not a single note was slurred, notwithstanding the stupendous difficulties of passage after passage." Cox makes it perfectly clear that Mendelssohn had the gift without which no artist, no matter how talented, can succeed: the ability to come over the footlights, to impress one's personality on the hearer. "Scarcely had he touched the keyboard than something that can only be described as similar to a pleasurable electric shock passed through his hearers and held them spellbound—a sensation that was only dissolved as the last note was struck and when one's pent-up breath seemed as if only able to recover its normal action by means of a gulp or sob."

Ferdinand Hiller, student of Hummel and friend of Mendelssohn —the friend of everybody, in fact: Chopin, Liszt, Schumann, Meyerbeer, Cherubini, Rossini, Berlioz, Brahms—was another pianist of the romantic period who scorned trash. He was an exponent of Bach and Beethoven (he had introduced the *Emperor* Concerto to Paris), a thorough musician (conductor of the Leipzig Gewandhaus concerts, among other things), a serious composer and a highly respected pianist. So was Charles Hallé, born in Westphalia, who ended up in England as founder of the Hallé Orchestra. Hallé was playing at the age of four and giving concerts at eleven, studying in Paris at seventeen and settling in England at twenty-nine. His repertoire was solid: Bach, Beethoven, Mozart and the best in chamber music. In his autobiography he claims to have been the first important pianist to have played a Beethoven sonata in London, but this is a highly doubtful claim. As Hallé tells the story of his concert in London in 1848:

When Mr. Ella [John Ella, director of the Musical Union, a concert-giving agency] asked me what I wanted to play, and heard that it was one of Beethoven's pianoforte sonatas, he exclaimed "Impossible!", and endeavoured to demonstrate that they were not works to be played in public; that, as far as he knew, no solo sonata had ever been included in any concert programme, and that he could not venture upon offering one to his subscribers. I had to battle for several days before he gave way. He consented at last, and was then much surprised to find that the sonata I had chosen (Op. 31, No. 3 in E flat) pleased so much that several ladies who heard it arranged afternoon parties to hear it once more.

Hallé did much to popularize Beethoven, especially the later sonatas. By 1852 he was giving semipublic recitals in his own home at which he played nothing but Beethoven. These attracted so much attention that in 1861 he started giving similar recitals in St. James's Hall, playing the thirty-two sonatas in a series of eighteen recitals. Apparently he was the first pianist in history to play the cycle. This fine musician conducted symphonic music and opera throughout England, did much to establish Berlioz, served as the head of the Royal College of Music in Manchester, and represented the best in his art. He also has come down in history as the man who invented an automatic page turner. Hallé, who always played from the printed note, developed a mechanism operated by the foot that turned pages. People would go to his concerts just to see the spectacle of leaf after leaf turning over, ghostlike, without the intervention of human hands. Musicians like Richard Hoffman were a little distressed. "It was so disquieting to see them turned by this unseen agent that it rather disturbed the musical *entrain* to which one would like to yield while listening to a great artist." George Bernard Shaw reviewed Hallé as late as 1888. "Sir Charles is not a sensational player, but nobody who has heard him play the *largo* of this sonata [Beethoven's D major, Op. 10, No. 3] has ever accepted the notion that his play-

Sir Charles Hallé, the first pianist in history to play the cycle of Beethoven sonatas in public. That was in 1861. He also invented an automatic page turner.

ing is 'icy and mechanical.'. . . The secret is that he gives you as little as possible of Hallé and as much as possible of Beethoven."

The most important "classical" pianist of the nineteenth century, the keyboard equivalent of Joseph Joachim on the violin, was Clara Schumann, née Clara Wieck. Nowhere does the dichotomy between the "pure" musician and the "pure" virtuoso so show up. Clara was conscious of her role and took it very seriously. She deliberately set herself up as the keeper of the tradition, and when the name of Liszt was mentioned she picked up her skirt and moved fastidiously away. In her youth she, like everybody else, had been carried away by Liszt, but as she grew older she reconsidered. "Before Liszt," she would say, "people used to play; after Liszt, they pounded or whispered. He has the decline of piano playing on his conscience." In 1856 she refused to contaminate herself by playing at the Mozart Festival in Vienna because Liszt was the conductor; nor would she appear at the unveiling of the Schumann memorial at Zwickau (her husband's birthplace) because Liszt was present. When she edited the complete works of Schumann, she struck off his dedication of the great C major Fantasy to Liszt. Her dislike for Liszt was almost pathological, and it may be that anything she said about him is suspect, such as the tale she told Edward Speyer in her late years. Liszt, she said, had always urged Schumann to compose a piano quintet. When Schumann finished his great Piano Quintet in E flat, Liszt came to Leipzig and insisted on hearing it that very night. Clara ran all over town trying to round up four string players. The performance was scheduled for 7 P.M. Liszt turned up at nine. After he heard the quintet (said Clara) he put his hand patronizingly on Schumann's shoulder. "No, no, my dear Robert. This is not the real thing. It is only *kapellmeister* music." It might well be that Liszt did not like the work, but certainly he was too polished and worldly a gentleman to say so in the words Clara attributed to him. She was rabid on the subject. (Liszt and his school spared no love for her, either. Ernest Newman quotes Liszt as saying, "If you want to hear Schumann's works played as they should *not* be played, listen to Clara"; and Hans von Bülow would parody her style to his pupils. "*So spielt Frau Schumann,*" he would say, in contempt.)

One thing about Clara: she always *knew* she was right. She had been the great prodigy, she was the great pianist, she had been married to the great composer. Wrapped in this triply secure blanket she always had a tendency to speak as if guided from On High. Her early life cannot have been too happy. To begin with, she was not a precocious baby. Quite the opposite; and not until after her fourth birthday did she begin to speak or understand speech. She also came from a divided household. About five years after her birth in 1819, her parents separated. Her father remarried in 1828. Friedrich Wieck was a pianist of the old school, and when she began to show talent at the age of five, he trained her very carefully and with ferocious discipline. It is not that he overworked her; he was too good a teacher for that. For a long time she was not allowed more than two daily hours of practice. But Wieck was a domineering, arrogant man. He pushed Clara's life in one direction only, taking charge of every detail. When she did not come up to his mark he did not spare his temper, and he must have continually been crushing the sensitive child. In her diary of 1827 she is found writing, "My father, who has long vainly hoped for a change of mood on my part, remarked today that I am still idle, negligent, unmethodical, self-willed, etc., especially in piano playing and practicing. . . . He tore the copy [of a Hünten set of variations] to pieces before my eyes, and from today will not give me another lesson, and I may only play scales, Cramer's etudes, and Czerny's studies on the trill." Her life was all music, music, music. Later on in life Clara was to say sadly, "My father never allowed me to read."

At the age of eight she was playing concertos by Mozart and Hummel. The following year she made her debut at the Gewandhaus at a concert given by a Fräulein Perthaler of Graz. Clara, one of the assisting artists, played the treble part of Kalkbrenner's *Variations for Four Hands on a March from Moses*. The year after that, Robert Schumann entered the Wieck household, full of aspirations to be a pianist. He developed into a fair one, though not on a virtuoso level; but whatever aspirations he had were blasted when he injured the fourth finger of his right hand. He had invented a contraption to strengthen it; instead, it ruined him for good. So he turned to composition, which he had been intending to do anyway. At that time, Robert took a brotherly interest in the nine-year-old Clara. By 1830 she had developed pianistically to a point where she was making concert appearances through Germany. One of the things she was playing at that time was Chopin's *Variations on Là ci darem la mano* (Schumann had "discovered" it), and she was the first—outside of the composer—to feature it in public. Wieck may have been a musician of the old school, but he had an open mind and knew an effective piece when he heard it. He let Clara keep it in her repertoire.

But on the whole he was not *that* revolutionary. In her early days, Clara's repertoire, guided by her father, leaned heavily on Herz, Kalkbrenner, Hünten and Hummel. She was not yet twelve, and thus in any case was not ready for bigger game. But by 1833 her tastes developed (Schumann must have been the moving factor here, in addition to her innate good judgment), and she began playing Bach and Schumann in public. She also introduced a good deal of Chopin's music to Germany. Her father fortunately let her develop musically as her instincts dictated. In a letter to a friend (1834) he wrote that "I shall have much to say to you when we meet about the new romantic school in which Chopin, Pixis, Liszt in Paris and several of Robert Schumann's disciples write. . . . It forms, as I am convinced, the bridge to the piano music of Mozart and Beethoven. Its difficulties are certainly unprecedented, but this successively was the case with the music of Mozart and Beethoven in their day." Wieck could be very perspicacious. When he heard Liszt for the first time, in 1838, he was bowled over, and his busy mind immediately set to work, weighing this and that. "It was the most remarkable concert of our lives, and will not be without its influence on Clara; and that Clara does not follow his many follies and eccentricities—of that an old schoolmaster will take care." The old schoolmaster was broad-minded and perfectly willing to take the best from any source for his Clara.

Although Liszt had been the first to give unaided solo recitals, it was Clara who even more than Liszt broke the eighteenth-century format. Up to about 1835 the artist generally had to engage an orchestra, was expected to play his own music with it, had to arrange for guest artists to share the program, had to vary his program with short pieces, had to end with an improvisation. But by 1835 Clara was, for the most part, playing with just a few assisting artists, and moreover presenting nothing but the best. Mendelssohn had paved the way. In Berlin, on November 9 and December 1, 1832, he had played Beethoven's *Waldstein* and the E flat Sonata (Op. 27, No. 1), both apparently the very first time that these two sonatas had ever been played in public. When Clara played the complete *Appassionata* in Berlin in 1837, it was the first time it had been heard there, as far as anybody can ascertain. What is more, she played from memory. Leschetizky maintained that she was the first pianist in history to do so in public. For this she was called, in some circles, "insufferable." Up through the 1840s it was held that to perform the work of a master without the notes was bad form: it showed disrespect to his art. Clara's avoidance of the printed music aroused wide comment, much of it unfavorable. Bettina von Arnim, Beethoven's friend, spoke of Clara as "one of the most unendurable persons" she had ever met. "With what pretension she seats herself at the piano and plays without the notes! How modest, in comparison, is Döhler, who places the music before him!" But there were others, and important ones, who greeted her with admiration; and the poet Franz Grillparzer referred to her as that "innocent child who unlocked the casket in which Beethoven buried his mighty heart." (It is interesting to note, as a turn of the wheel, that as Clara became old, she did not trust her memory and often used the printed music—always, when playing concertos.)

Clara and Robert Schumann were married on September 12, 1840, over violent objections from Wieck. One can understand his distress at Clara's "throwing herself away" on a penniless, eccentric composer. But his actions in fighting the marriage were reprehensible. He refused to give his consent, made the lovers go to court, spread word that Robert was a drunkard, and in general behaved like one possessed. From this point he rapidly passed out of Clara's life, which was entirely taken up with Robert and their children. There were Marie, Elise, Julie, Emil (died at fourteen months), Ludwig (a mental defective), Eugenie, Ferdinand and Felix. Naturally her public appearances were sharply curtailed. She took care of her family, listened to Robert compose, did a great deal of thinking. "The less I play in public, the more I despise mechanical virtuosity. Concert pieces such as Henselt's etudes, the fantasias of Thalberg and Liszt, have no longer any appeal for me." This opinion partly represents the influence of Robert, purest of musicians.

But unless a pianist works four, five, six hours a day, terrible things can happen to the technique. Robert realized this. "In the more deep-lying aspects of musical education, Clara has not stood still but advanced. She lives only in good music and consequently her playing has increased in intelligence and feeling. But the development of her technique to the point of infallibility—for that she has no time. The fault is mine, yet there is nothing to be done about it. Clara realizes that I must make full use of my powers, now that they are at their best." At her strongest Clara never had a technique

Clara Schumann in middle age, at the height of her career. She was the most important classical pianist of the mid-century.

Clara Schumann in the last years of her life. "Nobly beautiful and poetic," George Bernard Shaw called her.

on the order of a Liszt, Thalberg or Mendelssohn. But, then again, hers was not the kind of playing in which technique is the be-all and end-all.

During her marriage she did make a few concert tours. Those years were also enlivened by the appearance of "Herr Brahms from Hamburg," to meet her Robert. After her husband's mental breakdown in 1854, Clara had to resume her career. This she did, with formidable programs, including the *Hammerklavier*. She was then thirty-five years old, and there was considerable steel in the lady. Jenny Lind, her close friend, begged her to include in her programs something that the public would understand. Clara was firm. "I will yield to popular demands only insofar as they do not betray my own convictions." She might have mentioned Robert's convictions, too; through her life his spirit was the moving force. To the end of her days, in his memory, she played every concert dressed in black, bent over, head almost touching the keys.

It did not take Clara very long to conquer Europe. She had been one of the pioneers of good music to begin with, and by 1860, four years after Schumann's death, romanticism had been fully accepted by the public. So had "her" type of program. She re-entered the life of a touring pianist, with a very heavy schedule. One of her activities was the espousal of the music of Brahms. She naturally set her beloved Johannes up against the hated Liszt-Wagner combine of The Music of the Future. Between Clara and Brahms existed a very close relationship. There is no doubt that he was in love with her. There also seems no doubt that she was attracted to him, and had not the shade of Robert eternally stepped between them . . .

In 1878 she took her first teaching position, as head of the piano department of the Frankfort Conservatory, and she remained there until 1892. Deafness had set in, and her last public appearance had taken place in 1890. She died in Frankfort in 1896, a year before Brahms. Her most famous pupils were Fanny Davies, Adela Verne, Leonard Borwick, Nathalie Janotha and Clement Harris. Carl Friedberg, who later settled in the United States, also had a few lessons with her.

She never was one of the heroic pianists, and she never modified the technique that her father had given her. It was playing that avoided any kind of violence or excitement, or any kind of excessive physical movement. Fingers were kept close to the keys, and the keys were squeezed rather than struck. Chords were played from the wrist, not from the arm and elbow. She had hands large enough to take tenths with ease. Her father had drilled into her the axiom that the blow of the finger on the key should never be audible. Only the musical sound should be heard. Apparently, even with this hands-close-to-the-keys technique, she was able to draw a full, colorful tone. All her hearers are united on this. Her father had concentrated on tone from the moment she approached the piano. "I laid down as the first and foremost principle," he wrote, "the necessity for the formation of a fine touch, just as singing teachers rely on the culture of a fine tone in order to teach singing well." Clara's pupil Franklin Taylor once described Clara's sound:

Nothing ever sounded harsh or ugly in her hands; indeed, it may fairly be said that after hearing her play a fine work (she never played what is not good) one always became aware that it contained beauties undiscovered before. This was, no doubt, partly due to the peculiarly beautiful quality of the tone she produced, which was rich and vigorous without the slightest harshness, and was obtained, even in the loudest passages, by pressure with the fingers rather than by percussion. Indeed, her playing was particularly free from violent movement of any kind; in passages, the fingers were kept close to the keys and squeezed instead of striking them, while chords were grasped from the wrist rather than struck from the elbow.

Her musical conceptions were big. Amy Fay called her "a healthy artist," and George Bernard Shaw, when he first heard her, immediately realized what a "nobly beautiful and poetic player she was. An artist of that sort is the Grail of the critic's quest." Clara always did her best to subordinate herself to the intentions of the composer as she saw them. The great Austrian critic, Eduard Hanslick, like everyone else, remarked on this and on her penetrating understanding of every kind of music. "In one or another aspect of virtuosity, she may be surpassed by other players, but no other pianist stands out quite as she does, at the radial point of these different technical directions, focusing their respective virtues on the whole harmony of beauty." She always tried, says Hanslick, "to give a clear expression to each work in its characteristic musical style. . . . She could be called the greatest living pianist, rather than merely the greatest female pianist, were the range of her physical strength not limited by her sex. . . . Everything is distinct, clear, sharp as a pencil sketch."

The pencil sketch image is apt, for with her temperate use of the pedal and her avoidance of pronounced rubato effects, the playing would be intimate and even prissy against the tumultuous orchestration of the Liszt school. She detested speed and empty passagework. If a student tried "to rattle through any rapid figuration with mere empty virtuosity," Adelina de Lara has written, Clara would throw up her hands in despair. "*Keine passagen!*" she would cry. "Why hurry over beautiful things? Why not linger and enjoy them?" This was anti-virtuosity with a vengeance. Clara's restrained rubato greatly disturbed some of the late romantic pianists. As the wife of the composer she was considered the supreme authority on Schumann's music and—especially in England—her word and her Schumann playing were law. When Paderewski arrived in England and played Schumann he was received with coolness at first, for Clara had accustomed the British public to a restrained, almost rubato-less Schumann. Paderewski, of course, employed an extravagant rubato, and he was the antithesis of Clara. He himself tartly, and with a mean glint in his eye, said that the music of Schumann "as performed by that very old lady," was a tradition, "and I was disturbing that tradition; when it was fortissimo, I played fortissimo, which Madame Schumann, poor lady, could not produce." But that was toward the end, when the high priestess was playing wrong notes and trying to hear the music through her failing ears. She was entitled to her little idiosyncrasies, and one cherishes the picture of the dear old Frau Schumann playing her husband's concerto in her last years, coming on stage

a rather dumpy old lady in a cap. She was greeted with long-continued applause. She seated herself at the piano, and after half a dozen elusive settlings of herself and shaking out her gown, just as the conductor was about to begin, she popped up and went among the instrumentalists, in order to give a special direction to the first oboe for a certain passage in which she desired him to follow her. She then came back to the piano and again went through the settling process already experienced. At last she was ready. . . .

XVI

Tyrant and Intellectual

NOW CAME THE MUSICIAN-PIANISTS, faithful to the music in their fashion. True, the dictates of the age gave them more leeway than any mid-twentieth-century pianist could enjoy. The artist was still touched by God and had responsibility to precious few under that Power. But by the 1860s almost gone were the potpourris, the fantasias on Auber and Rossini, the improvisations and acrobatics, exhibition for the sake of exhibition. The artist was now an "interpreter," and he played real music: Bach, Beethoven, Schubert, Chopin, Mendelssohn, Heller, even Schumann. If an operatic transcription were put on a program, it invariably would be one of the transcendental exercises of Liszt, and not the puerile note-spinning of Herz or Thalberg. Recital programs began to solidify into the type of chronological program that is still entrenched: a bit of Bach and Scarlatti, Beethoven, Chopin and the other romantics, with a Liszt rhapsody topping everything off and sending the audience home happy. Of course the pianists also played the fashionable but temporary compositions of which every age has its ample supply.

Rather than piano playing being funneled through Paris, as it was in the 1830s, several major schools began to appear—the severe German style, the warm Russian one, the elegant French school and the eclectic English one. In the meantime the piano itself was being developed into substantially the instrument we know today. Thanks to the iron frame, tension on strings could be brought up to some sixteen tons per square inch by 1865 (as against thirty today). And everyone was buying pianos. By 1850 France was producing ten thousand annually; England, twenty-five thousand. Pitch rose with

244 · THE GREAT PIANISTS

the increased tension. The virtuosos kept demanding brilliantly voiced instruments with higher and higher pitch.

Then there was the development of the reading public: not the literary one, but those who could read music to play on their pianos. The amateur throve, and music publishers were kept busy feeding him music. All new orchestral and chamber music was simultaneously published in piano reduction so that the informed amateurs could keep up with the latest things. The amateurs even started looking into the music of Beethoven and Schubert. Naturally the last few Beethoven sonatas were considered tricky. Von Lenz, certainly a Beethoven admirer, threw up his hands at Op. 111. In the triplet variation he gravely counted 1,944 thirty-second notes and decided that the task of playing them was beyond human possibility. Clara Schumann had demonstrated, however, that a good deal of music hitherto thought forbidding was anything but; and Hans von Bülow proved it once and for all.

It was von Bülow more than anybody else who by the force of personality, skill, perseverance and rasplike intelligence established the supremacy of the German school for several decades. He was the archetype of the German *Tonkünstler*: demanding, dictatorial, testy, chauvinistic, convinced of his superiority, possessed of a fine musical culture plus executive ability and leadership, and also of a virulent, pathological anti-Semitism (which he may have picked up from his idol, Richard Wagner). He was as important a conductor as he was a pianist, and he brought the Meiningen Orchestra to a point where the musicians played their music from memory. The most valued member of the Wagner circle, he conducted the world premiere of *Tristan und Isolde* in 1865 and of *Die Meistersinger* in 1868. During the *Tristan* period he was married to Liszt's daughter Cosima. Wagner and she had an affair, three children resulted, and eventually she divorced Bülow for him.

Von Bülow was born in Dresden in 1830, went through the usual prodigy period and then really started work. From the very beginning he had a sharp mind and a determination to conquer, and in a letter to his mother the fifteen-year-old boy gives an indication of the progress he had made and the tasks he had set himself, while studying with Louis Plaidy at the Leipzig Conservatory:

With regard to my piano playing you may set your mind at ease. *"Je travaille comme un nègre,"* I can truly say. Every morning I play trill exercises, simple and chromatic scales of all kinds, exercises for throwing the hands (for these I use a study of Moscheles, one of Steibelt, and a two-part fugue of Bach's, which I play with octaves in both hands; it was Gold-schmidt [Otto Goldschmidt, pupil of Mendelssohn and later husband of Jenny Lind] who recommended me to do this), toccatas of Czerny, which Herr Plaidy gave me, and Moscheles' and Chopin's studies; so that I don't find any others of Bertini, Cramer or Clementi necessary. I have enough to do with the Chopin studies, which fully take the place of all these others, and I hope you will think I am doing right. I finished Field's A major Concerto yesterday; I have only studied the first movement—Herr Plaidy thinks the others are not worth much—and at my next lesson I shall begin Mendelssohn's D minor Concerto. Besides these I am studying myself Bach's fugues, Klengel's canons, Oberon's *Zauberhorn*, Hummel's fantasias, a Beethoven sonata (the *Pastorale* in D major), and am keeping up my old pieces, such as Chopin's *Tarantella* and nocturnes, Henselt's variations and *Frühlingslied* and Hummel's B minor Concerto.

The turning point in the boy's life came in 1849, when he met Liszt in Weimar. Naturally von Bülow was swept off his feet, "... quite a perfect man... admirable! astounding!" But von Bülow was not to study with Liszt at that time, although he must have known that his life was in music. He went instead to the University of Berlin, where he nominally studied law but kept busy contribut-ing to a political journal. He also wrote music criticism, producing fervid articles praising The Music of the Future. And he did not neglect his own piano studies:

After frequently hearing Liszt, I have now made a special study of what was particularly defective in my piano playing, namely, a certain amateur-ish uncertainty, a certain angular want of freedom in conception, of which I must completely cure myself. In modern pieces, especially, I must culti-vate more *abandon*, and when I have conquered the technical difficulties of a piece I must *let myself go* to a greater degree, according to how I feel at the moment; and, if one is not devoid of talent, of course anything absurd or unsuitable does not come into one's mind.

It is interesting that von Bülow, even at the age of twenty, put his finger so accurately on what was to be the chief defect in his play-ing—a want of freedom and spontaneity. He was to be one of the finest musical minds of the century, but he was too disciplined ever to let his emotions take over, and his playing tended to be cold and overplanned. He did not, ever, let himself go. But this is anticipating. In 1850 von Bülow heard Liszt conduct *Lohengrin* and could hold out no longer. He asked for lessons, and Liszt gladly took him in, telling his mother that "Hans is evidently gifted with a musical organization of the rarest kind. His executive talent will easily place him in the front rank of the greatest pianists." Liszt was correct, and von Bülow turned out to be his first great pupil. He was just as attracted to the podium, and his subsequent career fluctuated between keyboard and orchestra. If von Bülow had worked hard up to then, he was a maniac under Liszt. "I devote the greater part of my time, four or five hours daily, exclusively to the cultivation of technique. I make martyrs of the eventual founders of my material prosperity; I crucify, like a good Christ, the flesh of my fingers, in order to make them obedient, submissive machines to the mind, as a pianist must." He also found time to work on his doctorate, write music reviews, compose and make enemies. "My unpopularity here is unbounded."

By 1853 he was ready for concerts. After two years of public appearance he taught at the Stern Conservatory in Berlin, where he also wrote critical articles for newspapers. He carried his Liszt worship so far as to marry Cosima, Liszt's daughter, who stayed with him for twelve years before leaving him for Wagner. Von Bülow became, successively, conductor of the Royal Opera in Munich, director of the Munich Conservatory, a traveling virtuoso, director of the court theater in Hanover, director of the court orchestra at Meiningen, teacher at the Raff Conservatory in Frankfort and the Klindworth Conservatory in Berlin. He visited America three times. The first time was in 1875–76, when he was brought over by the Chickering piano firm and finished 139 out of a scheduled 172 concerts. (Steinway, in 1864, had negotiated with von Bülow for a tour, but nothing had come of it.) His contract called for a payment of $20,000, which was more than double the salary he later got as conductor of the Meiningen Orchestra. The tour was a mixed success and was not helped by Bülow's sarcastic remarks about America. Those were front-page items. His second and third American tours, in 1889 and 1890, were more successful.

When he first came to America, he was the most famous pianist to tour there since Rubinstein in 1872–73. The American press was fascinated with the diminutive, acerbic Bülow, and some lively pen portraits resulted, such as this one in the *Music Trade Review*, written by a man who clearly was a militant democrat:

Mr. von Bülow presents a soldier-like appearance, and we believe that in every sense he deserves to be looked upon in this light. He knows how to command as a leader, and, what is more important, how to obey as an interpreter; he appears, hat in hand, straight, erect, the brochette of decorations in his buttonhole... bows low before the public—a detestable habit, derived from old customs when the despised and nearly excommunicated actors were considered the unworthy servants of the public—and at last sits down at the piano.

His temper was easily aroused. In Baltimore he objected to the Chickering sign on the piano, walked over to the instrument and removed it. "I am not a travelling advertisement," a Baltimore reporter quoted him as saying. He put the sign face down on the stage "and cast it a glance of hatred as if it were a loathsome reptile. He then lapsed into German in which the terms '*Lump*' and '*Schweinhund*' were audible." On the day of the rehearsal he kicked the sign. "Thus was he appeased with blood."

At first Bülow was impressed with America, "this very curious but very comfortable and truly magnificent country." By comparison, "Europe is old and lame." He carefully studied American women, and some curiously otophilic tendencies made themselves felt. "I love particularly the form and character of their ears. A beautiful ear is a woman's magic charm; well-rounded and chiseled, it acts like a magnet." In Chicago there was an eruption. The papers there attacked him for too-serious programs, and Bülow was furious. At one of his concerts he told the audience that the critics "think that American education is not mature enough for the best composers and that I should therefore play pieces like [*Home*] *Sweet Home*, *Last Rose of Summer* and *Yankee Doodle*. I have to reply, first, that I am a German artist and therefore always worship in the temples of the great masters. And, second, that American audiences are the best before which I have had the honor to play anywhere in the world. Nevertheless, permit me as a kind of prelude to give you a sample of this so-called popular music." He then played *The Marsellaise* in a purposely slipshod, burlesque, exaggerated manner.

Through his life he cut a wide swath through Europe and American, terrifying and amazing people with his intellect, his temper, his sarcasm (Brahms once said, "Hans von Bülow's praise smarts like salt in the eyes so that tears run") and his undisputed musicianship. His temper was legendary. As a teacher he was a holy terror. Often he would take over Liszt's classes and attempt to weed them out. He told one of Liszt's young ladies that she should be swept out of the class "not with a broom but a broomstick. Go home!" To a girl who played Liszt's *Mazeppa*, the Étude that describes the galloping of a horse, von Bülow's compliment was that her only qualification for her playing the work was that she had the soul of a horse. In his own concerts he would glare the audience down, commenting audibly on its manners. He had two pianos on stage, switching from one to the other as his fancy took him. Amy Fay was amused. "His expression is proud and supercilious to the last degree, and he looks all around at his audience when he is playing. . . . His face seems to say to his audience, 'You're all cats and dogs, and I don't care what you think of my playing.'" Even toward the end he continued his eccentricities; age did not mellow him. Harold Bauer remembered him coming on stage with his silk hat and cane, and drawing off his gloves (as Liszt used to) before settling down at the piano. And woe betide the audience if it did not pay attention!

He was a martinet who had to have things his own way and he must have been impossible to work with. James Huneker heard him in 1876 in Philadelphia, playing the Tchaikovsky B flat minor Concerto (he played the world premiere in Boston the previous year). Benjamin Johnson Lang was conducting, and, says Huneker, Lang's presence seemed quite superfluous, "as Bülow gave all the cues from the keyboard, and distinctly cursed the conductor, the band, the composition and his own existence." He would lecture to the audience, walk out on concerts, take offense at criticism, and in general act as though he had a first mortgage on the entire universe. Once in Vienna he was supposed to conduct the *Egmont* Overture. Instead he came on stage, told the audience that since the critic of the *Fremdenblatt* had found fault with his previous performance of the *Egmont*, and as he would not like to wrong Beethoven again, he would instead conduct the Brahms *Academic Festival* Overture. This was petty, but there could be authentic grandeur in the old man. Kaiser Wilhelm, tired of von Bülow's temperamental eccentricities, had said, "If anybody doesn't like the way things are going in this country, let him shake the dust from his shoes." At von Bülow's last

Berlin concert he finished, put down his baton, bent down, took out a handkerchief, dusted his shoes and went off to Egypt, where he died soon after (in 1894).

As a pianist he was famous for what was called, again and again, his "passionate intellectuality." But some omitted the word "passionate." His memory was prodigious (sometimes he relied too heavily on it, with consequent wrong notes). He played—and conducted, too —without the music before him. According to Richard Strauss, he had small hands and could stretch just an octave. His repertoire was all-embracing, but his specialty was Beethoven and he was the first pianist to concentrate on that composer. More to the point, he introduced the last five sonatas all over Europe, and often he would play all five on one program. He did this in Vienna in 1881, and Hanslick was beside himself with admiration. The feat had never before been done there. In New York, between April 1 and 11, 1889, he gave a series of recitals at the Broadway Theatre that encompassed twenty-two Beethoven sonatas. On one of those concerts he included Op. 109, 110 and 111; and on another he presented the *Hammerklavier*, repeating the fugue as an encore. His technique was not entirely up to it, but few seemed to mind, for it was agreed that the musical message came through. The perceptive Henry Krehbiel, who reviewed the concerts, wrote that von Bülow's playing was able "to disclose the beauty of law and order and symmetry, to exemplify that cardinal element of beauty—repose." Krehbiel described the playing as objective but not without temperament. "Those who wish to add intellectual enjoyment to the pleasures of the imagination derive a happiness from Bülow's playing which no other pianist can give to the same degree."

But others were less kind. James Huneker—he was an out-and-out romantic, anyway—dismissed von Bülow as "all intellect: his Bach, Beethoven, Chopin and Brahms were cerebral, not emotional. He has the temperament of a pedant." There was undoubtedly a strong element of pedantry in his playing, just as the man himself was didactic beyond compare. Clara Schumann objected to his approach. "To me he is the most wearisome player; there is no touch of vigor or enthusiasm, everything is calculated." One critic said of von Bülow that his tone rang like steel, and he was almost as hard; and Amy Fay was reminded of looking through a stereoscope, "All the points of a piece seem to start out vividly before you." If the obituary

Hans von Bülow: intelligent, waspish, dictatorial. He was the first of Liszt's many great pupils.

Arabella Goddard, from 1853 to about 1890 the most important British pianist. At her debut she played the *Hammerklavier*, which in those days took a great deal of courage.

notice in the *New York Times* of February 15, 1894, is accurate, von Bülow's playing must have dropped to a dismal low in his last years:

It was very plain that his fingers were no longer what they had been. His technique was painfully deficient during his last visit to New York and his performance of Beethoven's *Emperor* Concerto at a Symphony Society concert filled his friends with pity. For some years the doctor had shown signs of failing powers, mentally as well as physically. He had always been a little eccentric, but his eccentricities began to overstep the limits of mental balance, and it was no serious surprise to his friends in America when it was made known in January, 1893, that he had been placed in a private institution suffering from mental disorder in an acute form.

Putting everything together, it is obvious that von Bülow's playing was clear, analytical, precise and probably cold. His was an analyst's approach to music and to the keyboard. Bruno Walter much admired him, but regretfully added that "a certain didactic element in his playing may have deprived it of some of the spontaneity manifested in his orchestral work." Josef Hofmann was blunter. Von Bülow's playing, wrote Hofmann, was "almost always pedantic, though unquestionably scholarly." Nevertheless, it was playing that must have packed tremendous authority. And von Bülow's example in programing nothing but the best in music was followed by many pianists of the day.

One of them was the talented Arabella Goddard, who at her debut in London in 1853 played the *Hammerklavier* from memory and who in 1857 began concentrating on the last five sonatas. Many encyclopedias state that Goddard was the first to play the *Hammerklavier* in England, but this is not true. Alexandre Billet, a French pianist, had performed it in St. Martin's Hall on May 24, 1850. Goddard had been born in France of English parents, and studied with Kalkbrenner and Thalberg. Moscheles heard her in 1854 and was much struck. "Miss Goddard conquers enormous difficulties with consumate grace and ease; her touch is clear and pure as a bell." Her husband was the important British critic James William Davison (she had formerly studied with him), and he spent a good deal of time promoting her. A French journal good-humoredly poked fun at the situation, and said that whenever a pianist approached the shores of England, Davison was sure to be standing on the cliffs of

Dover and shouting, "No pianists wanted here! We have Arabella Goddard!" Punch in 1860 took note of the marriage:

A fact long known to him, kind Punch must be
Allowed to congratulate his rara avis on,
Hail to the Lady of the Keys! From G
The music of her life's transposed to D,
And Arabella Goddard's Mrs. Davison.

She visited America in 1876 at the end of a world tour she had started in 1873. Apparently she made little impression in this country. She struck Americans as being a correct but passionless player. According to one critic, "Romantic music did not seem to move her, and though she could play the notes of Chopin accurately, she could not convey his thoughts. But her renderings of Bach's preludes and fugues were at once forcible, solid, and crisp. She had a firm, even touch, but it lacked variety and never lent itself to the production of tone color." On her return to England, Goddard did relax and play some music of a lighter kind not normally associated with her. George Bernard Shaw wrote about her in 1899, when her career still had some years to go (she was born in 1836 and lived until 1922). He called her an extraordinary pianist. "Nothing seemed to give her any trouble. There was something almost heartless in the indifference with which she played whatever the occasion required: medleys, fantasias, and potpourris for 'popular' audiences, sonatas for Monday Popular ones, concertos for classical ones; as if the execution of the most difficult of them were too easy and certain to greatly interest her. . . . She was more like the Lady of Shalott working at her loom than a musician at a pianoforte. I can see her now as she played; but I confess I cannot hear her, though I can vouch for the fact of her wonderful manipulative skill." For a quarter of a century she was the most famous English pianist, and she could not have stayed in the front rank that long, said Shaw, without great ability on her part.

Among others who followed von Bülow's stringent, no-nonsense programing were Walter Bache, Robert Fischhof, Agnes Zimmermann, Robert Freund, Franz Rummel, Ernst Pauer and Wilhelmina Clauss-Szavardy. Most of these pianists are forgotten today. Bache, English-born, studied with Moscheles and Liszt, and settled in London as pianist and conductor. The Czech-born Clauss-

Szavardy, who made her first concert tour in 1849, was immediately spoken of as Clara Schumann's rival. She concentrated on Scarlatti, Bach and Beethoven, and enjoyed a great reputation. She was not a powerful pianist—neither was Clara—but she must have been an artist. Hanslick described her in 1855: "The characteristic reflective quality of her playing, the tenderness and gentility of her interpretive style, more than made up for what she lacked in strength." Fischhof and Freund were Liszt pupils and intelligent musicians who ended up teaching, respectively, at the Vienna and Zurich conservatories. Zimmermann, German-born, made England her home and, with her pianistic vigor and excellent musicianship, kept Arabella Goddard on her toes. Rummel studied and taught at the Brussels Conservatory, and then toured Europe and America with great success. (His son, Walter, also became a respected pianist who specialized in the music of Bach and Debussy.) Pauer, who settled in London, was a scholar as well as a good pianist. He gave historical recitals throughout Europe, did considerable writing, and even compiled a dictionary of pianists. He taught, lectured, investigated virginals music and published some studies of pianists that are worth reading: a valuable man. His son, Max, achieved fame as a fine teacher and thoughtful artist.

Somewhat of a different school was Julius Epstein, the last representative of Viennese classicism. As a pianist he was clear, crisp and cold. He could play anything, knew everything, and sat before his instrument "like a model-drill sergeant under inspection." The best description of his playing was set forth by a British writer, W. H. Beatty-Kingston, in two words, "surpassing respectability." Epstein was popular enough, busy enough and successful enough to have his clothes made by Ebenstein, the prince of Austrian tailors; and for his concerts he wore lavender gloves, dazzling white linen and mirror-like boots. His son Richard achieved some fame as a pianist and seems to have picked up many of his father's traits. Richard, who died in 1919, lived long enough to make a few records, and his performance of Chopin's C sharp minor Waltz, on an Odéon disc, is played virtually without pedal and virtually without charm. Like father, like son. He settled in New York and was best known as an accompanist, appearing frequently with Sembrich, Fremstad, Culp, Destinn, Elman, Kreisler and others.

But the Pauers, Freunds, Baches and the others were not the pianists who captured the public imagination. For, starting with von

Bülow, the great figures of the Liszt school started appearing. Anton Rubinstein stormed out of Russia. The pupils of Theodor Leschetizky began coming out. With all of these the romantic age of piano playing caught its second wind.

· XVII ·

The Children of the Abbé

THE 1850s AND 1860s saw the first great deluge from the Liszt atelier. As a teacher Liszt was the magnet with more pull than anybody else in Europe. Pianists would go to other teachers first—Liszt, after all, did not take beginners, and he looked askance at child prodigies—but they would clamor to get near the old master as soon as their preparatory work had been finished. The most popular of the preparatory teachers were Theodor Kullak and Carl Reinecke. Kullak, a pupil of Czerny, had started out as a virtuoso and in 1846 was appointed pianist of the Prussian court. But he retired from concert work to start, with Julius Stern and Adolph Bernhard Marx, the Berliner Musikschule, better known as the Stern Conservatory. Five years later, Kullak broke away to found his own Neue Akademie der Tonkunst. Through his hands passed some of the world's best talent, en route to Liszt. Kullak wrote many theoretical works, and his *Octave School* is still in use. As a pianist he was an exponent of the elegant school of Thalberg.

Kullak was a martinet who ran his classes on the best Prussian principles. One of his pupils, Mabel Wagnalls, wrote a piece about him for the *Etude* music magazine. Every pupil had to be in place before he entered the classroom, and no one could leave before him. Nobody was allowed to talk in his presence, and an unwritten law prohibited even asking questions. Kullak insisted on clear playing. "Microscopical accuracy," Wagnalls called it. "There were no corners ignored in the pieces he taught; every spot was scoured bright and polished." Occasionally he would scrawl on a pupil's music "100 times." They hated him for that but, as Wagnalls wryly wrote, "To practice a pianissimo passage of sixty-fourth notes with one hand at a time, counting four to each note...will, if repeated 100 times, considerably improve your command of that particular run." At least the man was scrupulously fair. "We were all reproved with equal force and commended with equal caution."

Reinecke taught at the Leipzig Conservatory, was considered a fine Mozart player, and represented the conservative element which was against the Music of the Future. He insisted on a fixed and quiet hand position and would even have his pupils practice with a coin on the back of the hand, à la Clementi. He was also a good violinist and conductor and a prolific composer. His cadenzas to the Beethoven and Mozart concertos are still used by pianists. Still another important teacher was Karl Klindworth, who studied with Liszt, lived in London for fourteen years, and then went to Russia in 1868 as professor at the Moscow Conservatory. It was there that he brought out his famous piano reductions of the Wagner operas. He also started his critical edition of Chopin's music, an edition in use for many years and still valuable. He settled in Berlin in 1882 and established a piano school; a year later he closed it and retired to Potsdam, where he taught privately.

But it was Liszt who put the finishing touches on a good number of the major pianists of the century. From England they came to him, and from France and Germany, Italy and Russia, Scandinavia and America, all piling over one another, panting to sit at the knees of *Der Meister*. By the 1860s, the Liszt factory was mass-producing pianists. Liszt never claimed to be a professor, and his teaching consisted of advice and illustration. What a pianist got out of it depended upon his background and his own genius. Liszt never formed a "school" as such. But from his classes in Weimar, Rome and Budapest did emerge much major talent.

Von Bülow was one of the most important of the early Liszt students, but the greatest, pianistically speaking, was Carl Tausig, who died in 1871 at the age of thirty. Tausig—the phenomenon who was considered Liszt's peer, whom Rubinstein called "the infallible," who had mastered the entire literature as it was then known. Liszt himself did not disagree with any of these estimates of Tausig. He spoke admiringly of the young man's "brazen" fingers (*"tes mains de bronze et des diamants"*) and said that on Tausig would fall the mantle of the Liszt tradition. Never had such talent, Liszt said, come into his hands. The very first time he heard the boy he sent an enthusiastic letter off to his Sayn-Wittgenstein. "A little piano-playing prodigy from Warsaw named Tausig, age thirteen, [Tausig was actually fourteen] came to see me. . . . He'll probably spend a year or two at Weimar. He's an amazingly gifted boy whom you'll enjoy hearing. He plays everything by heart, composes (fairly well), and seems to me destined to make a brilliant reputation for himself very quickly." The letter is dated July 21, 1855. Liszt at first had refused to hear Carl, saying that he had no interest in prodigies. But Carl's father sneaked him to the piano. Peter Cornelius, the composer who was so important a member of the Liszt-Wagner circle, was present and reported that when Tausig started to play, Liszt was taken completely aback. The boy, wrote Cornelius, was "a very devil of a fellow. He dashed into Chopin's A flat Polonaise and knocked us over with the octaves." In later life the A flat Polonaise was to be one of Tausig's very special warhorses. As he explained to von Lenz:

"I told you that it is a specialty. . . . My left hand is so formed that it runs by itself over the four notes, E, D sharp, C sharp, B—it is a kind of *lusus naturae*" (smiling). "I can do it as long as you like; it does not tire me; it was written for me. Stroke those four octaves with *both* hands; you cannot play them so loud." I tried it. "See! see! very good, but not as loud as mine, and after a couple of measures you are tired—and so are the octaves! I do not think that anyone else can play this passage just as I do—but how few understand it! It is the tramp of the horses in the Polish Light Cavalry!"

Von Lenz may have been exuberant, as always, but he called Tausig the living impersonation of Chopin. "He played like him, he felt as he did, he *was* Chopin at the piano." As von Lenz was so well acquainted with Chopin, his remark must carry weight, but most people would have disagreed. For one thing, Tausig was a much more heroic pianist than Chopin. For another, he was an interpreter who played other people's music, something that Chopin rarely did. Most pianists and critics of the day agreed that Tausig carried pure virtuosity to heights that Liszt himself had only suggested. And he did it in an opposite manner from his master. Where Liszt was all flamboyance and color, it was Tausig's ideal to achieve his stupendous effects without making the least physical fuss. Like Thalberg, he prided himself on his ability to sit motionless at the piano, and he abhorred what he called *Spektakel*. His infallible fingers would be

MUSICAL AMERICA

Carl Reinecke, who taught at the Leipzig Conservatory. Many of his pupils went on to Liszt.

Carl Tausig, perhaps Liszt's greatest pupil. Many considered him the most flawless pianist of the century. He died in 1871 at the age of thirty.

working miracles, and the only sign of tension in his entire figure would be an imperceptible tightening of one corner of the mouth.

Some called him Tausig the Terrible. Liszt called him an "iron eater." He was a cocky teenager when he came to Liszt, and Louis Ehlert, who observed him, said he was a combination of "gypsy wildness, repulsive rudeness and prejudice." Somehow he managed to get his wildness under control and pass as a human being. Ehlert marvelled, "To what battles must he have not submitted his soul, and what strength of will he must have possessed, to have curbed to his will so demonic a nature." Tausig's playing at that time was to Ehlert "a sort of piracy that snatched effects when and how they were to be found." This was the boy who developed into the most finished pianist of his time; a pianist who emphasized clarity, balance and proportion.

Liszt sent Tausig to Wagner, and the composer was impressed. "You have given me great pleasure with little Tausig," he wrote. ". . . He is a terrible youth: now I am amazed at his eminently developed intelligence, now at his mad nature. He must become something quite extraordinary if he becomes anything at all." Wagner noted that already he smoked cigars and drank tea to excess and had too great a fondness for cheese and sweets. Wagner loved to walk. Tausig hated it and after the first short stroll complained that he had already walked for hours. Wagner was half irritated, half amused. "Thus has my childless marriage been suddenly blessed with a rich catastrophe, and I enjoy rapid draughts of parental cares and troubles." Carl played the piano with such brilliance that he made Wagner tremble. Later, Tausig was to prepare for Wagner the piano score of *Die Meistersinger*.

As the boy grew up he learned to control himself, but never could be described as a gentle human being. A Liszt pupil, Oscar Beringer, called Tausig a driven man, irritable and sarcastic, with hair already turning gray at twenty-seven. He practiced compulsively, all day long except for the four hours twice a week he devoted to teaching. (In 1866 he had established an Academy for Advanced Pianists in Berlin.) As a teacher he was a perfectionist, and wrong notes drove him crazy. Beringer says that Tausig read philosophy in his spare time and was one of the best chess players in Berlin.

He was a short man with burning eyes, almost as despotic as von Bülow. Amy Fay has described one of his lessons. She had prepared a Chopin scherzo, and Tausig stood over her uttering such cries of encouragement as "Terrible! Shocking! Dreadful! O *Gott!* O *Gott!*" His idea of teaching was to push the pupil aside, play the passage himself and tell the pupil to do it just so. In Amy Fay's unforgettable phrase, whenever Tausig said to do it just so, "I always used to feel as if some one wished me to copy a streak of forked lightning with the end of a wetted match." Tausig hated teaching, and he avoided it as much as he could, dashing into his classes only when he had a free moment in his concert schedule.

He was not only a piano virtuoso, but also an all-around musician. In addition he pursued studies in philosophy and the natural sciences. He even found time to get married (to a pianist, Josephine Vrabeley), though that did not last long. Wagner was fond of him, and Tausig made several piano reductions of the Wagner operas. His original music and transcriptions are no longer in the repertoire, though his once-famous transcription of Bach's organ Toccata and Fugue in D minor occasionally gets a hearing. Seventy years ago it seemed to be against the law not to open a recital with the Bach-Tausig D minor Toccata and Fugue. Tausig also arranged, charmingly and effectively, some Strauss waltzes. Will there ever be a day in which the Strauss-Tausig *Man lebt nur einmal* will again be popular (Rachmaninoff made a stupendous recording of it)? Or his fantastic revision of the Weber *Invitation?*

To his pupils and most of the public, Tausig was an enigma. Amy Fay's reaction on hearing of his death from typhus gives an idea of what he meant to most people:

Was it not terrible that he should have died so young? Such an enormous artist as he was! I cannot get reconciled to it at all, and he played only twice in Berlin last winter. He was a strange little soul—a perfect misanthrope. Nobody knew him intimately. He lived all the last part of his life in the strictest retirement, a prey to deep melancholy. . . . He entirely overstrained himself, and his whole nervous system was completely shattered long before his illness. He said last winter that the very idea of playing in public was unbearable to him, and after he had announced in the papers that he would give four concerts, he recalled the announcement on the plea of ill health. Then he thought he would go to Italy and spend the winter. But when he got as far as Naples, he said to himself, "*Nein, hier bleibst du nicht* (No, you won't stay here)"; and back he came to Berlin. He doesn't seem to have known what he wanted, himself; his was an uneasy, tormented, capricious spirit, at enmity with the world. . . .

Wagner and his wife were shocked at Tausig's death, but, after all, he was only a Polish Jew. Cosima has several entries in her diary. "We have certainly lost a great pillar of our enterprise, but that leaves us indifferent." Tausig had conceived the idea of establishing a Society of Patrons for the Bayreuth enterprise that came to fruition in 1876. Cosima and Wagner decided that Tausig had had a sad life because he was "conscious of the curse of his Jewishness."

Goodness knows what he would have developed into had he not died at so early an age. As early as 1864 Brahms was awe-struck by Tausig's talent. He wrote a letter to Clara Schumann in which he said he would play his two-piano Sonata (later turned into the D minor Piano Concerto) with Tausig. "This will surprise you most of all, for I expect you will have a terrible opinion of Tausig." Brahms knew his Clara. "But he is really a remarkable little fellow, and a very exceptional pianist, who, incidentally, as far as it is possible for a man to do, is constantly changing for the better." There is no doubt that Tausig was in the process of growth, and it was a growth that was observed by his contemporaries. The first time Hanslick heard Tausig, he complained of his habit of "jabbing at the keys. . . . He has a habit of striking single notes with a force that simply makes the piano groan." But Hanslick a few years later had to change his opinion, pointing out that Tausig had developed a much more finished style. Joachim, no mean judge, gave a concert with Tausig in 1866, and this usually measured man went into hyperbole describing the pianist. Tausig, he flatly said, "is the greatest pianist playing in public at present. He has a richness and a charm of attack, a varied repertoire, an absence of all charlatanism—in short, an almost uncanny perfection for a man only twenty-four years old." (Tausig was really twenty-six at the time.)

It seems to be true that until his death Tausig had no equal. He combined Liszt's force and color with von Bülow's intellectuality. Eugen d'Albert, one of the greatest of the Liszt pupils, equated Tausig very closely with Liszt. He said that Liszt's musical conceptions were grander, but that Tausig had a more wonderful, more accurate technique coupled with a good deal of poetry. Huneker described him as having the pianissimo of Joseffy, the liquidity of Thalberg, the resistless power of a Rubinstein. Tausig, quiet as he was, could rouse an audience to madness. He had all the virtuosity in the world, and one of his innovations—no longer with us, in our severe century—was to play the prestissimo unisons at the end of the Chopin E minor Concerto in broken octaves. When he did this the musicians themselves would applaud hysterically, and the conductor would rap the podium with his baton until it broke. Tausig was the perfect pianist, the one who coupled mechanism with discipline and musicianship. At his death von Bülow wrote a tribute full of words like "surpassingly great . . . gold . . . concentrated feeling . . . Here is the whole history of piano playing, from the beginning to this day."

Just as Tausig was Liszt's favorite male pupil, his favorite among the ladies was the Munich-born Sophie Menter. Because of her robust, electrifying style, they called her in Paris *l'incarnation de Liszt*. Young, pretty, confident, she came to Liszt in 1869 after having worked with Tausig and von Bülow. "No woman can touch her," Liszt said. He especially admired her "singing hand." So did all the others, and her concerts got a type of reception normally reserved for prima donnas. In Copenhagen the students unharnessed her horses and drew her coach through the streets. Critics were ecstatic. Walter Niemann described her style as "a blend of virtuosity and elegance; a great, round and full Lisztian kind of tone; fiery temperament; a masculine weight on the keys; plasticity; a through-and-through distinguished craft of shape and form; in whom soul, spirit and technique are fused in harmony and union." Quite a bit of prose. But Niemann's remarks are supported by George Bernard Shaw, who wrote about Menter in 1890. Menter, he said, "produces an effect of magnificence which leaves Paderewski far behind. . . . Mme. Menter seems to play with splendid swiftness, yet she never plays faster than the ear can follow, as many players can and do; and it is the distinctness of attack and intention given to each note that makes her execution so irresistibly impetuous."

She was popular enough to make a success with music that no other pianist would touch. When Dionys Pruckner, a pupil of Liszt, introduced the E flat Concerto to Vienna in 1857, Hanslick destroyed concerto, pianist and composer. He poked fun at Liszt's use of the triangle as well as at the musical content, and the result was that no pianist dared bring the work to Vienna again. None, that is, but Menter. In 1869 she decided to beard Hanslick with the concerto, triangle and all. Anton Rubinstein told her she would be crazy to play it, and everybody warned her of the disaster that would be hers when Hanslick let loose. To all of which she replied, in her Bavarian dialect, "*Wenn i dös nit spielen kann, spiel i garr nit—i muss*

ja nit in Wien spielen" ("If I can't play it, I won't play at all—I don't
have to play in Vienna"). She did play the concerto and made a grand
success with it.

Menter always put on a show. The American pianist Edward
Baxter Perry heard her in the late 1890s and sent back a rather catty
report to the *Etude.* "Although fully fifty years of age," he wrote,
"she was attired, except for her jewels, like a girl of sixteen.... I
never knew a lady to appear in the concert room wearing so many
jewels. They included a complete tiara of gold and diamonds; two
necklaces, one of five or six ropes of jewels and the other a kaleido-
scopic display of gems of every kind and color; while pins, brooches,
butterflies and brilliants were thrust into every portion of her attire." The London-based pianist and composer, Francesco Berger,
swore that at every concert Menter carried her will and especially
valuable pieces of jewelry in a reticule suspended from her waist and
secreted under her voluminous skirts. At the concert attended by
Perry, Menter played one of her specialties, a piece named *Rhapsodies.* What that meant, it turned out, was a composite of three Liszt
rhapsodies, Nos. 2, 6 and 12, "with briefer fragments from a
number of others." At the close of this potpourri, "We were left
dazed, confused, breathless and, I may add, nearly deafened by this,
undoubtedly the most brilliant and astounding concert number ever
rendered on any program."

The dynamic Sophie married the famous cellist David Popper in
1872. They were divorced in 1886. She did some teaching and from
1883 to 1887 was at the St. Petersburg Conservatory. Probably the
best of the Liszt ladies, she nevertheless had some competition from
a few others—especially from Anna Mehlig, who enjoyed a brilliant
career and who visited the United States as early as 1869. Another
of Liszt's better female pupils was Adele aus der Ohe, who came to
Liszt at the age of twelve as one of the few prodigies he accepted and
who stayed with him for seven years (1877–1884). Liszt liked her
and said her touch was as soft as velvet and as strong as a man's.
Previously she had studied with Kullak, where Amy Fay came across
her, "a little fairy of a scholar, ten years old.... I heard her play a
concerto of Beethoven's the other day with orchestral accompaniment and a great cadenza by Moscheles, absolutely *perfectly.* She
never missed a note all the way through." Aus der Ohe came to
America in 1886 and became a very popular artist, touring the country for seventeen consecutive seasons. It was she who played the

(*Above left*) Adele aus der Ohe. She worked with Liszt for seven years. In 1891 she played at the Carnegie Hall inaugural in New York. Her piece was the Tchaikovsky Concerto in B flat minor, with the composer conducting.

(*Above right*) Sophie Menter, Liszt's favorite female pupil. The dynamism of her playing, her blend of virtuosity and poetry, put her in a class by herself until the flowering of Teresa Carreño.

Julie Rivé-King, the first of America's great woman pianists. After her studies with Liszt, she returned to America to give over 4,000 solo recitals and make over 500 appearances with orchestra.

Tchaikovsky B flat minor Concerto under the composer's direction at the opening week of ceremonies in Carnegie Hall in 1891. Her repertoire was big, and she was one of the first pianists to feature both Brahms concertos. She played the B flat as early as 1899 in Boston. Either she was a brilliant pianist who liked to engage large-scale works, or she had a lot of misplaced confidence, as indicated by a typical program she played in Boston on March 9, 1891. It consisted of Beethoven's *Waldstein*, Chopin's B flat minor Sonata, the Schumann Fantasy and Liszt's *Don Juan Fantasy*. Most men, no matter how gifted as virtuoso thunderers, would think twice about playing so demanding and physically taxing a program.

One of the Liszt ladies could have made an equally brilliant career had she wanted to—little Vera Timanoff, from Russia. She seems to have been the kind of girl who bounces from teacher to teacher. At the age of fifteen she was working with Tausig, playing things like the *Winter Wind* Étude with such magnificence that Tausig told his class he could not have done better himself. In Liszt's class she made such an impression that he called her "*la crème de la crème*." But Timanoff never cared to play much in public, and she ended up as a teacher in St. Petersburg.

Julie Rivé-King, on the other hand, made a fine public career. Rivé-King was the first great American woman pianist. Born in Cincinnati in 1857, she was playing in public at the age of eight and was then brought to New York, where she worked with William Mason and Sebastian Bach Mills. In 1872 she followed the crowd to Europe, studying with Reinecke, finishing with Liszt, and returning to America in 1875. Rivé-King immediately started making an important contribution to the American musical scene. It was the kind of contribution Gottschalk could have made but didn't. Her repertoire seemed endless and her industry inexhaustible. In the eighteen years following her return she gave more than four thousand solo recitals and appeared with orchestra over five hundred times. She was to the piano in America what Theodore Thomas was to the orchestra, and she helped establish a new standard in repertoire and performance. Her playing must have been excellent—sane, serious, well equipped. She was not a grand virtuoso like Fannie Bloomfield Zeisler, who replaced her as the outstanding American woman pianist, but her work cannot be underestimated.

As for Amy Fay, the sharp-eyed and intelligent American girl from Bayou Goula, Louisiana, her claim to fame is not in her piano playing but in her charming account of musical life in Germany in the 1870s. Amy went to Europe in 1869 and studied with Tausig, Kullak, Liszt and Deppe. While abroad she wrote long letters home, and they were published under the title *Music Study in Germany* through the influence of Henry Wadsworth Longfellow. *Music Study* must have gone through twenty editions. It is a minor classic, brightly written, full of shrewd observations about the great and near-great, and it is prime source material for anybody interested in pianists of the period. Amy was probably not a very good pianist herself. She settled in Chicago and for many years gave lecture-recitals or, as she called them, "piano conversations." As late as the 1920s she was giving recitals here and there, but nobody took them very seriously. She died in 1928. Poor, dear Amy! One would like to have known her. Throughout her book she comes to life as a pert, attractive mind, and she looks on life with a breezy, unaffected American manner. She managed to re-create an age, in her book, with startling fidelity.

In the years that Amy was hopefully hopping from one teacher to another, she had plenty of company from fellow Americans, all of whom seem to have studied with the fashionable professors, topped off with a helping of Liszt. There was William Sherwood, out of Lyons, New York, who worked with Kullak, Deppe and Liszt. After making a fine European career, he returned to America as a pianist, composer and teacher (in Chicago and Boston) and became one of the most respected American musicians of the nineteenth century. Neally Stevens studied with von Bülow, Kullak and Liszt, and she was highly regarded both as pianist and teacher. Blindness did not keep Edward Baxter Perry from following his profession. Indeed, he did more than most people. He left Boston to study with Kullak, Clara Schumann and Liszt and came home to concertize, teach, and give more than 150 lecture recitals every year. Another Bostonian of the Kullak-Liszt-Deppe axis was John Orth; and from nearby New Hampshire came James Tracy, who also made the trek and returned to teach at the New England Conservatory.

Then there was the foreign-born contingent that studied with Liszt and settled in America. Among them were the Polish-born Alexander Lambert (active in New York), and the German-born Richard Burmeister. Burmeister worked with Liszt for three years before coming to America and taking a position with the Peabody Conservatory in Baltimore. Carl Stasny, also German, ended up at the New England Conservatory. And Emil Liebling, born in Austria, came to America in 1867, returned to Weimar to study with Liszt, and ended up the best teacher and pianist in Chicago. Liebling lived to be a *doyen* and was very amused at the fuss the Liszt pupils kicked up. He was more modest than they were about his relations with old Franz. "I enjoy to this day," Liebling wrote in 1900, "the enviable distinction of being the only living pianist who escaped being his favorite pupil."

The one important Italian pianist who emerged during the nineteenth century was Giovanni Sgambati (his mother, however, was English), whose career started at the age of five, when he began to give private recitals. At six he was playing in public. He studied with Liszt in Rome, and Liszt detected elements of Tausig's style in him. This surprised Liszt, for Italians ordinarily had nothing Germanic about their approach. He told Franz Bendel that Sgambati played German composers—Bach, Beethoven, Schumann—"with perfect independence and mastery of style." (Bendel, by the way, was a pupil of Liszt and was reputedly one of the big technicians of the day. On a visit to Boston he had the honor of playing at one of Patrick Gilmore's monster jubilee concerts—in an auditorium large enough to contain a chorus of ten thousand and an orchestra of five thousand. History does not record Bendel's feelings while playing in such a vastness.) Sgambati then followed Liszt to Germany and, on his return, settled down as a pianist, teacher, composer, conductor, critic and esthetician. He was a classicist and was a potent force in reintroducing to Italy the instrumental tradition lost since the days of Scarlatti. Naturally he was German-oriented, and Alfredo Casella was sourly to remark, many years later, that Sgambati was the pioneer of German infiltration into Italy. But even before he studied with Liszt, Sgambati was playing the classic composers; they were in his blood. Most of them were unknown to Italians at that time. Sgambati continued his work as director of the Accademia di Santa Cecilia, adding Liszt and Wagner to his musical enthusiasms.

Hans von Bronsart and Dionys Pruckner, two able Liszt pupils, came before the public around the mid-century. So did Alexander Winterberger and Josef Wieniawski (brother of the famous violinist). The unusual Count Geza Zichy came a little later. This distinguished Hungarian nobleman lost his right arm in a hunting accident at the age of fifteen. Already a talented pianist, he refused to let the catastrophe stop him. Instead, he became history's first one-armed pianist. It became his *idée fixe* to show the world that a cripple was not necessarily handicapped, and he slaved for six years to perfect his left-hand technique and prepare a repertoire of arrangements for concert use. In 1873 he met Liszt and worked with him until 1878, after which he started a solo career. Since he was extremely wealthy, he played only for charity during his forty-odd years before the public. Naturally the critics were awe-struck, though not so awe-struck that their stock of adjectives and superlatives was swallowed up. And Zichy was probably very good. Hanslick called his playing "the greatest marvel of modern times on the piano." "Zichy," he said, "has attained a perfection as astonishing as it is dazzling. With five fingers he is able to imitate the ordinary play of ten, with the art of arpeggios adroitly worked out, by the aid of perfectly graduated nuances from piano to forte." This is not the conventional talk of a critic looking for polite words to describe a handicapped musician. Hanslick was really impressed.

· XVIII ·

Thunder from the East

HE LOOKED LIKE BEETHOVEN and he played like Beethoven, making the piano erupt volcanically and not always being very disciplined about it. Wrong notes, broken strings—these did not matter. The audience went home limp, knowing it had run into a force of nature. The Russian with the thick, ugly hands was elemental and, by general agreement, was recognized as the greatest pianist after Liszt. And his resemblance to Beethoven was a psychological factor very much in his favor. Could Beethoven have had an illegitimate child? people would ask. Was Anton Rubinstein's "Russian" birth a cover-up? Was this the reincarnation of Beethoven? Perhaps nobody took this gossip very seriously—but there the resemblance was, and Liszt referred to Rubinstein as "Van II." Moscheles, who had been on intimate terms with Beethoven, looked at the young Russian and was struck by the likeness. "Rubinstein's features and short, irrepressible hair remind me of Beethoven." Rubinstein himself never went out of the way to capitalize on the physical relationship. On the other hand, he certainly never played it down. Nor did he remind people that he was born in 1830, three years after Beethoven's death.

He was a shambling Russian bear, immensely powerful, with extraordinary hands. Each finger seemed thicker than the key on which it rested. No wonder he hit in the cracks. There is a photograph of those hands in Rudolf Breithaupt's *Die naturaliche Klaviertechnic* with the caption "Absolute ideal type (in pianistic, not esthetic, sense). Strong, padded, colossal hand with huge ridge and wonderfully massive reticulae . . ." A sloppy dresser who quietly sat before the piano and evoked cataclysms, he was in some respects a

269

Anton Rubinstein in 1842, at the age of twelve. Even at this age he already was slamming into the piano, snapping strings right and left. This lithograph was made in Paris.

forerunner of Vladimir Horowitz. "Strength with lightness, that is one secret of my touch. . . . I have sat hours trying to imitate the timbre of Rubini's voice in my playing," he told an interviewer. Nobody had a more sensuous piano tone, and he explained to Rachmaninoff how it was to be achieved: just press upon the keys until the blood oozes from the fingertips. There were other sides to his nature. One of his pupils, an American named Alexander McArthur, said that he had a temper and sometimes acted "like a dozen madmen let loose." He was a gambler and womanizer. But he was the pianist who succeeded Liszt in the grand line.

He had studied in Moscow under Alexander Villoing, making his debut at the age of nine in 1839. Villoing took him to Paris. In those days Rubinstein imitated Liszt, trying to lift his hands as high as possible, to shake his hair the same way, use the same hand positions. Rubinstein was not the only ten-year-old pianist roaming through Europe at that time, and he recollects in his autobiography that child prodigies were all the fashion around 1840. He mentions Sophie Bohrer, Karl Filtsch, "the Englishman Palmer, the two sister violinists, Maria and Theresa Milanolo." Rubinstein made something of an impression. Even at the age of thirteen he was a piledriver, snapping strings right and left. There followed some study in Berlin, under Siegfried Dehn; then Vienna, where he gave some concerts and lived for a while in 1846.

Some writers give the impression that he studied with Liszt. But Rubinstein never did. He was part of the Liszt circle and may have picked things up from them, but Liszt never took him as a pupil. Rubinstein did play for Liszt in 1846 in the hope of becoming a pupil, but Liszt refused and very coldly said, "A talented man must win the goal of his ambition by his own unassisted efforts." This from the usually so generous Liszt! It is the only known case of his turning down a brilliant talent. Did he scent a powerful rival? Or was there something in the sixteen-year-old youth that he did not like? Personalities have been known to clash. Rubinstein was living in acute poverty at the time, and Liszt did not help him. Liszt's reception must have wounded Rubinstein deep down. In later years the relationship between the two was friendly enough, on the surface, but Rubinstein in his autobiography does get some digs in. He describes his sufferings in Vienna and Liszt's indifference. "It was now two months since I had called on Liszt. My prolonged absence had at last reminded him of my existence. He took it into his head to pay me a visit; and one day he made his way up to my attic, accompanied by his usual retinue, his so-called courtiers, who followed him wherever he went." Then, writing about his reunion with Liszt in 1871, "We met as old friends sincerely attached to each other. I knew his faults (a certain pomposity of manner, for one thing) but always esteemed him as a great performer—a performer-virtuoso, indeed, but no composer."

And so, Rubinstein never had a famous teacher. Perhaps he never needed one. Josef Hofmann, his greatest pupil, claimed that Rubinstein was "a born genius. All that he did was done instinctively, which, of course, is far superior to procedure by rule or instruction because it is vital." He alternated between giving concerts and teaching. In 1854 he started a four-year tour of Europe, breaking it up with a lengthy stay in Paris. His good friend there was Saint-Saëns, and for a while the two were inseparable. Saint-Saëns conducted orchestras for Rubinstein, and vice versa; and when they were not collaborating in public, they were home playing four-hand music. "We made music with passion simply for the sake of making it," Saint-Saëns wrote many years later. The Frenchman was amused, in recollection, at the figure he and Rubinstein must have cut in Paris—he frail, slim, a dandy, precise in manners, pale and consumptive-looking; Rubinstein shaggy, leonine, sloppy, powerful, athletic. Rubinstein's genius and basic musicianship made a big impression on others beside Saint-Saëns. Rubinstein was even proficient in improvisation, a form then on its way out, and Karl Goldmark tells of an evening when Rubinstein went to the piano and took a motive from the last movement of the Beethoven Eighth Symphony:

He counterpointed it in the bass; then developed it first as a canon, next as a four-voiced fugue, and again transformed it into a tender song. He then returned to Beethoven's original form, later changing it to a gay Viennese waltz, with its own peculiar harmonies, and finally dashed into cascades of brilliant passages, a perfect storm of sound in which the original theme was still unmistakable. It was superb.

By then Rubinstein's playing had solidified into the type it was to remain—playing of extraordinary breadth, virility and vitality, immense sonority and technical grandeur in which all too often technical sloppiness asserted itself. When carried away, Rubinstein did not

The brothers Rubinstein—Nicholas and Anton—in 1868. Nicholas was a brilliant pianist who made very few public appearances.

Anton Rubinstein bore such a striking resemblance to Beethoven that there were rumors to the effect he was an illegitimate son of the composer.

care how many false notes fell under the piano and wiggled on the ground. Thus the more academic, spit-and-polish pianists, especially the German-trained ones, were apt to wonder what all the excitement was about. William Mason reported that in fast passages Rubinstein would lose control, his fingers would run away, and he would anticipate climaxes. Heller, writing to Hallé in 1862, was merciless:

What exaggerations of the less salient points, and what negligence in the more important passages! One felt the boredom of those agile and powerful fingers that had nothing to put into them, as when they give the circus elephant an empty salad bowl to swallow.

And Clara Schumann (naturally) was equally bitter. When she heard him play the Mendelssohn C minor Trio in 1857, "he so rattled it off that I did not know how to control myself . . . and often he so completely annihilated fiddle and cello that I . . . could hear nothing of them." A few years later he gave a concert in Breslau, and Clara attended. She noted her disapproval in her diary, "I was furious, for he no longer plays. Either there is a perfectly wild noise or else a whisper with the soft pedal down. And a would-be cultured audience puts up with a performance like that!" Even Amy Fay, the breeze from America, was disturbed by Rubinstein's pounding. She heard him play "a terrific piece by Schubert"—presumably the *Wanderer* Fantasy—and it gave her such a violent headache that the rest of the performance was ruined:

He has a gigantic spirit in him, and is extremely poetic and original, but for an entire concert he is too much. Give me Rubinstein for a few pieces, but Tausig for a whole evening. Rubinstein doesn't care how many notes he misses, provided he can bring out his conception and make it vivid enough. Tausig strikes *every* note with rigid exactness, and perhaps his very perfection makes him at times a little cold. Rubinstein played Schubert's *Erlkönig*, arranged by Liszt, *gloriously*. Where the little child is so frightened, his hands flew all over the piano, and absolutely made it shriek with terror. It was enough to freeze you to hear it.

Those who cared less for pure craft than for spirit found much to praise. The German critic Rellstab called him "the Hercules of the piano, the Jupiter Tonans of the instrument." To the pedantic von

Bülow he was "the Michelangelo of music." Hanslick expressed the majority point of view in a review written in 1884. First Hanslick complained that Rubinstein's programs were too long—over three hours and with more than twenty pieces, including three sonatas (Schumann's F sharp minor, Beethoven's D minor and also his Op. 101 in A). But nevertheless the playing gave pleasure because of its sensual element. "His health and robust sensuality flood the listener with refreshing candor." Rubinstein's virtues, wrote Hanslick, were rooted in his "unsapped natural strength and elemental freshness. So also are the faults into which his rich, but frequently unbridled, headstrong talent easily tempts him." Hanslick ended his review with a neat line, "Yes, he plays like a god, and we do not take it amiss if, from time to time, he changes, like Jupiter, into a bull." And so, to many listeners, his wrong notes were of little importance. Rafael Joseffy compared his tone to that of a "golden French horn," and Huneker wrote that "the power and passion of the man have never been equaled."

But Rubinstein could play delicately when he wanted to. All are agreed that few pianists could display greater lightness, grace and delicacy. It is true that he seldom displayed that side of his nature. He learned early in life that people paid their money to hear his thunder, not the delicate patter of raindrops. He was expected to thunder, and thunder he generally did. His programs, like his style, were gargantuan. Rubinstein was an iron man with a colossal repertoire and an equally colossal memory until his fiftieth year. Then he began to have memory lapses and had to play from the printed note. When he did not have the music before him, the results were apt to be distressing. Paderewski heard him toward the end and remembered great moments alternating with memory slips and chaos.

But even in his last years his programs would run to formidable lengths. His series of historical recitals were famous—seven consecutive concerts covering the history of piano music, and each program enormous. To give an example, the second program consisted of sonatas by Beethoven—the *Moonlight*, D minor, *Waldstein*, *Appassionata*, E minor, A major (Op. 101), E major (Op. 109) and C minor (Op. 111). The fourth concert was devoted to Schumann and contained the Fantasy in C, *Kreisleriana*, *Études symphoniques*, Sonata in F sharp minor, a group of short pieces and the *Carnaval*. These did not include encores, which he sprayed liberally at each concert. What is more, he played every repeat of every piece on the programs except in the music of Bach and Handel. He told his students that in those two composers the repeat signs could be disregarded, but in Haydn, Mozart and Beethoven the repeats "are an integral part of the structure. To omit them is *lèse-majesté*." (It is hard to see why repeats in Mozart and Beethoven are structural, while in Bach and Handel they are nonstructural; but that was the nineteenth century for you.) Rubinstein apparently was never tired; the audience stimulated his adrenals to the point where he acted like a superman. Arthur Friedheim reported that he once went to a Rubinstein concert, and that "as a first encore he played Chopin's B flat minor Sonata; as a second the seven pieces of Schumann's [Friedheim means Mendelssohn's] *Characterstücke*. The audience roared its delight at the copious liberality of the Old Lion."

It was natural that America should beckon. The Steinway piano firm invited Rubinstein to give a cross-country tour in the 1872–3 season, and a series of careful negotiations ensued. Rubinstein specified that he was not to play in beer gardens or in the Southern states (but he did, after all, play in the South). He wanted a good deal of money, and it had to be in gold, for he distrusted American paper money and banks. All being satisfactorily settled, Rubinstein and the violinist Henri Wieniawski (who shared the tour, along with a troupe of instrumentalists and singers) set foot in the United States. The contract called for two hundred concerts at two hundred dollars a concert, and Rubinstein lived up to it. He was in America for 239 days and gave 215 concerts, topping them off in New York with seven farewell recitals in nine days. These were his famous historical programs, and he would have played them in eight days except that he had to break up the series with a Boston recital on May 21. He left for Europe on May 24, 1873. Rubinstein was an iron man, but even he felt the strain:

May Heaven preserve us from such slavery! Under these conditions there is no chance for art—one simply grows into an automaton, performing mechanical work; no dignity remains to the artist; he is lost. . . .

During the time I remained in America we travelled through the United States as far as New Orleans, and I appeared before an audience two hundred fifteen times. It often happened that we gave two or three concerts in as many cities on the same day. The receipts and the success were invariably gratifying, but it was all so tedious that I began to despise myself and my art. So profound was my dissatisfaction that when several years later I was asked to repeat my American tour, I refused pointblank. . . .

Wieniawski, a man of extreme nervous temperament, who, owing to ill health, quite often failed to meet his appointments in St. Petersburg—both at the Grand Theatre and at the Conservatory—never missed one concert in America. However ill he might be, he always contrived to find strength enough to appear on the platform with his fairy-like violin. The secret of his punctuality lay in the fact that by the terms of his contract he had to forfeit 1000 francs for every non-appearance. The proceeds of my tour in America laid the foundation of my prosperity. On my return I hastened to invest in real estate.

So it all ended happily. But the tour was a nightmare in which nerves were taut and tempers high. After a while, Rubinstein simply refused to speak to Wieniawski. The feeling was mutual, for Wieniawski got second billing to Rubinstein and resented it. High feelings and acrimony aside, Rubinstein made a major impact on America. This kind of piano playing and such forceful personality had been unknown in the New World. Rubinstein received more attention from the press than any other figure until the arrival of Paderewski in 1891. One little by-product of the press is a description of Rubinstein's hands by Mrs. William H. Sherwood, wife of the eminent American pianist. She wrote that the fingers were short and fat at the base, tapering exquisitely, "and that the nails were like bits of pink enamel sunk in velvet pads." (He had an enormous hand. Josef Hofmann has written that Rubinstein's fifth finger "was as thick as my thumb—think of it! Then his fingers were square at the ends, with cushions on them. It was a wonderful hand.") Also there was George Bagby's recitation, *Jud Brownin Hears Ruby Play*. Rubinstein was referred to as Ruby, just as Paderewski later was to rejoice in the name of Paddy and a British queen was to be referred to as Lizzy. All over America people were chortling over Jud's experiences at a Rubinstein recital, the climax of which was:

By jinks, it was a mixtery! He fetched up his right wing, he fetched up his left wing, he fetched up his center, he fetched up his reserves. . . . He opened his cannon—round shot, shells, shrapnels, grape, canister, mines, and magazines—every living battery and bomb a-going at the same time. The house trembled, the lights danced, the walls shuck, the sky split, the

ground rocked—heavens and earth, creation, sweet potatoes, Moses, nine-
pences, glory, tenpenny nails, Sampson in a 'simmon tree—Bang!!! . . .

With that bang! he lifted himself bodily into the air, and he came down
with his knees, fingers, toes, elbows and his nose, striking every single
solitary key on the pianner at the same time.

. . . I knowed no more that evening.

From 1861, one of the things closest to Rubinstein's heart was the
St. Petersburg Conservatory of Music, the first one in Russia. Rubinstein helped found it, was its first director, and rounded up an
imposing faculty. He ran into a great deal of opposition from the
Russian "Five"—Balakireff, Borodin, Cui, Rimsky-Korsakoff and
Mussorgsky—who looked on Rubinstein with suspicion and hostil-
ity. They were aiming at a Russian school and they claimed—quite
correctly—that Rubinstein esthetically was a German-oriented conservative. Rubinstein was a cosmopolite, though like so many Russians he was always being impelled back to his homeland. He once
wryly remarked that the Germans called him a Russian and the
Russians called him a Jew. This Russian Jew with Teutonic music
leanings made no bones about his conservatism. He was as reaction-
ary as a musician could be; and, while he visited Weimar constantly,
he detested everything it and Liszt stood for. In his autobiography he
gives an indication of his musical tastes:

As to the degree of musical appreciation possessed by the different na-
tions, I believe that Germany stands today at the head of the musical world,
and this in spite of the fact that she is eaten up with pride in her patriot-
ism, and sense of superiority to all other countries. Culture has but slender
chance in a nation so absorbed in its bayonets and its unity [these prophetic
words were written in 1889]; but in spite of all these drawbacks, it must be
confessed that Germany is the most musical nation in the world. . . .

And now, with the supremacy of Bismarck on the one hand, and Wagnerism on the other, with men's ideals all reversed, dawns the critical
moment for music. Technique has taken gigantic strides, but composition, to
speak frankly, has come to an end. . . . Its parting knell was rung when the
last incomparable notes of Chopin died away. It may prove but a temporary
paralysis, and who can say how long it may endure? Between the fifteenth
and seventeenth centuries painting stood at the zenith of its power, but
during the eighteenth century deterioration set in; and I believe that music
is passing through a similar crisis. . . . When and how it will end, no one

can know. One thing is beyond denial. All that enchanted us, all that we loved, respected and worshipped, and admired, has ended with Chopin.

In protest against this kind of philosophy, and against Rubinstein's conservatory in St. Petersburg, Balakireff founded a competitive Free School (as opposed to Rubinstein's court-endorsed and court-subsidized venture). But it was the St. Petersburg Conservatory that was to thrive, and also the Moscow Conservatory. That was founded by Rubinstein's younger brother, Nicholas, in 1866. Nicholas himself was a splendid pianist. A pupil of Kullak, he did not do much concert work but was reputed to play almost as well as his famous brother. Anton said that if Nicholas really had worked at it, he could have been the better pianist of the two. That this opinion is more than mere fraternal affection is upheld by no less a connoisseur than Emil von Sauer, one of Liszt's best pupils. Sauer in 1895 wrote a comparison of the two:

It is difficult to say which was the better pianist. In every way as different as the brothers were in personal appearance—the one dark, almost to blackness; the other very fair—so different was their playing. The playing of Nicholas was more like that of Tausig, only warmer and more impulsive. Perhaps Anton Rubinstein was the more inspired performer of the two, but he was unequal. Nicholas never varied; his playing both in private and in public was always the same, and kept up the same standard of excellence.

Nicholas remained head of the Moscow Conservatory until his death in 1881. But Anton gave up the St. Petersburg Conservatory in 1867. After twenty years of concertizing, composing and conducting, he returned to it in 1887. Finally he divorced himself from its operation in 1891. During his last four years there, he resumed his historical recitals for the benefit of the students. Every Sunday evening for thirty-two weeks he gave a different program, lecturing about the music as well as playing it. After 1891 he made Dresden his headquarters and worked there with his most famous pupil, Josef Hofmann. His last concert took place in St. Petersburg on January 14, 1894. He died on November 28 of that year.

Among his legacies was a formidable mass of music, virtually all of which has dropped from the Western concert repertoire. In Russia, however, his D minor Piano Concerto and his opera, *The Demon*, are still performed. But most of his piano and orchestral pieces, his chamber music and songs, seem to have been permanently retired unless an unprecedented shift in values takes place. His *Kammenoi Ostrow* and Melody in F survive as background music; otherwise, gone are the G major Concerto, the *Staccato* Étude and the *Étude on False Notes*, the cello sonatas and the once-so-popular *Ocean* Symphony.

But the memory of his piano playing still lives in the millions of words written about it. And had he lived another ten years—he was only sixty-four when he died—he could have left us some recordings. . . .

· XIX ·

French Neatness, Precision, Elegance

BUT SAINT-SAËNS, who was born only five years after Rubinstein but outlived him by twenty-seven, did leave a few recordings. Saint-Saëns is, chronologically, the ealiest-born pianist ever to record (but not the first pianist: Landon Ronald recorded a piano version of the *Liebestod* from *Tristan und Isolde* on a seven-inch Berliner disc in 1900). When we hear Saint-Saëns on the faded discs, we are hearing the playing of a man who was born in 1835. He developed into one of the most prodigious musicians of all time. Neither as composer nor pianist is he one of the immortals (although he excelled in both of these branches of his art), but for all-around musicianship and natural gifts, he was on the level of a Mozart or a Mendelssohn. When he was *two* years old it was found that he had absolute pitch. Before reaching the age of five he played the piano part in a Beethoven violin sonata. He learned Latin, geometry and history with equal ease. At six he was composing (a song called *Le Soir* was his first piece). At seven he was studying with Stamaty. At eight he was playing in public. At eleven he made his formal debut, playing a Mozart concerto, Beethoven's C minor Concerto, a sonata by Hummel, a prelude and fugue by Bach, and pieces by Handel and Kalkbrenner. All these he played from memory. As an encore he volunteered to play any of the thirty-two Beethoven sonatas. Small wonder that his fame penetrated all over Europe and even America. An item in the *Boston Musical Gazette* of August 3, 1846, states that "there is a boy in Paris, named St. Saëns, and only ten and a half years old, who plays the music of Handel, Sebastian Bach, Mozart, Beethoven, and the more modern masters, without any book before him."

With all of his gifts, it was not too surprising that Saint-Saëns should have decided against the drudging life of a touring virtuoso. He played the piano throughout his life, but he was never a concert pianist as such. Indeed, it was primarily as an organist that he was best known at first, for he became organist at the Madeleine in 1858 and remained there until 1877. During those years he also became professor of composition at the École Niedermeyer. Among his pupils were Fauré and Messager. Everyone who came in contact with him went away impressed with his phenomenal mastery of the materials of music. Among these was Richard Wagner, who pays tribute to Saint-Saëns' score reading—and ends up with one of the curtest and most snobbish dismissals in the history of music. Wagner is discussing Saint-Saëns' talent,

which was simply amazing. With an unparalleled sureness and rapidity of glance with regard to even the most complicated orchestral score, this young man combined a not less remarkable memory. He was not only able to play my scores, including *Tristan*, by heart, but could also reproduce their several parts, whether they were leading or minor themes. And this he did with such precision that one might easily have thought he had the actual music before his eyes. I afterwards learned that this stupendous receptivity for all the technical material of a work was not accompanied by any corresponding intensity of productive power; so that when he tried to set up as a composer I quite lost sight of him in the course of time.

Hans von Bülow was more generous, and rated Saint-Saëns as a score reader and all-around musician greater than Liszt. Von Bülow told the conductor Carl Zerrahn that once he and Wagner were in conversation, with Saint-Saëns in the same room. Saint-Saëns, who could not follow German, became bored and picked up the full-score manuscript of *Siegfried*, not yet completed, put it on the piano and began to play. Wagner and von Bülow stopped talking. Never, said von Bülow, had he heard such score-reading, and it was all *prima vista*. Scarcely an effect was lost; the player seemed intuitively to grasp the whole structure of the work, and he reproduced it in its transformed shape without a second's hesitation. Wagner was speechless. "I too can play from score," said von Bülow, "but neither I nor any living man could have performed that feat after Saint-Saëns. He is the greatest musical mind of our time."

It was not only music that interested Saint-Saëns. He dabbled in

Camille Saint-Saëns, extraordinary pianist and prodigious musician. He was not a concert pianist as such, and for the most part appeared in public only in his own music.

Francis Planté. Born in 1839, he made a series of records around 1930.

criticism, literature, poetry, astronomy (he was a member of the Astronomical Society of France), archeology, science in general and the occult sciences in particular. Many of his essays make stimulating reading, and his own reminiscences are fascinating. In addition, he was no mean musicologist, and he was one of the first to make a close examination of the pre-Beethoven clavier approach.

In one of his books, *Harmonie et Mélodie*, he describes himself as an eclectic. "This is perhaps a great defect, but it is impossible for me to correct it: one cannot alter one's nature." By all accounts his piano playing, however, was anything but eclectic. It represented a classic tradition, and his records bear this out, even though he unfortunately recorded nothing from the standard repertoire. His discs, made in 1904 and 1919, are devoted to his own music—the *Valse mignonne*, *Valse nonchalante*, a piano arrangement of two sections of his *Suite Algérienne*, and also the first movement of his G minor Piano Concerto, played by him with what now would be considered reckless and unmusical speed. (But tempos in the last quarter of the twentieth century are much slower than those of the nineteenth, as the recordings of musicians born before 1900 amply demonstrate.) His records indicate that he was an expert, somewhat dry pianist, and that was the opinion of most of his contemporaries. Saint-Saëns seems to have had a fluent technique, considerable flexibility, a *sec* touch, restricted dynamics and a tendency toward speed. Harold Bauer said that he played most things too fast. There seems to have been nothing he could not do in the way of technique, but emotionally he was reined in. Leopold Mannes, who heard him play an entire afternoon, was reminded of "a dry well." But Claudio Arrau, who also attests to the dryness, was more impressed. He remembers Saint-Saëns "leaning back with a big beard and a huge belly, playing the piano with *incredible* ease. . . . The most even scales you can imagine, and great power in the fingers. Ice cold, but amazing."

Saint-Saëns, however, was primarily a composer and not a pianist. The Frenchman who achieved most acclaim as a pianist in the middle of the nineteenth century was Francis Planté, whose tremendous life span (1839–1934) exceeded even that of Saint-Saëns. Planté was known for his elegance and precision, and was by far the most important French pianist until the arrival of Pugno. Something in French training—and, perhaps, in the French character—seems to inhibit instrumental flamboyance à la Liszt or Paderewski. To this day the French style has remained one of suppleness, of elegance and logic, of finger technique in the classic style (from hand and wrist rather than from arm and shoulder, resulting in the clear but percussive tone in fortissimo passages that so many French pianists display).

All of these characteristics Planté seems to have had in good measure. He graduated from the Conservatoire at the age of eleven and created a furore. "The suavity and charm of sound, exquisite delicacy of touch, brio and clarity of hard and brilliant passages, the extravagant bravura that the eleven-year-old boy executed like a Thalberg..." So writes Marmontel. Considering that Marmontel was Planté's teacher, his opinion might not be entirely unbiased. But it was echoed by everybody else. In Planté's early teens he was fully accepted as a colleague by two of France's greatest instrumentalists, the violinist Delphin Alard and the cellist Auguste Franchomme, and became their pianist in a trio. At an age when most young people have only the rudiments of style, Planté was playing Beethoven and Schubert with his two distinguished elders.

Fétis tells a story about Planté that has been picked up by most subsequent writers. In Fétis' words, "came a day in an official salon where he had been asked to play. The noise of conversation was such that it was impossible for him to be heard over it, and he was not able to get a moment of silence or attention. Justly offended by such lack of regard and politeness, M. Planté escaped after playing the piece he had started, went home, packed up, and left for far away in the Pyrénées." Planté had been born there and, according to Fétis, he sulked there for ten years. This would have made him a most sensitive Planté indeed. But the story, especially the part about those ten years, does not hold water. It could easily have been that Planté did walk out on a concert and return to the Pyrénées, but it could not have been for ten years, as he was playing in public during the time he is supposed to have retired to his kingdom and locked the door, like the Prince in the Andersen fairy tale.

At any rate, by 1872 Planté was considered supreme among French pianists. Fétis uses every adjective in his not inconsiderable vocabulary to describe his playing, "... a style truly incomparable in its astonishing variety of expression, marvelous feeling for nuances, from the most delicate to the strongest; the mellowness, suppleness and grace of finger; the phrasing so rich and free; his charm, at the same time penetrating and passionate; his intelligent aims; his exquisite and pure taste..."

His playing might have been elegant, but there were peasantlike aspects to his personal life. Like all French peasants, he was inclined to stinginess; and, again like all French peasants, he wanted to own his own land. Even as a great virtuoso he would stay at small hotels, eat at cheap restaurants, travel third class by railway, save every franc. Finally he had enough francs to make his dream come true, and he bought a villa in the country. There, at Mont-de-Marsan, is where he retired. And it was there, in 1928, that he celebrated the start of his ninetieth year by inviting friends to a pair of private concerts. Looking back on his career with a certain amount of grim humor, he told an interviewer, André Gresse, "I represent seventy-five years of piano playing at eight hours a day." At the first concert, the venerable pianist played Chopin's Third Ballade, Weber's C major Sonata, a Beethoven sonata, pieces by Schumann, Fauré, Gluck, Boccherini and Brahms, and finally a Liszt group including the E major Polonaise, the Overture and *Pilgrims' March* from *Tannhäuser*, and the *Rákoczy March*. That was in the afternoon. After a hearty dinner, the old man sat down to Chopin's F minor Ballade and E major Scherzo, Beethoven's *Les Adieux* Sonata, pieces by Mendelssohn and de Sévérac, Berlioz' *Mephisto Serenade*, pieces by Rubinstein, two Liszt rhapsodies and Liszt's *Mephisto Waltz*. He then gave many encores, ending with Chopin's A flat Polonaise.

It was at that time that he also made some recordings for French Columbia. It is a little embarrassing to discuss them. Even granting his extreme age, his playing is spasmodic to say the least; and the curious thing is that instead of the finesse and delicacy for which he was celebrated, the impression is one of uncontrolled power—something like Mark Hambourg in his bad moments—and uncertain rhythms. Isidor Philipp at ninety played much better.

Following Planté as exponents of the French style were Louis Brassin, Louis Diémer, Raoul Pugno and Édouard Risler. Brassin, who studied with Moscheles, was primarily noted as a teacher. He was associated with the Stern Conservatory, the Brussels Conservatory and the St. Petersburg Conservatory from 1878 on. He died in Russia. Today his name is remembered, if it is remembered at all, by his transcription of the *Magic Fire Music* from *Die Walküre*. At the turn of the century it was a recital favorite (Hofmann made a wonderful recording of it). Diémer, who took first prize at the Paris Conservatory in 1856, was described by Hanslick as a delicate and graceful artist (but, on the other hand, by Mark Hambourg as a "dry-as-dust player with a hard, rattling tone," suggesting that between the Russian-trained products of Leschetizky, of whom Hambourg was one, and the classically oriented French pianists, there could be nothing in common). To the French, Diémer was famous as "the king of the scale and the trill." Married to a wealthy woman, he gave free concerts and never had to teach. Lazare Lévy has summarized Diémer's art, "The astonishing precision of his playing, his legendary trills, the sobriety of his style, made him the excellent pianist we all admired." Diémer taught at the Conservatoire, where he succeeded the ancient Marmontel in 1887. Among his pupils were some of the most distinguished pianists and musicians in French history: Édouard Risler, Alfred Cortot, Robert Lortat, Marcel Dupré, Jean Verd, Marcel Ciampi, Lazare Lévy, E. Robert Schmitz and Robert Casadesus. During his career, Diémer played the first performance of many French works, including Franck's *Variations symphoniques*. His career, incidentally, had at one time been threatened with a complete halt, for he had been called up for seven years of military service. Rossini's wife raised the money to buy him out.

Diémer recorded five sides from 1904 to 1906. One of them is his own *Valse*, an idiotically banal composition but nevertheless difficult. Diémer plays it with dryness but impeccable finger work, gliding over long pianissimo scale passages with incredible feathery ease. He must have been one of the more finished technicians in pianistic history.

Pugno was an altogether brilliant pianist. He took first prize at the Conservatoire when he was fourteen, later following with firsts in *solfège*, harmony, fugue and organ. But even before then he had been a remarkable prodigy. He made his debut in 1858 at the age of six (the piece he played was named *La jeunesse de Mozart*), much to the delight of his father, who *wanted* him to be a professional musician. Pugno always maintained that a pianist could not amount to much unless he started at four. Apparently the only instruction that Pugno had up to the age of ten was supplied by a woman named Josephine Martin. At the Conservatoire he studied with Mathias, the Chopin pupil. But after his brilliant start Pugno neglected the

MUSICAL AMERICA

Raoul Pugno in his own studio in Paris. At the turn of the century he was considered the greatest French pianist. He also was a chamber-music player and made many appearances with the great Belgian violinist, Eugène Ysaÿe.

Édouard Risler, who finished his studies in Germany and became one of the first French pianists to concentrate on Beethoven.

piano in favor of teaching, organ playing and composition; and it was not until 1893 that he resumed his concertizing—with grand success.

He excelled as a chamber music player and, in 1896, joined forces with Eugène Ysaÿe, the great Belgian violinist. They were together for many years. Both were men of exceptional size and rotundity. The two colossi on the stage almost made it buckle. Pugno's touch was light, and his technique was incredibly flexible. This is not hearsay. In 1903 he made an elaborate series of recordings for the Gramophone and Typewriter Company in Paris. For some reason he seemed intrigued by recordings and would come to the studio, sit at the wretched upright and rattle off piece after piece. In this he was unique among pianists of his decade. He recorded eighteen known sides; and there are rumors that there were additional unreleased Pugno discs. On the known series he played Handel, Scarlatti, Weber, Chopin, Mendelssohn, Chabrier, Liszt and one of his own compositions, a genre piece called *Sérénade à la lune* (not a very distinguished work).

These recordings reveal him to have been a pianist with extraordinary finish and lightness. His passagework is limpid, always clearly etched and accurate, and there is an incredible deftness of execution. In Chopin's *Berceuse* he employs imaginative pedal effects that clearly come through the old recording; and the quasi-glissando scales toward the end of Liszt's Eleventh Rhapsody are amazing in their speed and clear articulation. Here and there the playing has mannerisms that are not admissible today, such as a tendency to rush phrase endings or insert ritards; but those were characteristics of the period, and Pugno abused them far less than did most pianists of the time.

Édouard Risler studied with Diémer at the Conservatoire, took various first prizes, and went off to finish his studies in the Liszt school. He worked with Bernhard Stavenhagen and Eugene d'Albert in the 1890s, and was probably the first French pianist to make a big impression in Germany. Thanks to the infusion of Liszt blood, Risler was unique among French musicians of the time in being so strongly attached to the music of Beethoven and Wagner that he began to specialize in both. As a Wagnerian he spent the summers of 1896 and 1897 at Bayreuth, working as a stage manager, and then took part as a coach in preparing *Die Meistersinger* for the Paris Opéra. One result of his Wagnerism was Risler's arrangement of *Das Rhein-*

gold for two pianos, which he frequently played with the young Alfred Cortot. Cortot always maintained that it was Risler who had lifted French pianism out of the doldrums. Up until him, French pianists were schooled in the light, fluent virtuoso technique stemming from Kalkbrenner, Herz and Stamaty. It was elegant but superficial. Along came Risler. At his first Paris concert after returning from Bayreuth, his program consisted of six Beethoven sonatas. Later he played the Beethoven cycle (he was to play it nine times between 1907 and 1914), the entire *Well-Tempered Clavier*, and major works by Schubert, Weber, Liszt and the new French school, in the process educating not only the French public but also his fellow musicians. Some, however, could not be educated. Risler was anxious to play a Mozart concerto and he showed the French conductor Édouard Colonne the score. Colonne laughed. "Really boring," he said, "and if I were you I'd play something else."

As for his Beethoven playing, the big influences on Risler were von Bülow and d'Albert. By 1906 Risler was playing the cycle of thirty-two sonatas. Berlin critics were entranced with his delicate touch—and also his ringing fortissimo. Risler employed a wide dynamic palette. He was a specialist in pedal effects and, if Oscar Bie is accurate, he anticipated Gieseking. Bie wrote that Risler "had discovered those last delicate nuances that lie precisely between tone and silence. His tones seem not to begin and not to cease; they are woven out of ethereal gossamer." Risler also learned from the Liszt school how to overcome his Gallic instincts and come crashing down on the piano. "It is true," wrote Arthur Dandelot, "that Risler in his maturity, a very corpulent man, had great muscular force in his arms and fingers." His recording of Liszt's Eleventh Rhapsody, made around 1910, does suggest great force. Some of the accents are explosive. The playing on this disc has character and technical finish, and suggests a major artist.

But in late life Risler changed his style, reverting to French classicism. In 1920 *Le Monde Musical* remarked that Risler had remade his playing. Toward the end he all but abandoned the pedal, and it was in this period that musicians used to call him "the pale pianist." He was pale in sound, in expression, in interpretation.

Risler ate himself to death. After his wife died he apparently gave up on everything and indulged in various excesses, of which food was one. His doctors begged him to give up his *excès de nourriture* but he didn't. He died in 1929.

· XX ·

The Lisztianers and Leschetizkianers
Take Over

THE LATTER HALF of the nineteenth century—and, indeed, the first quarter of the twentieth—was dominated by the pupils of Liszt and Leschetizky. In the last decade or so of Liszt's life there flocked to him a remarkable aviary who were to fly all over the pianistic life for years to come. Consider: Eugene d'Albert, Conrad Ansorge, Arthur Friedheim, Arthur de Greef, Alfred Reisenauer, Rafael Joseffy, Frederick Lamond, José Vianna da Motta, Moriz Rosenthal, Isaac Albéniz, Emil von Sauer, Alexander Siloti, Bernhard Stavenhagen, Constantin von Sternberg. But the list of important Leschetizkianers is equally impressive. It was Paderewski who put Leschetizky securely on the map as a teacher. Paderewski, however, was by no means the best product of the Leschetizky atelier, though certainly the most famous. There were (alphabetically) Ernesto Bérumen, Fannie Bloomfield Zeisler, Alexander Brailowskv, Richard Buhlig, Severin Eisenberger, Annette Essipoff, Ignaz Friedman, Ossip Gabrilowitsch, Katharine Goodson, Mark Hambourg, Helen Hopekirk, Mieczyslaw Horszowski, Edwin Hughes, Annette Hullah, Bertha Jahn, Frank La Forge, Ethel Leginska (née Liggins), Benno Moiseiwitsch, Elly Ney, John Powell, Ernest Schelling, Artur Schnabel, Arthur Shattuck, Martinus Sieveking, Josef Slivinski, Paula Szalit and Paul Wittgenstein.

Nearly all of the pianists in this grandiose roster of Liszt and Leschetizky pupils were romantic pianists (Schnabel and Horszowski being two important exceptions). They specialized in the literature from Beethoven on, seldom playing Mozart or Schubert, and playing Bach generally in transcriptions by Liszt, Tausig or d'Albert. They were exponents of the big line, the grand effect, the

291

tempo rubato. Not that they were very sure of what rubato really was, though to a man and woman they said they were. Constantin von Sternberg, in his little book called *Tempo Rubato*, poked fun at Chopin's description and the whole mystique resulting therefrom. Sternberg knew an old gentleman who had taken lessons with Chopin. This gentleman would talk about nothing but tempo rubato. Unfortunately he never gave the same definition twice. Sternberg tried to pin him down. "Ah, my young friend, no one but a Pole understands tempo rubato. That is why only a Pole can play Chopin, and of all the Poles there is only one—but, come to think of it, no—no—he cannot, either." Sternberg believed, correctly, that no artist from Bach on—or before, for that matter—could play in strict metronomic tempo even if he wanted to. Years before writing his book Sternberg had studied with Moscheles, the classicist, who once sat down to show him how to play a Beethoven adagio in strict time, yet with expression. "And then he sat down at the piano and played a most beautiful rubato, for he was a consummate artist. And when he finished he commented upon how strictly he had kept time."

Sternberg's idea of rubato was "balance." What is added in one place is to be taken away in another. What is stolen is to be restored. (The word "rubato" comes from "*rubare*," to rob.) But Paderewski, the great Polish master of rubato playing, thought that the concept of stealing followed by restoration was nonsense. "We duly acknowledge the highly moral motives of this theory, but we humbly confess that our ethics do not reach such a high level. . . . The value of notes diminished in one period through an accellerando cannot always be returned in another by a ritardando. What is lost is lost."

The argument still continues, though in a less heated way, for the second half of the twentieth century has had far less interest in rubato playing than did our forefathers. Rubato was only one of the many pianistic questions that agitated the theorists of the last quarter of the nineteenth century. Was there a system of muscular mechanics that would lead to a relaxed and infallible production of tone and technique? Ludwig Deppe thought so. He advocated the principle of "muscular synergy," in which the hand must be freed of the hampering weight of the arm. He was one of the first who interested himself in weight and muscular relaxation, though Moscheles had hinted at it years before. "The arm," Moscheles had written, "should be like lead, the wrist a feather." Deppe, who had considerable influence during the period after 1870, found some of his theories adopted by Leschetizky, and also by Rudolf Breithaupt in his "throw" technique.

In England there was Tobias Matthay, who, in such books as *The Act of Touch* and *The Visible and Invisible in Pianoforte Technique*, broke down the elements of piano playing into a fearsome system. We learn that there are six ways of arm functioning: poised-arm element, the forearm-rotation element, forearm weight, whole-arm weight, forearm down-exertion, upper-arm forward-drive. We learn about touch-forms, weight-touch, touch-construction, weight-transfer, rotary relaxation, rotation-stresses, duration-inflections.

For several decades, starting about 1880, this kind of talk was all the rage. There was a complete revolution against the old fixed-hand position. The new words were weight and relaxation. Arnold Schultz has written, in the introduction to the 1962 edition of Otto Ortmann's *Physiological Mechanics of Piano Technique*, "The winds of doctrine blow hard, and this particular wind swept everything before it. For many years it must have been an exceptional teacher indeed who did not go through the ritual of lifting his student's arm and then dropping it while he spoke the magical words like an incantation."

And this is true. Harriet Brower, in her two volumes entitled *Piano Mastery*, interviewed (up to 1915) scores of eminent pianists, many of whom were also teachers. The great majority of them spoke solemnly about weight and relaxation. Thus Mischa Levitzki: "The principle of relaxation plays a very large part; supple, yielding wrists, arms that hang quite free from the body..." Thus Leopold Godowsky: "Perhaps the most important principle of all—one that I have been elucidating for many years—is relaxation." Thus that admirable artist and ensemble player, Carl Friedberg: "As you see, the condition of the arm is quite loose and relaxed." Thus Ernest Hutcheson: "It may be that nothing can be done until the pupil learns to relax shoulders and arms." Thus Almon Kincaid Virgil, teacher and inventor of the Virgil Practice Clavier (a dummy keyboard that had a big vogue a few generations ago): "I have always taught... the principle of relaxation." Thus Ruth Deyo, the American girl who specialized in MacDowell's piano music: "One of the essentials... is immediate relaxation." Thus Martinus Sieveking: "My method of using relaxed weight..." Thus Harold Henry, a prominent teacher of the day: "Firmness of the hand and relaxation of the arm . . ." Thus Augusta Cottlow, a well-known American pianist and teacher at the turn of the century: "The secret of relaxation lies in the suppleness of the wrist." And so on, ad infinitum.

But most modern theoreticians ridicule the ideas of Matthay, Breithaupt and the other nineteenth-century weight-and-relaxation specialists. In the 1920s, Otto Ortmann cast the stern eye of science (backed by dispassionate laboratory readings) on the subject and demonstrated that it is physically impossible to play even a moderately rapid scale without a tightening, in one degree or another, of wrist, elbow, even shoulder. Ortmann's conclusions included "the need for a partial return to the older school" of Reinecke and Clementi; and he wrote that "undue stress on relaxation has seriously restricted velocity and technical brilliance."

Much was also written about the "Leschetizky system." It must have been a magical system that produced artists as opposed as Artur Schnabel and Ignaz Friedman. Whatever Leschetizky did have, it seemed to work. He himself had been a fine pianist in his day. He was born in Poland (where his name was spelled Leszetycki) in 1830, studied with Czerny in Vienna, concertized and settled in St. Petersburg as a teacher. There he married a singer named Anne Carlowna de Friedbourg. From that point on he married only his pupils. His other three wives were Annette Essipoff, Eugenia Donnemourska and Marie Gabrielle Rosborska. In 1878 he went to Vienna, where he spent almost the rest of his life.

He was a romantic who had little interest in music before Beethoven. Of the *Well-Tempered Clavier* he once said, "Go ahead and play it if it interests you, but why waste time on it when there is all of Beethoven, Schumann, Chopin, Liszt and Brahms to master?" His own repertoire was based on those composers, and he was a most able executant. Arthur Friedheim heard Leschetizky play in London. The old teacher was over seventy, "but he played the Chopin scherzo in a manner that was more than masterly. I mention this because there is a general impression that he was never much of a performer."

Unlike the genial Liszt, Leschetizky was a despot as a teacher. His pupils never knew what to expect. He could be quixotic, generous, kind, choleric, sweet, sarcastic and explosive: a dangerous package. When he took pupils he entered into their private and spiritual lives, wanting to know everything about them and wanting them to consider him a second parent. He took only advanced pianists. If a prospective student had less than what Leschetizky considered a minimum of preparation, the student would have to work a year or more with a *Vorbereiter*—an assistant who would prepare the pupil in Leschetizky basics. Those basics included a good deal of technical drill, a curved hand position and a relaxation of muscles. Pupils would eagerly submit themselves to a heavy preparatory drill because of Leschetizky's prestige. One of his students came to the conclusion that the secret of his success was, simply, authority. "Because of the position of authority which the adulation of hundreds has enabled him to assume, he can insist on an amount of technical drudgery that would appall the average student."

But what was it, exactly, that Leschetizky gave? It has been pointed out that Malwine Brée's book about the "system"—she was a Leschetizky assistant whose book was endorsed by the master himself—is not only inconsistent but (according to such twentieth-century authorities as Ortmann and Schultz) full of anatomical impossibilities. To Ethel Newcomb, another assistant, the secret was in the hand. Leschetizky, she wrote, "would discuss the hand from every point of view; what this sort of hand should do, and why another kind of hand should be held differently and should be required to do otherwise. That is why he often said he had no method. 'To make a pupil play three notes on the piano expressively and with variety of touch, that is my method,' he would say." But to Edwin Hughes, the Leschetizky method was simply "his remarkable ability for taking pains." Fannie Bloomfield Zeisler wrote that "during the five years I was with Leschetizky, he made it very plain that he had no fixed method in the ordinary sense of the word. Like every good teacher, he studied the individuality of each pupil and taught him according to that individuality. It might almost be said that he had a different method for each pupil, and I have often said that Leschetizky's method is to have no fixed method." Arthur Shattuck echoes Bloomfield Zeisler. He contrasts Leschetizky with Liszt, who was primarily a coach and an inspirational force. Leschetizky, says Shattuck, "did not merely [like Liszt] tell a student to do this or that, or suggest a sunset, the reflection of a ruined temple in a pond, or the patriotic emotion that inspired a composition to be written—he showed the student clearly how to produce the effects which the composition demanded. He discovered the students' physical handicaps and found a remedy for them. He explained generously and specifically the art of obtaining (developing) a beautiful, singing tone, to produce a big tone without hardness, a pianissimo tone that would carry to the last row of the top gallery."

Tone, tone, tone! Paderewski had his say about Leschetizky and tone. "The method of Leschetizky is very simple. His pupils learn to evoke a fine tone from the instrument and to make music and not noise. There are principles, you will agree, that are to be uniformly inculcated in every pupil—that is, breadth, softness of touch and precision in rhythm. For the rest, every individual is treated according to the nature of his talent. In one word, it is the method of methods."

If Leschetizky could do this—if he could give his students this kind of tonal resource—he must have had a system of some kind. But where is it? His students have written much, in glorious disagreement, about his teaching. One does not find mention of a method in an essay by Ossip Gabrilowitsch about Leschetizky. The Leschetizky method, he says, is not a set of manual exercises, or fingerings, or hand position. "No. The 'Leschetizky method' might much more accurately be described as the 'Leschetizky attitude' towards music and indeed towards life itself." Gabrilowitsch says that all of Leschetizky's great pupils were individualists. "What a wizard must have been the man who succeeded in developing their musical and pianistic gifts without destroying that which is more precious than anything else in art—individuality!" And Schnabel once said about Leschetizky's teaching, "It was a current which activated or released all the latent vitality in a student's nature. It was addressed to the imagination, to taste, and to personal responsibility. It was not a blueprint or a short cut to success. It did not give the student a prescription, but a task. What he arrived at was truthfulness of expression, and he would not tolerate any violation or deviation from what he felt to be true."

All this approaches metaphysics rather than describing a system. Perhaps the closest anybody has come to describing what it actually might have been was an anonymous pupil writing in the February 1899, issue of *Musician*. "Leschetizky teaches his pupils to save their bodies fatigue by devitalizing (that is the word he uses) the muscles not called into play. Let anyone support the extended arm of another, and then at a given word allow the arm to drop. If it falls to the side instantly and quite limp, it is said to be devitalized, but many people will find difficulty in letting the arm go entirely in this way with all their muscles relaxed." Apparently Leschetizky concentrated on muscular relaxation with those of his pupils who were physically tense.

He himself denied that he had a method. In a letter dated June 5, 1915—this was five months before he died—to Carl Stasny of the New England Conservatory of Music, he wrote, "I am personally against any fixed principle in instruction. Every pupil must, in my opinion, be treated differently according to circumstances. . . . My motto is that with a good, yes, a very good teacher, no printed method will be effective, and only he is a good teacher who can practically demonstrate every possibility to his pupils." This, of course, Leschetizky could do. In his studios were two pianos—a Bechstein and a Bösendorfer (he also had a Steinway in his own room)—and he was constantly illustrating at the second piano. Among his strictures was the falsity of the concept that long hours of practice were beneficial. He would not think of a student working six, seven, eight hours a day. "No one can do that without being mechanical, and that's just what I'm *not* interested in. Two hours, or three at most, is all anyone should require if he will only listen to what he is playing and criticize every note." Presumably he was talking about repertoire rather than technical drill, for his assistants did not stint on exercise assignments to the aspirants. Leschetizky maintained that there were three indispensables for pianistic greatness and would ask prospective pupils three questions, "Were you a child prodigy? Are you of Slavic descent? Are you a Jew?" If all three of these attributes came together, Leschetizky would rub his hands with glee. (He himself was not Jewish, by the way.)

Like most musicians of his generation, Leschetizky's attitude toward the printed note was one of great freedom and leeway. As a student of Czerny, he had a direct link with Beethoven; and Czerny had taught him that Beethoven's piano music was not to be played with strictness. Thus, freedom of delivery was what Leschetizky demanded; and he demanded it in all music. A pedantic, inelastic interpretation of Mozart or Beethoven drove him wild. If his own recorded performances (on piano rolls) of Mozart's C minor Fantasy (K. 475) and Chopin's D flat Nocturne are a reliable guide (piano rolls are *so* untrustworthy), Leschetizky's freedom extended even toward textual changes. Yet he was nineteen years old when Chopin died, and he could very well have had a precedent for the cadenzas he added to the Nocturne. Perhaps Leschetizky heard Liszt play it that way; or perhaps he had access to a manuscript in Chopin's hand

Theodor Leschetitzky and
one of his pupils, Marguerite Melville-Liszniewska.

Julius Schulhoff, whose
artistry in 1850 deeply impressed Leschetitzky.

that contained the variants. Some of Chopin's pupils, including Mikuli, did have written copies of variants that differ considerably from
the published versions.

Leschetizky liked strong hands and muscles. The modern piano,
he said, was not made for a light, trilling, tinkling touch, but "for
the play of little hammers." He would call upon a physical giant like
Sieveking to display his muscles, and he would exclaim over them.
Noted a pupil, "It has become a matter of pleasant rivalry among the
young ladies under him to see which one can show the best bunches
of muscle between her white fingers and along her forearm."

If there was one thing upon which Leschetizky concentrated, it
was tone. He himself had first become super-conscious of tone when
he heard the Bohemian pianist, Julius Schulhoff, around 1850, in
Vienna:

Under his hands [Leschetizky wrote] the piano seemed like another instrument. Seated in a corner, my heart overflowed with indescribable emotions as I listened. Not a note escaped me. I began to foresee a new style of
playing. That melody standing out in bold relief, that wonderful sonority—
all this must be due to a new and entirely different touch. And that cantabile, a legato such as I had not dreamed possible on the piano, a human
voice rising above the sustaining harmonies! I could hear the shepherd sing,
and see him. Then a strange thing happened. He had finished and had
awakened no response. There was no enthusiasm! They were all so accustomed to brilliant technical display that the pure beauty of the interpretation was not appreciated. . . . Dessauer, coming toward me, a slight sneer of
disapproval on his face, asked me what I thought of it. Still very much
moved, I answered: "It is the playing of the future." . . . Schulhoff's playing
was a revelation to me. From that day I tried to find that touch. I thought
of it constantly, and studied the five fingers diligently to learn the method
of production. I practiced incessantly, sometimes even on the table-top,
striving to attain firm finger-tips and a light wrist, which I felt to be the
means to my end. I kept that beautiful sound well in my mind, and it made
the driest work interesting. . . . In the meantime, Schulhoff had conquered
Vienna. Heard in a large hall, his playing produced the proper effect.

All of Leschetizky's pupils were agreed that in his teaching
Leschetizky concentrated more on tone than anything else.
Paderewski, Hambourg, Schnabel and Gabrilowitsch testify that
Leschetizky could not stand an ugly sound; and, says Hambourg,

"he focused his teaching largely on the quality of sound to be produced." According to Hambourg, Leschetizky had suffered through his career as a concert pianist from the disability of having had a thin, bony hand; and he had observed that pianists with fat hands, such as those of Jaëll and Rubinstein, had the most beautiful tone. He also had observed that for brilliance and lightness, the thin, agile hands of Liszt were best. Thus, Leschetizky came to the conclusion that the thin hand had to use considerable key pressure, whereas the fat and heavy hand had to be trained to play with the least amount of pressure.

And it is true that the most famous of Leschetizky's pupils were noted for their tone. This applied as much to the clear, virile sound of a Schnabel as to the colorful and resonant tone of a Paderewski, Friedman or Gabrilowitsch. The secret of Leschetizky's teaching, if there is any secret, was his ability to make his students hear themselves and the tone they produced (something in which very few teachers have ever been successful). In any case, in the mystique of teaching, pupils can make the teacher as much as teachers can make the pupil: if a teacher produces a comet, he is sure to attract meteors. Leschetizky was largely responsible for a comet like Paderewski, and had he not produced a Paderewski he most assuredly would not have been the household word (in musical circles, anyway) that he did become; nor, the chances are, would the young geniuses have rushed to him the way they did. Which is not intended to take anything away from Leschetizky, one of the great teachers in history. If he represented a romantic pattern not especially palatable to this age of ours, all we can do is remember that our patterns may look remarkably silly three generations from now.

XXI

An Archangel Come Down to Earth

LESCHETIZKY'S MOST FAMOUS pupil was the most publicized, most admired, most successful and most legendary pianist after Liszt. With his great aureole of hair, his romantic and courtly presence, his hold over the public, his noble tone, his almost palpable magnetism, poetry, glamour and mystery, Ignacy Jan Paderewski was pianism personified to a good portion of the globe. When Burne-Jones saw him walking the streets of London, he rushed to tell all his friends that he had seen an archangel come down to earth. (Shortly after, the two were introduced, and a famous portrait resulted.) In his more than half a century as a headliner, he earned an estimated ten million dollars. Much of it was made in the United States. As Henry T. Finck gravely explained, "He has a house in Paris, a château in Switzerland, and he has expensive habits and hobbies; so has his wife. He needs, therefore, vast sums of money. These are most easily earned in America."

But was he the greatest pianist of his time? Most of his colleagues did not think so, and his career presents the case of a pianist popular beyond imagination who was not taken too seriously by his fellow pianists. Rosenthal went to hear the phenomenon in London and is said to have come out of the concert shrugging his shoulders. "Yes, he plays well, I suppose, but he's no Paderewski." Reisenauer was once spoken to about Paderewski's culture, his linguistic ability, his fine mind. "Yes," said Reisenauer, "he knows everything—except music." But others of his colleagues were not so much envious as respectful and admiring, with a how-does-he-do-it-on-what-he's-got attitude. "See what Paderewski's personality has accomplished for him," said Sauer. "His long, curly, blond locks, a kind of melancholy atmosphere that he always surrounded himself with, were just what hero-worshipers were looking for. It meant dollars for Paderewski."

He was a public idol, but those who had to work with him were not enchanted with his personality. He seems to have been vain, spoiled and something of a bully, picking on people who were in no position to fight back. Alexander Greiner, manager of the concert and artists department of Steinway, said that he was always surrounded by sycophants and was a terror backstage. Greiner first met him in 1927. Paderewski had an 11 A.M. appointment to try out some pianos for his oncoming tour. He turned up at 4 P.M. and tested six instruments. On each of them he played the entire *Études symphoniques* by Schumann. Greiner was surprised. All other pianists played a few scales and immediately knew if the instrument was or was not to their liking. Greiner said that he never heard Paderewski play well. "I never did understand Paderewski's success as a pianist and do not understand it today."

And it is a fact that when pianists and critics with long memories get together and talk about the fabulous pianists they have heard, Paderewski's name comes up surprisingly seldom. Hofmann, Rachmaninoff, Godowsky, Busoni, Rosenthal, even Pachmann—these are the legends to the professionals. Not Paderewski, and one reason is that most professionals tend to respond primarily to craft. Paderewski was not a great technician—his records from 1911 on amply bear this out—and often he would take the easy way, simplifying difficult passages, or slowing up when the going got too hard. And, too, Paderewski did not help his great career when he appeared in public at an age when he could no longer control his playing. In this he did a disservice to himself and to his art.

Yet nobody could have so thrilled a public for so long without having had something that few artists in history could equal. Wrong notes and all, there was nobility of tone and a sense of style, plus a projection of personality that was awesome. Paderewski took care that his surroundings were in accord with his public image. What with his private railroad car, his chef and butler, his masseur and private physician, his tuner, his wife, and *her* aides, his tours could not be demeaned by so ignoble a word. They were not tours. They were royal processions. He made an impact on women that, in hysteria and abandon, rivaled the triumphs of Liszt. Women would line up to worship the hands insured for a hundred thousand dollars (today they would be insured for ten million). When he left for

STEINWAY AND SONS

Paderewski in 1923, on his return to the concert stage after his term as Prime Minister of Poland.

An unidentified caricature from an American newspaper. The period is probably around 1910. Note the two inscriptions: *Recital Cage or the Feminine-Kiss-Fender*, and *My Hair Help Yourselves*.

Europe, women would rush to the pier to see him off. Paderewski always made good copy, and reporters were never far away. The *New York Sun* of April 23, 1896, had a fairly representative story:

As the White Star steamship Teutonic moved majestically out from her pier yesterday noon, there was heard above the blaring of the band, the shouting of the seamen, the general tumult incidental to the occasion, a high chorus of shrill tones. It was the farewell of Paderewski's feminine admirers.... Previous to the parting chorus, they had mobbed the long-suffering pianist, pressing around him, shaking his hands, giving him flowers, pestering him for autographs, and begging him in tearful voices to come back again soon.

One girl got three autographs from Paderewski, the story goes on to say, "One to frame and hang in my bedroom, one to paste inside the piano to improve its tone, and one to carry with me always." Paderewski could well put up with these bacchantes. He had just earned three hundred thousand tax-free dollars for three months' work in the United States. Much of it came from women. In 1899 a newspaper reporter named Alan Dale described a Paderewski audience, "There I was, simply girled in. A huge and dominant gynarchy seethed around me. There were girls in shirt waists of silk and of flannel; there were girls in loose corsets and in tight corsets. There were large and bouncing girls, and short and stubby ones. There were girls in hats and girls in bonnets. There were girls who wore wedding rings and girls who didn't. There were girls..." As Henry C. Lahee wrote in his *Famous Pianists*, Paderewski was the subject of more newspaper comment than any pianist in history, "and he has been the victim of a greater amount of female adulation than any pianist since Liszt." Of course, Lahee primly adds, "All this had more to do with the business sagacity of his manager than with his art, though it undoubtedly has been greatly assisted by the personal appearance and romantic history of the pianist." The sagacious business manager cited by Lahee was Hugo Görlitz. Many years later, in a reminiscent mood, Görlitz told Leonard Liebling that he had invented the mad rush down the aisles which prevailed in New York concert halls until the fire department stopped the practice in the 1940s. According to Liebling, Görlitz, at each of the early Paderewski concerts, would give fifty tickets to students on condition that they stampede "as though overcome with a mad desire to get a nearer view of Paderewski performing his magic."

Paderewski did not immediately spring to fame, and he bounced around for a very long time before arriving. In a way he was self-taught, for although his musical impulse manifested itself at the early age usual for anyone who is going to develop into an important pianist—four, or thereabouts—he had no systematic instruction until he was twelve. This is an important fact to remember, for he had been badly trained, and that helps explain his later difficulties. He did not have the chance to build up the set of reflexes a gifted child should have had, and thus his life ended up a struggle with the technical difficulties of the piano. His lack of basic training can also account for his nervousness before the public. All artists are nervous before going on, but Paderewski was pitiable and often had to be pushed out. Down deep, he must have lacked confidence, knowing better than anybody else his limitations.

It was not until he entered the Warsaw Conservatory at the age of twelve that he received decent instruction. But his bad technical habits were by that time ingrained, and he received no encouragement at the conservatory. He was told, repeatedly, that he had no talent and would never make a pianist. The strange thing is that by all odds these predictions should have turned out true, for Paderewski had started serious training too late and had nothing but determination to offer. When he toured Russia three years later it was with a remarkable lack of success. This gave support to his teachers' predictions. From all accounts, Paderewski on this initial tour sprayed the air of Russia with false notes. He returned to the Warsaw Conservatory, then studied in Berlin and, finally, with Leschetizky in Vienna. Paderewski was twenty-four at the time, and only a dogged person in love with the piano would still have been looking for a career at that age, much less looking for a piano teacher. But Leschetizky was the answer. "He taught me more in those few lessons than I had learned in the whole twenty-four years preceding that time," Paderewski later said. Leschetizky at first despaired of doing anything with the persistent Pole. He put him on Czerny exercises and worked with him on tonal production. "It's too late! It's too late!" Leschetizky would cry. "Your fingers lack discipline! You do not know how to work!" But work he did, with a dedicated intensity that almost scared Leschetizky.

Paderewski made his official debut in Vienna in 1887 and played in Paris the following year. It was in Paris that the craze started. His recital was a sensation, and the two most important conductors, Colonne and Lamoureux, hastened to invite Paderewski to play with their orchestras. Paderewski was not ready. At that time he had no concertos in his repertoire, and only one recital program. He worked up a second program in three weeks, nearly killing himself. In 1890 he was in London, billed as The Lion of Paris. This the British public did not like. Such flamboyant advertising was in bad taste and definitely un-English. So was that enormous head of golden-red hair. A young critic named George Bernard Shaw found a few things to admire, however. "His charm lies in his pleasant spirit and his dash of humor. . . . He makes a recital as little oppressive as it is in the nature of such a thing to be." But soon Shaw was complaining of Paderewski's rhythm. "The license of his tempo rubato goes beyond all reasonable limits . . . an immensely spirited young harmonious blacksmith."

He came to America in 1891, under the auspices of the Steinway piano firm, and made his debut in the new Carriage Hall on November 17, 1891. Walter Damrosch conducted the orchestra. The audience was not big, most of it was papered, and the gross that night was only five hundred dollars. But never again. Though the critics had reservations, the audience went wild. "He is not the ideal pianist," said the *New York Times*. The public gave no heed. On his opening program Paderewski played two concertos—the Saint-Saëns Fourth and his own A minor. His schedule in New York called for three concerts with orchestra, including six concertos, in one week, plus solo groups at each concert. Paderewski was to shudder, in later life, at this insane schedule. He practiced seventeen hours daily for an entire week, and at the end of his series he had become the biggest attraction New York had ever seen. Steinway immediately increased his tour. He had been engaged for eighty concerts with a guarantee of thirty thousand dollars. Instead he played 107 concerts, with an agreeably appropriate raise in his net income. His programs were far from fluff. In Chicago he played five Beethoven sonatas— the *Waldstein*, the *Appassionata* and the last three, and also Bach's *Chromatic Fantasy and Fugue* in addition to the expected pieces by Chopin, Liszt and himself (the Minuet in G, of course). Emil Liebling, Liszt's fine pupil and the dean of pianists in Chicago, commented on Paderewski's magnetism. He did suggest that Beethoven was not Paderewski's strong point. "Both Joseffy and Rummel have presented this sonata [the *Waldstein*] to us in all its glory, and far superior to Paderewski both technically and emotionally." But Paderewski nevertheless impressed Liebling as "*sui generis*" and a "sublime" artist.

It is possible that he never played at his best after his 1891 tour. Midway through, he threw a muscle during a concert. Despite excruciating pain he finished. Medical men diagnosed torn and strained tendons. He lost the use of his fourth finger and had to refinger everything. After the tour he got all kinds of treatment in Paris. But he was never completely cured, and for all one knows he was never again the pianist who came to America in 1891.

Many of America's musicians were at first bowled over. "It seems to me," wrote William Mason, "that in this matter of touch, Paderewski is as near perfection as any pianist I have ever heard, while in other respects he stands more nearly on a plane with Liszt than any other virtuoso since Tausig." The knowledgeable Mason then put his finger on exactly what was special in Paderewski's playing. "It possesses that subtle quality expressed in some measure by the German word *Sehnsucht*, and in English as 'intensity of aspiration.' This quality Chopin had, and Liszt frequently spoke of it. It is the undefinably poetic haze with which Paderewski invests and surrounds all that he plays which renders him so unique and impressive among modern pianists."

By 1896 Paderewski had made three tours of the United States, and had netted (according to Hugo Görlitz) half a million dollars. He was the greatest drawing card in American musical history. At one concert, in Chicago, the receipts were $7,382—unheard of in those days. Four concerts in one week—two in Chicago, two in St. Louis —brought in $21,000. Audiences would refuse to leave the hall and often insisted on encores for a solid hour. As many as a thousand people would clamber on the stage and insist on shaking hands with the pianist. In Texas whole schools traveled many miles to see him. All over America, crowds waited at railroad crossings to see his private car pass, hoping to get a glimpse of the Paderewski profile. Often crowds would line the streets from hotel to concert hall.

Of course he was constantly in the news; and when he wasn't, he strove to make his own news, as when he tipped a cab driver two hundred dollars, getting thousands of dollars of publicity for the outlay. Sometimes he was unconsciously funny, as in an 1896 *New*

York Herald interview. He was asked about musical taste in the United States and how it had progressed since his first visit in 1891. "It is a solid, wholesome growth," Paderewski said, very seriously. "I have one way of judging: four years ago my receipts for one performance in Chicago, for instance, were $2,000. Three years ago they were $3,500. This year they were $7,348; this is, understand, for one night only. In St. Louis, three years ago, for two nights the receipts were $3,000. This year for two nights they were up to $9,000."

But the honeymoon did not last too long. Critics began to accuse Paderewski of pounding, of wrong notes and erratic rhythms. As early as 1900 he began to get bad reviews, and by 1916 judgments like this were being written: "uneven and unsatisfactory reading, with faulty technique, punching on the part of the left hand, and plenty of wrong notes." To many critics his worst feature was "the blurred rhythms"; and another annoyance was his increasing "breaking of hands." Paderewski was far from the only pianist who used this breaking device; it was heard from many romantic pianists. In "breaking," the left hand slightly anticipates the right hand. Word about Paderewski's pianistic fallibility was getting around, and the critic of the *Los Angeles Graphic*, on October 28, 1916, wrote that if he were still teaching piano he would forbid his students to attend a Paderewski recital. "It is a pity that so great an artist should lose prestige with the portion of the world that lives in the same art as he—for I have not heard one musician voice an opinion other than the one here expressed." And the famous critic H. T. Parker, in Boston, called Paderewski "a pale reflex of his former self."

It made no difference. Paderewski remained "the world's greatest pianist" and the supreme drawing card in music. He made several world tours, he luxuriated in his Swiss villa and his California ranch, and he composed until 1917. Little of his music has remained in the repertoire. During World War I, he worked hard for Poland, raising money and acting as the spokesman of his people. After the war he became the first Premier of Poland. He had a racist streak in him and, in some newspaper interviews, fulminated against the "foreign blood" that was emigrating to America. He said that it would spoil "the pure, rich Anglo-Saxon strain" that had made America great. In his will he left forty thousand rubles "to start economic associations to open little stores in [Polish] villages to help fight Jews who mostly run these stores and refuse to be assimilated."

He recorded copiously, but unsatisfactorily. In difficult music his tempos are always on the safe side, and his playing is ultra-careful. His ability to shape a telling phrase comes through the discs, and so does a suggestion of what must have been one of the most glorious sounds in pianistic history. But he never had much technical authority, and his rhythms do tend to be flurried and eccentric. His best recording is probably the disc of Liszt's Tenth Rhapsody. The opening is marvelous: stately, noble, big in every way; and the glissando sections are done with grace and style. At the coda, though, his weaknesses become apparent, and the final pages are a rather desperate scramble. Obviously Paderewski triumphed through manner rather than solid craft. His performance on records of the Wagner-Liszt *Spinning Song* is also probably typical of him at his best. On the other hand, some of his recordings, such as the Rubinstein *Valse Caprice*, have almost as many notes left out as there are in, and many of those that are in are false. If Paderewski sounded like this, or like the work on his 1906 piano roll of Chopin's A flat Ballade, his playing must have been utterly impossible.

Not that it made any difference. Audiences to the very end battered at the doors to attend a Paderewski recital. Anybody who said that he was not the greatest living pianist would have been mobbed. In the public eye, "Paderooski" was the personification of the piano. As a composer he enjoyed fair success, mostly because of his personal popularity. None of his music except the Minuet in G is heard any more in America, however, and very little even in his native Poland. Even Paderewski's trimphant return to the concert stage in 1923, after his term as Prime Minister of Poland, failed to salvage his music.

He kept playing to the end of his life: a tired old man whose trembling fingers tried unsuccessfully to evoke the grandeur of his youth. But in his great days before the turn of the century he was a phenomenon: a man who hewed for himself, by sheer force of will, an improbable and fantastic career despite the fact that he had fewer pianistic gifts than many of his colleagues. The man had style and a big heart; and he had immense dignity and glamour; and he could produce golden sounds; and he was an unparalleled showman. And so while his competitors were counting his wrong notes, he was counting his dollars.

XXII

The Little Giant, and Other Liszt-Made Giants

OF ALL THE BRILLIANT talent that crowded Liszt's last classes at Weimar, he was proudest of the diminutive Eugene (or Eugen) d'Albert—tiny in size, but with such a heroic approach to the keyboard that he was called The Little Giant. In his relatively short career before the public—short because though he lived to the age of sixty-eight (he died in 1932) he became more interested in composing than in playing the piano—he was considered by many the greatest virtuoso of his age, and Liszt could think of no better compliment than to refer to him as the second Tausig. Liszt first ran across d'Albert in 1882, and he wrote to Sayn-Wittgenstein on Nov. 24:

There was also an artist, an *extrordinary* pianist, by the name of d'Albert. Richter [Hans Richter, the eminent conductor] introduced me to him in Vienna last April. Since then he has worked at Weimar, without interruption, under my tutelage. Among the young virtuosos from the time of Tausig—Bülow and Rubinstein naturally remain the Senators and Masters —I know of no more gifted as well as dazzling talent than d'Albert.

"Our young lion," as Liszt called d'Albert ("Albertus Magnus" was another of Liszt's pet names for Eugene), had come from Scotland, the son of a French father and a German (though some authorities say English) mother. In 1876 he went to London, studying under Ernst Pauer. His harmony and counterpoint teacher was Sir Arthur Sullivan. D'Albert would bring reams of compositions to him, and Sir Arthur would say, "Good gracious, my dear boy, do you expect

310

The Little Giant—Eugene d'Albert. Liszt referred to him as "The second Tausig."

me ever to get through this?" The composer of *Pinafore* and *Mikado* was not the most gifted of teachers. Perhaps experiences like this soured d'Albert on England. He went to Vienna and ended his studies at Weimar. It was in Germany that he found his spiritual home. He considered himself half German to begin with; and after a few years in Germany he considered himself *all* German. He was rabid on the subject; and, being the peppery, testy, hair-triggered man he was, he was constantly bringing the fight to the "enemy." As early as 1884, when he was twenty years old, he wrote to a German paper correcting a biographical note:

DEAR SIR:

... Permit me to correct a few errors I find therein. Above all things I scorn the title "English pianist." Unfortunately I studied for a considerable period in that land of fogs, but during that time I learned absolutely nothing; indeed, had I remained there much longer, I should have gone to utter ruin.... Only since I left that barbarous land have I begun to live. And I live now for the unique, true, glorious, German art.

Naturally when World War I came he felt no allegiance to England and considered himself a German. By that time he had taken strong roots in Germany, having succeeded Joachim in 1907 as director of the High School of Music in Berlin. And by that time, too, he was well established as a composer. His *Tiefland*, the seventh of his twenty operas, had made an enormous success (it is still occasionally revived), and his second hit, *Die toten Augen*, was finished right in the middle of the war, in 1916. The British called him a renegade. But d'Albert had given England fair warning. Long before the war he had written a letter to the *Times* declaring his intention to slough off forever his allegiance to a country that was in his opinion unworthy to harbor any artistic talent. D'Albert's life was nothing if not tempestuous. That included his private life. He had six wives, the second of whom was the equally tempestuous, brilliant, handsome Venezuelan genius of the keyboard, Teresa Carreño. *That* marriage did not last long. Carreño could give even d'Albert lessons in temperament.

The great days of d'Albert as a pianist extended roughly from Liszt's death to the early years of the twentieth century, a span of some twenty years. After that he was too busy composing to keep his

technique in virtuoso shape—or probably (judging from his recordings) in any shape at all. But in his day he must have been extraordinary. He was considered not only the greatest Beethoven pianist, but
also the best all-around pianist and the successor of Liszt. "The
crown of piano playing in our time has been won by Eugene
d'Albert.... On him the mantle of Liszt has fallen in our
generation.... The seriousness of Brahms's concertos, the murmur-
ing of Chopin's *Berceuse*, the titanic power of his A minor Étude, the
grace of Liszt's *Soirées de Vienne*, the solemnity of Bach move under
his hand, without one taking the least from the other. It is objectivity, but we do not cry out for subjectivity: it is personality, but we
do not miss the rapport with eternity." So wrote Oscar Bie around
the turn of the century. As a progressive composer himself, d'Albert
investigated the modern school and was one of the first to play Debussy in Germany. Ernest Hutcheson well remembered the surprised look on d'Albert's face when the pieces were hissed by
German audiences.

His performances of Beethoven were considered definitive. Bruno
Walter has written of the impression d'Albert made on him, "I shall
never forget the titanic force in his rendition of Beethoven's Concerto in E flat major. I am almost tempted to say he did not play it;
he personified it. In his intimate contact with his instrument he
appeared to me like a new centaur, half piano, half man." Nearly
every critic found himself using the word "titanic" in relation to The
Little Giant. Indeed, when d'Albert made his New York debut on
November 18, 1889, Henry Krehbiel found him *too* titanic for Chopin. But when d'Albert got around to playing the Beethoven Fourth
and the *Emperor*, Krehbiel hurled the adjectives: "magnificent...
strong... reverent... profound." "Fingers of steel," Krehbiel concluded.

D'Albert left many recordings, most of them extremely rare.
These discs can cause nothing but embarrassment. He made them at
a time when his technique was in deplorable condition; and even
considering the freedom and actual license granted to performers in
the last century, his playing is eccentric, sloppy and undisciplined.
Once in a while, as in the Weber *Invitation* or Chopin's F sharp
Nocturne, there are hints of the grand—indeed, overwhelming—
style he must have had at his peak. Otherwise the playing is inexplicable, full of wrong notes, memory lapses and distorted rhythms;

and one can only conjecture that he went to the studios with a what-the-hell attitude, figuring that nobody would hear his discs and they would be nonexistent in a few years.

Other pupils of Liszt's last years made no such immediate impact as d'Albert, but they had much longer careers. One of the most discussed and possibly the greatest was Moriz Rosenthal, who continued playing until the 1940s. Rosenthal was Polish, studied under Mikuli in Lvov before coming to Liszt, and was considered one of the most stupendous technicians ever to touch a keyboard. A short, rather portly man with a massive head and fierce Kaiser Wilhelm mustaches, he stormed the piano as few before or since ever did. And yet he had a wide dynamic palette which included delicate sounds that could compare with de Pachmann's feather pianissimos. Hanslick threw up his hands and called Rosenthal a conjuror. Fellow pianists were amazed. "I heard Rosenthal in Berlin when he was about twenty-seven," Josef Hofmann has written. Hofmann would have been thirteen at the time. "He was *terrific*, and I started pounding the piano at our Berlin home for six hours daily, trying to imitate Rosenthal."

Indeed, it was probably not until the young Vladimir Horowitz that pianism once again encountered such speed, power and endurance. When Rosenthal played the Liszt E flat Concerto, one of his specialties, it was like a thunderbolt. And, like a thunderbolt, it was uncontrolled. The young Rosenthal tended to belabor the piano, and Hanslick gently chided him. "Through many years of acquaintance with modern piano virtuosity, I have almost forgotten what it is to be astonished, but I found young Rosenthal's achievements indeed astonishing." But also too violent. "Such impetuosity may well subside with the years, as it did with Liszt and Tausig." And when Krehbiel heard Rosenthal on his first American tour, in 1888 (in company with a young violinist named Fritz Kreisler, who got fifty dollars a performance), he said pretty much what Hanslick had said. He heard Rosenthal play, among other things, Liszt's Third Rhapsody and *Don Juan Fantasy*, and wrote, "To New Yorkers there is nothing novel in brilliant pianoforte playing, but it can fairly be questioned whether an audience composed of experienced and discriminating music lovers in this city was ever before stirred to such a pitch of excitement . . . a phenomenal master of the mechanical side of piano playing" but, said Krehbiel, a little lacking in poetry.

The young Moriz Rosenthal—speed, power, endurance.

Rosenthal in the last year of his life.

That was to come. As Rosenthal grew older he bore out Hanslick's prediction by developing, along with his remarkable virtuosity, a good deal of finesse. And in his last years, when he could no longer thunder, he concentrated on beauty of tone and liquid phrasing. Fortunately he left many recordings—over forty—though nowhere near the amount a pianist of his prestige should have made. He did not make his first disc until he was past sixty. The only concerto he was assigned was the Chopin E minor—a "straight," curiously stolid performance. His Edison disc of the Chopin C major Étude (Op. 10, No. 1) and the F major Prélude are of extreme beauty, however; and in his own *Papillons* and his Strauss paraphrases he is all over the keyboard in great style. Elegance, plasticity, charm and control, not to mention a staggering technique (much of it in pianissimo work, more difficult than any amount of fortissimo banging) mark his playing here. In his last years, when he lost his strength, he substituted a dynamic range that went from a triple pianissimo to mezzo forte, and his disc of the Schubert-Liszt *Soirée de Vienne* in A minor, as well as some Chopin mazurkas and waltzes, testify to the unerring stylistic insights of the grand veteran, then well in his seventies. (But a posthumously issued disc of the Chopin B minor Sonata and other works does him a disservice. There are flashes of greatness, but when he made those discs Rosenthal had lost control.)

He was a witty man, and a malicious one. In all the thirty years he knew him, Arthur Shattuck said, he never heard Rosenthal say a kind word about any of his fellow artists. Some of the bons mots attributed to Rosenthal are well known, though stories attributed to musicians are hard to pin down. They have a habit of being attributed to too many other people. At any rate, Rosenthal is supposed to have said, when he heard that Arthur Schnabel had been rejected by the army, "Well, what did you expect? No fingers!" On one occasion, when a group of pianists were signing a joint letter, the last one to pick up the pen found only a tiny space for his name. "What am I supposed to write down here?" he indignantly asked. "Your repertoire," said Rosenthal. Once he was forced to listen to a prodigy. The conversation is said to have run something like this:

"How old are you?"

"Seven, sir."

"And what would you like to play for me?"

"Please, sir, the Tchaikovsky concerto, sir."

"Too old!"

It may have been this prodigy whom Rosenthal met a few years later and asked, "Tell me, how old are you still?"

Emil von Sauer made his impact differently than Rosenthal. Instead of hurling thunderbolts, he caressed the piano in a suave, polished manner. Born in Hamburg, he had studied with Nicholas Rubinstein at the Moscow Conservatory from 1879 to 1881. Then he went to Liszt, but he took a rather dim view of being called a Liszt pupil. On one occasion he even denied it. He told an interviewer in 1895, "It is not correct to regard me as a pupil of Liszt, though I stayed with him for a few months. He was then very old, and could not teach me much. My chief teacher has been, undoubtedly, Nicholas Rubinstein."

Liszt or no, Sauer gained the respect of the toughest of all critics —his own colleagues. Even Josef Hofmann, not notoriously generous to many pianists, called Sauer "a truly great virtuoso." He left about thirty recordings before his death in 1942, including performances of both Liszt concertos that he made at the age of seventy-seven. In these records Sauer stands revealed as a smooth pianist who inclined toward relaxed tempos and exactitude of detail rather than explosive bursts of temperament. He was a sensitive and eminently satisfactory artist, one with style and taste, at once poet and virtuoso.

Alfred Reisenauer, who unfortunately left no recordings, also must have been something out of the ordinary. His keyboard approach was quite different from Sauer's. Reisenauer is forgotten today (he did not even rate a listing in the 1955 edition of *Grove's Dictionary*), but in the 1890s it was he who many critics thought most resembled Liszt. Liszt himself seems to have been of the same opinion and is reported to have said that Reisenauer did very closely approach his style, "yet without imitation." He accepted Reisenauer as a pupil in 1874, when the boy was only eleven (of the hundreds of Liszt pupils, only half a dozen or so came to him as prodigies), and he saw him through his first public concert in 1879.

Reisenauer was a very fat man. Liszt put it most delicately, "*Malheureusement trop sujet à l'embonpoint.*" He was big and his playing was big. Like Busoni, he was attracted to the colossal items of the repertoire—pieces like the *Hammerklavier* and the more elaborate of

Emil von Sauer, suave and polished.

Rafael Joseffy: the poet, the Patti of the Piano, the colorist.

the Liszt operatic paraphrases. He had an urge to travel and was one of the first pianists to tour Siberia, Persia and Asia Minor. Most critics considered him a stupendous technician and a romantic colorist who was uneasy in the pre-Beethoven repertoire. His forte was romantic music. Clarence Adler, who studied with him in Leipzig during the summer of 1907, says that Reisenauer had an unparalleled tone production. "Such richness and quality! I used to think of gold." Unfortunately he was an alcoholic. He could put away a full bottle of champagne with each lesson—and he gave many lessons. There are stories of him weaving to the piano and letting his reflexes take over. Johannes Magendanz, a pupil of Klindworth, once wrote an interesting little sketch of Reisenauer:

When that bulky man seated himself at the piano, and sat there like a rock, a picture of massive imperturbability and sovereign competence, one felt assured that a treat was in store as only few could offer. I remember only a few of the things he did: the *Chromatic Fantasy and Fugue*, the A major Sonata and A major Rondo by Mozart, the C major Fantasias by Schubert and Schumann, all the Préludes by Chopin, Beethoven's *Hammerklavier* and *Diabelli* Variations, and among Liszt's works the Fourteenth Rhapsody and the *Fantasy from Auber's Muette de Portici*, which is rarely attempted. He never moved, whether he played pianissimo or fortissimo, even when evoking the sonority of an orchestra; his hands and fingers moved quietly over the keyboard. Never any thrashing; mellowness and fullness prevailed all of the time. He must have possessed enormous muscular strength which he could control at will. . . . You know, I suspect that Papa Liszt's cognac bottle gave the start to Reisenauer's love for drinking. Then we ought to remember that traveling in Russia and Siberia, the home of the fabulous drinkers, vodka at that, must have made matters worse. And it ended tragically in Lebau, a Russian city, where he was found dead in his hotel room after a brilliant recital.

The brilliant Rafael Joseffy was another favorite Liszt pupil and, from all accounts, one of the greatest pianists of the nineteenth century. He was a Hungarian, born in 1852, and he studied with Moscheles, Reinecke, Tausig and finally Liszt in 1870 and 1871. Joseffy, of all the Liszt pupils, was a miniaturist—the essence of delicacy and poetry, the master of a singing tone and pianissimo shadings. The Patti of the Piano, he was called, There was steel in his playing, too, but a well-tempered steel with a sharp cutting edge. If Huneker is to be believed, "Joseffy stands today [1911] for all that is exquisite and poetic in the domain of the piano. His touch is original, his manipulation of the instrument unapproachable, a virtuoso among virtuosi, and the beauty of his tone, its velvety, aristocratic quality, so free from any suspicion of harshness or brutality, gives him a unique position in the music-loving world. There is magic in his attack, magic and moonlight in his playing of a Chopin nocturne, and brilliancy—a meteor-like brilliancy—in his performance of a Liszt concerto. This rare combination of the virtuoso and the poet places Joseffy outside the pale of 'popular pianism.'"

Huneker was notoriously exuberant, and in addition he had been Joseffy's assistant for a while; but he was a brilliant critic and he knew the piano as well as any living mortal. His summation is echoed by anybody who ever heard Joseffy. He must have been the most supple and elegant of pianists—a de Pachmann, but with control, and also with a fine musical mind. He spent much of his career in America. After several years of concertizing in Europe, he made his American debut in New York on October 13, 1879, at Chickering Hall. With an orchestra conducted by Walter Damrosch, he played the Chopin E minor and Liszt E flat concertos, interspersing them with solo groups. Then he went on tour. A Boston critic stated, "We have never heard in any artist (Rubinstein, von Bülow, Essipoff included) a more near approach to absolute perfection in every element of technique and of execution. The evenness and ease of all the runs and arpeggios; the commanding, penetrating power, always expressively graduated and shaded; the positive intensity (so different from 'pounding') with which significant single tones were struck and made to vibrate through and through the listener..." This went on for a column, concluding with: "It was the general feeling that here is a man who unites *all* the qualities of a complete pianist with no weakness or flaws anywhere."

Joseffy finally settled in New York, making his home in Tarrytown. Mostly he taught, privately and at the National Conservatory of Music in New York City. In later years he played less and less in public. He would say that he was getting older and that he found it ever harder to do things he once did with ease. Thus his career was marked by relatively few concerts. What a shame that this aristocratic artist never recorded! He must have been a prince of pianists.

Somewhat in Joseffy's style was Arthur de Greef, the Belgian pupil of Liszt. Shaw heard him in London and was impressed. "Mr. de Greef is a true Belgian, spirited, brilliant, neat, confident, clever, and intensely happy in the consciousness of being all that. His execution is extremely ambidextrous and he has a prodigious musical gift, besides having a fair share of sense and taste." His recordings do indeed display sensitivity and musical culture.

Another elegant product of Liszt was Bernhard Stavenhagen, one of the last pupils (he actually was beside Liszt when he died) and a fine, serious artist. Hanslick called this German the perfect pianist. Unfortunately he left no recordings (to be accurate, he does seem to have made a Pathé record, but no American collector has come across it). Frederic Lamond, born in Scotland, was considered a Beethoven specialist and—unlike Joseffy, Reisenauer and Stavenhagen—did pile up a large discography before he died in 1948, the last but one of the important Liszt pupils. These recordings are puzzling. Whenever he had anything difficult to play, such as the *Muette de Portici*, or even the last movement of the *Moonlight* Sonata, he failed quite devastatingly. Obviously he was not a strong technician. But he was a stylist, and his pellucid performance of the first movement of the *Moonlight*, as well as his altogether grand playing of Liszt's Étude in D flat, show that he had imagination, if not fingers.

There was the strange Josef Weiss, who worked with Liszt in the 1870s. Some people thought he was great, and among his admirers was Gustav Mahler, Alma Mahler, in her biography of her husband, well remembered Weiss. She writes that the pianist had "a square, bald skull, with the merest tuft in the middle, and brown eyes wedged in slits, which could only mean insanity or genius." There *was* something strange about him, and even Mahler, his staunch supporter, had to admit that Weiss was too eccentric to play in public. The one time Mahler tried to help him was the last; it was not worth it. It seems that he engaged Weiss for a Mozart concerto, and the rehearsal ended up with the pianist throwing the music at Mahler's feet. The orchestra players, thinking that Mahler was being attacked, flung themselves upon Weiss. Then the newspapers took it up, exaggerating as usual. "WEISS HITS MAHLER ON THE HEAD." Weiss made at least one recording, a Parlophone disc of Liszt's Twelfth Rhapsody. It is an example of the Liszt school at its worst—eccentric, inaccurate, rhythmically unstable.

Arthur de Greef, still another well-known pupil of Liszt.

Arthur Friedheim, who copied many of Liszt's mannerisms.

Arthur Friedheim made a much better reputation. At first, Liszt fought shy of this Russian-born pianist. He did not like his playing, although he was forced to admit the individuality of his style. Or was the trouble Friedheim's teacher? Friedheim had studied in St. Petersburg with Anton Rubinstein; and, deep down, there was no love lost between Rubinstein and Liszt. Liszt played coy, and Friedheim had to play for him several times before being accepted as a pupil in 1880. Eventually Liszt became so fond of Friedheim that he made him his personal secretary.

Friedheim had an exceptionally broad style in the so-called grand manner. He also had such a hero-worshiping crush on *Der Meister* that he copied many of his mannerisms. Busoni, who heard him in 1883, was amused no end:

Pose is the order of the day. There is a pianist here called Friedheim, a pupil of Liszt, with long hair and a face that looks half severe, half bored. When he plays he comes forward and bows in such a way that his hair covers his face; then he throws his head back to tidy his mane. Then he sits down with a great deal of fuss, and looks around waiting until the audience is quiet; then he seizes the keys "as the wild beast seizes his prey," to quote Hanslick. But the loveliest thing is to see him during the *tuttis* of the orchestra. There he has room to show off all his tricks. He examines his nails, considers the audience, thrusts his hands into his hair, and does other silly things.

Friedheim settled in the United States in 1915. Even before making his home in New York, however, he had been invited to settle here as conductor of the New York Philharmonic. He was offered the position in 1898 and again in 1911. He was a good conductor, but he preferred to concentrate on the piano. Around 1912 he made three recordings for Columbia. They are not distinguished, and one of them is a curiosity—Chopin's *Funeral March*, in which Friedheim plays to the end of the trio and then, having no more room on the record, simply stops. And so he was content to record two-thirds of Chopin's *Funeral March*. On records his playing is reminiscent of the playing of Conrad Ansorge, who had studied with Liszt in 1885 and 1886. Both pianists sound heavy and not too accurate technically.

Two other Liszt pupils of great reputation who settled in America were Alexander Siloti and Constantin von Sternberg. Siloti came out of the Moscow Conservatory, where he had studied piano with Nicholas Rubinstein and composition with Tchaikovsky. He was with Liszt from 1883 to 1886. Then he returned to Moscow and became a professor at the conservatory. Among his pupils there was his cousin (two years younger than himself), Sergei Rachmaninoff. In 1890 Siloti left the conservatory to become a recitalist. He lived in Germany and came to the United States in 1922. From 1924 to 1944, a year before his death at the age of eighty-two, he taught at the Juilliard School of Music in New York. He had an immense hand, and his pupils still talk about the way he played the left-hand octaves in the Chopin A flat Polonaise, fingering them 2-3-4-5. Siloti made no records and played very little in public. His style has been described as a combination of vitality and refinement, backed by a big technique.

Sternberg also was Russian. He studied with Moscheles, switched to conducting and achieved a fine reputation before going back to the piano and to Liszt. In 1888 he became an American citizen, living first in Atlanta and then in Philadelphia. He was reputedly a fine pianist and was also an intellectual who contributed sensitive articles on piano playing and esthetics to various American publications.

The last of the major Liszt pupils to pass away was José Vianna da Motta, the Portuguese pianist who died in Lisbon on June 1, 1948. During most of his life, da Motta concerned himself with various musical activities in Portugal. On the few occasions he did concertize, he aroused admiration. A scholar, a reliable editor, a writer on musical subjects, a composer, a close friend and associate of Busoni, da Motta was a superior man as well as a superior musician. He made a few recordings toward the end of his life, and in them are traces of a noble style.

Did these pupils of Liszt have anything in common? One wonders, when thinking of pianists as dissimilar as Lamond and Rosenthal, Sauer and Friedheim, Joseffy and Reisenauer, or, for that matter, von Bülow and Tausig. Liszt, after all, founded no school and as a teacher was mainly an inspirational force. Most of the Liszt players did have "line," tone and a romantic approach. But, then again, the same could be said of the Leschetizky pupils. All that can be said is that Liszt was the greatest romantic pianist, and his pupils got, through osmosis if by no other means, the romanticism that he exemplified. Which meant concentration on tone, a good deal of bravura, freedom in phrase and rhythm (uncontrolled in some pupils, but delightfully handled by others of the caliber of Rosenthal, de Greef, Sauer and, one feels certain, Joseffy), and perhaps the notion that the piano and the pianist came first, the music second. But there was never any such thing as a Liszt school of playing. His students, having sat at his feet, rose to depart on their respective ways and play according to their respective philosophies, as have all students of all teachers from the beginning of time.

XXIII

Some of the Leschetizky Group

LESCHETIZKY DIED IN 1915 and some of his most famous pupils had careers extending past the sixth decade of the twentieth century. Among his early male pupils, though, two who commanded a great deal of attention were Mark Hambourg and Ossip Gabrilowitsch. There could not have been a greater disparity between the two. Hambourg was a big stylist and an inaccurate technician, while Gabrilowitsch was as polished and refined a musician as Joseffy must have been.

Hambourg came out of Russia as a child prodigy, making his debut in Moscow in 1888 at the age of nine. Two years later he played in London, and Paderewski, who heard the boy, advanced him the money to study with Leschetizky. Paderewski thought that Hambourg was the greatest natural talent he had ever heard and spread the word to such good effect that concert managers came around seething. A word from Paderewski was a password, and Hambourg's career was well launched. His Viennese debut was auspicious enough. Sophie Menter became ill, and Hambourg replaced her—at Leschetizky's suggestion—at the last minute in Liszt's *Hungarian Fantasia* with the Berlin Philharmonic, which was then making an appearance in Vienna. Hambourg swept all before him, and that night at a banquet Brahms proposed a toast to "the youth who has played this evening." He was sixteen then, and he almost immediately started touring. For many years he was in constant demand.

There was something volcanic about Hambourg's style. With complete disdain for anything so prosaic as technical accuracy, he would pile sonority on top of sonority. His records, and he made many, are often incredible. Through them, to be sure, one does get

326

something of the vitality of the man and the excitement that he must have brought to music. But one also gets a profusion of wrong notes, text changes, even halting passages that would make his playing inexplicable today.

Gabrilowitsch was a much more finished workman. He had as much right to be called (as he so often was) The Poet of the Piano as any pianist in this century. He studied with Rubinstein in St. Petersburg, won the Rubinstein Prize in 1894, finished off with Leschetizky after Rubinstein's death, and made his debut in Berlin in 1896. In 1900 he made his first American tour, and from 1904 to 1918 lived in Munich as conductor of the Konzertverein. Then he settled in the United States, becoming a citizen in 1921, and alternated between concertizing and conducting the Detroit Symphony from 1918 until his death in 1938. He had married an American in 1906. She was Clara Clemens, daughter of Mark Twain.

Gabrilowitsch was a much-admired man and musician. Slim, aristocratic-looking, with a mass of hair à la Paderewski and an unusually high wing collar (he probably wore it to minimize a long neck), he would sit quietly at the piano and coax it rather than pound. He had at his command an unusual variety of nuance and the utmost musical elegance. From the beginning critics raved about his tone. A critic in the *Deutsches Volksblatt* of Vienna wrote in 1906 about Gabrilowitsch's "singing touch, shadow-like pianissimos and the power which never seems to force itself upon one." That review could stand as *the* Gabrilowitsch review; in essence it was to be repeated ad infinitum.

Like most Leschetizky pupils he concentrated on the romantic repertoire, with a good deal of Russian music thrown in and—fairly unusual for a pianist of his schooling—a few Mozart concertos. One of his specialties was to give a concerto series—nineteen concertos at four concerts. This he first did in 1914, continuing it intermittently until his death. He also followed Rubinstein's lead in presenting a series of six historical programs, though those he played only early in his career.

He made pitifully few recordings. The most ambitious was the Schumann Piano Quintet, with the Flonzaley Quartet—one acoustic version (abridged) and one early electric (complete). Here can be heard the patrician art of Gabrilowitsch. It is characteristic that he was one of the very first of the great pianists to record chamber music. He also recorded the Arensky Waltz for two pianos with

Harold Bauer, and a lovelier piano disc has never been made. Gabrilowitsch and Bauer, two fine musician-pianists, started giving public recitals in 1915. They were not the first in America, however. Ernest Hutcheson and Rudolf Ganz had previously joined forces when their commitments permitted, as had, on occasion, Rosenthal and Joseffy.

Two of Leschetizky's pupils who attracted attention at the turn of the century were Josef Slivinski and Martinus Sieveking. Slivinski for a time was Paderewski's rival in England; and, indeed, Shaw set Pole against Pole, finding Slivinski much the better technician. "From the purely gymnastic point of view he, and not Paderewski, is the exponent of the Leschetizky technique; for in his case it has not, as in Paderewski's, become overlaid by a technique of his own; besides, being natural to him, it does not sound cruelly and artistically contradictory from him, as it often does from Paderewski. His steel finger is always elastic: it leaves the piano ringing unhurt." But later G.B.S. was to point out what to him were certain deficiencies in style. Slivinski retired in 1918 and settled in Warsaw to teach. In his concert days he was especially admired for his performances of Chopin, Schumann and Liszt.

Sieveking, who came from Amsterdam, was known as The Flying Dutchman. He was big—"more a house than a man," wrote Hambourg—and his hands matched. It is said that he could span a fourteenth or fifteenth. Today most reference books do not even list his name, but he used to command great respect for his brilliance, power and exuberant approach to the keyboard.

Ignaz Friedman and Benno Moiseiwitsch, among the most brilliant of the Leschetizky pupils, came out around the same time. Friedman was one of the most unusual and original pianists of the century. He was born in Podgorze in 1882 and displayed remarkable gifts from the beginning. At eight he was transposing Bach fugues at sight. He was a phenomenon but a completely undisciplined one, and when he went to Leschetizky the great man stroked his beard and advised him to find another line of work. But Friedman persevered and worked with Leschetizky for four years. He later said that Leschetizky was one of the few teachers who knew positively when the student had ceased to be a student and had become an artist.

Friedman's career officially started with his debut in Vienna in 1904. His program consisted of three concertos—the Brahms D minor, the Tchaikovsky B flat minor and the Liszt E flat. Busoni,

(Above left) Ossip Gabrilowitsch, one of the greatest Leschetitzky pupils. He was the son-in-law of Mark Twain.

(Above right) Ignaz Friedman, one of the most unusual and original pianists of the twentieth century.

(Below) Benno Moiseiwitsch. Like Gabrilowitsch and Friedman, he was a Leschetitzky product and one of the great romantic pianists of the century.

Godowsky and Rosenthal were in the audience. He became a very busy pianist, giving more than three thousand concerts all over the world. The outbreak of World War II found him in Australia, and he never returned to Europe. Making Sydney his home, he toured Indonesia, concertized in Australia and New Zealand, taught, continued composing and gave many recitals on the radio. A few years before his death in 1948, he had a stroke and lost control of his left hand. Some of his music is interesting; he composed over ninety works (and also found time to edit the Chopin works for Breitkopf and Härtel as well as a great deal of Schumann and Liszt for Universal). A few pianists play his charming Viennese-like waltz arrangements (he recorded three of them, inimitably). Nothing else of his is heard, but among his large output is a very clever set of virtuoso variations on the Paganini twenty-fourth Caprice, the one used by Schumann, Liszt, Brahms and Rachmaninoff. It could be an impressive recital piece in the right hands.

His style was completely his own, and it was marked by a combination of incredible technique, musical freedom (some called it eccentricity), a tone that simply soared, and a naturally big approach, with dynamic extremes that tended to make a Chopin mazurka sound like an epic. In his youth he was accused of uncontrolled banging, and the charge may be true. He must have had something of Rosenthal's approach in his make-up: a colossal technique that sometimes would run away. As he matured he was able to control his fingers, and whatever he did was because he specifically wanted it so. He handled a melodic line inimitably—deftly outlining it against the bass, never allowing it to sag, always providing interest by a unique stress or accent. As he thought big, he played big. His recording of Chopin's *Revolutionary* Étude is a remarkable, magnificent conception. To provide impetus, Friedman runs the left-hand arpeggios with tremendous speed—running the notes together so that they slur a bit up to the climactic E flat. The effect is heroic, though purists might wrinkle their nose. Equally remarkable are his records of a series of Chopin mazurkas and Mendelssohn's *Songs without Words*. Again he does not play by the book—he was a true child of the late romantic age and, especially in the Chopin, his rhythms, accents and volcanic approach are apt to unsettle conservative listeners. But the more one hears them, the more one admires. And his recording of Chopin's E flat Nocturne (Op. 55, No. 2) may well be the most beautiful, singing, perfectly proportioned performance of a Chopin nocturne ever put on records. Like him or not, Friedman was a force—a powerful, unusual, original pianist, sometimes erratic but always fascinating, and always full of imagination and daring. He never was a headliner in America, as Paderewski, Hofmann and Rachmaninoff were, but he did not have to defer in natural gifts and pianistic resource to any pianist of his time. His colleagues knew it. "He was a lazy artist, he wasn't a pusher," said Benno Moiseiwitsch. "But he was one of the few pianists of the caliber of Rosenthal and Rachmaninoff."

Moiseiwitsch, born in Odessa in 1890, settled in England in 1908. In Odessa he won the Rubinstein Prize at the age of nine before going to Leschetizky. His recitals immediately established him as an elegant pianist and also a "natural" one, natural in the sense that he played without strain or effort, the piano being an extension of his arms and hands. Moiseiwitsch was above all a lyric player, with remarkable fluency and subtlety. Rachmaninoff considered him his artistic heir and was greatly struck by the way Moiseiwitsch played his music. In his later years Moiseiwitsch's formidable technique dropped a bit, but never the sensitive musical impulse that always animated his playing. Like nearly all of the Leschetizky pupils, he represented the last vestiges of romanticism as it was actually practiced in the romantic period—which means pliancy, a perpetually singing line, concentration on inner voices and a free approach to the notes. In Moiseiwitsch's case, freedom was always tempered by impeccable musicality.

XXIV

The Chopinzee, the Buddha
and Others

ALTHOUGH LISZT AND LESCHETIZKY dominated the teaching of the latter half of the century, that did not mean other teachers and other pianists could not thrive. A pianist—or pianissimist, as he was sometimes called—like Vladimir de Pachmann belonged to no school, had no followers, and made his own rules as he went along. His only teacher of importance was Joseph Dachs in Vienna. Listening to de Pachmann's records, and he made very many from about 1910 to his death in 1933, it is hard to conceive how he could ever have been taken seriously; but taken seriously he was, and many considered him to be the greatest Chopinist alive. It was Huneker who nicknamed the little man the Chopinzee; and, indeed, that tiny figure with the round face and eccentric behavior could have had less appropriate nicknames.

A good part of his fame came from his shenanigans. De Pachmann would talk, mutter, grimace and lecture his way through a recital. He denied that he did this for effect, and insisted that the speech and the platform goings-on were necessary for him to express what was surging within his artistic soul. He said this so many times to the press that he probably ended up believing it. He would make speeches to the audience and play games with his listeners. George Bernard Shaw was terribly amused. "M. Vladimir de Pachmann," he wrote, "gave his well-known pantomimic performance, with accompaniments by Chopin." In those days de Pachmann's wife, Maggie Oakey, was still before the public as a pianist. De Pachmann would go to her recitals and sit in a back row. "Charmant! Magnifique! Brava!" he would loudly cry.

It was de Pachmann who, dressed in a horrid, smelly, old dressing

Vladimir de Pachmann, the Chopinzee and pianissimist.

De Pachmann in 1924, on vacation in the Catskill Mountains. The seventy-six-year-old pianist said it would never do to let his fingers stiffen and claimed that milking cows was better finger exercise than anything devised by the mind of man.

gown, would receive visitors. "It belonged to Chopin," he would explain. When it wore out, another, always owned by Chopin, would take its place. He wore socks owned by Chopin, gloves owned by Chopin and probably underclothes owned by Chopin. Fellow pianists sweated more than usual when, from the stage, they saw de Pachmann in the audience. They never knew what was going to happen. At a Godowsky concert he rushed to the stage at one point. "No, no, Leopold," he said, to the vast amusement of the audience and the fire-engine blush of Godowsky, "you moost play it like *so.*" He played it like so, and then told the audience he wouldn't have given the demonstration for just any old pianist. "But Godowsky," he said, "is *ze zecond* greatest liffing pianist." At a Busoni concert in 1919, he rushed to the stage and kissed Busoni's coattails. *"Busoni grösster Bachspieler, ich grösster Chopinspieler,"* he announced.

Once, during a recital in London, he crouched over the keyboard so that nobody could see his hands. He was playing one of his specialties, the Chopin *Minute* Waltz arranged in thirds. "Vy I do zis?" he asked the audience. "I vill tell. I see in ze owdience *mein alte freund* Moriz Rosenthal, and I do not vish him to copy my fingering." He created a furore at his London debut, and an interviewer asked him what he thought of London. De Pachmann drew himself up. "Zat is not ze qvestion, Madame. Ze qvestion is vat do London zink of Pachmann?" At another interview he went into, or pretended to go into, a rage. "You zit zere ven you should be on your knees before me," he screamed at the reporter.

His struggles with the ups and downs of the piano stool were legendary. One of his tricks was to raise it, lower it, fiddle around with the controls until the audience was desperate. Then he would rush into the wings and come out with a large book, placing it on the seat. No good. Then he would rip out one page, put that page on the seat, and smile beatifically at the audience. Now he was comfortable. Like as not he would stop in the middle of a piece and ask the audience what it thought of the performance. Of course there would be applause and cheers. Whereupon de Pachmann would inform the audience that it was deaf and idiotic; that he was playing terribly; that *now* he would play as only de Pachmann could.

As he grew older the tiny man wore his hair like Liszt. He always made good newspaper copy, and papers all over the world followed his adventures—how he would solemnly dip each finger tenderly into a glass of raw brandy before a recital. They would quote his immortal utterances—"Godowsky, he is the greatest composer since Chopin"; or "Liszt? Ah, yes he play very well, very well. But me, I play like a god." They even gave him columns in which he himself could philosophize. One of them, which he wrote when he was seventy-seven, is rather charming:

The doctors will say that nicotine is bad for you. Well, I smoke eight cigars every day. The doctors say you must have exercise, walk in the air or play with the ball. Well, I have never taken any exercise in my life, unless you count the four hours a day practice at the piano. I have a beautiful little summer house at Fabriano, in Italy, with a lovely garden, but I never walk in it. All the fresh air I want comes through the window. So there is my life. And I am seventy-seven. But I do not expect everyone to follow my example, for after all I am Pachmann, the unique. I laugh at your doctors.

All of this was well calculated to take everybody's mind off *how* he played. Perhaps in his early years—he was, after all, born in 1848 —he had the flexible technique and imagination of a major artist. He did retire for some years in his youth, dissatisfied with his progress, and devoted himself to intensive study. Thus, after a tour of his native Russia (he was born in Odessa) in 1869, he remained out of action for eight years. Then he emerged for a short European tour in 1877, and by 1880 he was a phenomenal success. Old musical dictionaries make statements like the following: "De Pachmann is a player of a highly poetic temperament, refined sensibilities and extraordinary personal magnetism. He is at his best in works demanding extreme delicacy of touch, for there he can legitimately display his marvelous velvety tone and ethereal pianissimo. In this respect he probably never had a superior, and certainly few equals." From the beginning he concentrated on Chopin. It was generally agreed, and he himself must have known it, that his style simply would not fit either the classic composers and Beethoven or the large-scale works of the repertoire.

One should give de Pachmann the benefit of the doubt. But if he did in concert what he did on his records, his listeners were treated to a wonderful display of choppy rhythms, wrong notes, simplifications and textual changes. De Pachmann was imperturbable. If the going got too hard, he merely slowed down to where the music was manageable, or he simplified. At his best he must have been a charming miniaturist, and one with the most beautiful of tones. His

ancestry was most likely in the Hummel-Cramer group of pianists—
those who stressed tone and pure finger technique without drama.
But—again, if de Pachmann's records are to be taken as a guide—it
is impossible to take him seriously. It is true that there is something
engagingly naïve about some of his recorded irresponsibilities, such
as his weird and pathetic attempt to play the Godowsky paraphrase
of Chopin's *Revolutionary* Étude for the left hand alone. De Pachmann could no more handle it than he could handle the Brahms B
flat Concerto, and the result is a ludicrous whatnot of chopped
lines, all-but-palpable desperation and wrong notes. In other,
simpler music, every once in a while a faded sort of charm, a deftly
turned phrase, peeps through. Occasionally there is even a moment
of elegance. And at his best he must have had a series of pianissimo
shadings not unlike Chopin's own. He is heard at his best in such
relatively simple things as Chopin mazurkas, which he projects simply, clearly and with undeniable charm. There is absolutely nothing
"romantic" about these interpretations; they avoid rubato, there is
very little fluctuation of tempo, and there certainly is no hint of the
eccentric Chopinzee. And every once in a while, as in his recordings
of Liszt's *Rigoletto* paraphrase or the second part of Liszt's E major
Polonaise, he unleashes sparkling, well-adjusted runs. He recorded
only the second part of the Polonaise, starting with the cadenza.
The disc is called *Cadenza and Polonaise*.

In any case, it is doubtful if de Pachmann was taken very seriously by his colleagues after the turn of the century. The pianist
who *was* taken seriously, the pianist's pianist, was Leopold Godowsky. Short, plump, round-faced, with inscrutable Slavic eyes (he
was born in Poland in 1870), he looked like Buddha and was aptly
nicknamed by Huneker The Brahma of the Keyboard. Others called
him The Apostle of the Left Hand. All conceded that his was—in
the studio, at any rate—the most perfect pianistic mechanism of the
period and very likely of all time. He was one of the most remarkable
pianists who ever lived.

The curious thing was that Godowsky, headliner though he was,
never could make the public impact his extraordinary gifts entitled
him to make. Perhaps there was something of Henselt in him. Before an audience his playing, according to some of the best judges of
his time, seemed to lose color and strength. Hypnotized by perfection as he was, it may be that in public he refused to take a chance,
worried about marring the unruffled perfection of his pianistics.

Leopold Godowsky in 1895, five years before his fabulous Berlin debut.

The Buddha-like aspects of Godowsky come out in this photograph, about 1925, at the height of his career.

That goes for his recordings, too. They are beautiful, as far as they go, but in only one case—the Grieg Ballade, made around 1928—does the playing begin to suggest the purity, elegance, authority, and transcendental pianistic command of the man. His effects were noted by all professionals in his audiences, but there could be no denying that concert work inhibited him. George Bernard Shaw indicates this in an 1890 review. Godowsky had played Schumann's *Études symphoniques*, and though he rippled through them with no trouble at all, "a certain shyness, rather engaging than otherwise, prevented him from standing on his merits emphatically enough to get full credit for his performance." His colleagues, who knew what Godowsky could really do, regretted this inhibition. Josef Hofmann once told Abram Chasins, after leaving Godowsky's home, "Never forget what you heard tonight; never lose the memory of that sound. There's nothing like it in this world. It is tragic that the public has never heard Popsy as only he can play."

To connoisseurs Godowsky was the ultimate phenomenon. Huneker hailed Godowsky's "fine equilibrium of intellect and emotion . . . purity of style, polyphony. . . . The superman of piano playing. Nothing like him, as far as I know, is to be found in the history of piano playing since Chopin. . . . His ten digits are ten independent voices recreating the ancient polyphonic art of the Flemings. . . . He is a pianist for pianists, and I am glad to say that the majority of them gladly recognize this fact." They did, even if his unruffled perfection reminded them of "a mathematician, or a chess player solving a problem."

The amazing thing was that Godowsky was virtually self-taught. None of his early instruction amounted to much, although he was concertizing at the age of nine. According to one story that was told about him, he heard the regimental band play a selection from *Martha* when he was three years old. A year later he played it correctly on the piano, not having heard it in the meantime—and, coincidentally, never having had piano lessons. Some haphazard instruction from musicians in his native Vilna followed, and by seven he was composing industriously. Godowsky's guardian (he had lost his father, a physician, when he was a baby) was in fair way to exploit him unmercifully, but the child was saved by a Herr Feinburg. Feinburg was a banker in Königsberg, and he financed Godowsky's studies at the Hochschule in Berlin. Woldemar Bargiel and

Ernst Rudorff were Godowsky's main teachers there. Some sources also mention Joachim.

Godowsky remained in Berlin through 1884 and then embarked on an American tour with the Belgian violinist Ovide Musin. Returning to Europe, he became associated for three years with Saint-Saëns. The great French musician is popularly supposed to have been Godowsky's only important teacher. Godowsky himself, perhaps proud of being a self-made musician, in later life discounted Saint-Saëns' contribution. "I went to Paris," he told an interviewer in 1924, "and played a good deal for Saint-Saëns, though he did not give me any lessons. When I played for him—even my own compositions—he would invariably say: 'Mais c'est charmant,' or 'Admirable,' or 'Épatant, mon cher!' or something of the same sort and, even though spoken from the heart, this hardly amounts to constructive criticism."

After Saint-Saëns, Godowsky was on his own. He concertized extensively, taught in America and, in 1900, conquered Berlin. He wrote a very long letter about his Berlin debut to W. S. B. Mathews, the Chicago critic. Dated December 24, 1900, it is a fascinating document that deserves to be printed:

. . . I was greatly astonished to find that I was well known among Berlin pianists and teachers, though many of the critics and the musical public knew nothing of my existence. Those that heard me before the concert predicted a great success; however, I was not so sure. Some artists have a success with the public, but the critics kill them; others are successful with the press, but make no impression on the public. There are claques here that work for certain artists. Then there is the antisemite press and public. Add to this professional jealousy, and you will get some idea of the difficulties I had to contend with. Imagine my surprise when I discovered that my concert was eagerly awaited by all musicians and music students. The Beethoven hall was crowded with a representative musical audience. All Berlin pianists were at the concert. When I came out I was so heartily greeted that I had to bow several times before I started. By some *unusual* good luck I was hardly nervous, and the first movement of Brahms [the Concerto in B flat], which was the first number, I played to my *absolute* satisfaction. This gave me courage for the following movements. The applause after the first movement startled me. It was terrific. It took a long time before I could begin the second part. After the last movement I was recalled I don't know how many times. After a pause of several minutes I came out to play my seven Chopin paraphrases and Weber's "Invitation." The musicians and public did not know what to expect. There was a general commotion. The hall looked remarkably festive, and electricity was in the air. I played first the study for the left hand alone, Op. 25, No. 4 (A minor). To describe the noise after this study would be impossible. The tremendous ovation was overwhelming. Then came Op. 10, No. 11, and Op. 25, No. 3, combined, Op. 25, No. 8 (sixths), Op. 25, No. 5 as a mazurka, Op. 10, No. 9 in C sharp minor [Godowsky means No. 4], Badinage, and Op. 10, No. 5 in G flat, followed by the "Invitation to the Dance." The success was greater than anything I have ever witnessed, not excepting a Paderewski enthusiasm. I could have repeated every study, but I did not care to have the concert too long. The public would have been too tired for the Tchaikovsky [Concerto in B flat minor], so I only repeated the Badinage and Mazurka. To tell how many times I had to come out after the paraphrases would be impossible. I could not count them. Pianists like Pachmann, Josef Weiss, Hambourg, Anton Foerster and the entire audience actually went mad. They were screaming like wild beasts, waving handkerchiefs etc.—The Tchaikovsky I played with a great deal of dash. The second movement I could not improve upon. At the end of the concert, I played as an encore the Scherzo from Saint-Saëns' G minor Concerto and the plain Black Key Study for the left hand. I refused to play more. The scene in the artist's room will never be forgotten by those who have witnessed it. People almost suffocated in the mad rush to reach me. Mrs. Godowsky and some friends could only reach me by going on stage and through the stage door. . . . All [criticisms] are so wonderful that I am told *nobody* ever got such notices. My success is the most *sensational* within the recollection of all musicians. Remember! I don't exaggerate the success—I can never do justice to it!

And so Godowsky entered Berlin as a conqueror. His big rival there was Busoni. Each would give several Berlin recitals during the course of a season, trying to outdo the other. Noël Straus, who studied with Godowsky in Berlin, remembered Godowsky leading with a Liszt recital and Busoni trumping it with a program of nothing but Liszt transcriptions. Godowsky taught in Berlin and, from 1909 to 1914, was professor at the Akademie der Tonkunst in Vienna. The war sent him back to America, where he settled. In 1930, during a recording session in London, he was incapacitated by a stroke and was never able to play again. He died in 1938.

Does one speak about Godowsky the concert pianist or Godowsky the pianist in his own studio? It was at home that he was transcendent, and it was from his home that all other pianists walked away talking to themselves. Godowsky's technique was not of the heroic kind; at least, he never favored enormous sonorities. But in independence of hands, equality of finger, ability to juggle polyphonic strands, and general pianistic finish, he may have been unique in keyboard history. His own music—and he composed and transcribed a great deal—is of such complexity, burdened with such elaboration of detail, crossed with so many inner voices, that none but he could play it. Most of his music has vanished, though big technicians will occasionally attempt his paraphrase on *Fledermaus* or (less frequently) *Artist's Life*. In his day it was said that he was composing for a future generation of pianists. If so, that generation has not yet arrived.

His most elaborate series—and they are probably the most impossibly difficult things ever written for the piano—are his fifty-three paraphrases of Chopin études. These are fantastic exercises that push piano technique to heights undreamed of even by Liszt. Godowsky wrote several for left hand alone (including the *Revolutionary* upon which de Pachmann foundered). Or he put two together, such as the two G flat Études (*Butterfly* and *Black Key*, under the title of *Badinage*). Or he put the bass of one étude into the right hand and the melody into the left. Godowsky was well aware that his tinkering with the Chopin études would be protested in many musical circles. In his foreword to the Schlesinger edition he wrote:

The fifty-three studies based on twenty-six études of Chopin have manifold purposes. Their aim is to develop the mechanical, technical and musical possibilities of piano playing, to expand the peculiarly adapted nature of the instrument to polyphonic, polyrhythmic and polydynamic work, and to widen the range of its possibilities in tone coloring.

Godowsky went on to add some personal remarks about the esthetic justification of so treating the Chopin études. These remarks have made no impact at all on the present age, which regards the paraphrases as sacrilege. But the dwindling band who admire Godowsky's treatment ignore the shout of heresy. They point to the diabolic ingenuity Godowsky displayed; to the polyphonic skill with which he fitted one étude into another; to the altogether original ideas about piano technique; to the extraordinary tonal applications. And there is no denying that, professionally speaking, the writing contains a transcendental quality that personifies the piano—the instrument itself. The Godowsky paraphrases *are* the piano, pushed to its logical (or, if you wish, illogical) extremes of the tightest kind of romantic polyphony. Nothing since Liszt has been so imbued with the idiom of the piano qua piano. And despite the enormous difficulties, the paraphrases were not intended to be played as bravura stunts. Godowsky had musical aims primarily in mind. It may be that those aims are old-fashioned and reflect an esthetic that is considered dubious today. But they do represent a philosophy where the piano itself was the be-all and the end-all, less a musical instrument than a way of life, and the paraphrases end up not music for the sake of music but (like so many of the Liszt transcriptions) music for the sake of the piano. Unfortunately the chances are that they will be entirely forgotten a generation from now unless the twentieth century experiences a complete esthetic turnabout.

On the other side of the pianistic scale from the philosophers and transcendentalists were the charmers: a passel of very popular composer-pianists who made an enormous success in their day and are now slipping (or have slipped) into oblivion. Alfred Grünfeld was one. He was a pianist somewhat in the de Pachmann style, though a stronger technician. He too was essentially a miniaturist who, as Hanslick said, understood to perfection the art of charming his Viennese listeners. He was born in Prague, worked in Berlin with Kullak, and eventually became court pianist in Vienna. The saving grace of Grünfeld was that he never pretended to be anything else than he was. "Alfred Grünfeld," Josef Hofmann once commented, "had a velvety touch, but he only played salon music really well." And Grünfeld seldom moved from the salon orbit. He was a sort of super-cocktail pianist showing off his little bag of tricks. Among those tricks were repeated notes. Grünfeld had a flexible technique and wrote a good deal of music for himself in which his repeated notes could stutter away. At that his playing had style, and his 1904 recording of Chopin's B minor Mazurka is not only technically accurate but quite limpid and tasteful. One of the first pianists to record —he cut some seven-inch Berliner discs even before 1904—he kept on, through the years, making discs of his own music, including Strauss potpourris and some rather disgraceful (because so banal) transcriptions of Schubert songs.

There were others who had charm. Xaver Scharwenka, that romantic Pole with dash and sensitivity, turned all the ladies' heads. What student has not played his *Polish Dance* in E flat minor? He recorded it, too, around 1911. There was a time when his B flat minor Piano Concerto was very much in the repertoire. Another Pole was Moritz Moszkowski, who (like Scharwenka) studied with Kullak and developed into a very well known pianist and composer. For a while his piano music was incredibly popular, and only recently has it dropped from the repertoire. There was not a pianist who did not play *Etincelles, La Jongleuse,* the *Capriccio Espagnol, En Automne* or the E major Concerto; and, indeed, no better salon music has ever born composed, or any so gratefully conceived for the piano. One of these days a pianist will come up with a program of Pieces Our Grandparents Loved. . . .

Still another Polish pianist who attracted considerable attention was Raoul von Koczalski. All pianists begin as prodigies, but von Koczalski was unusual even for that breed. He made his debut at *four,* toured at seven and was court pianist to the Shah of Persia while still a child. By the age of nine he had composed up to Op. 46, and at eleven he celebrated his thousandth appearance in public. One of his many records is fascinating. It is Chopin's well-known Nocturne in E flat (Op. 9, No. 2), "with authentic variants." As heard under von Koczalski's fingers, the Nocturne emerges with much additional fioritura. Von Koczalski probably got these variants from his countryman Karl Mikuli, the pupil of Chopin. If indeed they are authentic, the disc is a very valuable document. For it indicates that Chopin did not always play his own music as written and could embellish with the best of them.

Alexander Michailowski was a Polish pianist who never attracted much attention on the international circuit because he cut his playing off to teach in Warsaw (Mischa Levitzki and Wanda Landowska were among his pupils). His background included studies with Moscheles, Reinecke, Tausig and Mikuli. An indication of what he might have been like in his prime is contained on his Polish Syrena record of Chopin's B minor Scherzo, made when he was eighty (he died in 1938 at the age of eighty-seven). The playing is tremendous —full of fire, passion and temperament. Occasionally he loses control—no more than could be expected from a man of his great age—but a heroic voice is heard.

Out of Russia came Vassily Sapellnikoff, who in 1888 played the

Tchaikovsky B flat minor Concerto in Hamburg under the composer's direction (and recorded it for Vocalion in the early 1920s). He amazed George Bernard Shaw with his performance of the Chopin A flat Polonaise, "the middle episode of which comes from his puissant hands like an avalanche." Shaw, on hearing him several times, remained impressed. Sapellnikoff, he said, had "cultivated the purely musical and tactile quality of his playing to an extraordinary pitch, his left hand being a marvel even among right hands for delicacy of touch and independence and swiftness of action." Perhaps Shaw had heard him play the Tausig arrangement of Weber's *Invitation to the Dance*, with its spectacular left-hand passages. This is among Sapellnikoff's many recordings, and it bears out Shaw's observations about Sapellnikoff's left-hand technique. His records are the product of a fine musical mind and an elegantly schooled artist. The recording (slightly cut) of the Tchaikovsky concerto, incidentally, is quite sober, without any show-off quality or changes in the notes.

And out of Australia came Ernest Hutcheson, to study with Reinecke and Stavenhagen. A prodigy at five, Hutcheson at the age of twelve had toured with another eminent Australian, Nellie Melba. Hutcheson was a clear and logical player with a rather classic style. Somebody once said of him that he had genius for the *detail* of piano playing. Passion was not for him, but not many pianists have had equal finish, erudition or musical integrity. He came to the United States in 1900 and from that point did relatively little playing, contenting himself with teaching and administrative work. He taught first at the Peabody Conservatory in Baltimore; then became dean and finally president of the Juilliard School of Music. One of his feats was not inconsiderable. In the early 1930s he gave a series of fifty half-hour, coast-to-coast radio broadcasts in which he went through a great deal of the concerto literature. Those were the days when the discography was small—electrical recording was still finding its way—and Hutcheson introduced the delights of the Mozart, Bach, Beethoven and Brahms concertos (plus many others) to a very large audience.

About ten years after Hutcheson came out of Melbourne, he was followed by another Australian—Percy Grainger. Grainger was one of the eccentrics of music—a gangling figure with an aquiline face and a formidable mop of hair; a vegetarian; a health faddist; a man who, likely as not, would hike from concert to concert with a knapsack on his back; and a whale of a pianist. He also had a secret life

The phenomenon from Australia—Percy Grainger, one of the keyboard originals.

not known to many until a biography by John Bird appeared in 1976. The blond, blue-eyed, athletic Grainger had a relationship with his mother that was not very healthy (she eventually committed suicide) and was a flagellant and a virulent racist with a special antipathy to Jews.

Because he wrote so much music of the *Country Gardens* and *Molly on the Shore* variety, many refused to take him seriously as a pianist, especially toward the end of his life, when his great days before the public were long over. The younger generation of pianists used to chortle when his name was mentioned. No chortle was ever more unjust or misplaced. Grainger was one of the most gifted pianists of the century, and his credentials were impeccable: student of Louis Pabst, James Kwast and Ferruccio Busoni; friend of Grieg; exponent of modern music (Debussy, Delius, Albéniz) at the turn of the century. He had a free, easy swing at the piano, a superb tone, an effortless and completely natural technique. Naturally his playing had some romantic mannerisms, such as a tendency to ritard at phrase endings. But his recordings of Bach-Liszt (A minor and G minor organ fugues) are superbly clear and logically organized. His Liszt playing glittered; his Chopin and Schumann had strength, poetry and grace; and, of course, he was unapproachable in Grieg and in his own music. He was one of the keyboard originals—a pianist who forged his own style and expressed it with amazing skill, personality and vigor, a healthy, forthright musical mind whose interpretations never sounded forced and who brought a bracing, breezy and quite wonderful out-of-doors quality to the continuity of piano playing.

· XXV ·

The Ladies

AFTER SOPHIE MENTER, the honors were divided between Annette
Essipoff and the cyclonic Teresa Carreño, with honors probably
going to Carreño. Next to her, Essipoff probably looked and sounded
like a little gray mouse. Carreño had overpowering personality, overpowering talent, overpowering physical strength, overpowering technique. And on top of that she was one of the most beautiful women
of her time, in an Amazonian sort of way. In short, she was overpowering in every direction, and there seemed nothing she could not
do. She even appeared on the operatic stage. In 1872 she was on
tour in England with James Henry Mapleson, the impresario, as
piano soloist with his opera company. One of the singers was unable
to go on, and Mapleson talked Carreño into singing the role of the
Queen in Meyerbeer's *Huguenots*. She did so, first extracting from
Mapleson the promise (fulfilled) of a Carreño benefit concert.

They called her The Walküre of the Piano, and there was something wild about her from the moment she emerged from Venezuela,
a child of nine looking very much like Adelina Patti. People fell all
over themselves trying to help the talented girl. Louis Moreau
Gottschalk heard her in New York in 1862, called her a genius, gave
her a few lessons and promoted her career. The following year she
was touring. One of her stops was the White House, where she
played for President Lincoln and complained about the piano. Lincoln asked her to play his favorite piece, *Listen to the Mocking Bird*.
Carreño did and improvised some variations.

Three years later she was studying with Mathias in Paris and
making a big impression on Rossini and Liszt. Liszt offered to teach
her, an opportunity any pianist would have groveled for. But Teresa

The young Teresa Carreño, talented (also as an opera singer), temperamental, tempestuous and beautiful.

Carreño, the Walküre of the piano, the female Rubinstein.

showed her independence by refusing to follow him to Rome. She was thirteen at the time, and perhaps she did not know any better. Rossini and Patti wanted to make a singer out of her; she had a beautiful voice (mezzo-soprano). Anton Rubinstein heard her in London and gave her lessons whenever their paths converged. This was not too often, for Carreño became the idol of Europe and a busy virtuoso in her own right. Von Bülow called her "the most interesting pianist of the present age" when she made her Berlin debut in 1889. Carreño, in the full flush of her youth and aided by her exuberant nature, probably whaled the daylights out of the piano at that time. She was not too disciplined, and many Germans said that, fantastic as she was, she needed "schooling." By that was meant, of course, German schooling. But von Bülow was not to be deceived, lack of discipline or no. "A phenomenon," he said. "She sweeps the floor clean of all piano paraders who, after her arrival, must take themselves elsewhere." Not many are alive who heard her. Claudio Arrau did, and he calls her "a goddess. She had this unbelievable drive, this power. I don't think I ever heard anyone fill the Berlin Philharmonic, the old hall, with such a sound. And her octaves were *fantastic*. I don't think there's anyone today who can play such octaves. The speed and power."

Her private life was as tempestuous as her playing. In 1873 she married the violinist Émile Sauret. That broke up, and in 1875 she entered into a common-law relationship with a baritone named Giovanni Tagliapietra. She made concert tours with him, often deserting the piano in part of the program to sing duets at his side. For a while, indeed, she did leave the piano. In 1876 she was well received as Zerlina in Mozart's *Don Giovanni* with an opera company in New York. Naturally her husband sang the Don. A short time later she organized, with him, an opera company that toured Venezuela. If singers were not available or became ill, Carreño went on stage and sang. If conductors did not show up or walked out, Carreño conducted. That could go on just so long. Carreño left Tagliapietra to resume her concert career. In 1892 she married Eugene d'Albert. *That* must have been a battle royal, and they seem to have spent more time arguing than harmonizing. Two such egocentric, royal temperaments could not but clash. She had met him in 1891, and he was eleven years her junior. For a while they lived together, then decided to legalize the union. They took a castle in Germany, her studio at one end of it, his at the other. From there comes the story that one day d'Albert hastily rushed into the Carreño wing of the ménage. "Teresa! Teresa! Come quickly! My child and your child are fighting with *our* child!" The story is delightful but apocryphal, even though each did have a child by a previous marriage, and Teresa did bear two daughters to d'Albert. Not apocryphal, though, is a review that appeared in a German paper, "Frau Carreño yesterday played for the first time the second concerto of her third husband at the fourth Philharmonic concert."

Carreño and d'Albert were divorced in 1895, after three violent but presumably not uninteresting years. She made a few two-piano appearances with d'Albert before the rupture, and it caused some amused talk, for all musical Europe knew of their headlong collisions. But even if the marriage did not work, Carreño undoubtedly learned a good deal of the Liszt tradition from the great d'Albert, and she also learned to rein herself in. It was noted that after her years with d'Albert her playing had more control. She may have remained a Walküre, but she also developed into an artist. Her final marriage caused something of a scandal. In 1902 she married Arturo Tagliapietra, the brother of her second husband. This was considered bad form, but the marriage was the only happy one in Carreño's restless life.

She was a large woman with a large hand (exceptionally broad palm and thick fingers: very much like Rubinstein's), and she "played like a man." Her out-and-out virtuosity in her early days irritated some sensitive listeners. Grieg, in a letter to a friend, wrote disgustedly of her performances of Liszt's *Hungarian Fantasia* and Chopin's E minor Concerto, ". . . the devil is in these virtuosos who always want to improve on everything." According to Grieg, she made inexplicable tempo changes; and Grieg, a fairly close friend of hers, took the opportunity to give her a piece of his mind. She had been one of the first to include the Grieg Concerto in her repertoire, and she had no hesitation tinkering with it. Among her "improvements" was substituting octaves for the concluding arpeggios. This probably did not sit too well with the composer (though composers are generally more flexible on such matters than one might imagine).

Naturally The Walküre went in for big works. She had the power and technique to handle them, and she thundered through the *Emperor* Concerto, the Rubinstein D minor, the Liszt E flat, the Tchaikovsky B flat minor and the MacDowell D minor. (She had taught young Edward, and in 1888 she played the world premiere of his D minor.) In her later years, stately and white-haired, she was the queen of pianists and considered the equal of any, male or female. She could have recorded, and it is a tragedy that she didn't. She made some piano rolls, but they give no idea of what she must have been capable of.

Essipoff was almost an exact contemporary of Carreño (1851–1914 as against Carreño's 1853–1917). She was Russian-born and studied with Leschetizky, who married her in 1880. (They were divorced in 1893.) Essipoff as a pianist was efficiency personified. When she appeared in Boston on December 23, 1876, *Dwight's Journal* observed that "she seems organized for the piano; the beautiful movement of her hand and wrist is worth watching for itself . . . cat-like strength and subtlety . . . consummate technique . . . faultless . . . We fear it will be long before we hear any piano playing to compare with it, unless she come again." New York went wild about her, though the learned critic of the *Music Trade Review* was worried, "She sits so high and far away from the piano that we should have thought her outstretched arms would soon get tired." He screams about her technique. "Her left hand in single runs, thirds or octaves, does exactly what the right hand does."

Shaw heard her in 1888 and turned in a typical performance, "That lady's terrible precision and unfailing nerve; her cold contempt for difficulties; her miraculous speed, free from any appearance of haste; her grace and finesse without a touch of anything so weak as tenderness: all these are subjects for awe rather than for criticism." Essipoff, reports Shaw, played without any affectation or platform mannerisms. "When the applause reached the point at which an encore was inevitable, she walked to the platform without wasting a second; shot at the audience, without a note of prelude, an exercise about forty seconds long, and of satanic difficulty; and vanished as calmly as she had appeared. Truly an astonishing—almost a fearful player."

But Paderewski describes her as merely "a charming pianist." Paderewski gives a very interesting comparison between the efficient Essipoff and the volcanic Carreño. Essipoff's playing, he wrote,

in many ways was perfect except when it came to strong, effective pieces. Then she was lacking in force, as women pianists generally are. Quite different from Madame Teresa Carreño, who was a very, shall I say, strong

Annette Essipoff, Leschetitzky's second wife and for years a ranking pianist.

Fannie Bloomfield Zeisler, a Leschetitzky product, and one of the great ones.

pianist, even too strong for a woman. Carreño was one of the women pianists who had a very big tone, but it was not a beautiful tone, because a beautiful tone must include tenderness, and there was none of that, just brilliance. Essipoff, on the contrary, was quite the opposite. She was very feminine in her playing, and small poetic pieces she could play admirably.

Carreño and Essipoff were two among the many ladies who charmed music-lovers around the last quarter of the century. Liszt-ladies swarmed all over Europe and America, waving their master's credentials. And there were even a greater number of Leschetizky-ladies. The one with the greatest promise as a youngster was Paula Szalit, whom Artur Schnabel believed to have been the greatest child wonder in history. She came to Leschetizky at thirteen, and her fellow pupil Arthur Shattuck flatly said that even at that age she was "the sublimest recreative talent of her time." But Szalit went back to her native Poland and little was heard of her. The most prominent Leschetizky-lady after Essipoff was the American pianist Fannie Bloomfield Zeisler (though born in Austria, she was brought to Chicago at the age of four; she was, incidentally, a cousin of Moriz Rosenthal). If Carreño was The Walküre of the Piano, Bloomfield Zeisler was The Sarah Bernhardt of the Piano—or so she was called. In Chicago she worked with Bernhard Ziehn and Carl Wolfsohn, and then, on Essipoff's recommendation, went off to Vienna in 1878, spending the next five years with Leschetizky. For many years she was considered the greatest American pianist: a powerful technician with a staggering repertoire (in San Francisco she gave eight recitals in eighteen days without repeating a number). She once said that her specialty was being no specialist.

She was very petite. "Has any one in the audience ever seen her for the first time she appears without a feeling of compassion?" one critic wrote. "This small, slight, frail, delicate woman, who appears more to need assistance for walking than for playing, how can she dare attempt the gigantic task she often does of playing two or even three great concertos in one evening?" And the New York *Sun* in 1901 called her "an electric dynamo endowed with a human body and soul." But at one point the dynamo short-circuited, and she snapped. She had to go to a rest home and remained there for a while before returning home. On February 12, 1906, she disappeared from her home in Chicago and was found walking the streets in a state of what was described as "almost complete physical and mental exhaustion." It was diagnosed as "melancholia." (Shades of Robert Burton!) Today we would call it a nervous breakdown. But that fall she nevertheless was back on the concert stage. Nine years later, H. T. Parker of the *Boston Transcript* gave a pen portrait of her (calling her, as most writers did, Fanny Bloomfield-Zeisler; she herself did not hyphenate the name and spelled her first name "Fannie"):

> Some young artist, quick with memories of Rembrandt's pictures of Jewish women, ought to paint Mme. Bloomfield-Zeisler playing the piano, and it is easy to believe that the master himself would not have disclaimed her for a subject. As she sat yesterday afternoon in Jordan Hall, bent intently on the keyboard, she was pictorial indeed and rather in the fashion in which Rembrandt chose to limn and color his Jews. The sharp and strong Semitic profile; the deep-set and bright Semitic eyes; the full, hunched shoulders; the sinewy body; the dress rich in color and large flow of line; the whole impression of a vivid personality in vibrant play. . . .

She probably was one of the great ones. Certainly she was accepted in Europe and America as one of the most brilliant players of her time. From all accounts, her performances crackled with life and excitement. At her Golden Jubilee Concert, on February 25, 1925, she played the Schumann A minor and Chopin F minor Concertos (with the Chicago Symphony) and a group of solo pieces.

In addition to the Liszt-ladies and the Leschetizky-ladies, there were the Clara Schumann-ladies. Chief among those was the Polish-born Natalie Janotha, a vigorous and uninhibited type who in 1885 became court pianist in Berlin. Janotha would never, as long as the beast was alive, give a concert without her dog, Prince White Heather, somewhere on stage within her view; and she would ostentatiously place a prayer book on the piano. Without Prince White Heather or the prayer book, said Janotha, she could not possibly play a single note. She made four recordings in 1905. One of them was the Chopin Fugue, a student work of which she owned the manuscript. The disc states that the Fugue is "arranged from the manuscript," which may mean that Janotha touched it up. Her recording is the only known one of that piece. Another record is Mendelssohn's *Spinning Song*. The label of this old G&T disc states that the work is "played by Miss Janotha, who holds the record for the rapidity of her execution." She adds two chords to start the piece (get ready, get set . . .) and, during the course of the performance, interpolates a few extra scale passages. Total time: one minute, 35.4 seconds. Her own *Gavotte Imperiale* is a screamingly funny piece of music, and she bangs it out with great enthusiasm. On the basis of her records, she was anything but a sensitive pianist, and certainly not a good musician, but at least she could get around the keyboard.

Less flamboyant Schumann pupils were Fanny Davies and Ilona Eibenschütz. Davies, from England, was considered the successor to Arabella Goddard. She recorded the Schumann Concerto and the *Davidsbündlertänze* around 1928, and behind her neat, controlled, tasteful playing one can see the specter of Clara. The last surviving pupil of Clara was Eibenschütz, who came to her in 1886 at the age of thirteen, already a seven-year veteran of the concert stage. For Ilona had been one of the formidable prodigies in piano history. She studied with Clara until 1890. Apparently Clara spent a great deal of time trying to curb Ilona's fiery Hungarian temperament and tendency toward speed; nor was Clara ever sure that she had succeeded and even expressed some doubts to Brahms. Ilona entered the Brahms circle through Clara. Brahms was impressed enough to entrust her with the world premieres of some of his late works, notably Opp. 118 and 119, and she also played the British premieres when she moved to London. Shaw reviewed her London debut in 1891. He called her "a wild young woman." But it did not take her long to settle down, "and when she touched the first chord of Schumann's *Études symphoniques,* the hand lay so evenly and sensitively on it that at once I perceived that Ilona . . . would come away from it mistress of the situation. And she did." Eibenschütz developed into a very respected pianist. One of her few recordings—she made three or four in 1903—is of a pair of Brahms waltzes. She plays them very simply, with a swinging line, flexible rhythm, faster tempos than are customary today, and a complete avoidance of "romanticism." The results are ravishing. On another record is a pair of Scarlatti sonatas, played in an extremely fast tempo. She reveals herself to be a sound keyboard technician and a sensitive artist. Although she died, in 1967, at the age of ninety-five, she had a very short career, retiring from the stage after her marriage in 1902. She did, however, make a few private recordings in 1950, give a BBC interview in 1952 about her friendship with Brahms and, at the age of 89, she made a home recording of the Brahms A flat Waltz. All these have been transferred to LP discs. Sometimes Ilona's old fingers are unsteady, but stylistically she presents an order of playing long vanished from the earth.

Adelina de Lara, another Schumann-lady, might have been a good pianist; but the Clara Schumann Society in the 1950s did her no service by having her record several large-scale Schumann works. De Lara was seventy-eight at the time; and whatever her intentions, she did not have the coordination to put them into practice. Mathilde Verne, probably a better pianist and one of the more successful of the Schumann-ladies, achieved great fame as a teacher in London. Among her pupils were Solomon and Harold Samuel. Mathilde's sister, Adela, did not study with Clara, as some sources state. She worked with Marie Schumann, one of Clara's daughters, and then studied with Paderewski. A fine pianist, one who favored big works, she introduced to England the Brahms B flat Concerto.

Shaw's favorite lady was neither Lisztian, Leschetizkian nor Schumannian. She was Agatha Backer-Grøndahl, from Norway, "a great artist—a serious artist—a beautiful, incomparable, unique artist!" She had studied with Kullak, von Bülow and Liszt. Her career was short, and toward the end she played only her own music. Marie Krebs-Brenning, Clotilde Kleeberg, Berta Jahn, Tina Lerner, Ethel Leginska and the impulsive Elly Ney also were fine pianists whose names carried considerable weight. And there was Cécile Chaminade, who could play her own music as well as anybody around, and whose recordings of her *Scarf Dance* and other works, in the early years of the century, show her to have been an assured, competent pianist with a good technique, grace, a high degree of rhythmic drive and a good deal of pianistic finesse.

Helen Hopekirk must be mentioned. She came from Edinburgh, went off to study with Leschetizky, and made a big impression on him. At least, he is quoted in a reliable source as saying that Hopekirk was "the finest woman musician I have ever known." Hopekirk was appearing in public at eleven; went to the Leipzig Conservatory to work with Reinecke; ended up with five years of Leschetizky; came to America and taught at the New England Conservatory of Music; and later taught privately in Boston and Brookline. She was the composer of some popular songs, and also the author of some remarkable strictures, one of which appeared in *The Musician* of June 1912, and deserves some kind of immortality:

You will find that all musicians have noses that are broad at the base. Always look at a new pupil's nose, and never expect anything of a pupil who has a thin, pinched nose. If the pupil has a nose that is broad at the base, you can feel quite happy.

Hopekirk had a nose that was *very* broad at the base.

XXVI

Composers at the Keyboard

MOST GREAT PIANISTS have been composers. But after Liszt not many were *great* composers. The corollary holds, too: most great composers have been pianists. (Three big exceptions: Wagner, Verdi, Berlioz.) Which is the more valuable aspect of their work? In the cases of Mozart, Beethoven and Chopin, it was the composition, great as they were as pianists. In the cases of Brahms and Grieg, it also is composition though Brahms was trained as a pianist and in his youth might have been a good one. But he never practiced enough to keep his fingers loose, and pretty soon experts began to poke fun at his playing. William Mason said that it not only lacked finish, but that it was not musical, lacking style and contour. "It was the playing of a composer, not that of a virtuoso." In later years, when Brahms was forced to the piano, he would generally bluff the bass, vaguely rolling his hand around. He made a cylinder in 1889, and some years ago it turned up, in decayed condition. The recorded sound is primitive—Brahms plays a *Hungarian Dance*—and the surface noise fearsome, but through the chaos one does hear fragments of piano sound. Not enough can be heard to make any judgment.

Edvard Grieg, on the other hand, kept his piano technique in good shape, as his 1904 recordings indicate. He made nine sides of his own music and played it very skillfully. Grieg, however, never made any pretense at being a concert artist. Nor, in later life, did César Franck, though Franck had been a prodigy and had toured at the age of eleven. In 1838 he won the Grand Prix d'Honneur for piano at the Paris Conservatoire, and his father was most anxious to push him into a concert career. For several years Franck gave concerts, taught piano and wrote a handful of bravura pieces, now entirely forgotten. Later he concentrated on the organ and, of course, on composition. The chances are that Franck was an extremely gifted pianist.

So was the composer of *Carmen*. Marmontel, in his *Pianistes célèbres*, writes about his "regretted friend, and pupil, Georges Bizet," who "played the piano like Hummel, Heller and Chopin, with that exquisite perfection and that particular taste of the great virtuosos, the masters of the art of song." Bizet had something of Liszt's ability to hear a piece of music and immediately play it back. He did this once in the presence of Liszt himself. Liszt played one of his works to a group of musicians including Halévy. He finished and said that in all Europe only two pianists could play it—von Bülow and himself. Halévy prodded Bizet to the piano, and the young man played the most difficult episode right back. Whereupon a somewhat startled Liszt procured the manuscript and Bizet read it at sight, with verve, accuracy and rapidity. Liszt rose to the occasion with an apology. "Now there are three of us, and I must add, to be just, that the youngest of us is perhaps the cleverest and the most brilliant."

Although Isaac Albéniz had an impressive career as a pianist, it is primarily as a composer that he is remembered today. His was one of the more interesting lives in music, and certainly the most staggering childhood—a childhood that makes one wonder at the kind of precociousness which makes men out of some children. Albéniz had a talent that was on a Mozartean level. He made his debut as a pianist in his native Spain at the age of four—that would be in 1864—and was composing fluently at seven. He was a fantastic child, mature far beyond his years, blessed with a perfect ear, good looks, a healthy body and an independent mind.

Just how independent the next few years were to show. Naturally he was acclaimed as Spain's greatest prodigy, and his parents put him on display, taking him on concert tours. For these occasions his mother dressed him as a French musketeer, complete with uniform and rapier. Out on stage the manikin would gravely stride, hand on sword, bowing deeply. Freudians take note. There is no English biography of Albéniz, and no studies of his character have been made. But a deep and raging resentment must have been built up, and there must have been a psychic explosion at the indignities his parents were subjecting him to. And so he started running away from home. He was constantly running away from home. His parents would then alert the police, and Isaac would be carried ignominiously back. A typical escapade occurred when he was nine. Stimulated by reading Jules Verne, unhappy at having to perform like a trained monkey, he ran away, jumped into the first train he saw, and on the train met the Alcalde of the Escorial, who took him to the Casino there. Greatly amused, the Alcalde let him play the piano for the visitors and gamblers, and then put him on a train with a stern admonition to go home. Instead, at the first opportunity, Isaac jumped on a train going in the opposite direction and gave concerts at Avila, Zamora and Salamanca. He made some money but was robbed, and so he gave a few more concerts, playing his way home. Finally he made the break for good. He was giving a concert near a seaport, and he hid on a ship heading across the Atlantic to Puerto Rico. When the ship sailed, he was dressed in the musketeer's costume he was wearing when he ran away. He was twelve years old.

.Imagine! Off on his own, without a cent, determined to make his way in the world of men—at the age of twelve! Albéniz played the piano for the passengers, and they got up a fund for him. Goodness knows what kind of story he told the captain. We know that he was not sent home when the ship docked. The next that is heard about him, he is in Buenos Aires, penniless, sleeping in churches, begging in the streets. Finally he got some people interested in him and started giving concerts in South America. He did well. Affluent, confident, he went to Cuba. But his father by now knew where he was and got in touch with the authorities. Albéniz was taken into custody and brought to Havana, where his father was waiting for him. And what happened? The thirteen-year-old boy talked his father into letting him go alone to New York. There must have been a soft spot in the father's head. He let the child go and returned to Spain.

Whereupon Albéniz soon spent all the money he had and again was penniless. He would wait for Spanish ships to come into the harbor, so that he could carry baggage for the passengers. Or he would play in saloons. One of his tricks was to play popular music with his hands upside down. He beat his way to San Francisco in 1874. How he managed to survive is a mystery. But survive he did. The fantastic boy made his way back to Europe and gave concerts. Then, at the age of fourteen, he took lessons in Leipzig with the great Carl Reinecke. Finally, under a subsidy from the Spanish government, he entered the Brussels Conservatory. Now he was fifteen.

Isaac Albéniz. After a riotous boyhood, he became a fine pianist and an even better composer.

But a steady regimen did not attract him. He ran away to America once again.

In other words, Albéniz sowed his wild oats at an age when his contemporaries were eating them as porridge. When he returned to Brussels he was all but unmanageable. He kept bad company, lived riotously, and the Spanish ambassador himself had to call him to heel. After some weird escapades, Albéniz settled down to work. With no trouble at all he took first prize at the conservatory, where his teacher was Brassin. Then he went to Budapest in 1878 and got an audition with Liszt, who gladly accepted him as a pupil. Albéniz followed Liszt to Weimar and Rome. That completed his formal studies as a pianist.

The rest of his life was fairly quiet. He did much touring as a virtuoso pianist and was called The Spanish Rubinstein. Shaw reviewed his London appearances with a good deal of respect. By 1893 Albéniz was settled in Paris, a well-liked man, a close friend of Dukas, d'Indy and Fauré. That was the year he stopped playing the piano in public. By the end of his life, in 1904, he had composed hundreds of pleasant salon *morceaux*. Most of these are forgotten today, and so are his operas (in America, at any rate). But in the last three years of his life he set to work on a series of complicated piano pieces, and with them was assured of immortality. They were published in four books under the title of *Iberia*.

Nothing in Albéniz's previous work had led anybody to expect from him music of this complexity, muscularity and difficulty. His friend, the fine French pianist Blanche Selva, read the manuscript and was appalled. "It is unplayable," she said—a remark echoed by many later pianists who have struggled with *Triana, Fête-Dieu à Seville* and *El Puerto*. Albéniz reassured Selva. "You will play it," he said. She eventually did. But those twelve pieces in *Iberia* are reserved only for superior pianists. So, by the way, is the *Goyescas* by Enrique Granados. *Goyescas* is the only set of Spanish pieces for the piano that can be spoken of in the same breath as *Iberia*. Granados himself was an exceptionally fine pianist, but he never gave concerts, as Albéniz had done.

Had he wished, Edward MacDowell could have had a brilliant career as a solo pianist. He had received a few lessons from Carreño, studied in Paris with Marmontel and (in 1881) had taught piano at the Darmstadt Conservatory. As a matter of fact, he did a bit of concertizing in Europe, and Liszt was interested in the young American. But MacDowell's primary interest was composition, and after 1888 he seldom touched the instrument. From all accounts he had a brilliant virtuoso equipment.

Alexander Scriabin, too, was a pianist and a good one. He won the gold medal for piano at the Moscow Conservatory in 1891 (he was a classmate of Rachmaninoff), started concertizing and composing, and in 1898 became professor of piano at his alma mater. After leaving the conservatory for good in 1903 he made many concert tours, concentrating on his own music. He never did stop playing, and his last recital was given on March 27, 1915. He died about three weeks later. Scriabin's playing is said to have resembled that of Albéniz. Both have been described as elegant, light-fingered pianists, most at home in the shallower side of the repertoire, and both gifted with a fluent technique. Scriabin was a spontaneous kind of pianist and never played anything twice the same way. Ellen von Tideböhl, who was a guest on the famous tour for which Serge Koussevitzky chartered a boat down the Volga and conducted nineteen concerts in eleven towns (with Scriabin as soloist in all of them playing his Piano Concerto in F sharp minor), later wrote that Scriabin played the work differently each time, "according to the happenings of the day and his mood at the moment."

It is not generally remembered that Claude Debussy was a fine pianist who could have had a professional career had he so wished. All composers, of course, know something about the piano, but Debussy's equipment was of top-notch quality. His teachers included Mauté de Fleurville (a Chopin pupil and the mother-in-law of Verlaine) and Marmontel at the Conservatoire; and when he went to Russia it was as a piano teacher to the children of Tchaikovsky's patroness, Nadezhda von Meck. She called him "my little pianist." Debussy was especially good as a score reader, almost in Bizet's class; and, of course, his revolutionary piano music attests to his profound knowledge of the capabilities of the instrument. He added more to the piano than any composer since Chopin: new theories about pedaling, new ideas about sonority, a completely new concept of figuration and layout.

His ideal was to suggest a piano without hammers. Marguerite Long, an excellent French pianist who studied many of Debussy's works under his supervision, has described his playing:

Debussy was an incomparable pianist. How could one forget his suppleness, the caress of his touch? While floating over the keys with a curious penetrating gentleness, he could achieve an extraordinary power of expression. There lay his secret, the pianistic enigma of his music. There lay Debussy's individual technique; gentleness in a continuous pressure gave the color that only he could get from his piano. He played mostly in a half-tint but, like Chopin, without any hardness of attack. . . . His nuances ranged from a triple pianissimo to forte without ever becoming disordered in sonorities in which harmonic subtleties might be lost.

In a way Long's prose is as impressionistic as Debussy's music, but there were others, such as André Suares, who referred to the way Debussy pressed, instead of struck, the keys. Debussy's hand position was flat. Maurice Dumesnil, the French pianist, said that this was true even in chordal passages. "He seemed to caress the keys by rubbing them gently down in an oblique motion." Debussy told Dumesnil to "play with more sensitiveness in the fingertips. Play chords as if the keys were being attracted to your fingertips and rose to your hands as to a magnet." All pianists who worked with Debussy emphasize that his playing was not all clouds and dreamland. In his own virtuoso works, such as L'île joyeuse, he could be as brilliant as anybody. But he employed pedal mixtures and a kind of touch new in the history of music and piano playing. He liberated the piano from its hammers. This is not the kind of Debussy playing heard in the last quarter of the twentieth century, where the emphasis is on clarity and strict rhythm, and where the tone is hard if not actually steellike. Pianists seem to be proud of taking the impressionism out of Debussy.

Where Debussy was known primarily as a composer, Ernö von Dohnányi started as a pianist and made his first international success as a thundering virtuoso. When, fresh from studies with d'Albert, he toured Europe and America in 1899 and 1900, the young Hungarian was instantly accepted as one of the great pianists of the day. His playing had power and propulsion and extraordinary finesse. Naturally he was a romantic pianist (his recording of the Mozart G major Concerto contains everything that is considered bad style today), just as his own compositions are in the romantic style. Later on, Dohnányi was to concentrate on composition and teaching, with relatively little public playing. But when force of circumstances made it necessary for him to reappear on the concert stage, after

World War II, a very old man, it was still apparent that though age might have blunted his fingers, it had not taken away his broad, noble style.

Dohnányi's more famous countryman, Béla Bartók, was four years younger. Bartók, like Dohnányi, was a magnificent pianist—"a second Dohnányi," he was called— who was appointed professor of piano playing at the Budapest Academy in 1907. Bartók did not make concert tours and when he did play it was generally his own music. His recordings show that his approach to the piano was nowhere near so percussive as some of today's young virtuosos might think. Bartók, after all, was a pianist of the old school, where tone was still the most important thing, and he never banged out his music as so many of his successors do.

XXVII

Dr. Faust at the Keyboard

THERE WAS SOMETHING Faustian about Ferruccio Busoni, that rest-less, tormented man of pianistic genius, the theorist and intellec-tual, the avant-garde composer who worked out new scale systems, the titanic technician and master of pianistic effects. In a few pe-ripheral aspects he was like Godowsky. Both were transcendent technicians who largely worked things out for themselves. Neither had an important teacher and each could almost be said to be self-taught. Both were perfectionists. Godowsky could slave away for twenty-hour stretches; while Busoni, after a triumphant recital, would (according to Harold Bauer) sit at the piano all night, replay-ing and criticizing the program he had just finished. But there the resemblance ends. To Godowsky the *piano* was the thing; to Busoni, the *idea*. Godowsky was the personification of the piano, Busoni the personification of intellect, of interpretation on the piano. Busoni's life was spent in quest (Faustian again; and his greatest work, though unfinished, is his opera *Dr. Faust*). It was a quest for the ideal music: the ideal music that he could play, the ideal music that he could compose. In his youth his repertoire was all-embracing. As he grew older it became slimmer and slimmer; and toward the end he confined himself to nothing but Bach, Mozart and a few things of Beethoven. At his farewell concerts in Berlin in 1922 it was nothing but Mozart—twelve of the piano concertos. As early as 1907 he had described the shift in his musical values:

With regard to my musical tastes, I began . . . by getting beyond Schu-mann and Mendelssohn. I used to misunderstand Liszt, then I worshiped him. Later I was amazed at him, and then, as a Latin, turned away from him. I allowed Berlioz to take me by surprise. One of the most difficult things was learning to distinguish between good Beethoven and bad. Latterly I discovered the most recent French composers by myself, and when they became too quickly popular dropped them again. These are metamorphoses which cover twenty years, and all through these twenty years there stood unchanged, like a lighthouse in a stormy sea, the score of *Figaro*. But as I looked at it again a week ago, I found signs of weaknesses in it for the first time, and I rejoice in the discovery that I do not stand so far beneath it as I did—although on the other hand this discovery means not only a positive loss, but it also points to the transitoriness of all human achievement. And how much more transitory must my own be!

In 1922, two years before his death, he looked over his pianistic career and was profoundly dissatisfied. "I have devoted myself too much, I think, to Bach, Mozart and Liszt. I wish now that I could emancipate myself from them." Then comes an outburst that is positively Dostoyevskian. "Schumann is of no use to me any more; Beethoven only with an effort and strict selection. Chopin has attracted and repelled me all my life; and I have *heard* his music too often—prostituted, profaned, vulgarized. . . ."

Busoni's style at the keyboard must have been monumental and, for its day, eccentric. Critics, and also many of his fellow pianists, could not follow his ideas. He took nothing for granted and he restudied everything he played. Although his approach remained basically romantic—he was, after all, born in 1866—he threw overboard many of the excrescences of the romantic style and set the stage for the "modern" school of Hofmann, Rachmaninoff, Petri, Schnabel and the others. His Chopin playing aroused positive consternation. He was entirely without the *Kitsch* of so many of the romantic Chopinists; without the big rubatos, accelerandos, diminuendos and sentimentality. Even the tiny Préludes he played in a monumental and nonsentimental manner that many critics thought entirely without charm. Busoni in 1902 ticked off a critic who complained about his "modern" style:

You start from false premises in thinking it is my *intention* to "modernize" the works. On the contrary, by cleaning them of the dust of tradition, I try to restore them their youth, to present them as they sounded to people at the moment when they first sprang from the head and pen of the composer. The *Pathétique* was an almost revolutionary sonata in its day, and ought to sound revolutionary. One could never put enough passion into the *Appassionata*, which was the culmination of the passionate expression of its epoch. When I play Beethoven, I try to approach the *liberté, nervosité* and *humanité* which are the signature of his compositions, in contrast to those of his predecessors.

It was *idea* again. Busoni, despite an intensive study of the classic composers, was no great scholar. But he did have philosophic ideas about music; he was much more interested in idea than in color, or display, or technique, or the other things so dear to most pianists. He was one of the first pianists to *think* about music rather than merely play it; to think of its meaning and what the composer intended; to think of music in terms of an esthetic and then try to verbalize it: not sentimentally as von Bülow, Tausig and all the others had done, not in terms of pictures and programs, but on the basis of intellect. In this he was the direct ancestor of such modern pianists as Schnabel. He took much of the romantic nonsense away from piano playing.

But in the process he substituted some nonsense of his own, if his discs and piano rolls are an accurate indication of how he sounded in public. Of all the romantic pianists, Paderewski not excepted, Busoni was the most eccentric and even bizarre, judging by today's accepted standards. His rhythms could be wayward, his interpretations personal to the point of arbitrariness, his apparent disdain for the printed note in a class of his own. Take his piano roll of the Chopin Préludes. The shorter Préludes he often plays twice, going up to the codettas, restarting from the beginning and then playing them all the way through. In some of the pieces he changes the harmonies. His tempos often are completely outside the norm. Nobody today could appear in public with such interpretations. Indeed, no pianist would be allowed to enter a conservatory if he played Chopin in so wayward a manner. Nor is this piano roll unique. Time and again Busoni sets himself above the composer. Obviously he had virtuoso fingers and a very strong mind, but for a pianist with his gigantic reputation this kind of music-making is inexplicable. Nor did it have anything remotely in common with the work of great pianists of his day. In the history of piano-playing Busoni stands alone.

Yet it is clear, from all testimony, that his playing had extraordinary force and concentration. Perhaps it appealed more to the professionals than to the public. Intellectuals all over Europe and the United States were fascinated with his unique approach. In his concentration of idea and philosophy on music he was reflecting German metaphysical thought out of Hegel, Fichte and Kant. He even distrusted so basic a thing as temperament, though he must have had enough to supply a regiment of pianists. "Never be carried away by temperament, for it disrupts strength," he once wrote.

For Busoni was an Italian but, like Sgambati before him, he had entered thoroughly into the German ambience. Hugo Leichtentritt described him as "Italian by birth and instinct, German by education and choice." Alfredo Casella, however, insisted that even though Busoni had so strongly come under the influence of German philosophy and musical thought, he essentially remained a Tuscan. Busoni himself insisted that he was neither Italian nor German, but a cosmopolite.

He was born in Empoli, near Florence, of musical parents. His father, a clarinetist, was Italian; his mother, a pianist, was born in Trieste of German extraction. At the age of four Busoni was playing piano and violin. For a few years his father taught him (badly) and sponsored his debut at the age of seven in pieces by Mozart, Clementi and Schumann. By twelve he was a veteran of the concert stage and also of the Vienna Conservatory, where he claimed to have learned just about nothing. If ever a pianist was essentially self-taught it was Busoni; and what genius he must have had to triumph over his miserable training! If there was an influence on his playing, it was that of Anton Rubinstein. Busoni had heard him and been struck by his monumental conceptions.

Busoni developed into a strikingly handsome man, with a noble head, a magnificent build and an appearance of overpowering dignity and concentration. He looked every inch the artist. For a while he followed the life of a touring pianist. Then he started teaching—at the Helsingfors Conservatory, at the Moscow Conservatory, in Boston (he made his first American tour in 1891 at the invitation of the Steinway firm). In Weimar he taught advanced pupils to carry on the Liszt tradition. By 1902 he was settled in Berlin, which was to be his headquarters for the rest of his life—even though he interrupted his residence there several times, once to become director of the Liceo Rossini in Bologna, once to sit out the war in Zurich. From 1900 until his death he was constantly making concert tours of Europe and America. His best pupil was Egon Petri, who inherited

Ferruccio Busoni at the age of twelve, five years after his debut. He was already a veteran of the concert stage and the Vienna Conservatory.

his master's taste for the big pieces of the repertoire. Petri, who settled in America, was one of the best Liszt pianists of the century and a formidable exponent of the larger works of Beethoven, Chopin and Brahms: a superb technician, and a musician of intellect, refinement and strength. Another pupil was Dimitri Mitropoulos, who was to achieve fame as a conductor; he did not study piano with Busoni but was a composition student of his.

This is not the place to speak of Busoni's music, or of the ideas he sponsored in his *Sketch of a New Esthetic of Music*. His compositions have never firmly entered the repertoire, though they are strongly admired in some circles. As a philosophical musical thinker he could be brilliantly penetrating, then turn around and propound the tritest of platitudes. And he could be inconsistent. On the one hand he preached the necessity of getting close to the composers' intentions. On the other hand, like all musicians of the day, he had no hesitation about touching up music. When reproached for rewriting parts of Franck's Prelude, Chorale and Fugue, he answered quite simply (and, to him logically) that Franck did not always know how to obtain the effects he wanted. Busoni refused to see anything sacred and inviolate in the printed note, and in that he followed the classic and romantic tradition. He changed to suit himself. These changes he considered unimportant; and, in a strange way, they *were* relatively unimportant. For he left pianistic pedanticism to the pianistic pedants; and, as an interpretative artist, he succeeded in the main endeavor of interpretation—to bring out the Beethoven in Beethoven, the Liszt in Liszt, the Bach in Bach. A strong creative mind himself, he apparently was able to identify with these three composers of his choice; and who would argue about a few changed notes when the essential spirit of the composer was revealed? Anyway, it must be repeated once again, composers are far less finicky about having their music edited by imaginative musicians than most nonprofessionals begin to realize. (As Walter Piston once said to a musician who asked him how to play a certain work, "I don't care what ideas you have—as long as you have ideas.")

Thus in many ways Busoni was a romantic pianist, just as in many other ways he can be said to have founded the modern style. He was the transitional pianist of his time, as Moscheles had been a hundred years previously. In the first two decades of the twentieth century he represented the old transcendentalism of Liszt as well as the new attitude that one must rid the music of outmoded tradition

An informal photograph of Busoni. People in the background are unidentified.

A posed photograph of Busoni.

and study it from a fresh point of view. It may be true that today's taste would find Busoni's playing exaggerated. It is also true that in his day he was accused of overintellectualism and aridity. And yet it becomes clear that his conceptions must have been original, and they must have been titanic. And he did not waste his conceptions on minor pieces of music. He was a superman who thought nothing of giving fourteen concertos in four programs. When he played in New York in 1911, his program consisted of the four Chopin Ballades, six Liszt études, the two Liszt *Legends* and the *Don Juan Fantasy*. In London a typical program was the *Hammerklavier*, the four Chopin Ballades and the A flat Polonaise, and Liszt's *Fantasy on Robert le Diable*. He celebrated the Liszt centenary in Berlin with six programs of Liszt's music.

His playing was much discussed and thoroughly analyzed. If it was unconventional, it always was gigantic. Mark Hambourg says he had very narrow hands and that he had to do an extraordinary amount of technical work to keep in condition, "especially as he had not an easy method of playing. . . . Playing from his shoulders, and very little with the wrist, he produced weighty if somewhat angular effects. He used to tell me that the romanticism of Chopin and Schumann were distasteful to him, and that the grandiloquence of Liszt and the majestic structures of Bach were more akin to his nature." For most of his life Busoni specialized in Bach (and also composed some transcriptions that are still in use, notably of the Chaconne and the Toccata in C), Liszt and Beethoven, and one of his aphorisms was "Bach is the foundation of piano playing. Liszt is the summit. The two make Beethoven possible."

As a Liszt player he was colossal, releasing floods of tone, "chords like cast bronze, glittering runs, the mighty roaring of the arpeggios . . ." It was not Liszt as played by the Liszt pupils; there was too much concentration, too much tautness, for that. Ferruccio Bonavia in 1920 called Busoni an ascetic and set him up as the opposite of Liszt. Liszt, said Bonavia, represented sentiment; Busoni represented reason. Busoni, according to Bonavia, "commanded a wider range of tone than any living pianist, although his preference for cold, unemotional shades might have caused some to doubt it. . . . It led him to a quality of tone which can only be called 'white,' a quality that was cold and almost inanimate. From this perfectly even basis he would start and build up a climax that reached the extreme limit of what is possible to a pianist, an avalanche of sound giving the impression of a red flame rising out of marble. His intellectual control was remorseless."

Another aspect of Busoni's style was supplied in 1920 by the British critic H. Proctor-Gregg, who insisted that Busoni's rhythm was his greatest glory. "It is the controlled vitality of his rhythm that almost deifies him in Bach, Liszt and Weber. . . . He is the most educative pianist in the world, for though there is everything to absorb in that gigantic style, there is nothing to imitate." Proctor-Gregg, like many, could not understand Busoni's Chopin. "The poet of songs and dreams is 'hustled,' speeding up in fact, into an efficiency of vigour and invective that is quite frightening." But perhaps Proctor-Gregg's remark about Chopin being the poet of songs and dreams gives the show away. Anybody who could write that line would automatically insist on a prettified, ultra-romantic Chopin; and *that* Busoni was not prepared to give.

Those who could identify with Busoni's vision thought him not only the greatest of living pianists but most likely the only one. Hugo Leichtentritt, the German musicologist and critic, was one of Busoni's worshipers. He wrote that Busoni had "the most powerful individuality and the greatest technical mastery since Liszt and Rubinstein." Here was a musician with "an elevation, a spiritual force, an utter absence of materialism. The astounding boldness and clarity of his polyphonic playing, the vehemence and elemental force of his brazen octaves and chords, his sweeping passages, the fascinating elegance of his ornamental work, the elasticity and precision of his rhythms, the surprisingly new and admirable treatment of the pedal, create marvels of sound the like of which has never been heard before."

One would give anything to hear this paragon. But the only evidence of his playing that we have are a few recordings, and those acoustic Columbias cannot possibly give an idea of what Busoni sounded like. His style was not compressible, and records in 1920 were not ready for the large-scale works in which Busoni was triumphant. Starting in 1919 he recorded many pieces, only a few of which were released. Those released include the Liszt Rhapsody No. 13, one of Busoni's arrangements of a Bach chorale-prelude, Beethoven's *Ecossaises*, the first Prelude and Fugue from Bach's *Well-Tempered Clavier*, and Chopin's A major Prélude, G flat Étude

(*Black Key*) and F sharp Nocturne. He hated making records, and described his agonies to his wife in a letter dated November 20, 1919:

My suffering over the toil of making gramophone records came to an end yesterday, after playing for three and a half hours! I feel rather battered today, but it is over. . . . Here is an example of what happens. They wanted the *Faust* Waltz (which takes a good ten minutes), *but it was only to take four minutes*. That meant quickly cutting, patching and improvising, so that there should still be some sense left in it; watching the pedal (because it sounds bad); thinking of certain notes which had to be stronger or weaker to please this devilish machine; not letting oneself go for fear of inaccuracies; and being conscious the whole time that every note was going to be there for eternity; how can there be any question of inspiration, freedom, swing or poetry? Enough that yesterday for nine pieces all of four minutes each (half an hour in all) I worked for three and a half hours.

His unhappiness in the recording studio might reflect some of the curious things that happen on his discs. The Thirteenth Rhapsody (in an abridged version covering two sides of a disc) is glorious on the first side—strong, original, full of deft touches and color applications. But on the second side there is a mad race to the end, and one can see Busoni fighting the time restriction in an effort to get as much as possible on the wax. There were no time troubles involved in most of the other pieces, however, and these can be studied as more representative. The C major Prelude from the *Well-Tempered Clavier* is simple, flowing and beautiful. Toward the end, however, there are arbitrary inflections that today would be condemned as over-romantic. The Fugue contains much variation in tempo, and huge ritards at the ends of sections. Pianistic mastery, yes; but dubious Bach playing according to the dictates of modern scholarship. Edward Dent, his biographer, has described the way this Prelude and Fugue sounded in concert:

He played the first Prelude of the *Forty-Eight*, and it became a wash of shifting colors, a rainbow over the fountains of the Villa d'Este; he played the Fugue, and each voice sang out above the rest like the entries of an Italian chorus, until at the last stretto the subject entered like the trumpets of the *Dona nobis* in the Mass in B minor, though in the middle of the keyboard, across a haze of pedal-held sound that was not confusion but blinding clearness.

All very romantic and described in equally romantic prose; but can this be Bach? Again modern scholarship would say no. And still once again it must be pointed out that pianists of Busoni's generation reflected *their* age, not the latter half of the twentieth century.

Listening to Busoni's recording of the A Major Prélude and *Black Key* Étude, it is easy to see why his Chopin playing was called cold and uninteresting. If Busoni was looking backward in his Bach interpretations, he was hinting at the future in Chopin. He takes the tiny Prélude very directly, without much charm and inflection. Then he repeats the piece and modulates (using the rhythm of the Prélude) into G flat. The Étude receives as straightforward a reading as the Prélude. Little color is present, though the playing is strong and direct. Busoni adds an extra measure, just prior to the concluding octaves. Was this deliberate, or did he absent-mindedly repeat the previous measure? At another spot he breaks one measure into two.

But these recordings are unjust to Busoni. He was no Grünfeld who made pretty-pretty sounds. As well confine the Atlantic Ocean in a milk bottle as confine Busoni to records. He was not noted for playing this kind of four-minute music, and the chances are that he was not particularly good at it (as his records suggest). He was rather the pianist of the *Hammerklavier*, of the Liszt B minor Sonata and *Don Juan Fantasy*, of Bach's *Goldberg Variations* and Beethoven's *Diabelli*. In music like this he must have been one of the most fascinating, brilliant, large-scaled and controlled pianists in musical history: an artist with a burning message and a sense of mission, as removed from a mere piano manipulator as a sparrow is from an eagle.

XXVIII

Perfection Plus

BUSONI WAS THE FIRST of the great modern pianists. He was followed by Sergei Rachmaninoff and Josef Hofmann. Rachmaninoff was a late starter who turned from conducting and composing to the piano because of economic necessity. But Hofmann, that most remarkable of prodigies, was startling audiences in 1882 when he was six years old. Thus, though three years younger than Rachmaninoff, he deserves priority.

To those who have it in their heads that Hofmann and Rachmaninoff represented a romantic age of piano playing, it may come as a surprise to hear them called "modernists." And, as one listens to their records, it is easily apparent that they took more liberty in phrase, tempo and rubato than do most pianists who belong to the twentieth century proper. But time alters perspective, and modernists they were, in their day. Compared to most of their great colleagues, Busoni included, they took remarkably few liberties, and their performances were models of textual accuracy against the performances of the Lisztianers and Leschetizkianers. Hofmann and Rachmaninoff represented the first reflection of the modern attitude that the printed note is the all-important guide for the performer. This was something new in history, though today we take it for granted. And, as the printed note became more and more important (because of the disappearance of such traditions as improvisation and embellishment and the old idea of the virtuoso as hero), so did the "message" of the composer. All of a sudden the composer tended to become more important than the virtuoso.

Anton Rubinstein's attitude had been, in his own words, "Just play first exactly what is written. If you have done full justice to it and then still feel like adding or changing anything, why, do so." But "No!" said Rubinstein's greatest pupil, Hofmann. Hofmann's attitude was that the performer had enough to do to play the notes as written without adding anything of his own. A lifetime, said Hofmann, would not suffice to bring out the possibilities of a Beethoven sonata or any equivalent work. "I venture to prove to any one who will play for me—if he be at all worth listening to—that he does not play *more* than is written (as he may think), but, in fact, a good deal *less* than the printed page reveals. . . . The true interpretation of a piece of music results from a correct understanding of it, and this, in turn, depends solely upon scrupulously exact reading. . . . A purposed, blatant parading of the player's dear self through wilful additions of nuances, shadings, effects, and what not, is tantamount to a falsification; at best it is 'playing to the galleries,' charlatanism. The player should always feel convinced that he plays only what is written." (Apropos of this statement, Hofmann followed his own precepts. His playing of course had great freedom, poetry and individuality, but textually it remains breath-takingly accurate. In his best recordings, which are an unreleased series he did for H.M.V. in the mid-1930s, one can take dictation from his playing. Even in the left hand, every value—every rest, every dotted note, every phrase mark—is reproduced with blueprint accuracy.)

Yes, Hofmann was a modernist, with far fewer mannerisms than any pianist of his rank. In his little book, *Piano Playing*, he has some interesting observations to make about the shift in styles that led to the modern approach:

At first there was childlike simplicity. Then, with the further development of the art we find the tendency toward enormous technical accomplishment and very great complexity. Fifty years ago [1875] technic was everything. The art of piano playing was the art of the musical speedometer—the art of playing the greatest number of notes in the shortest possible time. Of course there were a few outstanding giants, Rubinsteins, Liszts and Chopins, who made their technic subordinate to their message; but the public was dazzled with technic—one might better say pyrotechnics. Now we find the circle drawing toward the point of simplicity again. Great beauty, combined with adequate technic, is demanded rather than enormous technic divorced from beauty.

It was not that Hofmann had anything against technique. Rosenthal had said, "I have found that the people who claim that technic is not an important thing in piano playing simply do not possess it"—and Hofmann agreed with him. Hofmann, who had a perfect technique for the music he played, was quite aware that a Rubinstein concerto or the Chopin E minor cannot be played without technique to burn. But technique, to Hofmann, was merely a set of tools from which the skilled artisan draws what is necessary. "The mere possession of the tools means nothing; it is the instinct—the artistic intuition as to when and how to use the tools—that counts."

Nor did Hofmann, who self-consciously fought the exaggerations of romantic pianism, fear that "objectivity" would necessarily mean sterility:

It is sometimes said that the too objective study of a piece may impair the "individuality" of its rendition. Have no fear of that! If ten players study the same piece with the same high degree of exactness and objectivity—depend on it: each one will still play it quite differently from the nine others, though each one may think his rendition the only correct one. For each one will express what, according to his lights, he has mentally and temperamentally absorbed. Of the distinctice feature which constitutes the difference in the ten conceptions each one will have been unconscious while it formed itself, and perhaps also afterward. But it is just this unconsciously formed feature which constitutes legitimate individuality and which alone will admit of a real fusion of the composer's and the interpreter's thought.

And Hofmann did play with a mixture of classic purity and romantic elegance. Many connoisseurs consider him the most flawless pianist of the century and possibly the greatest. He had all of Godowsky's technique (though the two pianists were aiming at different things) with more color and much more fire. His style combined an aristocratic musical line, a perpetually singing tone, and a range of dynamics from the most ethereal pianissimo to tigerish surges in which the piano erupted. His control was amazing, and remained so until his last few years before the public, when a combination of factors began to affect him; but even then his playing was thrilling. Yet, after the novelty of his prodigy days was forgotten, it took Hofmann some time to be recognized as the perfect pianist he was, for his playing was alien to the standards of the day. It contained none

of the egomania of de Pachmann and the other favorites, nor did it
have the blazing, super-sensational virtuosity of a Rosenthal (though
Hofmann's virtuosity was on a par and was much better controlled).
It was regular, clear, logical, sensitive playing, with the notes correctly positioned and proportioned, the basses wonderfully organized, all animated by an extraordinarily subtle poetry. As a matter
of fact, Hofmann's playing until the 1920s might even have had its
moments of pedanticism. Certainly the records he made from 1911
to 1920 have nowhere near the titanic force, freedom and originality
that were in evidence when he played the same pieces during the
two decades after 1920.

It is rather startling to hear Hofmann's recordings of specific
works against those of the Liszt pupils. Hofmann is clear, elegant
and unflurried, almost chaste, with an incredible fluency and with
none of the heavings, sighings, sentimentalities, eccentricities and
sloppy technique of some of the Lisztianers. Indeed, in 1907 the fine
American musician Edward Burlingame Hill felt it necessary to
come to Hofmann's defense:

As an artist, Hofmann is so normal as to baffle the critics not a little. In
these days of ultra-modern music, when intensity and sensational effect
play so large a part, when the neurotic temperament is regarded as
commonplace, it is strange to be confronted by an artist who looks as if he
were in training for some athletic sport, his muscles solid, who plays as
healthily as he looks. In his interpretations one is struck by the absence of
sentimentality.

That was written twenty years after Hofmann's American debut
at the age of ten. Nothing like it had ever been heard in this country, and not until the appearance of the young Yehudi Menuhin was
there to be a comparable debut. Hofmann, born in Cracow on January 20, 1876, had been playing in public since the age of six, and
he may have been the most completely equipped prodigy in musical
history. At nine, in Berlin, he played the Beethoven C major Concerto with no less a conductor than Hans von Bülow. He had been
taught by his father, Casimir, who was a very good promoter in
addition to being a good musician (pianist, conductor, composer).
Enough advance interest in the boy was built up so that his American debut on November 29, 1887, rated the Metropolian Opera
House. He played the Beethoven C major, a set of variations by

Rameau, a Chopin group consisting of the *Berceuse*, E flat Nocturne and E minor Waltz, the Weber-Liszt *Polacca* and a group of improvisations. Adolf Neuendorff conducted.

There was not a critic who was not bowled over. "That wonderful boy," Hofmann was called. Krehbiel pointed out that Josef's technique was phenomenal, and that he was anything but a trained monkey. "It would be difficult... to convince a musician that the exquisite phrasing and lovely shading... the solidity of style and lucidity of exposition... were acquired by an exercise of a merely imitative faculty, no matter how abnormally developed.... Ripeness, maturity, precision, pianistic genius... Bewildering." The *New York Times* was no less extravagant. "Josef Hofmann was born to be a pianist, and as such today at the age of 10 he is in the front rank.... Perhaps the one thing which struck the educated hearer most forcibly was the fact that the boy did not play like a boy. It was not necessary to think 'That is extremely good work for a child,' because it would have been extremely good work for a man."

So successful was the debut that Josef became the rage, and he was—to put it mildly—exploited. His November 29 appearance at the Metropolitan Opera was followed by appearances there on December 1, 3, 6, 13, 15, 22, 27 and 31; January 2, 18, 21 and 25; and February 1, 8, 15 and 18. In the meantime he was playing in Brooklyn, Boston, Philadelphia and Baltimore. In all he played fifty-two concerts in about ten weeks, sharing the program with other musicians. After a while, wrote Krehbiel, the concerts "degenerated into a craze so silly and irrational that a sordid father and grasping managers did not hesitate to encourage it with mountebank tricks."

The boy's repertoire was very large. In addition to the Beethoven C major, he had several other concerted works at his fingertips: the Beethoven C minor, the Mozart D minor, Mendelssohn's *Rondo brillant* and G minor Concerto and Weber's *Concertstück*. Solo pieces included works by Pirani, a good deal of Chopin, Rubinstein, Gottschalk, Bach, Weber, Moszkowski, Kalkbrenner (the Duo for two pianos, which Josef played with his father), Mozart and himself. One of Josef's compositions was the "*Polonaise Americaine*, composed, scored for orchestra and conducted by Josef Hofmann." In addition to his inflexible mastery, Josef startled musicians by the accuracy of his ear. Once, at the Metropolitan Opera, he heard a tuning fork supposed to be at 440-A. Josef said it was a shade sharp, and it was.

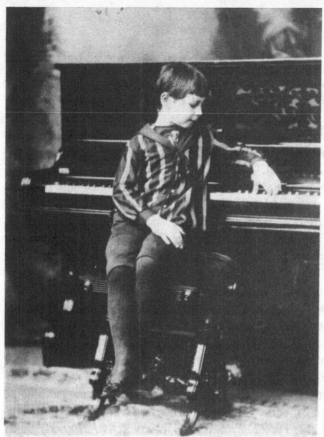

Josef Hofmann at the age of ten, in a photograph taken at the time he was giving his long series of concerts in New York and arousing the interest of the Society for the Prevention of Cruelty to Children.

Hofmann shortly after the turn of the century. His colleagues regarded him as a superman.

On November 26, 1887, three days before the debut, the attention of the New York Society for the Prevention of Cruelty to Children was alerted by a notice in the public press. The notice said that Josef Hofmann was to play an excessive number of concerts under the management of Henry Abbey. From November 29 on, the Society kept close watch, and tried to see to it that Josef was licensed to give no more than four concerts a week. But the boy played more anyway, and Elbridge T. Gerry, president of the Society, issued a complaint to the Mayor of New York, Abram S. Hewitt. Musicians took up Gerry's cause. Among the letters to the press was one by that fine and respected pianist, Ernst Perabo. He was very worried about Josef:

Just because he does not make faces or turn somersaults before the piano, people think that the work is easily done. The more easily he grasps, executes and interprets, the more expensive is the fuel; excellent work exhausts the finest fibre, and the nervous system once ruined, leaves him a wreck. We were told of an examination by Mayor Hewitt and several physicians. With all due respect for their learning, what, pray, can these persons know of the mental freight he is carrying in his memory, of intricate, abstruse, scientific difficulties, representing from eight to ten hundred pages of repertory?... If his present career be continued, he will be deprived of a normal childhood.

Perabo was alluding to a physical examination given Josef on February 2, 1888. The boy appeared to be in excellent health, but a newspaperman noted that "his face, however, looked pale and there were dark rings under his eyes." No wonder. The previous Wednesday he had played in New York. Friday had seen him in Philadelphia. On Saturday he had given another New York concert before leaving for Boston, where he had played on Monday; and he had returned to New York to play on Wednesday. He was not yet eleven years old.

Suddenly his father canceled all concerts. Casimir Hofmann let the press know, on February 21, that he did not want to take a chance with his son's health. The *Times* reporter looked in on Josef and returned with a quote that should have earned him a raise, "What do they want to make a little boy like me work so hard for? I am not able to do it." But other reporters smelled something, and word got around that a wealthy man had put up a sizable sum of money for Josef's retirement and study. Casimir heatedly denied this. But he was lying. Alfred Corning Clark, a New York philanthropist, was the donor of fifty thousand dollars—on condition that Josef be withdrawn from the concert stage until he was eighteen. Clark's name was kept a secret. When Abbey heard of Casimir's decision, he promptly started a fifty-seven-thousand-dollar suit for breach of contract. A subsequent medical examination revealed that Josef, while not suffering from any organic disease, was beginning to show signs of "mental derangement." Whereupon Abbey withdrew the suit—he had to, or he would have been run out of town by an excited citizenry—and on March 28 Josef sailed for Europe with his family.

Looking back at his childhood, Hofmann insisted that he had been perfectly happy playing those concerts and that no favor had been done for him by calling them quits. He told an interviewer:

I should never have stopped appearing in public. That retirement for six years was kindly and generously meant by Alfred Corning Clark, who financed it to the amount of $50,000. My family meant well too, but I see now that much of that time was wasted.

Public appearance is a spur to ambition. If a child is obviously going to be a professional musician, he will be a better one for encountering professional appraisal, at least in homeopathic doses, and with the use of discretion about his health. . . . Public appearance is the test, the yardstick by which a musician can know if he is advancing. . . . No, it was not necessary for me to retire, I believe. I really wasn't ill. Six months would have restored me, but six years made my ambition go slack.

Back in Europe, the Hofmann family made its headquarters in Berlin. Josef studied there with Moszkowski and then, starting in 1892, with Anton Rubinstein in Dresden. He had forty lessons with Rubinstein—once a week in the winter, twice a week in the summer. Rubinstein had heard Josef play the Beethoven C minor Concerto at the age of eight, and had said that he was a boy such as the world of music had never before produced. According to Hofmann, he was the only private pupil Rubinstein ever accepted. Rubinstein must have been an unsettling teacher, the kind of teacher that only a brilliant student can profit from. He never played for Hofmann and was capricious in his advice. Hofmann wrote, many years later:

Rubinstein was much given to whims and moods, and he often grew enthusiastic about a certain conception only to prefer a different one the next day. Yet he was always logical in his art, and though he aimed at hitting the nail from various points of view he always hit it on the head. Thus he never permitted me to bring to him, as a lesson, any composition any more than once. He explained this to me once by saying that he might forget in the next lesson what he told me in the previous one, and by drawing an entirely new picture only confuse my mind.

Rubinstein insisted on textual fidelity. This surprised Hofmann, who had heard many Rubinstein concerts and taken note of the liberties employed by the great Russian. He once got up enough nerve to ask Rubinstein to reconcile the paradox. Rubinstein gave the answer teachers through the ages have given, "When you are as old as I am now, you may do as I do." Only Rubinstein added, "If you can."

As a sort of graduation, Rubinstein arranged for Hofmann's debut as a mature pianist. It was in Hamburg, on March 14, 1894, and Hofmann played Rubinstein's D minor Concerto with the composer on the podium.

After his debut in 1894 Hofmann entered upon the life of a touring pianist. He was especially popular in Russia to the point where, in 1912, he gave twenty-one consecutive concerts in St. Petersburg, not once repeating a piece. In all he played 255 different works during that marathon. Apparently, once he had a piece in his fingers, it was there for good. That was fortunate, for he was one of the few pianists who never practiced. At most it might be an hour a day when he had a tour coming up; usually nothing it all. His wife's diary contains an entry during the Russian tour in 1909:

Jef [her pet name for Josef] did a marvellous thing, really. He did not know what he was to play, and made eye-brows when he saw the Brahms [the *Handel* Variations] on the program. He has not touched, seen or thought of it for 2½ years, since he played it in Libau, April, 1907, and he went thro' it without a thought or hesitation. It is spooky.

Spooky indeed. He soon became one of the pianistic headliners of his generation, and to his colleagues he was a legend for the finish and craftsmanship of his playing. He made the United States his headquarters during World War I, became a citizen, was appointed first head of the piano department of the Curtis Institute of Music when it was created in 1924 and became its director in 1927. He remained there until 1938. One of the most famous concerts ever given in the United States took place at the Metropolitan Opera on November 28, 1937, when Hofmann celebrated the fiftieth anniversary of his American debut. In 1955 the solo portion of this concert was issued commercially by Columbia. Subsequently, the entire concert, including Rubinstein's D minor Concerto and Hofmann's own *Chromaticon* for piano and orchestra, was made available through the International Piano Library (now the International Piano Archives at the University of Maryland). The last years of his life were tragic. He became an alcoholic and his concerts combined moments of greatness with actual incoherencies.

Hofmann composed a large number of charming salon pieces under the name of Michael Dvorsky (Russian for "Hofmann," meaning "man of the court"). He kept this pen name secret for many years. In 1916 he was asked whether he and Dvorsky were one and the same. No, no, said Hofmann. He told a reporter from the Cincinnati *Post* the story of Dvorsky's *Chromaticon*, "I am flattered indeed that the public thinks the work is mine. But it really isn't. Every artist receives numbers of manuscripts. At the time I received this one, I had looked over twenty-five or thirty and I found this one very much worth while. I do not know the composer, but selected the concerto entirely on its own merits." Dvorsky, said Hofmann with a straight face, was "an interesting and invalid young French composer, at present inhabiting the Spanish *villa d'eau* of San Sebastian."

Blessed with one of the most remarkable ears in musical history, Hofmann could startle his colleagues with Liszt-like tricks in which he played back music, correctly, without ever having seen the printed note. Maurice Aronson, Godowsky's assistant, liked to tell the story of Godowsky's *Fledermaus* transcription. It seemed that in Berlin, around 1900, Hofmann and Godowsky became close friends —which they remained throughout life—and Hofmann would drop into Godowsky's studio to listen, open-mouthed, while Godowsky was working out *Fledermaus*. Hofmann's father finally ran into Godowsky and said, "What have you done to Josef? He sits home all day and plays Strauss waltzes." A week or so later, Hofmann visited his friend and played the entire transcription, note for note. He, of course, had never seen the music; in fact, Godowsky had not even written it down. It should be added that Godowsky's *Fledermaus* is one of the most fantastic, resourceful and complicated stunts ever written for the piano. And Rosina Lhevinne says that Hofmann once heard Josef Lhevinne play Liszt's *Lorelei*, which somehow Hofmann had never studied or heard, and played it that very evening as an encore at his concert. This ability stood Hofmann in good stead because, curiously, he was a poor sight reader. Nevertheless, as a young man he built up a repertoire that included just about everything of importance from Beethoven up through some music by Brahms, and also a good deal that was not of importance. In his youth, incidentally, Hofmann played many more concertos than the seven or eight he ended up with in the last twenty years of his career.

Hofmann was short, and he had small hands. In the days when pianists sported heads of hair à la Paderewski, Hambourg, de Pachmann and Grainger, Hofmann wore his neatly cut: another touch of "modernism." (Rachmaninoff went him one better by favoring a convict-like trim.) Steinway made several pianos especially for Hofmann, with keys shaved a fraction of an inch. It was not that Hofmann was inoperative on a standard instrument, but he found the custom-built model a little more comfortable. His style on it was one of the phenomena of twentieth-century pianism. Above all he had tone: a magical tone, never hard even at moments of greatest stress; a shimmering, tinted, pellucid tone. His playing had a degree of spontaneity, of "lift," of dash, daring and subtle rhythm, that was unparalleled. Perhaps only his close friend Rachmaninoff was titan enough to stand by his side as an equal. But even Rachmaninoff never had Hofmann's poetry, color and vitality. Nobody so made the piano sing.

When he played, there was the feeling of a tremendous and original musical personality. His rubato was carefully measured, yet it flowed freely and naturally. His playing always had breathing space, and his basses exceptional clarity. (Hofmann used to despise what he scornfully called "right-hand pianists.") Never did the playing sag, never were there dead spots, never did the tensile quality slacken. A strong classic element was represented in the purity of his pianistic approach. And his interpretations, romantic but not exaggerated, had a measure of classicism. The grand manner, of course, was always present: roaring surges of tone when the music demanded it;

Hofmann and his son, Anton. Note the strong likeness between Anton and his father at the age of ten (see page 361).

delicate applications of color; the complete gamut. There also was a feeling of spontaneity, and those who knew his playing well were aware that he never played the same piece twice exactly the same way. To say that Hofmann's was a personal style means little; every great pianist's style is personal. To say that it was the quintessence of aristocracy may mean a little more. The finish and refinement of his playing were unique. Only Godowsky approached him in that respect, and Godowsky never had Hofmann's red blood.

For Hofmann, though not a thundering virtuoso on the order of a Rosenthal or Friedman, had equal force and could thunder with the best of them when he wanted to. He could also match fingers with any of them. Those who heard his Carnegie Hall performances of Liszt's *Don Juan* in the middle 1930s have memories of technical feats that even so stupendous a workman as Simon Barere later failed to approximate in the same piece.

Nor is it likely that any pianist of the century had Hofmann's incredible control of dynamics. His pianissimo had many levels of shading, and he seemed to have a brain built into each of his velvet fingertips. When he played Chopin's posthumous D flat Étude the piano did things that pianos are not supposed to do. Hofmann's fourth and fifth fingers sang out the melody over the perfect staccato of the accompaniment; and the thumb of his left hand was finding inner voices that none but he ever seemed able to discover: three strands going at once, in the most elegant and controlled polyphony. When he really let go, his fortissimo attack had an almost savage quality. There was actually something frightening about it, all the more in that he used it sparingly and with meaning. Even when, toward the end of his career, he was out of pianistic condition, his interpretations were never less than fascinating. At his last New York concert, in 1948, Hofmann played Chopin's B minor Sonata. At one point in the last movement—measure 68—he did not like the way things were going and in a frenzy brought his left hand down and smashed the keyboard with his palm, *sforzando* as marked. It was like the roar of a wounded lion. But even in his great days of the 1920s and 1930s there were always such moments, when Hofmann got carried away, losing his classic poise, and when in a frustrated madness he would try to burst the flesh that held him back.

· XXIX ·

The Puritan

THE TALL, DOUR, LANK, unsmiling figure of Sergei Rachmaninoff, with its seamed face and head of close-cropped (almost shaved) hair invariably reminded the public of a convict on the loose. No audience ever saw him unbend, ever saw that sorrowful Russian face relax, ever saw the least crack in his gravity. But at the piano those marvelous, infallible hands created bronzelike sonorities, welding the bronze into structures of imposing architectural solidity. Just as Hofmann was the great colorist, so Rachmaninoff was the great pianistic builder of his day. He was the Hamlet to Hofmann's Mercutio, and the latter knew it. He once told Rachmaninoff, "I dare say that I do not plan how to build a composition and occasionally it happens to sound well." This was a monumental oversimplification with a grain of truth in it, for Hofmann was the most spontaneous-sounding of pianists. Rachmaninoff could never work that way. Under his hands the music would emerge with inexorable logic—beautifully organized, impeccably delivered, never capricious, and year in and year out sounding much the same way. And it was playing buttressed by one of the colossal techniques in pianistic history, with a powerful left hand that probably left Dreyschock's far behind.

At any Rachmaninoff concert one noted the sharp rhythmic thrusts (these were his trademark), the virility and the sense of sonority that the man had. And, above all, a musical elegance in which phrases were shaped with exquisite finish. When he played a Liszt transcription of a Schubert song, one immediately realized how unimaginative and unmusical most singers were. Only the very greatest vocal artists—a Lotte Lehmann or an Elisabeth Schumann—could shape a phrase with equal finesse and authority. But there

390

never was any *Kitsch* to Rachmaninoff's playing, even when the music was *Kitsch*. So big were his musical thoughts, so aristocratic his instincts, that he ennobled whatever he played.

His was not an instinctive way of musical interpretation. He studied every piece as a composer as well as a pianist, and he worked out its essential musical structure, emotional as well as formal. In every piece he aimed at one culminating moment—what he called "the point." According to his friend Marietta Shaginyan he once raged at himself after a concert, "Didn't you notice that I missed the point? Don't you understand—I let the point slip!" Writes Shaginyan:

On a later occasion he explained that each piece he plays is shaped around its culminating point: the whole mass of sounds must be so measured, the depth and power of each sound must be given with such purity and gradation, that this peak point is achieved with an appearance of the greatest naturalness, though actually its accomplishment is the highest art. This moment must arrive with the sound and sparkle of a ribbon snapped at the end of a race—it must seem a liberation from the last material obstacle, the last barrier between truth and its expression. The composition itself determines this culmination; the point may come at its end or in the middle; it may be loud or soft, yet the musician must always be able to approach it with sure calculation, for if it slips by, the whole structure crumbles, the work goes soft and fuzzy, and cannot convey to the listener what must be conveyed. Rachmaninoff added, "I am not the only one who experiences this—Chaliapin too."

Professionals stood in awe of Rachmaninoff's workmanship, and of his ability to accomplish with apparent ease things that were next to impossible. Unlike many of the great pianists, he had enormous hands, and the murderous figurations in his own music, with its very wide stretches, were a result of the unusual conformation of his hands. He grasped a chord with unparalleled security, and his technique did not have a weak spot anywhere. The accuracy and deftness with which he could skim through the most complicated passagework left his colleagues breathless in respect and envy. If Hofmann was the Tintoretto of pianists, Rachmaninoff was—at least in one respect—the Canaletto. Never was there a blurred line or a vague color. Using the pedal with great tact, letting his fingers and not his feet do the work, Rachmaninoff was able to unfold the notes with fantastic clarity. "You have to peer into every corner," he once said, "take every screw apart, so that you can then easily put the whole together again."

Stylistically there were few vagaries in his playing or, for that matter, in his platform presence. His rhythms had no eccentricities, his ideas were unsentimental, he adhered closely to the printed note, he sat quietly before the instrument. Probably no pianist ever had his sheer finish, his authority, his unruffled, unflawed perfection. Not for him were the spontaneous approach of a Hofmann, the anarchism that Friedman sometimes displayed, the intellectualities of a Busoni, the scholarship of a Schnabel. Instead he was the pianist of control—a romantic pianist who carefully avoided exaggeration, an extraordinary technician who never went in for mere show, a tempered man and a tempered artist with a naturally big style and a sense of virile, unforced poetry. Most connoisseurs put him on a par with Hofmann as the greatest pianist of the time in that kind of repertoire (from, roughly, Beethoven through Liszt; hardly any Bach or Mozart, no moderns except salon moderns). And Rachmaninoff, of course, played his own music inimitably. Hofmann and Rachmaninoff were very close friends. Hofmann thought that Rachmaninoff was the greatest living pianist, and Rachmaninoff thought that Hofmann was the greatest living pianist. Henry Pleasants, as a young critic in Philadelphia, interviewed Rachmaninoff and asked him who he thought the greatest pianists of the day were. Rachmaninoff, always deliberate, thought a long time. "Well," he said, "there's Hofmann." He thought some more. "And there's me," and he closed his mouth and didn't say another word.

The amazing thing is that Rachmaninoff became a professional pianist late in life through economic necessity. Up to then he had used the piano primarily to introduce his own music. Born in 1873, he concentrated almost exclusively on his own works, and it was not until after the Russian Revolution of 1917 that he started to build up a concert repertoire. At the Moscow Conservatory he had concentrated much more on composition, working with Arensky (harmony) and Taneiev (composition). His piano teacher was Nicolai Zverev; and he was also helped by his cousin, Alexander Siloti, who had recently returned to Russia after studies with Liszt. Among Rachmaninoff's classmates were Josef Lhevinne, who was to develop into a magnificent pianist, and Alexander Scriabin. Nobody thought of Rachmaninoff as a pianist at that time, even though he passed the piano examination with honors. He was the Moscow Conservatory's fair-haired boy as a composer; and when he was graduated in 1892 he received the Great Gold Medal, the highest honor, for his opera *Aleko*.

At the Conservatory he scared everybody. He seemed to have the entire literature of music in his head. Anything he heard he never forgot. More: he could go to the piano and play back, note for note, anything he had ever heard—sometimes years later. He was a fabulous sight reader. His was an incredible musical organization; his mind was a musical blotter that soaked up and retained every kind of aural impression. He could take the most difficult pieces—the Brahms *Handel* Variations, say—and memorize it in two days, giving a finished performance. Scriabin's murderous C sharp minor Etude (Op. 42, No. 5) gave him a bit of trouble. "Difficult etude!" he told one of his classmates. "I spent an hour on it."

But other things interested him more than the piano. It was not that he was unacquainted with the literature of the piano. He had started taking lessons at four, at his own request, and his parents had seen to it that he had good instruction. He even had toured Russia, three years after graduating from the Conservatory, as accompanist for the Italian violinist Teresina Tua. During that tour he had been given the chance to play solos. But he cut it short and left Tua, for piano playing bored him. He found much more interest in conducting and, of course, composing. His familiar Prelude in C sharp minor, which he grew to loathe as much as Paderewski loathed the Minuet in G, was composed as early as 1893, and it made him famous. England invited him to appear in 1898, largely to see the person who was the composer of THE prelude. (He found it published in England under such titles as *The Burning of Moscow, The Day of Judgment* and *The Moscow Waltz*.) In Russia he busied himself conducting operas in the Imperial Theatre. He also directed orchestral concerts, and as late as 1933 the composer-pianist Nikolai Medtner recalled a concert that Rachmaninoff had given in 1904:

I shall never forget Rachmaninoff's interpretation of Tchaikovsky's Fifth Symphony. Before he conducted it, we heard it only in the version of Nikisch and his imitators. True, Nikisch had saved this symphony from a complete fiasco (as conducted by its composer), but then his pathetic slowing of the tempo became the law for performing Tchaikovsky, enforced by conductors who had followed him blindly. Suddenly, under Rachmaninoff, all this imitative tradition fell away from the composition and we heard it as

MISHKIN
N.Y.

(Left) Sergei Rachmaninoff in 1909, as he looked during his first American tour.

(Right) Rachmaninoff in the early 1920s. This is as close as he ever came to smiling in public.

(Below) Sergei Rachmaninoff.

DRAWING BY HAROLD C. SCHONBERG

if for the first time; especially astonishing was the cataclysmic impetuosity of the finale, an antithesis to the pathos of Nikisch that had always harmed this movement.

Even more unexpected... was the impression of Mozart's G minor Symphony, which had long been labeled dull—a thing in rococo style. I shall never forget this symphony as conducted by Rachmaninoff; it suddenly came toward us, pulsing with life and urgency.

(In America, Rachmaninoff did little conducting after he established himself as a pianist. But his recording of his own third Symphony with the Philadelphia Orchestra, around 1940, bears out Medtner's remarks. Rachmaninoff conducts as he played the piano —with drive, authority, complete command and that rhythmic snap which was so peculiarly his own.)

For a while, Rachmaninoff lived in Dresden, using that city as a base of operations and introducing his C minor Concerto—one of the most popular ever written—to various European cities in 1908. His first American tour took place the following year. He played only his own music, including the new D minor Concerto (dedicated to Josef Hofmann, who never played it, saying that it was not for him). Walter Damrosch was the conductor at the premiere, in New York on November 28, 1909. Rachmaninoff did not like America and wrote a complaining letter home.

... You know, in this accursed country, where you're surrounded by nothing but Americans and the "business," "business," they are forever doing, clutching you from all sides and driving you on.... I am very busy and very tired. Here is my perpetual prayer: God give me strength and patience. Everyone treats me nicely and kindly, but I am horribly bored with it all, and I feel that my character has been quite spoiled here.

He may have been bored, but he made enough of an impact to be offered the post of conductor of the Boston Symphony Orchestra. Rachmaninoff would have none of it. He returned to his homeland, made European tours, became one of the idols of musical Russia, and made his last appearance there as a pianist on September 5, 1917. Three weeks after the Revolution he was invited to appear in Stockholm. He and his family left Russia for good on December 23. They were exiles. He played twelve concerts in Stockholm, paid off his debts, caught his breath and looked around. To take care of his wife and daughters he had to make a living, and composition alone was out of the question. The career of orchestral conductor apparently did not appeal to him, and he never liked teaching. So he turned to the piano.

This meant a complete shift in his musical philosophy. He had to develop a virtuoso equipment (which he of course had; but it needed pointing up in the repertoire) and build up a series of concert programs (which he did not have). For a man of forty-five, this was no easy assignment. His choice must have been complicated when, in 1918, the Boston Symphony Orchestra offered him a proposal to conduct 110 concerts in thirty weeks. Ossip Gabrilowitsch had first been sounded out as the successor to Karl Muck, but he suggested Rachmaninoff. He wrote to the board of trustees that nobody admired the orchestra more than he, "and indeed I fully realize that an offer to become its conductor—if such an offer were made to me—would be a very great honor, but I am willing to see that honor bestowed on one who is worthier of it." Gabrilowitsch was that kind of man. Rachmaninoff, however, refused. He also turned down an offer from the Cincinnati Symphony Orchestra. In both cases he was tempted, but he knew that he did not have the repertoire. Encouraged by the offers, however, he moved to America and took up residence. Many musicians, including Hofmann and Gabrilowitsch, immediately rushed to offer advice and to use their influence. Before he knew it, Rachmaninoff was well established as a pianist. The Prelude in C sharp minor naturally followed him around wherever he went, and with an internal sigh he played it wherever he went. But once in a while he steeled himself and refused to play it. Huneker wrote about such an occasion in 1918:

> The Rachmaninoff "fans"—and there were thousands of them in the audience—clamored for the favorite piece of the Flatbush "flappers." They swayed toward Serge in serried masses. They clustered about the stage. . . . But the chief thing is the fact that Rachmaninoff did not play It. All Flapperdom sorrowed last night, for there are amiable fanatics who follow this pianist from place to place hoping to hear him in this particular Prelude, like an Englishman who attends every performance of the lady lion tamer hoping to see her swallowed by one of her pets.

Huneker was a romantic attuned to the romantic style. Rachmaninoff's playing disturbed him, and it is interesting to note that this piano specialist and scholar (for he was one) had very little to say about Hofmann and Rachmaninoff. Huneker's tastes were more toward Joseffy, Godowsky, Rosenthal and others of that school. For Hofmann and Rachmaninoff represented something new, and something that Huneker found inhibiting. They were of the new breed of pianists who adhered much more closely to the notes than did the old-timers: new pianists whose rhythm was tight and whose rubato was restrained. It was not the kind of playing that the older generation particularly liked, and when Rachmaninoff played a Beethoven sonata, Huneker was not exactly captivated:

The oldsters were reminded of von Bülow. The same cold white light of analysis, the incisive touch, the strongly marked rhythms, the intellectual grasp of the musical ideas, and the sense of the relative importance in phrase-groupings proclaimed that Rachmaninoff is a cerebral, not an emotional artist. Not Woodrow Wilson himself could have held the academic balance so dispassionately. Even the staccato Princeton touch was not absent.

But most others hailed the purity of the playing, its emotional directness and its avoidance of super-romantic effects. It was apparent that a giant was on the scene. Rachmaninoff was dubbed The Puritan of Pianists (as much for his looks as for his sober interpretations), and the name was used admiringly, not in any pejorative sense. Rachmaninoff also rapidly changed his mind about America, and on a British tour in 1922 he wrote, "I extol America to all the English and they get so angry." By the middle 1920s Rachmaninoff was an international pianistic idol, and Ernest Newman in London was writing, "In a world that teems with fine pianists I know none finer than Rachmaninoff." W. J. Henderson, America's most respected critic, wrote in 1930 of Rachmaninoff's performance of Chopin's B flat minor Sonata:

The logic of the thing was impervious; the plan was invulnerable; the proclamation was imperial. There was nothing left for us but to thank our stars that we had lived when Rachmaninoff did and heard him, out of the divine might of his genius, re-create a masterpiece. It was a day of genius understanding genius. One does not often get the opportunity to be present when such forces are at work. But one thing must not be forgotten: there was no iconoclast engaged; Chopin was still Chopin.

This kind of review followed Rachmaninoff to the very end, and it was no less than he deserved. Fortunately he left a large number of recordings—mostly of his own music, though he did record Schumann's *Carnaval* and Chopin's B flat minor Sonata and, with Fritz Kreisler, Schubert's Duo in A, Grieg's C minor Sonata and Beethoven's G major (Op. 30, No. 3). He started his great Victor series in 1920, though those discs had been preceded by a few now-forgotten Edison hill-and-dale (vertical-cut) discs. In 1941 Rachmaninoff suggested to Victor (according to the biography of Sergei Bertensson and Jay Leyda) that he record a series of his recital programs. Victor rejected the idea, and the loss is posterity's. Rachmaninoff was still in wonderful form in 1941. But two years later he was laid low in the middle of a concert tour. It was cancer. He was put into a hospital in Los Angeles, and he knew his end was near. He looked at his hands. "My dear hands. Farewell, my poor hands." A month later he was dead.

XXX

Some Headliners of the Day

HOFMANN AND RACHMANINOFF were legends to their colleagues in that they were flawless executants as well as imaginative, re-creative musical minds. But that did not mean that all other pianists had to pack up and go home. The castle of piano playing has many rooms, and one of the most popular tenants in that castle was Harold Bauer, who was born in 1873 in London. Bauer was one of the very few exceptions to the rule that every great pianist must start as a child prodigy. He started as a violinist—he had been a prodigy on *that* instrument, at least—and was well along on his career as a string player when Paderewski heard him play the piano. Bauer was around twenty at the time. Paderewski was impressed with the young man's easy approach to the keyboard, and by the lovely tone he drew from it. "You must be a pianist. Besides," he added—and on this, Paderewski was the ultimate authority—"you have such beautiful hair." Bauer ran all over asking musicians how he could make some kind of showing at the piano "with my musical understanding and my imperfect technique." But, according to Bauer, Paderewski was really in no way responsible for his change from violinist to pianist. Bauer by that time had made up his mind that he could never be a great violinist; and although he continued to give recitals, he began to concentrate more and more on the instrument that eventually was to give him a world-wide reputation. Who was Bauer's teacher? Nobody seems to know. Bauer himself does not mention any piano teacher anywhere in his autobiography, nor does any reference book that lists Bauer. His parents had taught him to read notes, and it may be that Bauer really is that miracle: a self-taught pianist. Apparently, he did have a few lessons from an aunt when he was a child. Others mention lessons from a pianist named Deryck Cooke. In an article he wrote for the *Musical Quarterly*, Bauer said that the greatest influence on his piano playing was a dancer, Isadora Duncan. He watched her and was struck by the way she translated music into motion. Bauer wondered if he could reverse the process, translating motion into music, and he worked out a series of muscular movements that enabled him to overcome a deficient technique.

By 1900 he was well established as a pianist. His musicianly, cultivated style made him especially fit for chamber music, and he appeared very often in trio with Kreisler and Casals, or in sonata recitals with Thibaud, Ysaÿe, Marsick or Gérardy. Bauer generally preferred joint recitals to solo ones. He considered himself a musician, not an entertainer. Yet, despite the handicap of a late switch to the piano, he was anything but a technical cripple. Virtuosity, however, was the last thing in his mind. It was typical that when he made his American debut in 1900 it was with the Brahms D minor Concerto. He scored a mild success. In later years Bauer could afford to be amused at the rather feeble impact he made, and he described his first American tour as "one of the least impressive visits ever made to the United States by an artist who had acquired some status in Europe." He eventually settled in America and in 1919 formed the Beethoven Association, which, until it was disbanded in 1940, was an important element in the musical life of New York, presenting great musicians in chamber music.

Bauer was an interesting combination of the new and the old style of playing. His programs virtually never contained fluff, and he was interested in the then modern school, introducing to America major works of Debussy and Ravel. A fine musician and a man of integrity, he played the piano and made music with unfailing taste. But in his attitude toward the printed note he was a romantic (and his editions of Schumann's piano music should be approached with great caution). Bauer said, in so many words, that it was impossible to follow the printed note even if the musician wished to do so. He believed that the markings of the composers were only "superficially related to the music. . . . Experience has taught me that the average composer's written indications are sometimes, but not always, right, whereas his verbal directions for performance (supplementing those already written) are almost invariably wrong. . . . Personally, although I have sought every opportunity of consulting a composer prior to playing his music in public, it is only very rarely that I have derived any benefit from his suggestions." According to Bauer, nobody can ever possibly know the exact intentions of the composer, "for the simple reason that musical notation permits of only relative, and not of absolute, directions for performance, and must therefore be an approximation which no two people can interpret precisely in the same way." Bauer inveighed against the "futility of blind respect to the text." He approvingly related an incident which had taken place when he was a young man in Paris:

I was turning the pages for Paderewski during a rehearsal of a Brahms trio he was about to play with his friends Gorski and Salmon. A discussion arose regarding a diminuendo that Paderewski wished to replace with a crescendo. "*Cela ne va pas*," objected the cellist, supported immediately by Gorski. "Brahms has written 'diminuendo' here for all three parts." I can still hear Paderewski's impatient reply: "*Il ne s'agit pas de ce qui est écrit. Il s'agit de l'effet musical.*" (The point is not what is written, but what the musical effect should be.)

I remember thinking at that time that it was quite proper for a genius such as he was to take liberties which must be denied to the ordinary man. Later I came to feel that the ordinary man who fails to realize what lies in the music beyond the printed indication is just . . . an ordinary man.

But Bauer's own well-tempered playing, his judicious tempos and sensitive interpretations, his absence of musical egocentricity and exaggeration, placed him as an artist squarely in the modern school. He had the taste and imagination to adapt his romanticism to the twentieth century. Others did not, and foundered.

Bauer, being English, represented a tempered sort of eclectic romanticism. There were others in his day who were closer to pure romanticism, and most of those had Slavic blood. The vintage year of 1873, which brought forth Rachmaninoff and Bauer, was followed by the birth of Josef Lhevinne. Lhevinne belonged in the company of the giants of any age, and this despite the fact that he was not one of the international headliners. He did not tour very much, and he contented himself with teaching, playing far fewer recitals than many pianists who were infinitely less gifted. He made very few records; the sum total of his American discs fills only a single LP disc. It seems that he was a quiet, not very ambitious man and certainly not a colorful one. The Lhevinne clipping folder in the

Harold Bauer. He switched from violin to piano at about the age of twenty, a feat unique in pianistic annals.

Josef Lhevinne, a super-virtuoso blessed with a poetic temperament.

Music Division of the Lincoln Center Library is voluminous, but it is curiously negative. No matter how hard the journalists tried, they never managed to make Lhevinne very interesting. He had little to say except platitudes. Yet the finish of his playing, his extraordinary technique and ease of delivery, his innate musicality were at once the joy and the despair of his competitors.

A fellow student of Rachmaninoff's at the Moscow Conservatory, Lhevinne studied with Safonoff and made his debut in the *Emperor* Concerto with Anton Rubinstein conducting. As early as 1906 he made his American debut. (That was the year a young man named Arthur Rubinstein came over for the first time.) Lhevinne's remarkable powers were quickly recognized. His tone was like the morning stars singing together, his technique was flawless even measured against the fingers of Hofmann and Rachmaninoff, and his musicianship was sensitive. He was one of the modern romantics who did not have to pull music apart to get its message across. Even when he played Chopin's Étude in thirds and the octave Étude in B minor— his double notes and octaves were fabulous—he never tried to make a stunt of the music. One of his little tricks, the utmost he would permit himself in the way of outward panache, was to take the octave glissandos of the Brahms *Paganini Variations* prestissimo, staccato and pianissimo. He accomplished this, one guesses, with a rigidly tight wrist that was propelled by sheer nervous impulses. It provided a quasi-glissando that sounds impossible of achievement; but Lhevinne did it, to the amazement of pianists who heard him, and to the utter disbelief of those who didn't.

Then there was the popular Mischa Levitzki, an American who was born in Russia, worked with Michailowski in Warsaw, Dohnányi in Berlin and Stojowski in New York. Levitzki was an elegant, finished pianist, and his death in 1941 at the early age of forty-five deprived the world of an unusually gifted artist. Also Russian-born was Simon Barere, who died at the piano in Carnegie Hall on April 2, 1951, while playing the Grieg Concerto with the Philadelphia Orchestra. Barere was a virtuoso-plus: not one of the remarkable musical minds, but a playing mechanism startling for speed, accuracy and disregard of difficulties. Barere, too, had a fine, colorful tone. The harder the music—*Don Juan Fantasy, Islamey*—the more Barere reveled in it, and the faster he played it. Yet the man was also capable of poetry, as witness his recorded performances of Chopin's

Alfred Cortot, a combination
of intellect and elegance.

Olga Samaroff, née Hickenlooper, from Texas.

C sharp minor Scherzo and Liszt's *Sonetto del Petrarca* Sonetto
No. 104.

The outstanding exponent of the French school after Pugno was
Alfred Cortot, a remarkable and unusual pianist. Born in Switzerland of French pianists, he was first taught by his sisters. When he
went to Paris in 1886, he failed the Conservatoire examination. He
attended the classes of Émile Descombes on an unofficial basis and
then studied with Diémer, in whose class he received the *premier
prix* in 1898. Among his friends were Risler and the brilliant young
violinist Jacques Thibaud. When Anton Rubinstein visited Paris,
Cortot played for him the first movement of the Beethoven *Appassionata*. Silence. Finally Rubinstein said, "My boy, don't you ever
forget what I am going to tell you. Beethoven's music must not be
studied. It must be reincarnated." Cortot never did forget those
words. He also *almost* played for Saint-Saëns, who used to wander
through the Conservatoire to see how the solfège and harmony
classes were going. He would ask each student what his instrument
was. Stopping in front of Cortot, he asked, "And you, my little one,
what do you play?" Said Cortot, "I am a pianist." Lisped Saint-
Saëns, "Oh, do not let us exaggerate, my little one." André Benoist,
later to be an important accompanist, was one of Cortot's classmates
and remembered him as not the most gifted in the class, but certainly the most determined and the hardest worker. Benoist did not
admire Cortot and said that he "would use any means to arrive at his
ends, which in his case were fame and power." Cortot, said Benoist,
also had a good opinion of himself. "How he strutted!"

After graduating from the Conservatoire, Cortot plunged into the
musical life of Europe, and not only as a pianist. He became an
assistant conductor at Bayreuth. Back in Paris he formed La Société
de Festival Lyrique. In 1902 he married Clotilde Bréal, Romain Rol-
land's first wife. In 1902 he also conducted the first Paris performance of *Götterdämmerung* (and also, though this was not a Parisian
premiere, conducted *Tristan und Isolde*; he was a great Wagnerian
who had all of the operas memorized and could play them all
through at the piano). He allied himself with his contemporaries and
introduced, as conductor and pianist, many works of the new
French school; he joined Casals and Thibaud in a trio that achieved
international fame; and he succeeded Pugno in 1917 as professor of
the highest piano class at the Conservatoire. As a teacher there, he
produced some important pianists, among them Clara Haskil,

Yvonne Lebure, Youra Geller and Magda Tagliaferro. With Auguste Mangeot he founded the École Normale de Musique. There his pupils included Dinu Lipatti, Samson François, Igor Markevich and Dino Ciani. In addition he wrote books and treatises, edited music, concertized, recorded.

How could he possibly find time to keep his fingers in shape? The answer is simple: he didn't. Cortot was always making mistakes or having memory slips. These would have been fatal with a lesser man. With Cortot they made no difference. One accepted them, as one accepts scars or defects in a painting by an old master. For, mistakes and all, it was obvious that Cortot had a big technique, and was capable of all kinds of fireworks when the music demanded it, as witness his fabulous recording of Liszt's Hungarian Rhapsody No. 11. And, as an interpretive artist, he was one of the strongest minds of his age.

There was in his playing a combination of intellectual authority, aristocracy, masculinity and poetry. Cortot retained a few mannerisms of the old school, but above all he was an intellectual player—a profound musician whose fine mind came through every note he played. He never made an impression merely as a technician, and he left flamboyance to the big virtuosos. Cortot was much more the re-creative musician, with severe elegance and logic to his playing, and with much more force (emotional as well as physical) than most French pianists have ever displayed. One guesses that, as with Risler, his German training modified his French approach. Cortot had a unique style, and a Cortot performance could always be recognized (and still can be recognized from his records; he made hundreds) by its sharpness, point, clarity of line, unmistakable rubato, sheer intelligence—yes, and by its wrong notes, too. Unfortunately he continued before the public too long; and both his final appearances and his final recordings were a disservice to his memory. During World War II, Cortot played in Germany and was considered a collaborationist by the French. He was allowed to resume his career in 1946 and continued playing until 1958. Some of his last appearances, marked by failing fingers and failing memory, were disastrous. At his best, though, he was one of the important pianists of the century—a man with a repertoire that apparently encompassed the entire history of music, an artist of formidable resource and all-embracing musical culture. Certainly no French pianist of his time approached him, though Yves Nat and Robert Lortat had their admirers. So did Isidor Philipp and Marguerite Long. The last two, however, became much better known as teachers (at the Conservatoire) than as soloists.

Philipp's greatest pupil was a child from Brazil named Guiomar Novaes. This young lady at the age of fourteen received a grant from the Brazilian government to study in Europe, and she chose the Paris Conservatoire. The year she applied, 1909, there were two vacancies for foreign students, and 387 applicants. Novaes played for a jury consisting, among others, of Debussy, Fauré and Moszkowski. Her pieces were the Paganini-Liszt Étude in E, Chopin's A flat Ballade and Schumann's *Carnaval*. She took first place, and the jury asked her to repeat the Ballade. There is a letter by Debussy in which he writes with amazement about the little Brazilian girl who came to the platform, forgot about public and jury, and played so beautifully, with such complete absorption.

Apparently her technique and musical ideas were completely formed at that time. One of her first pieces for Philipp was the Op. 81a Sonata (*Les Adieux*) by Beethoven. "No, no," said Philipp. "The second movement is much too fast. Play it slower." Novaes thought it over for a moment and then replayed it, with some difference in detail but in exactly the same tempo. This happened several times, and Philipp gave up. "Even at that age she had a mind of her own," he later said. By the end of the following year Novaes was a concert veteran, having played with the Chatelet Orchestra under Gabriel Pierné (this was her official debut), under Sir Henry Wood in England and on tour in Italy, Switzerland and Germany. In 1915, at the age of nineteen, she made her American debut, at Aeolian Hall in New York, and threw the critics into a tizzy. Aldrich of the *New York Times* called her "a musician by the grace of God." Sanborn in the *Globe* described her as "the young genius of the piano." Finck of the *Post* compared her to his ideal, Paderewski, and wrote that "more inspired playing has never been heard in Aeolian Hall." It was Huneker who, a year or so later, gave her a title that may have been a little off, geographically, but which stuck for a long time. In a *Times* review he called her "The Paderewska of the Pampas."

In her youth and early touring days Novaes had a very large repertory. In later life it narrowed. But whatever she played, she played perfectly, with an aristocratic approach, a perpetually singing line and complete spontaneity. Part of her appeal was in her natural approach to the keyboard. She was one of the few pianists about whom one felt that the instrument was a welded extension of her arms and fingers. A more natural, relaxed, effortless style could not be found anywhere. Her tone, in its color and subtlety, recalled the magic note-spinning of the great romantic pianists three generations ago (the generation, of course, in which Novaes was trained). Her technique was supple, she never strove for effect, and at all times her playing was intensely poetic and extremely feminine. When in the late 1950s she played the Schumann concerto with the New York Philharmonic under the direction of André Cluytens, the performance was strikingly reminiscent of Josef Hofmann's. It had much the same suppleness, tonal subtlety and unswerving rhythm.

Novaes' playing was never cut and dried. Again like Hofmann, she seldom played the same piece of music twice the same way. Each time she brought to it a slightly different point of view, and each time the new approach seemed perfectly natural and inevitable. Her microgroove records do not do her justice; they sound stilted next to her concert work. Curiously, the acoustic series she did for Victor in the early and middle 1920s give a much better idea of her worth, and those early performances of Liszt's *Gnomenreigen*, Philipp's *Feux follets*, the Paderewski Nocturne in B, Gottschalk's *Brazilian National Anthem* (a horrendously bad piece of music, but of appalling difficulty) and the Richard Strauss–Godowsky *Ständchen* are among the supreme treasures of the early piano discography.

The English school produced a much-loved pianist in Harold Samuel. Born in London and trained at the Royal College of Music, Samuel at first was a virtuoso pianist. As early as the turn of the century, however, he became interested in Bach, and in 1906 he seems to have introduced the *Goldberg* Variations to London. Then came a fallow period. He was not enough of a virtuoso to compete with the digital demons, and he had to turn to accompanying to keep alive. But in 1919, at the age of forty, he returned to the concert stage with a Bach program in Wigmore Hall. From then on, Bach and Samuel were inseparable. By 1921 Samuel was giving Bach weeks—six consecutive programs without repeating a work. Thus he was instrumental in breaching the Bach-Liszt, Bach-Tausig, Bach-Busoni castles, although the tradition of playing Bach as arranged by the great virtuosos lingered on for another two decades or so. (Today many of the younger pianists have never even heard the

Bach-Liszt Prelude and Fugue in A minor, or the Bach-Tausig Toccata and Fugue in D minor, which a generation ago opened every second recital.)

Samuel was a Bach *pianist* and was never attracted to the harpsichord. After one of his New York recitals Wanda Landowska lectured him on the desirability—nay, the necessity—of presenting the *Well-Tempered Clavier* and the other Bach clavier works on the instrument for which they were originally written. Samuel listened dutifully to the great lady. Finally he managed to get a word in. "But Madame Landowska, I don't *like* the harpsichord." As it happened, Landowska's point of view was the one that eventually was to prevail, and in the 1950s most pianists thought twice about playing Bach in public. That should not detract from Samuel's pioneer work. And his Bach playing was of the utmost elegance, flexibility, transparency and logic. He reflected the modern style in its lack of elaborate, Busoni-like ritards, in its strict adherence to the text, and in its rhythmic steadiness. In matters of scholarship Samuel might be faulted. Bach scholarship has gone a long way since Samuel died in 1937. But when the plump Harold Samuel came trotting out, beamed at the audience and took it into his confidence, comfortably settled himself and placed his big hands (he could take a twelfth) in position, it was an experience that only a great artist could supply.

Switzerland's most famous pianist—until he became an American citizen—was Rudolph Ganz. (Edwin Fischer then replaced him as Switzerland's favorite pianistic son.) Ganz had a busy life as concert artist, conductor, composer and educator. He was born in 1877 and was still playing in 1962 at the age of eighty-five. His early training took place in Zürich. Then he finished off in Berlin with Busoni and started making the international rounds. He was a brilliant pianist with a good deal of life and *joie de vivre* in his playing. It was clear, spirited and unaffected. In the first few decades of this century Ganz—like Ricardo Viñes, the Spanish pianist, and George Copeland, the American—allied himself with the avant-garde, introducing important works by Busoni, Ravel, Dukas, Bartók, Debussy, Dohnányi, Loeffler, d'Indy, Korngold and others. He also was one of the pioneers of recording, and some of his discs were made before 1910.

Three ladies active in America early in the century were the Russian-born Tina Lerner, the Hungarian-born Yolanda Mérö and the American-born (Texas) Olga Samaroff, née Hickenlooper. Each was a skilled and popular pianist, but of the three it was Samaroff who had the most brilliant career and the longest. She had been the first American girl to be admitted to the Paris Conservatoire. Then, in 1900, she returned to America to work with Ernest Hutcheson, going back to Europe to finish her studies with Ernst Jedliczka in Berlin. Her debut established her as an important artist. She created a sensation in London with her performance of the Tchaikovsky B flat minor. It was about that time that she changed her name. Hickenlooper was more of a burden than any young artist could be expected to assume. A formidable woman, a fiery and temperamental pianist, she was constantly on tour even through her years of marriage with Leopold Stokowski. They were married in 1911, divorced in 1924. After leaving the concert stage she became, for two years, music critic for the *New York Evening Post*. Then she taught at the Juilliard Graduate School and at the Philadelphia Conservatory. Among her best-known pupils were William Kapell and Rosalyn Tureck. Tureck at first was an exponent of contemporary music but later turned to Bach. She was one of the few young pianists of her day to defy the new musicology and specialize in Bach on the concert grand.

XXXI

New Philosophies, New Styles

AFTER CHOPIN, the significant advance in piano tech.nique came from two composers—Claude Debussy in France and Serge Prokofieff in Russia. Debussy experimented with, and finally resolved, a new approach to the keyboard. Up to him, French piano music had followed the course of the nineteenth century, Fauré composed elegant piano music largely influenced by Chopin and Schumann, though with a great deal of harmonic and melodic ingenuity. (It was Fauré's style that in turn led to such works as Falla's *Noches en los jardines de España* and d'Indy's *Symphonie sur un chant montagnard français*.) Saint-Saëns, perhaps the first of the neo-classic composers, wrote a very large quantity of fast-running, smoothly written virtuoso pieces in which Liszt and Chopin are combined. The remarkable Chabrier left a handful of prophetic piano works that were to influence Satie and Poulenc—pieces that were harmonically years ahead of their day, sophisticated and amusing, but nevertheless expressed basically in nineteenth-century language. In Russia, Scriabin in his later piano works (starting around the Fifth Sonata; his previous piano works are graceful evocations of Chopin) started to build harmonies on fourths instead of triads, and in the process began to turn out music of fearsome complexity. Some of it is tinged with impressionism, some of it has new ideas about sonority and layout, and all of it gave contemporary pianists something to think about. Nevertheless the music was, as pertains to pianistic resource, primarily of the nineteenth century. Also in Russia, the composer-pianist Nikolai Medtner wrote much skillful keyboard music that had elements of the new style, though, like Rachmaninoff's, it was basically conservative.

It was Debussy who pointed to the twentieth century, who gave to the world entirely new color combinations, with a use of pedal effects that went far beyond anything Chopin had dreamed of. Debussy's piano style vibrated with quadruple pianissimos and it contained altogether a new kind of digital figuration. Maurice Ravel, too, worked somewhat in this style, and in a way he had priority, with his *Jeux d'eau* of 1901. At any rate, Debussy and Ravel worked simultaneously, though differently. Ravel's piano music was the sharper, the clearer, the more classic, the more indebted to Liszt. In Ravel's piano music the pianist manipulates the keys. In Debussy's, the piano appears almost to have ceased being a keyboard instrument. Harmonies billow up and figurations float through them, foglike and mysterious. (There were exceptions. Pieces like *L'île joyeuse* and *Feux d'artifice* are of a neo-Lisztian virtuosity; and in a work like the Toccata from *Pour le piano,* or in many of the études, Debussy could be as objective and "hard" as Ravel.) Debussy's characteristic harmonies are often exotic, based on the whole-tone scale or suggesting a gamelan orchestra. As Edward Lockspeiser writes in his biography of Debussy, "With the *Estampes* the piano not only leaves the practice-room and the drawing-room; it even leaves the concert hall. It becomes the poetic instrument of a wandering, imaginative spirit, able to seize upon and define the soul of far-off countries and their peoples, the ever-changing beauties of nature, or the innermost aspirations of a childlike mortal observing the fresh and most moving wonders of creation." Lockspeiser continues:

... the unrivalled accuracy and intelligence of the craftsman compelled a severely practical approach to the keyboard, in which we see the composer analyzing and defining the vast complexity of the instrument's purely physical properties, all of which, ultimately, are to be obtained by the action of ten human fingers upon the piano's unchanged, material mechanism. If the piano was to be transformed into an instrument of illusion—Debussy insisted that performers of his music should imagine the piano as an instrument without hammers—the transformation could only be effected by the closest analysis of touch and vibration, of keyboard harmony and figuration, of the immeasurable scale of contrasts in tone and register—in short by analysis of all the technical resources of an instrument whose very defects and limitations were to be turned by Debussy into newly discovered virtues.

In his last piano works, the two books of Études, Debussy codified his theories much as Chopin had done in *his* Études almost a hundred years previously. In Debussy's synthesis, every aspect is examined—scales, seconds, thirds, fourths, octaves, ornamentation, repeated notes, arpeggios, chords. And his Études end up being to the early twentieth century what Chopin's two books were to the nineteenth. In the meantime, Ravel was still continuing along somewhat parallel paths; and in his *Gaspard de la nuit* he created a virtuoso piece, expressed in the new language, that may be the most significant contribution of its kind after Liszt.

But it was not the impressionistic style of Debussy and Ravel that was to dominate the piano writing of the decades after 1910 (though certain elements of Debussy's figurations can be traced in some twelve-tone music). Debussy and Ravel were complete in themselves. They had a few followers—Cyril Scott in England, some of the French composers, Kodály in some of his early piano music—and, of course, the theories of Debussy entered the language of music, after which the piano (and music itself) could never again be the same. But the new creators, the Young Turks, had different ideas. Debussy wanted to suggest a piano without hammers. Prokofieff, Bartók, Stravinsky and Hindemith had the opposite view. Nonsense, they said in effect. The piano *is* a percussive instrument, and there's no use trying to disguise the fact. So let's face up to it and treat the piano as a percussive instrument.

Young Serge Prokofieff, the pianist of steel, came raging out of Russia, playing his own music and startling the West with his vigor, his exuberance, his wild rhythm, his disdain for the trappings of romanticism. The anti-romantic age was under way. Prokofieff was a marvelous pianist and a perfect illustrator of his own theories. With his Piano Concerto No. 1 and his *Suggestion diabolique* he demonstrated in a fearsome manner the austerity and power of the new idiom. Gone were romantic color, wide-spaced arpeggios, inner voices, pretty melodies. This was music of revolution, as many Western critics immediately pointed out. Prokofieff at the piano attacked the music with a controlled fury, blasting out savage and complicated rhythms, giving or asking no mercy. He went about it almost without pedal, and with a percussive, metallic-sounding tone. How his teacher must have fretted at the demon she had spawned! For his teacher had been none other than Annette Essipoff, the great pianist and exponent of the Leschetizky method. Essipoff had stopped concertizing in 1908 and settled down as a teacher in the St. Petersburg Conservatory. Prokofieff would walk through the halls of the school poking fun at the composers so dear to the gentle Essipoff's heart. "They say you can't give a recital without Chopin? I'll prove that we can do quite well without Chopin." He said nasty things about Mozart, "What kind of harmonies are these—I, IV and V!" There were constant clashes between Prokofieff and Essipoff, and after the first year she sorrowfully noted, "Has assimilated little of my method. Very talented but rather unpolished." In his biography of Prokofieff, the Russian musicologist Israel Nestyev nevertheless indicates that the years Prokofieff spent with Essipoff were not wasted. "Prokofieff's brilliantly individual style of playing," writes Nestyev, "with its clear-cut finger technique, steel-like touch and exceptional freedom of wrist movement bore the stamp of the Essipoff-Leschetizky school." Which may be, though once Prokofieff was on his own he discarded everything that was romantic in that particular school. Yet, as his own recordings illustrate, he could produce a singing tone and pure legato when he felt like it, and he did not pound his music nearly as much as today's young heroes of the keyboard do.

He was good enough, though, to win the Rubinstein Prize for piano in 1914. How he ever got away with it is a mystery. Instead of a classical concerto, as was prescribed, he announced that he would play his own D flat Concerto. When the directors of the St. Petersburg Conservatory heard about this breach of the rules, they raised a storm. So did Prokofieff. Then they agreed it would be all right—if each member of the jury had a copy of the concerto before the competition. It so happened that Jurgenson in Moscow was in the process of printing it, and Prokofieff begged him to have it ready on time. Jurgenson did. "When I came out on stage," Prokofieff wrote, "the first thing I saw was my concerto spread out on twenty laps—an unforgettable sight for a composer who had just begun to be published." Prokofieff managed to impose his very strong will on the directors to the extent that they looked away from further breaches. Instead of a prelude and fugue from the *Well-Tempered Clavier*, Prokofieff played one from the *Kunst der Fuge*. He did, however, bow to the inevitable, and included as his virtuoso piece the Liszt arrangement of Wagner's *Tannhäuser* Overture.

Even before the competition he had played the D flat Concerto in public, and his new, anti-romantic style was immediately noted. One critic pointed out the salient characteristics very accurately, "His tone was somewhat dry, but he played with amazing assurance and freedom. Beneath his fingers the piano does not sing or vibrate. It speaks with the stern and precise tone of a percussion instrument . . . the tone of the old-fashioned harpsichord. But it was precisely the convincing freedom of his playing and the clear-cut rhythm that won the composer such enthusiastic applause." Naturally this unorthodox style created antagonism. Until his approach was accepted—it took at least a decade, and even then there were agonized howls in conservative circles—he was derided as a madman, a hammerer, a cacophonist. In his own country he could not break the barrier, and that is one reason he left. None of the important Russian organizations would play his music—or, at least, not to the extent that Prokofieff would have wished. There also was the turmoil after the Revolution of 1917. Prokofieff left Russia and did not return until about ten years later.

He headed for America by way of Japan. The effect he made upon the United States was startling. America had never heard anything like it; and Prokofieff and his music were described as "Russian chaos," "carnival of cacophony," "Bolshevism in art." As for his approach to the piano: "Steel fingers, steel wrists, steel biceps, steel triceps—he is a tonal steel trust." Prokofieff played a good deal of his own music. He soon found that as a concert pianist he could not compete with the Paderewskis, Hofmanns and Rosenthals of the day, especially when he programmed things like Beethoven's Sonata in A (Op. 101), Chopin Études and other romantic music he secretly so despised. His lack of success depressed him, and also the failure in Chicago of his *Love for Three Oranges*, when Mary Garden staged it in 1921. Prokofieff had some hard words to say about the conservatism of American audiences:

I wandered through the enormous park in the middle of New York and, looking up at the skyscrapers bordering it, I thought with a cold fury of the wonderful American orchestras that cared nothing for my music; of the critics who were repeating for the hundredth time, "Beethoven is a great composer," while balking violently at new works; of the managers who arranged long tours for artists playing the same hackneyed programs fifty times over. . . .

And so he went off to make his headquarters in Paris. That was the Paris of the 1920s, and the intellectual climate was much more stimulating than anything America could offer. Prokofieff began to find a hospitable audience. He did visit the United States several times during the 1920s and 1930s and continued his activities as a pianist for at least a decade. More and more he concentrated on playing only his own music. From 1927 he made reappearances in Russia, and by 1935 was again a permanent resident there.

As a pianist Prokofieff was the New Man of the century. He had little in common with the past, and his playing was completely original. His influence upon the century's piano philosophy was profound. This was the kind of approach needed to play Bartók, Stravinsky and the other moderns. It was functional pianism, stripped clear of artificial device, bleak and powerful, unpadded, impatient of bar lines and orthodox metrics and agogics. Prokofieff himself had little sympathy for Stravinsky's neo-classicism. The least neo-classic of composers (Prokofieff's *Classical Symphony* represents a *jeu d'esprit* rather than an attempt to evoke the past), he represented a sort of contemporary Russian nationalism. It is true that Stravinsky, who also had his moments of nationalism, did compose a bit of piano music that ran parallel to Prokofieff's in at least one respect—the use of the piano as a percussive instrument. And the greatest of the piano percussionists was Bartók. Bartók's Op. 1, the Rhapsody for Piano and Orchestra (also a piano solo) is one of his few conservative pieces, the kind of Hungarian evocation that Liszt might have written had he lived another twenty years. From that point, Hungarian nationalism was diverted from its Lisztian course. Bartók's first two piano concertos, his *Allegro barbaro* and his piano suites, his folk-song arrangements and his sonatina, had Prokofieff's demonic force coupled to an implacable rhythmic complexity and a disdain for consonance that were outside anything in Prokofieff's experience. As Bartók conceived the instrument, the piano was indeed a hammer clavier. He composed a series of studies and also six books of graded pieces named *Mikrokosmos*. The *Mikrokosmos* is so named because of the brevity of the pieces in the collection. These six volumes codify Bartók's pianistic and harmonic theories.

The Bartók-Prokofieff-Stravinsky style, with the addition of the contributions of the German twelve-tone and then serial composers, led into a good deal of the piano writing from the 1930s to the 1970s, as exemplified in America by such composers as Aaron Copland and Elliott Carter. Some composers, true, continued to write in the romantic manner through all the turmoil. Among them were Francis

Serge Prokofieff. This photograph was made in New York in 1918 for his American debut.

Serge Prokofieff.

Poulenc and Darius Milhaud, whose pianistic style stemmed from Satie and Fauré back to Chabrier. For a long time they were dreadfully out of fashion. Poulenc has made a comeback. Milhaud has not.

The brittle, anti-romantic style was the one that attracted the most comment. It was of the avant-garde; and in the 1920s and 1930s the young composers flocked to the avant-garde. In America during those years the young Leo Ornstein, stimulated by Prokofieff, made a big (though brief) career with his uninhibited, hammerlike attack. He had his predecessors. Around 1910 Percy Grainger was causing a stir by the near-tone clusters in such works as his *Gumsuckers March*. Whether or not Henry Cowell heard Grainger, he carried Grainger's innovation one step further by introducing actual clusters, played by fists, elbows and forearms. Cowell also explored the possibilities of string resonance, making the pianist lean over and pluck the viscera of the instrument. Charles Ives, in the *Concord* Sonata, went so far as to have the pianist use a long piece of wood to depress many keys simultaneously. Around the same time Arnold Schoenberg was introducing new ideas of piano technique, and in his Three Pieces (Op. 11) and Six Little Pieces (Op. 19), from 1908 and 1911 respectively, introduced the expressionist style to the piano. Cowell and Schoenberg were eventually to lead to the post-Webern serialists and even far beyond, to the Dada of John Cage and the aleatory of Karlheinz Stockhausen as expressed in the piano playing of David Tudor.

During the 1950s and 1960s, Tudor was the world's outstanding exponent of ultra-avant-garde pianism. He was one of the few pianists who could decipher the new types of notation favored by the new school; and, at a representative concert, the piano itself was the least of his worries. Tudor at these events could be found more or less simultaneously hitting a keyboard, manipulating one of several tape recorders, standing up to lean into the piano and sweep its strings, kneeling down to rap its sounding board, swiveling around to blow a whistle or kazoo—or at times merely looking intently, with frozen immobility, at the keyboard for four minutes or so. That last example of contemporary piano playing occurs in a piece by Cage named 4′ 33″. This is a work of silences, in which the pianist merely looks at the keyboard, a stop watch in hand. Generally Tudor did not work from music composed on the two staves. He had to decipher such sets of directions as follows (from Cage's Variations):

Six squares of transparent material, one having points of four sizes. The 13 very small ones are single sounds; the 7 small but larger ones are 2 sounds; the 3 of greater size are 3 sounds; the four largest 4 or more sounds. Pluralities are played together as "constellations." In using pluralities, an equal number of the 5 other squares (having 5 lines each) are to be used for determinations, or equal number of positions, each square having 4. The 5 lines are: lowest frequency, simplest overtone structure, greatest amplitude, least duration, and earliest occurrence within a decided-upon time. Perpendiculars from points to lines give distances to be measured or simply observed. Any number of performers, any kind and number of instruments.

Naturally Tudor and the specialists who followed him could not "practice" this music, in the traditional sense of the word. And it could take them months merely to make a plot of what the composer wanted. In more orthodox music Tudor was a brilliant technician and sight reader, but in the advanced music he had to work out his own exercises—exercises in coordination, in leaps, in the type of figuration encountered in this repertoire.

Very little of this music has made headway with the public. For that matter, the piano music of Stravinsky and Bartók can scarcely be described as popular. But whether or not they have been fully accepted, elements of their style—from Prokofieff and Stravinsky through Schoenberg, Webern and Cage—have nevertheless entered the musical vocabulary of the mid-century. Other factors played a part, and not all were necessarily musical. The entire century has been one of shift in emphasis away from the romantics. Playing only a part in the general upheaval was the sophistication and intellectualism of the new music. There was the shift in emotional and social values after the First World War. There was the new scientific revolution, as potent as the industrial revolution a hundred years previously. There were the developments in musicological research, where for the first time a thorough and documented investigation began to be made into performance practices of the baroque and renaissance.

In the realm of the piano and pianists, it all meant that the concept of the Virtuoso-as-Hero was being retired to an honored place in history. As a replacement came the scholar-pianist, the musician-pianist, the re-creator of the composers' thought, the abdication of technique qua technique. Virtuosity, indeed, became something of a dirty word. Clara Schumann, after all, had eventually triumphed; and how she must have laughed from Above!

One of the important movers in the new thought, though she was not primarily a pianist, was Wanda Landowska. She was the one who demonstrated how Bach, Handel, Scarlatti, Couperin and the others sounded on the instrument for which their music was originally conceived. It would be a mistake to consider Landowska a classicist, though. She had been born in an age of romantic playing, an age dominated by the figures of Liszt, Leschetizky and their pupils. Thus she grew up with certain romantic traditions of performance, and those traditions remained with her to the end, whatever the stringency of her musical scholarship. For the learned, birdlike lady was no mean showman, either in her personality or her music-making. She knew how to hold an audience breathless, and when she gave a recital it was to the accompaniment that all great artists receive—deathlike silence and attention.

Her stage entrances were unforgettable. When she gave her 1949 series devoted to the first book of Bach's *Well-Tempered Clavier*, in New York's Town Hall, she had the stage fixed up as though it were her living room—the harpsichord dominating, a studio lamp to the left of the keyboard, the stage nearly darkened. Fifteen minutes before the start of the event the audience was already firmly in place. Mme. Landowska made everybody wait a good while before she decided to come out. Finally the stage door opened and The Presence approached.

It seemed to take her a good five minutes to walk the twenty or so feet to the instrument. Her palms were pressed together in prayer à la Dürer, her eyes were cast to the heavens, and everybody realized she was in communion with J. S. Bach, getting some last-minute coaching and encouragement. She looked like the keeper of the flame as, dressed in some kind of shapeless black covering, her feet shod in what appeared to be carpet slippers (they really were velvet ballet slippers), she levitated to the harpsichord. It was one of the great entrances of all time.

Her playing was on an equally romantic level, and who is to say it was not closer to Bach than the dry munchings of some later harpsichordists? As an executant she had a miraculous equality of touch, with a left hand that seemed to have a brain of its own. Her registrations were, to say the least, colorful. But no artist in this generation (and, one is confident, in any generation) could with equal deftness clarify the polyphonic writing of the baroque masters. And none could make the music so spring to life.

Her secret was a lifetime of scholarship, plus perfect technical equipment and resilient rhythm, all combined with a knowledge of just when *not* to hold the printed note sacrosanct. Of course, that alone demands a lifetime of knowledge. (Landowska's great contemporary, Pablo Casals, would tell his students much the same thing. "The art of not playing in tempo—one has to learn it. And the art of not playing what is written on the printed paper." But no modern teacher would dare utter such heresy.) She was a genius at underlining the dramatic and emotional content of a piece. When she held on to a fermata, worlds tottered and the sun stopped until she went on to the next phrase. Everything she did had meaning and emotional significance. She took liberties, all kind of liberties, but like all great artists she could get away with them. In short, her entire musical approach was romantic: intensely personal, full of light and shade, never pedantic. In such pieces as the twenty-fifth of the *Goldberg* Variations she could outline the melody with a freedom and yet with a controlled passion that could tear one's heart out; and this she was able to do with no heart-on-sleeve ostentation. Her rubato, incidentally, was a perfectly calibrated means of expression. It was not for nothing that she had Polish blood.

A woman of strong opinions, she had a pretty good idea of her worth. There was no false modesty in her. One of the great stories of music concerns her meeting with another Bach specialist, also a woman. They got into a discussion of Bach ornamentation, and suddenly the air grew frigid.

"Very well, my dear," Landowska was overheard saying. "You continue to play Bach your way and I'll continue to play him *his* way."

Thanks to Landowska, Bach all of a sudden began to sound thick on the piano. One by one, pianists stopped playing Bach-Liszt, Bach-Tausig & Co. Then they began to think twice about playing any kind of baroque music, including even Scarlatti. The piano repertoire, it began to be felt, was large enough without the necessity of reverting to transcriptions—and Bach and Scarlatti on the piano were, in a way, transcriptions no matter how faithfully the original notes were played.

In line with this kind of purity came the emphasis on the sanctity of the printed note and the back-to-nature study of the composers' manuscripts. This has continued past mid-century, will continue,

Wanda Landowska at the harpsichord. Her theories had a strong influence on twentieth-century pianism.

Landowska: "You play Bach your way and I'll play him *his* way."

and is something new in the scheme of things. There was scarcely a pianist prior to World War I who did not make changes in the music to suit himself. Some made sweeping changes, like Paderewski and Busoni. Some, like Hofmann and Rachmaninoff, were much more restrained. But a pianist like Arthur Schnabel flew in the face of all his Leschetizky training and became a scholar as well as a great artist, going to the sources, painstakingly collating the composers' manuscripts with all printed editions. The search was on for textual truth. Today's younger virtuosos have been trained to the point where they would as soon cut off their hands as knowingly change a note, a phrase, a dynamic indication. Whether or not this concentration on textual truth has led to emotional inhibition is a point that teachers throughout the world would do well to discuss. It probably has. For slavish adherence to the text can be a fine prop to support a musician without ideas of his own. Not only that, but many musicians, afraid to tamper with holy writ, end up obeying the letter but not the spirit of the music. With all the advance in scholarship, many young artists nevertheless still do not realize that the baroque, classical and many romantic composers fully *expected* their music to be somewhat changed by the interpreter.

In line with the prevailing intellectualism, one of the concomitants of the new school of piano playing was a lessening of interest in the romantic composers. Prokofieff's prediction began to come true: there actually started to be recitals without Chopin. The Polish composer, of course, continued to be played, but with nowhere near the staggering frequency he had previously enjoyed. Indeed, the race of Chopin specialists began to disappear; and by the 1980s there were very few left, save for several of the older generation of pianists. After the First World War a new school of artists came to the fore, all of them conditioned by the new precepts. A few of them had been active before 1918, but not until after that did they really start to dominate the scene as representatives of the modern style. The ambience in which they worked and lived had nothing in common with the world of the Liszt and Leschetizky pupils who had dominated the previous generation. For better or worse, the style had changed, and it was the style that has remained in existence to the present day.

XXXII

The Man Who Invented Beethoven

To MANY OF THE LAST generation there was but one Beethoven pianist and his name was Artur Schnabel. This may have been a little hard on such Beethoven specialists as Wilhelm Backhaus, Edwin Fischer, and Rudolf Serkin, but in the public eye Schnabel and Beethoven were synonymous. It was granted that Schnabel played Mozart as none other, and that he probably was the greatest Schubert pianist of the century, and that he also had a sure way with Brahms. But it was to Beethoven that he kept coming back, and as far as the public was concerned, Schnabel was the man who invented Beethoven. The Beethoven piano music, at any rate.

Schnabel was a short, cigar-smoking man with a big head, a stocky body and stubby fingers. He looked anything but the popular conception of a pianist. At the keyboard he was a rather unimpressive sight. Most popular pianists are necessarily showmen, and have been so since Liszt. Nearly all of the romantic pianists lifted their hands high; smoke came from their nostrils and lightning from their eyes, and their audiences screamed and carried on. But that did not apply to the new school of pianists. Schnabel never lifted his hands high, nor did he shake his head or try to see the Deity on the roof of the concert hall. Yet when he played, there was cathedral silence in the auditorium. His concerts were not circuses; they were communions. And when the audience dispersed, it was with the feeling of having been cleansed.

Schnabel will not be forgotten. For one thing, he was a legend, and legends tend to increase with the years. For another, he taught many pupils, and they carry on his tradition. For still another, he made very many records, among them the thirty-two Beethoven sonatas. Schnabel was the first in history to accomplish that feat on records, though in recent years it has become almost a commonplace. It took Schnabel several years—from 1931 to 1935.

No more atypical pianist came from the Leschetizky atelier. (Previous to Leschetizky, Schnabel had studied with Leschetizky's wife, Annette Essipoff, who had prepared him for *Der Meister.*) By the age of twelve—an assured, mature, intellectual twelve—Schnabel was an ex-prodigy who already was bored with mere technique. And he had plenty of technique. But he found other things to interest him than showpieces. Leschetizky said (was it supposed to be a compliment or not?), "Artur, you will never be a pianist. You are a musician." Yet it was romantic old Leschetizky who had put Schnabel on the Schubert sonatas and seen him through his debut in 1893. At the age of sixteen, a concert veteran, Schnabel had already met Brahms, started composing, taken on a number of musical jobs, and had accompanied the contralto Therese Behr, whom he eventually married. She was six feet tall, he but four inches over five feet.

Chamber music was at first Schnabel's primary interest. With Alfred Wittenberg and Anton Hekking he founded the Schnabel Trio. A later trio consisted of himself, Carl Flesch (whom many considered the Schnabel of the violin) and Jean Gérardy. Still later there were Schnabel, Flesch and Hugo Becker. Naturally Schnabel was anything but a romantic pianist. Yet his repertoire was very wide. On his early American tours he included such works as the Chopin Préludes and Schumann's C major Fantasy; and veteran observers around Berlin in the 1920s still speak of the power and brilliance of his Liszt. Yes, Liszt. His pupils say that he could illustrate anything on the piano; that he had studied and memorized virtually the entire literature; and that his technique, which could be unreliable toward the end, was staggering when he was in form.

In later years Schnabel seldom, if ever, played romantic music. It became distasteful to him. At a public forum he was once asked why his repertoire was so restricted.

My answer [said Schnabel] is that now I am attracted only to music which I consider to be better than it can be performed. Therefore I feel (rightly or wrongly) that unless a piece of music presents a problem to me, a never-ending problem, it does not interest me too much. For instance, Chopin's studies are lovely pieces, perfect pieces, but I simply can't spend time on them. I believe I know these pieces; but playing a Mozart sonata, I am not so sure that I do know it, inside and out. Therefore I can spend endless time on it. ... Children are given Mozart because of the small *quantity* of the notes; grown-ups avoid Mozart because of the great *quality* of the notes.

For many years Schnabel was anything but a popular success as a concert pianist. When he came to the United States in 1921 he played to small houses and lesser acclaim. The same thing happened in 1922, whereupon Schnabel, unhappy with his reception, decided to remain in Europe. There, at least, he was appreciated for his musicianship. It was in 1927, the year of the Beethoven centennial, that he first played the cycle of sonatas, in seven Sunday programs. The following year, 1928, was the Schubert centennial, and Schnabel busied himself with that composer's piano music. His 1930 tour of America—he had changed his mind and returned—was his first big success here. And when he played in this country in 1935, with his Beethoven recordings behind him, it was as a recognized master and also the head of what amounted to a cult.

Some of his pianistic colleagues, to whom workmanship was more important than content, could not understand his success. By that time Schnabel could not have been less interested in technique, and these critics pointed out certain limitations in his equipment, suggesting that an artist who had to struggle through the finale of the *Appassionata*, who messed up the fugue of Op. 101—let's not talk about the fugue of the *Hammerklavier!*— was after all perhaps not much of a pianist. And there could be no denying the fact that in the last twenty-five years of his life Schnabel never had the massive grasp of the keyboard shown by a Backhaus, a Hofmann or a Lhevinne. In his public appearances, and even in his recordings (done, of course, in pre-LP days, when there was no such thing as tape splicing), there were places where Schnabel's fingers were painfully extended. Pianistic holes there were in plenty.

But those who were pedantic enough to judge a pianist only by his wrong notes entirely missed the essence of Schnabel. The magnitude of his creative accomplishments left technical considerations far behind. His Beethoven had incomparable style, intellectual strength, and phrasing of aristocratic purity. The important thing was that even when his fingers failed him, his mind never did. Schnabel was always able to make his playing interesting. A mind came through—a logical, stimulating, sensitive mind. And when

Schnabel had his fingers under control, which was more often than not in his literature of Mozart, Beethoven and Schubert, he took his listeners to an exalted level. He was especially impressive in the knotty last five Beethoven sonatas. If ever a musician achieved identification, it was Schnabel as he sang forth the slow movement of Op. 110, the icy galactic vision of the last pages of Op. 111, the lyric patterns of Op. 109. There were no tricks, no excesses; just brain, heart and fingers working together with supreme knowledge.

His playing had an inner calm and certainty that carried over into his own life and his deportment on the concert stage. He once played the Brahms B flat Concerto with the New York Philharmonic under Bruno Walter. This concerto was one of his specialties, and he must have played it over a hundred times in public. In the slow movement of this performance occurred what must happen to every artist at one time or another—a memory lapse. Schnabel went one way, the orchestra another, there was a horrified gasp from the audience and the music came to a dead stop. Walter was appalled. Schnabel merely grinned, shrugged his shoulders, got up from the piano and walked over to the podium. Two elderly gray heads bent over the score, there was a muttered injunction to the orchestra, Schnabel returned to the piano and the music began again. To any other pianist, the mental shock and embarrassment would have been impossible to overcome. Not to Schnabel. He continued to play as beautifully as he had done before. Perhaps even more beautifully, determined to make the audience forget the lapse.

He was also a composer, and anybody who has written about Schnabel has pointed out the Schnabelian paradox: that a musician so steeped in the classic tradition should have composed such advanced music. Schnabel's compositions are abstract, frequently atonal, complicated and difficult to grasp. He never, incidentally, took advantage of his own position to record his music, something he could easily have done. For a while, shortly after his death in 1951, his admirers tried to bring his music before the public, sponsoring well-prepared concerts. These attracted very little attention, and the chances are that Schnabel's music has disappeared for good.

There was a time when Schnabel maintained he was *not* a Beethoven specialist. He said that he had not worked out the correct way of playing Beethoven until after 1918. But he later had to accept the charge of specialization, especially after his edition of the sonatas was published in 1935. It was, and is, a fabulous edition, one that

can be studied with interest and profit—even if it is a dangerous
guide (and a guide that Schnabel himself often refused to follow).
Musicologists tend to scoff at it; and, in all truth, only experienced
artists should consult it. Schnabel collated every Beethoven manuscript and first edition he could get his hands on and then went to
work to supply a guide to interpretation that is a stupendous
achievement whether or not a reader agrees with it, and many do
not. The correct musical expression was uppermost in Schnabel's
mind. He indicated his own preferences in fingering (sometimes
wildly unorthodox), his own pedalings, often his own phrasings. He
made no bones about his editorial changes. "The slurs as well as the
accents and indications relative to touch were noted by the composer
in such an obvious and confusing flightiness and carelessness—
especially in his early works—that the Editor felt himself not only
musically justified, but in duty bound to change them occasionally
according to his best judgment, sense and taste; to abbreviate, to
lengthen, to supplement, to interpret. Changes of this kind are not
especially noted. . . ." Thus anybody using the Schnabel edition has
no way of knowing where the text leaves off and Schnabel's emenda-
tions begin. With characteristic thoroughness, Schnabel added footnote after footnote to the text, some of them of alarming complexity.
As the music grows more complex, so do the notes, and by the time
he gets to the last sonatas Schnabel is in full philosophical flower.
His introduction to the slow movement of Op. 110, admittedly one
of Schnabel's more elaborate exegeses, will give the idea:

With the lavish abundance of interpretation-signs, seventeen in number
(not counting the pedal-signs) all in sharp contrast one to the other, and
extending only over the few notes from the "Recitativo" to the "Adagio ma
non troppo" Beethoven wished to impart an exhaustive, forcible description
of his conception of unrestrained expression. Owing to the inequality of the
bar-lengths, the complete freedom of plastic form becomes apparent as
well. The "Recitativo" contains, according to the manner in which one
explains the second bar, either 85½, or 85, or 83 semiquavers. The first
bar has exactly 28 of them (7/4), the third 20 (5/4), and the fourth 10, of
which 6 already belong to the "Adagio" (10 = 4 and 2 × 3). The only
disputed bar is the second one. Beginning with the first note: is it a semiquaver or an appoggiatura? Probably both: an appoggiatura for which place
and value were indisputably determined. It makes its appearance at the
same time as the chord, and has the value of the two chords 9/4. If one

Artur Schnabel in the 1920s, the musical *chevalier sans peur et sans reproche*.

Schnabel listening to a playback at
a recording session in the 1940s.

Artur Schnabel.

counts the first semiquaver as part of the bar, and gives the last three quavers their full value (the Editor considers their appearance as triplets, as in most editions) then the result is: 33½ semiquavers, i.e. too many for ¾; with the last quavers as triplet 31½, without the demisemiquavers at the beginning 31, i.e. in both cases not enough for ¾. Next to the first note stands . . .

This is about a third of the footnote. It is not surprising that Schnabel's musical approach could be analytical. He maintained that music was only a series of symbols of notes and notations, set out in various patterns that obeyed certain definite rules of harmonic successions, of tonal attractions and of formal construction. A group of chords, a marking of *piano* or *crescendo*, were all clear signs of the composers' intentions; and whether set down by Beethoven or Debussy, they meant exactly what they said. That was all there was to it, and to Schnabel it turned to dust the assumption that Mozart's forte should sound as though it came from the next room, or that Debussy's piano should sound as if perpetually immersed in water. The ideal interpreter of all composers, therefore, was the one who could perform what was written, interpret the signs by accurate judgment and intelligence. So he told a pupil, Marcella Barzetti, and it is a viewpoint not unlike Stravinsky's. Stravinsky wanted a literal and objective translation of the notes he had written, no more and no less. It is not surprising to find Schnabel and Stravinsky thinking along the same lines, for Schnabel was a modern pianist, one of the very few modern (i.e., entirely unromantic) pianists who came from the Leschetizky group. The other would be Mieczyslaw Horszowski, a sound and sincere artist who, like Schnabel, had dedicated himself to chamber music and the classic composers and was still giving concerts at the age of ninety-three. Schnabel's fierce integrity, brilliant intellect—and waspish tongue, too—made him the leader of the German school of piano playing and one of the most respected musicians of the century.

· XXXIII ·

Romanticism Still Burns

IN THE GENERALLY antiromantic age during the period after World War II, at least two great pianists remained to carry the flag of romanticism. One was Arthur Rubinstein, whose career mounted and mounted to the point where many considered him the greatest living all-around pianist: an artist at home with Beethoven, a Chopin player in the great tradition, and a specialist in Spanish and impressionistic music. The case of Vladimir Horowitz is more complex. He never had Rubinstein's poise and *joie de vivre*, or his emotional health. What he did have was the most brilliant technique of his day and possibly the greatest (in his prime) in pianistic history; and, with that technique, a thunderous sonority, achieved without banging, that had not been heard since the great days of Anton Rubinstein.

Arthur (for years his manager, Sol Hurok, billed him as "Artur") Rubinstein and Vladimir Horowitz were the two pianistic superstars of their period. Possessed of big egos, they had an uneasy off-and-on friendship. In his autobiography, Rubinstein admitted that Horowitz was the better *pianist*, but he consoled himself with the belief that he was the better *musician*. Both pianists invariably played to sold-out houses. The Rubinstein audience came expecting to be enveloped with a genial presence and a bath of warm tone. Rubinstein concerts were comforting. Horowitz concerts, on the other hand, were demonic. People always were in place long before the pianist made his appearance and, if any performer could be said to have been a legend in his own time, it was Vladimir Horowitz. There was a feeling of electricity in the hall that Rubinstein never evoked. Horowitz almost *scared* people. His entrances and exits were genial

433

enough, but while he was at work there was a feeling of high voltage in the auditorium, and there still is (he continues to play, at the age of 83, at the point of writing). Rubinstein was still playing at 90; he died in 1982 at the age of 95.

Different as their styles were, the two men complemented one another as apostles of high romanticism. Horowitz was born in Kiev in 1904 and studied with Felix Blumenfeld at the Conservatory there. Blumenfeld had been a pupil of Anton Rubinstein. For a while Horowitz toyed with the idea of being a composer, but the Russian Revolution and consequent liquidation of the family fortune forced him to the keyboard. He was well established by 1924, when he gave about twenty-five concerts in Leningrad alone, never repeating a program or even an individual piece. In 1925 he went to Berlin and sprang into fame when he played the Tchaikovsky B flat minor Concerto as a last-minute replacement for an indisposed pianist in Hamburg. When Horowitz unleashed his powers in the opening cadenza, the conductor, Eugen Pabst, did not believe what he was hearing. He left the podium to watch Horowitz's hands. The audience went wild, and word about the brilliant newcomer spread.

In 1928 he made his American debut, playing the Tchaikovsky with the New York Philharmonic under Sir Thomas Beecham. It was also Beecham's American debut. That must have been a concert to remember. Both Sir Thomas and Horowitz were, of course, determined to put their best foot forward. The conductor, apparently, could not have been less interested in his soloist (at least, that is the Horowitz version of the occasion), and at the rehearsals quickly and perfunctorily went through the concerto, insisting on much slower tempos than Horowitz was used to. Horowitz was unhappy. At the concert he dutifully followed his conductor and felt his audience slipping away. When the last movement started, Horowitz decided to go down with all guns firing. He took off in a burst, leaving Sir Thomas far behind with a startled look on his face. Beecham and the orchestra never did catch up although, as Horowitz says, "We almost finished together." Next day the critics greeted Horowitz as the whirlwind he was. "That unleashed Cossack from the steppes."

A long and brilliant career was to follow. Horowitz became the most sought-after pianist before the public. He concertized extensively; he made friends with his idol Sergei Rachmaninoff; he married Wanda, the daughter of Arturo Toscanini; he played with orchestras (toward the end his concerto repertory dwindled to the

Tchaikovsky, the Brahms B flat and the Rachmaninoff D minor). But his career was interrupted by several sabbaticals. Horowitz has had physical and emotional problems. In 1936 he stopped playing for two years. Then from 1953 to 1965 he did not give any concerts, though he made a few recordings. His return to Carnegie Hall in 1965 was an unforgettable event. He had been away, after all, for twelve years, but he had never been forgotten. Pianists still talked about him with awe, much as chess players talk about Bobby Fischer. Days before the evening of the concert, there was a queue at the Carnegie Hall box office. Every pianist who could get a ticket was there. Horowitz did not disappoint. There were a few wrong notes and hesitant passages, but the old magic and brilliance were there.

He resumed his career, though there was to be another interregnum between October, 1969, and May, 1974. After he had resumed playing, he did not give many concerts, and he no longer would play with orchestras. His fees assumed astronomical proportions, and usually there was some kind of television tie-in to create additional revenue. Horowitz was probably the highest-paid musician in history. In 1982 he played in London for the first time in thirty-one years. His 1983 tour of America and then Japan was a catastrophe, with memory lapses at every concert and a seeming loss of physical control. It later turned out that he had been playing in what amounted to a drugged state. The medications he had been taking were dropped, and the veteran bounced back in 1985 and 1986 with concerts in London and Europe and a pair in Russia—Moscow and Leningrad. The Moscow concert received an international telecast, and the viewers could see how hyperemotional the event was for Horowitz and the Russians. He played well, often substituting finesse and color for strength, and there were flashes of the Horowitz of the 1960s in some of the performances. He still had more authority, a greater aura, more magnetism than any other musician before the public.

The impact of Horowitz on the American pianistic scene was massive in more ways than one. His audiences always seemed to be half full of pianists, listening closely and trying to figure out how Horowitz did the things he did. Then they went home and tried to copy him. What happened was that for a long time American concert halls were studded with young people who came on stage playing Horowitz programs and trying to ape his mannerisms. Of course they couldn't, and the concert halls were flooded with raw and ugly sound as pianists tried to duplicate the Horowitz sonority. Knowledgeable listeners would wince as the youngsters draped themselves in Horowitz's phrasings, Horowitz's tempos.

Horowitz never liked to be known as a stunt man. Aside from some extraordinary *tours de force* that he himself wrote as recital-closers—a transcription of Sousa's *Stars and Stripes Forever*, arrangements of several Liszt rhapsodies, and so on—he considered himself an artist who used his technique for musical ends. But, unfortunately, he was too rich technically for such a modest disclaimer, and his audiences generally came to see him turn the piano upside down. Many of them must have been disappointed. Horowitz generally saved the fireworks only for the last piece on the program. In addition he was one of the quietest of pianists when seated before the instrument. His movements were precise, his body almost immobile. And many of his hair-raising technical accomplishments were hair-raising only to the professionals in the audience.

As a technician Horowitz was one of the most honest in the history of modern pianism. He achieved his dazzling effects by fingers alone, using the pedal sparingly. Notes of scales could not have been more evenly matched (his Scarlatti was technically fabulous); chords could not have been attacked more precisely; octaves could not have been sharper or more exciting; leaps could not have been hit more accurately. No matter how difficult and complicated the piece, Horowitz would make it sound easy. He had worked out his own technique, one that ran counter to established traditions of hand and arm. His hands were turned out; he used a low wrist and flat fingers; the little finger of his right hand was always curled tight until it had to strike a note. When it did, it was like the strike of a cobra. Professionals never could figure it out. "I don't know how Horowitz does it!" exclaimed Alexander Greiner of the Steinway firm. "He plays against all the rules and regulations of piano playing we were taught—but with him it works." And above all there were his stupendous fortissimos—that orchestral body of tone that only Horowitz could produce. In such a work as the Rachmaninoff Third Concerto he swamped the orchestra, thundering out the last-movement climax in a manner that not even Rachmaninoff himself had ever achieved. Yet always there was the feeling of something in reserve, always the feeling of a controlled intensity. Those million volts of technique were well harnessed, but there was something

Vladimir Horowitz: Unparalleled tension and sonority coupled to one of the most flawless techniques in instrumental history.

Horowitz in 1962. Although at this time he had not been before the public for almost ten years, he was still actively engaged in a series of recordings.

almost frightening about so much energy under the control of one person. One almost felt that there was a demon trying to get loose. Surely that tensely controlled figure was wound up too tight? What would happen if the demon ever got loose? But it never did.

Naturally any pianist with this all-embracing technique, and with a whiplash quality that could make all of his colleagues seem tame, was going to be accused of shallowness. In some circles Horowitz has never been accepted as a great interpreter. A colossal workman, yes; but an artist whose playing was neurotic and out of focus. Virgil Thomson dismissed him as "a master of musical distortion," a pianist "out to wow the public and wow it he does." The new school of critics, trained in the antiromantic school of the day and out of touch with the period that Horowitz really represented, referred scornfully to his "affettuoso" style and his "teasing" of the line. Michael Steinberg in the new edition of *Grove's Dictionary* set forth the opinion of Horowitz prevalent among the young revisionists. "It is nearly impossible for him [Horowitz] to play simply, and where simplicity is wanted, he is apt to be of a teasing, affettuoso manner, or to steamroll the lines into perfect flatness. . . . Horowitz illustrates that an astounding instrumental gift carries no guarantee about musical understanding."

But what Thomson and the younger critics have failed to recognize is that Horowitz was not necessarily out to wow the public, any more than a beautiful woman is out to catch a man every time she walks down the street; it is not her fault if heads turn to follow her. Generally speaking, Horowitz applied his bravura only to pieces that demanded full bravura. When he played Chopin mazurkas or the Schumann *Kinderscenen,* on the other hand, it was with a simplicity and singing line that had nothing to do with virtuosity.

And many contemporary critics who did not grow up in the romantic school of piano playing failed to realize that when Horowitz brought out an inner voice or pointed a crescendo to its logical climax, he did so as a representative of a certain tradition. For in many respects Horowitz was a romantic throwback, an atavist. He was not an intellectual pianist. He did not consider the printed note sacrosanct. He had no hesitation, for example, in completely rewriting Mussorgsky's *Pictures at an Exhibition* to make it pianistically more effective. Secure in his knowledge of the Liszt style, he would add cadenzas to Liszt rhapsodies and other works, knowing full well that the composer would have raised no objections to contributions on such a transcendental level. With Beethoven and Schumann, of course, Horowitz was much more careful, and if he made any textual changes he did them with the utmost discretion.

No pianist, it is unnecessary to say, has an all-embracing culture. Like any other, Horowitz has had his specialties. Most professionals would agree that Horowitz played Rachmaninoff, Liszt, Scriabin and Prokofieff with more flair than any pianist of his time. And one of the curious things about this extraordinary technician was that he had a surprising affinity for the miniatures of the repertoire. Scarlatti; Chopin mazurkas and waltzes; isolated pieces by Schumann; salon music by Moszkowski—these he played with grace, charm and unaffected simplicity. In the larger Beethoven, Schumann and Chopin works, he sometimes would become too engrossed in detail, and at those moments his playing could sound disconnected. At times, too, the nervous intensity with which he approached music could be unsettling. Inner repose was lacking. Yet he could turn around and play Schumann's *Arabesque* in a calm, rippling, spacious manner, or sing out the last movement of the C major Fantasy with wide-arched lines and a luminous quality of tone. A paradoxical and fearsome pianist. But no pianist of the day brought such sheer, incandescent excitement to the concert platform, and none was more of a legend.

There have really been three styles in his playing, and these can be followed in his long series of recordings. At first Horowitz was very much in the Rachmaninoff tradition—strong, clear, direct. In the 1960s, mannerisms began to creep into his playing, and it was here that the younger school of critics became disturbed. There were lingerings, outsized dynamics, a quality of neuroticism not present in his previous playing. In the 1970s some of the mannerisms approached caricature. Yet, in his 1986 concerts Horowitz pulled himself together and played in a much more direct manner, with charm and security, with a controlled freedom instead of eccentricity. It should also be noted that no matter what the critics may have said, pianists everywhere bowed down before Vladimir Horowitz. *They* knew what he was and what he represented, and to them he was *the* pianist of their lifetime, much as to violinists Heifetz was *the* violinist.

Horowitz basically was an introvert. Arthur Rubinstein was an extrovert who loved people, loved life and loved to play the piano. All this came out in his interpretations. And none but an artist in love with the concert platform would push himself so hard. Rubinstein was over seventy years old when he gave a marathon of ten Carnegie Hall recitals in one season. He gave the series because in 1961 he was entering what he considered his twenty-fifth American anniversary. It was on November 21, 1937, that he made his grand re-entry into New York. Up to then he had never been a headliner in America, though he had played here off and on since 1906. He himself explained the relative failure of his early tours. "When I was young," he once told an interviewer, "I was lazy. I had talent but there were many things in life more important than practicing. Good food, good cigars, great wines, women.... When I played in the Latin countries—Spain, France, Italy—they loved me because of my temperament. When I played in Russia there was no trouble because my namesake Anton Rubinstein, no relation, had conditioned the audiences there to wrong notes. But when I played in England or America they felt that because they paid their money they were entitled to hear all the notes. I dropped many notes in those days, maybe thirty percent, and they felt they were being cheated." In those years Rubinstein was unperturbed. "To hell with the German pianists and their exact fingers. Temperament! I was spoiled and I admit it. But as I have never played in Germany since 1914 I have at least escaped their criticism."

Rubinstein was born in Lodz on January 28, 1886, and was playing the piano at the age of three. Taken to Berlin, he played for Joseph Joachim, who took an interest in the child and kept an eye on his musical education. He made his debut at seven, studied with Heinrich Barth, started concertizing in his teens, discovered girls, wines, cigars and the good life, took a few lessons with Paderewski (and was not particularly impressed), and first played in the United States in 1906. Critics said that the young man needed seasoning. "I must admit," Rubinstein wrote in his autobiography, "that was also my opinion." For many years he lived in Paris. In 1926 he started to make records. Rubinstein always maintained that he was a sloppy pianist before he married, but his 1926 records tell us otherwise. All the basic Rubinstein qualities are already present. The playing is ardent, brilliant, full of color, and more accurate technically than he was in his later years.

A natural pianist with the hand of a natural pianist (broad palms, spatulate fingers, a little finger almost as long as his middle one, a mighty stretch that could take in a twelfth: C to G), Rubinstein found that he did not have to work too hard. He memorized almost instantly and practiced very little. When he had to give a recital he would give the music one quick look. "I couldn't sit eight, ten hours a day at the piano. I lived for every second. Take Godowsky. I was awed. It would take me five hundred years to get that kind of mechanism. But what did it get him? He was an unhappy, compulsive man, miserable away from the keyboard. Did he enjoy life? It made me think a bit."

But in the early 1930s Rubinstein went through a period of soul-searching. "Was it to be said of me that I *could* have been a great pianist? Was this the kind of legacy to leave to my wife and children?" He started working intensively. He also started his great series of recordings, a series that not only was eventually to take in Chopin virtually entire, but large segments of Beethoven, Schumann, Liszt, Brahms and the impressionists; chamber music from Beethoven to Fauré; and substantially the entire active romantic concerto literature. When he did return to America in 1937 it was as the giant he could have been from the beginning. To his overflowing temperament was added discipline. Color, technique and a fine musical mind he always had.

He was the romantic player *par excellence*—but the modern kind of romantic pianist. Bach and Mozart played little part in his repertory, though in the latter part of his life he was playing three or four of the Mozart concertos. Of Beethoven his repertoire took in a few sonatas through Op. 81a. From the early romantics the whole world of piano music up through Poulenc and Villa Lobos seemed to be at his disposal. And he treated that world like a *grand seigneur*. More than any contemporary player, Rubinstein's playing reflected a culture, an exuberance, a sheer masculinity and sinewy athleticism, that made him unique. Romantic as it was, it was nevertheless entirely unmannered and almost always true to the text. And it was playing expressed in a gorgeous tone, directness and emotional clarity.

Rubinstein developed into a romantic pianist who consistently avoided the meretricious aspects of romanticism and retained all that was good. He never broke a line and seldom bent a rhythm. He used little rubato and relatively little fluctuation of tempo. His playing represented sentiment without sentimentality, brilliance without nonsensical virtuosity, logic without pedantry, tension without neurosis. He could be dramatic without being affected or overemotive.

Arthur Rubinstein: extro-verted, warm-blooded, ro-manticist par excellence.

Rubinstein, in a picture taken at an actual Carnegie Hall recital.

But if there was no "ham" in his interpretations, there certainly was some in his stage deportment. Rubinstein put on something of a show, making a grand entrance, lifting his hands high at the keyboard, always conscious of his audience. Rubinstein well knew the value of charisma, an element he possessed in googol quantities. In an interview, he once said that the younger generation of pianists played better than he did, "but when they come on stage they might as well be soda jerks." Nobody ever accused Rubinstein of being a soda jerk. He adored playing in public, and his audiences adored him. The mutual love affair lasted as long as he lived.

He had a good deal of musical curiosity, though in the last part of his career he left the new music to the younger men. As a youth in Paris, he flung himself into the modern school. In 1904 he was playing Debussy and being booed for his trouble. Throughout the next few decades he interested himself in such composers as Prokofieff, Ravel, Stravinsky, Dukas, Villa-Lobos and others, to his great artistic satisfaction and to the distress of his finances.

The directness of his musical approach seemed so natural, indeed so inevitable, that one wonders why most pianists could not duplicate it. But style is, after all, the man, and Rubinstein as a man was polished, witty, highly intelligent, a great raconteur, probably emotionally uncluttered. As the man, so his music. His Chopin playing unfolded with suavity, poetry and aristocracy, and above all with ardor. It was all the more poetic because Rubinstein never felt the need to prove something to himself or his audiences or to counterfeit an emotion he did not feel. In his Chopin were none of the artificialities, stresses, underlinings, emotional frigidity or hysteria that make so much contemporary Chopin playing unsettling.

It is interesting to note that in his early years Rubinstein came under the same kind of attack as did Hofmann for his Chopin playing. Both artists threw over the romantic excrescences and adopted toward Chopin a much more direct approach. In 1960, on the occasion of the Chopin sesquicentennial, Rubinstein wrote an article for the *New York Times* about his development as a Chopin player:

...I heard quite a bit of Chopin during my childhood in Poland—mazurkas, polonaises, nocturnes, the whole beloved repertoire. All of it was played interminably, and most of it badly.

Why badly?

In those days both musicians and the public believed in the Chopin myth, as do many people today. That myth was a destructive one.

Chopin, the man, was seen as weak and ineffectual; Chopin the artist as an irrepressible romantic—effeminate if appealing, dipping his pen in moonlight to compose nocturnes for sentimental young women.

Pianists whose heads were filled with such nonsense had to play Chopin badly...

At my next recital [about 1902] I included Chopin and presented him nobly, I hoped, without sentimentality (sentiment, yes!), without affection, without the swan dive into the keyboard with which pianists customarily alerted the audience to the fact that they were listening to the music of Chopin.

What was the result of what I considered conscientious work? My interpretation was adjudged "dry." The audience and critics, it turned out, preferred the "good old Chopin" they knew from before—the mythical Chopin.

By the time I came to America four years later to make my New York debut, I felt I was a dedicated, deep-minded, well-educated musician. Technically, however, I did not feel well equipped. What happened? The critics said that technically I was "impeccable"—but lacking in depth! And also, as had happened in Europe, I was chastened for my "severe" interpretations of Chopin.

Stubbornly I continued programming Chopin in my concerts. And stubbornly the critics continued to criticize. Oh, yes, it was admitted subsequently, I could play Spanish music, and I certainly could play Ravel and Debussy. But Chopin? No.

Only very much later was the validity of my interpretation granted. Only then was I permitted to have my Chopin and to give him to audiences ...

This is all very amusing, but one wonders who those swan-dive pianists were. In his autobiography Rubinstein has some unflattering things to say about Hofmann, but Hofmann never took a swan dive into the keyboard. Paderewski did, and so did Pachmann. Of course there were pianists around the turn of the century who represented the worst aspects of romanticism—Mark Hambourg, for one—and it was those who were scorned by Rubinstein. It is also true that Rubinstein used much less fluctuation of tempo and was far less interested in inner voices than were the pupils of Liszt and Leschetizky. Thus, as early as the turn of the century, he was one of the first "modern" performers of romantic music. He continued to present his kind of Chopin until the late 1970s, which meant that he had a career of some eighty-three years before the public. Perhaps this is a world record. To the end, even when fingers and memory failed him, his playing remained that of a young man in love with music. He never developed into a philosopher of the keyboard. As Dr. Johnson's friend said, cheerfulness was always breaking in.

XXXIV

Twentieth-Century Schools

IT COULD BE SAID that Schnabel was the archetype of the modern German pianist. The school that followed him has been represented by such pianists as Wilhelm Backhaus, Edwin Fischer, Wilhelm Kempff, Rudolf Serkin and, more recently, Alfred Brendel. This school has its roots and alliances in the German and Austrian repertoire from Bach through Brahms (though all German pianists naturally have at one time or another investigated all aspects of the literature, and one like Edward Steuermann specialized in the Viennese atonalists and dodecaphonists). The German school of piano playing is one of scrupulous musicianship, severity, strength rather than charm, solidity rather than sensuosity, intellect rather than instinct, sobriety rather than brilliance. It is a school that stresses planning and leaves nothing to chance. Naturally these are only the general outlines.

Pianists within the group, being human, vary. Backhaus's monumental solidity and even impassivity were balanced against Serkin's exuberance. Claudio Arrau, Chilean-born but German-trained, has achieved international respect for the stupendous extent of his repertoire and the high finish of his pianism. And so on. Robert Goldsand, who received his primary training in Vienna, has a repertoire that is virtually equal to Arrau's in its catholicity. Goldsand, however, later worked with Moriz Rosenthal and went on to encompass a type of repertoire that few pianists of the German school have engaged. His Chopin playing, for example, is highly idiomatic, and it is hard to think of a German pianist who has ever been considered a great Chopinist (though Backhaus and Serkin have played Chopin in their day).

Claudio Arrau, in 1987, one of the last of the Old Masters. Few pianists
have had a larger repertoire.

Another atypical pianist of the German school was Walter Gieseking, whom many considered the century's greatest exponent of the impressionists. He was born in Lyons of German parents living in France. By the age of four he was playing the piano, and, at eleven, was working with Karl Leimer at the Hanover Conservatory. He made his debut at fifteen and the same year played the thirty-two Beethoven sonatas in a series of six recitals. In an autobiographical sketch Gieseking stated, matter-of-factly, that when he was sixteen he knew and played "the major part of Bach's works, almost all Beethoven, all Chopin and Schumann, pieces by Mendelssohn and Schubert." At any age this would be a feat. Gieseking brushed it off. "The most difficult part was memorizing them," he said, "and that wasn't very difficult." The remark was not that of a braggart. Gieseking had one of the fastest musical minds in twentieth-century pianism. He could—and often did—memorize a work overnight. He once visited the Italian composer Mario Castelnuovo-Tedesco and saw on the piano the manuscript of a suite. Gieseking sat down and tried it out (he was a dazzling sight reader), borrowed it for a day, returned the manuscript and played the work in a recital shortly thereafter. Goffredo Petrassi's difficult piano concerto he memorized in ten days. Gieseking had the kind of technique that made life easy for a pianist. He did not have to practice much. Once he told an admirer, Marcella Barzetti, that he never worked more than three or four hours a day. *"Wer badet hat's nötig, wer übt auch."* Or, in English, "The one who has to bathe obviously needs it." He never even had to go to school. "At the age of five I discovered I could read and write. I never needed to learn anything after that."

Gieseking played all of the German composers and went as far afield as the Rachmaninoff concertos. He was one of the few international favorites who interested himself in contemporary music, and he played major works by Korngold, Cyril Scott, Schoenberg, Szymanowski, Scriabin, Busoni, Hindemith, Casella and a bushel basket of now-forgotten names. But his greatest fame came as an interpreter of Debussy and Ravel. In his prime (about 1920 to 1939; after the war he sounded almost like a different pianist) there was no subtler colorist. His knowledge of pedal technique was supreme, and in particular he was a master of half-pedal effects. Never did he create an ugly sound. The sheer limpidity and transparency of his playing would alone have been memorable even if it had not been backed up by a fine musical mind. Gieseking had the tonal control to

Walter Gieseking, the German who specialized in the French impressionists.

play the triple pianissimos in Debussy so that, delicate as they were, they could be heard throughout a large hall. Somehow he had achieved complete identification with the music of Debussy, and here he was master of his own world.

He also was highly respected as a Mozart player, and until conceptions in Mozart style changed there were few to stand up to him. This takes some explanation. Gieseking's ideas about Mozart were essentially nineteenth-century ideas, over which were superimposed the twentieth-century concept of the sanctity of the printed note. We know, however, that Mozart expected to have his notes supplemented. And the nineteenth century played Mozart, when it played him at all, as a Dresden china doll with painted lips, adding romantic phrasings and dynamics and completely ignoring the essential Mozart quality—his exquisitely balanced formal relationships. These meant little to the past century. And, most of all, there was little appreciation of Mozart's strength. It was the musicologist. Alfred Einstein who, in the 1930s, began to focus attention on what he called "the daemonic element" in Mozart's music, and he helped establish the long-delayed fact that Mozart was anything but a small-scale, rococo, pretty-pretty figure. Gieseking represented the pre-Einstein school of thought. His Mozart, to be sure, had no exaggerated romanticism. But neither did it have the vigor, tensions, full-scaled dynamics and big tone that such contemporary pianists as Serkin have brought to the music; nor did it have the superb organization, delivered in so masculine yet lyric a manner, that was Schnabel's great contribution to Mozart playing. Next to these, Gieseking sounded almost effeminate.

During World War II, Gieseking remained in Germany, playing both there and in occupied France. In 1945 he had to go through de-Nazification proceedings and was not allowed to return to the concert stage until 1947. Many of his colleagues considered him a committed Nazi. When he returned to the United States there were demonstrations and crowd scenes in protest. In any case his playing had lost much of its magic, and in many of his concerts he seemed merely to be going through the motions. In his great days, however, he was one of the most important pianists of the century: an original artist with a magic touch; a pianist who knew more about the pedals and instrumental coloration than virtually anybody around; a musician with an enormous repertory and a mind that could seize upon the fundamental aspects of any piece and translate them into shimmering beauty.

In the late 1980s the three great veterans, the Grand Old Men of the piano still in action, have been Vladimir Horowitz, Claudio Arrau and Rudolf Serkin. Of these three, Horowitz, of course, represents a throwback to nineteenth-century romanticism. Serkin is the exponent of the Austro-German tradition. Arrau, also German-trained, is more eclectic—a pianist who seems to play everything from Bach to Prokofieff (he has looked at atonal and serial music as avant-garde as Boulez but has not felt impelled to play it in public).

Rudolf Serkin: probity, idealism, search for truth.

In his youth Serkin played Chopin, Schumann and other romantic composers. But as he grew older his repertory condensed until he was playing little but Bach, Beethoven and Schubert. He was born in Vienna and obviously was put on earth to be a pianist. "I started to play the piano before I can remember," he told Dean Elder. "My father made me play. He was a singer and gave up singing to teach his eight children. He tried teaching all of us either piano or violin. I hated the violin; it was so close to the ear." At the age of six he was playing in public. At nine he was sent to Richard Robert at the Vienna Conservatory for advanced study. There he made friends with the brilliant George Szell, six years his elder. Szell, one of the great conductors of the century, never lost his pianistic skill. At the Conservatory, Arnold Schoenberg was one of Serkin's teachers. When he was twelve he played the Mendelssohn G minor Piano Concerto with the Vienna Symphony. After graduation Serkin formed an association with the violinist Adolf Busch (he married his daughter Irene in 1935) and was one of the relatively few pianists of his time to feature the Bach and Mozart concertos. As early as 1921, Serkin gave a Bach concert with Busch. At the end, Busch pushed him out, telling him to play an encore. "What shall I play?" asked Serkin. "The *Goldberg* Variations," answered Busch, jokingly. Serkin took him seriously. He says that when he finished, there were only four people in the audience—Busch, Schnabel, Alfred Einstein and himself.

It was with a Mozart concerto under the direction of Arturo Toscanini that Serkin made his American debut in 1936. He remained in America and became a citizen. Serkin has been one of the great exponents of chamber music, and the summer music school he created in Marlboro, Vermont, has consistently attracted some of the finest talents in the world. As a pedagogue, he was associated for many years with the Curtis Institute of Music in Philadelphia.

Through the years, he concertized steadily. In his concerto literature he sometimes went far afield, playing such things as the MacDowell D minor, the Reger F minor, concertos by Bartók and Prokofieff, and the Strauss *Burleske*. Eventually his concerto repertoire became confined to Bach, Mozart, Beethoven and Brahms. His recitals as often as not would contain only the last two sonatas of Schubert or the last three of Beethoven. He was Schnabel and Clara Schumann come back to life, and his interpretations have had equivalent authority. The century has not seen a pianist of greater probity and purer ideals. Serkin has spent his life searching for the truth as he sees it, and at the keyboard he expresses his vision in austere terms that nevertheless manage to make use of a singing line that came right out of the nineteenth century.

Serkin has never felt comfortable in the record studios but, nevertheless, has compiled a large discography through the years. Claudio Arrau also has a voluminous discography that goes back to the 1920s and covers the major part of the solo and concerto literature. Recognized everywhere as a great pianist, Arrau has never managed to make the kind of impact on the United States that he has made elsewhere in the world. Nobody has ever disputed his mastery. But for some reason many American critics have found his playing too calculated on the one hand and too eccentric on the other. He has a tendency to play slow movements slower than anybody else, and even in fast movements he can drag tempos. He has been charged with giving performances that are charmless, over-serious, lacking in spontaneity. Yet he can confound his critics by, to cite one example, his extraordinary, vital and understanding performances, on records, of the Liszt *Transcendental* Études.

Of course he was, as all great pianists have been, a prodigy. He says that at the age of four, "before I knew the alphabet," he taught himself to read music and was able to sight-read Beethoven sonatas. At five he was playing in public. At nine he already was practicing nine hours a day. Here was one pianist whose enthusiasm and dedication never flagged. As a young man he was known to work twenty hours a day to get a work ready. Arrau, as reported in Dean Elder's *Pianists at Play*, says that he had the physical capacity to do that. "I never tired physically from practicing."

In 1913 Arrau went to Berlin and studied with Martin Krause, a Liszt pupil. He made a sizable reputation as one of the up-and-coming pianists, as much for the extent of his repertoire as for his technical infallibility. His repertoire included a Bach cycle (twelve concerts), a Mozart cycle, a Weber cycle (the four sonatas), a Schubert cycle, a Schumann cycle, the Beethoven cycle. He played most of the piano music of Chopin, Brahms, Debussy and Ravel and had in his fingers a tremendous amount of Liszt. With Josef Szigeti, he played the cycle of Beethoven violin sonatas. He had about seventy concertos in a repertoire that extended from Bach through Stravinsky.

Arrau is a hard pianist to categorize. Possessing a stupendous technique, he nevertheless has never used it for display purposes. He is a literalist, in that he closely examines all the texts of the music he plays and scrupulously adheres to the printed note once he has made up his mind about the version he will use. Yet he avoids the curse of literalism by putting a strong mind and a decidedly romantic piano sound into his interpretations. Perhaps he can best be described as an eclectic of the German school.

The English school of the first half of this century, represented at its best by Myra Hess, Clifford Curzon and Solomon Cutner (who played under the name of just Solomon), possessed a certain affinity with the German. There always has been a German connection. First Handel and, then, Mendelssohn exerted their great influence on British music. Thus, the English school to this day concentrates largely on the German classics from Bach through Brahms.

Dame Myra Hess was one of the most beloved pianists of the century. The most prominent of the Matthay pupils, she made her debut in 1907 at the age of seventeen. For a while she did two-piano work with her cousin, Irene Scharrer, a fine pianist and also a Matthay pupil. Recognition came slowly to Hess, and for a while she considered giving up. Her calm, sensitive, intelligent, unostentatious playing must have sounded very tame alongside the fireworks of the big virtuosos. But she persevered, and as the modern school gained ascendancy she came to fame as one of the admired artists of the day; a position she held from the 1920s until her death. During World War II, she was responsible for concerts at the National Gallery in London, where she participated in a great deal of chamber music, often playing imperturbably away during bombing attacks.

Solomon, whose career was cut short by a serious illness, began as a phenomenal prodigy under the tutelage of Mathilde Verne. He made his debut at the age of eight, playing no less than the Tchaikovsky B flat minor Concerto. But he later stopped playing in public for a long time. When he returned to the concert stage after studies in Paris, it was as a completely mature artist of uncommon elegance. In his cultured, precisely tooled playing was the golden mean. Like Hess, he was a pianist of clarity (though with a much stronger technique than Dame Myra ever had), textual accuracy, delicate color and classic proportion: one of the most finished pianists the century had to show. There was nothing of the entertainer in him, as there has been in so many of the big virtuosos. His repertoire was serious, and he played it seriously, but with an uncommon amount of poetry, suppleness and infinite degrees of shading. He was one of the great masters. Fortunately he made many recordings.

Curzon was in much the same class. A product of the Royal Academy in London, he finished up his studies with Schnabel, Landowska and Nadia Boulanger. He alternated concert tours with teaching. Toward the end of his career, he concentrated on Mozart, Beethoven and Schubert. His appearances became infrequent, but when he did play, his concerts were rare events to which all cognoscenti thronged. Many considered him to be the greatest living Mozart player. He brought to Mozart a pellucid sound and an aristocratic approach that had a suppressed but always evident kind of nervous tension. An extraordinary colorist, his pianissimo alone seemed to have about twenty degrees of shading.

These three British pianists had in common an approach that was a combination of German intellectualism and British civilization. British musicians in general tend to be eclectic, in the best sense of the word. They have taken the best that the European schools have to offer and modified it to their national temper. The English school is an urbane one, seldom passionate and seldom even dramatic, but never closed-in. That is why it is more closely allied to the classical school than to the others. Old J. B. Cramer put his mark on the English school late in the eighteenth century, and Mendelssohn the classicist was the dominating force in the nineteenth. Their ghosts haunt British music and British pianists to this day.

The spooks in the castle of French music are Henri Herz, Pierre Zimmerman and Antoine François Marmontel. Their influence is still felt, for through them came a continuity of teaching at the Paris Conservatoire that extended through Isidor Philipp and touches even the present day. Most French pianists of the nineteenth century, and most French pianists now, incline toward elegance, facility, a shallow tone and fast tempos. Marguerite Long has described her school: "Lucid, precise, slender. If it concentrates above all on grace rather than force, guarding primarily its equilibrium and sense of proportion, it nevertheless does not bow to any other in its power and the profundity of its inner emotion." But few would agree with her remark about power and profundity. French pianists do not "get into the keys," as the professionals say. Rather, most of them are on top of the keys, playing with finger and wrist rather than arm and shoulder. This leads to the fluid brand of pianism exemplified by Robert Casadesus in his younger days (later his style broadened and became more eclectic) or by the near-percussive, but extraordinarily alive and original, playing of Jeanne-Marie Darré. She followed the normal course of *les enfants prodigues;* starting at five, in the Paris Conservatoire at nine, studies with Marguerite Long and Isidor Philipp, winning first prize at fourteen, making her debut at fifteen. Her graduation recital was typical: she played all five piano concertos by Saint-Saëns. She would think nothing of playing such programs as the twenty-four Chopin Préludes, followed by the twenty-four Études. In her great days she played with a kind of thew and abandon not normally associated with French pianists— and yet she remained quintessentially French: musically sophisticated, rhythmically alert, intelligent, technically flexible and musically charming. Her repertoire was representative of French pianists—eclectic in repertoire, though with certain gaps. Very few of them, for example, play Brahms. On the other hand, very few non-French pianists can begin to approach most French pianists in their own music. Gieseking was the outstanding exception and that only in Debussy and Ravel; he did not play Fauré, Chabrier or the modern French composers. Of the younger generation, one of the most interesting French pianists is Cyprien Katsaris, a strong individualist with glittering fingers. He has unconventional ideas about repertoire. For his New York debut in 1986, his centerpiece was Beethoven's *Eroica* Symphony in the Liszt transcription, and he surrounded it with a group of seldom-played, late Liszt works. Very much his own man, Katsaris has been trying to get a nineteenth-century quality into his playing, and often, as in his disc of Grieg *Lyric Pieces*, he succeeds. Elsewhere he can be mannered, but he has a pronounced musical profile that puts him in a class far above the cut and dried exponents of the international school of modern pianism.

There is no Spanish school as such. José Iturbi, the most famous Spanish pianist of the period immediately prior to World War II, did study in his native Valencia but, like most of the important Spanish musicians, went to Paris to be finished off. The most impressive Spanish pianist to have emerged after the war is Alicia de Larrocha, a tiny woman who tosses off things like the Albéniz *Iberia* and Granados *Goyescas* as though they were basic Czerny.

De Larrocha went through the usual child-prodigy stage in her native Barcelona and was already being talked about when she was five years old. She was a tiny child who grew up to be a tiny woman. People wonder how she, with her apparently small hand, can manage the stretches in the Granados and Albéniz pieces she plays. As a matter of fact, her teacher, Frank Marshall, put her on stretching exercises, and she can squeeze out a tenth. She made her American debut in 1955 and then went back to Spain to teach. A series of her Spanish records interested an American impresario, and when she returned she was enthusiastically greeted. Soon she became the pianistic queen of the United States. By far the most popular female pianist in America, she can make as many as seven or eight appearances to full houses in New York alone.

Her specialty is Spanish music, in which she is supreme among living pianists. It is hard to imagine the piano being played better than it is in her Epic recording of the *Goyescas*. She also has developed into one of the world's major Mozartians. Her Mozart playing is featured by impeccable finger work, bracing rhythm, intelligent layout, and a strong feeling for the arialike operatic elements of the slow movements. Her repertoire is wide, covering as it does Bach, Mozart and most of the nineteenth century through Rachmaninoff. Some critics, however, feel that her performances of romantic music, steady and accomplished as they are, lack the color and flexibility she brings to her Spanish repertory.

Many major pianists have come from Latin America and South America ever since Teresa Carreño stormed out of Venezuela in the 1860s. Players from that part of the world seem to have a good deal of poetry and controlled temperament coupled to an eclectic repertoire. They show different influences—not surprising, considering that most of them have gone to Paris and Germany and, latterly, the United States to finish off their studies.

Cuba gave the world Jesús María Sanromá, Jorge Bolet, Horacio Gutiérrez and Santiago Rodriguez. Claudio Arrau and Rosita Renard came from Chile. The case of Renard is fascinating. She was born in Santiago in 1894 and was sent, as a very young woman, to Berlin for studies with the Liszt pupil Martin Krause, who was also the teacher of Edwin Fischer and Arrau. When World War I came, Renard went to New York and made her debut there in 1917. She was immediately hailed as one of the greatest living pianists, the true successor of Carreño. After the war, she returned to Germany and, finally, back to Chile, where she taught and helped reorganize the Santiago Conservatory. Nothing more was heard of her for two decades. After World War II, the great conductor Erich Kleiber was in Chile and needed a pianist for a Mozart concerto. Renard's name was mentioned, and she played for Kleiber. He was overwhelmed. They gave concerts together, and he urged her to return to New York, which she did in Carnegie Hall on January 19, 1949. The critics were as astounded as Kleiber had been. Plans were made for her return, but the next year she was dead, of encephalitis. Fortunately, the Society of the Friends of Music of Bogotá recorded the Carnegie Hall concert, and lucky are those who possess the two-disc album. It has become a very expensive collector's item, as much for its musical value as for its rarity. Renard's performances of Bach, Mendelssohn, Chopin and Ravel are testimony to a patrician musical mind, a marvelous set of fingers, a singing tone and the other characteristics of late-romantic playing.

From Argentina came Martha Argerich, a woman born to play the piano. She made her debut at five, which put her into the Josef Hofmann category, then went to Europe when she was fourteen and worked with Friedrich Gulda, Nikita Magaloff and Arturo Benedetti Michelangeli. In 1965 she won the Chopin Competition in Warsaw. Her playing can be undisciplined but is always of interest. She has a great deal of temperament, apparent in both her private life and her music, and her technique is one of the most brilliant to be found anywhere in the world today. For a while she was associated with the excellent Brazilian pianist Nelson Freire, who in one respect at least must have made her feel retarded. He made his debut at four.

Another major pianist who can be termed Argentinian is Daniel Barenboim, who was born in Buenos Aires of Russian parents. He made his debut there when he was seven. Studies in Europe followed, after which the family moved to Israel. Barenboim is today probably better known as a conductor than as a pianist, but he has never let his fingers get out of practice and continues to concertize. His specialties are Mozart, Beethoven and Brahms, though in recent years he has also turned his attention to the large-scale Liszt works, which he plays in as grand a style as the modern manner permits.

Central Europe has spawned many superior artists, but there is no Central European school as such. The major pianists from Hungary, Czechoslovakia and the Balkan countries generally have ended their studies in the West. Dinu Lipatti from Rumania worked with Cortot in Paris. His death in 1950, at the age of thirty-three, took away a pianist who would have been one of the major figures of the century. He had everything—technique, style, a beautiful sound, sensitivity, musicianship, elegance. Clara Haskil, also from Rumania, was another who worked in Paris and made a fine reputation as a Mozart player. The ties between Paris and Rumania were very close in the days before World War II. After the war, most Rumanian pianists were sent to Moscow. Radu Lupu was one; he studied with Neuhaus and then went off to win the Van Cliburn Competition in 1966. He also won the Enesco Competition in 1967 and the Leeds in 1969. Now resident in London, he has achieved great success as a player of the Austro-German classics, especially Schubert. The polished and urbane Rudolf Firkusny came out of Czechoslovakia to study with Schnabel, while Ivan Moravec, another admired Czech pianist, worked with Michelangeli. Generally, with the Central Europeans, an eclectic brand of pianism resulted; a brand marked by stringent musicianship without the severity of the German school and a natural elegance without the tonal shallowness of the French school.

Hungary, which claims Franz Liszt, has had its share of major pianists in the twentieth century. After Dohnányi and Bartók there came, after World War I, Tamas Vasary, an elegant artist who has specialized in romantic music. The period after World War II produced three remarkable young men: Andras Schiff, Dezso Ranki, and Zoltan Kocsis. Schiff staked out an area dominated by Bach and Mozart. Ranki became a famous Bartók specialist in addition to having a repertory extending from Mozart through Stravinsky. Perhaps the most talented of this gifted group is Kocsis, who seems to play everything. He has an extraordinary technique that enables him to deliver the notes with utter clarity; his interpretations are marked by intelligence, spirit and temperament; and he produces a lovely, singing sound from his instrument. Occasionally, as in his recording of the Rachmaninoff D minor Concerto, his facility can lead him into tempos that are abnormally fast. Usually, however, he plays with taste and style.

Poland, which in the nineteenth century was a reservoir of great pianists, was quiescent after the Russians took over the country. Perhaps the gifted Krysztian Zimmerman, a winner of the Chopin Competition, will carry on the tradition. The one Yugoslavian pianist talked about these days is Ivo Pogorelich, who became famous when he did not make the semifinals of the Chopin Competition, at which point Martha Argerich resigned from the jury and made loud noises about injustice. Pogorelich—young, very handsome, eccentric—suddenly was in demand. He has talent, too, though there are those bemused observers who have decided that he wants to be the Glenn Gould of the romantic piano. Everything he does is unconventional. That includes his concert dress, which as often as not has been leather clothes. He has attracted a predominantly young audience that adores him, identifying with his rebellious attitude toward the establishment. His tempos have often been completely outside any normal parameters. In his 1985 Carnegie Hall concert, he played Beethoven's last sonata, Op. 111 in C minor. Pianists of an older generation used to bring in the C minor Sonata at about 25 to 27 minutes, playing all the repeats. Clifford Curzon took 25'40". Myra Hess, 26'25". Rudolf Serkin, 25'50". Pogorelich: 31'31".

Of course, many pianists are impossible to classify and fit no school. Gina Bachauer was an example. She was born in Greece of parents whose lineage was Austrian. When a child, she heard a recital by Sauer and announced that she wanted to be a pianist. She studied in Greece and, at eleven, was placed under the tutelage of Waldemar Freeman, a Busoni pupil who had moved to Athens. After winning the gold medal of the Athens Conservatory in 1929, she went to Paris and worked for three years with Cortot at the École Normale. She also had lessons with Rachmaninoff. When she gave her New York debut in 1950, she was entirely unknown. Usually there is word of mouth about a talented artist, but nobody apparently had heard a thing about this lady from Greece. Bachauer stunned the New York critics with her tremendous technique, her grand style and big, singing line, the breadth of her conceptions and her affinity for all periods of music. Not since the great days of Carreño had there been a woman who so "played like a man." She suddenly was in demand all over the world and became one of the most popular artists of her time.

Unlike most modern pianists she was a romantic with a virtuoso approach to the keyboard. Like Horowitz, she was a throwback. Unlike Horowitz, she played in an unmannered, unaffected way, never placing effect above substance. She died in Greece when, at a rehearsal of a Beethoven concerto, she suffered a heart attack. Her death caused real sorrow in the musical world. Bachauer was not only a popular and respected international musician; she also was a beloved figure—extroverted, generous with her time and money, helpful to young musicians, completely lacking in malice.

If there is an Italian school, it is represented by the puzzling and redoubtable figure of Arturo Benedetti Michelangeli, the most important Italian pianist after Busoni (if Busoni be considered Italian). Purely as a playing machine, Michelangeli is a legend to his colleagues, who put him in the Horowitz class as a super-virtuoso. Some of his playing is startling in its sheer pianistic polish and perfection. His fingers can no more hit a wrong note or smudge a passage than a bullet can be veered off course once it has been fired. In addition he is a complete master of tonal application, as evidenced in his performance of *Gaspard de la nuit*. By any standards this is one of the triumphs of modern pianism. The puzzling part about Michelangeli is that in many pieces of the romantic repertoire he seems unsure of himself emotionally, and his otherwise direct playing is then laden with expressive devices that disturb the musical flow. He also is an eccentric who drives his managers crazy by cancelling more concerts than he plays. In any event, he was the only Italian pianist of the century, until the arrival of Maurizio Pollini, to achieve an international reputation. More modest careers have been made by Aldo Ciccolini and Maria Tipo. Ciccolini is a neat, fleet-fingered, objective pianist of the modern school who has centered on the French school, especially Saint-Saëns and Satie. Tipo, another objectivist, created a good deal of talk in the 1970s with a brilliant disc of Scarlatti sonatas and a sensitive one of Schumann's *Davidsbündlertänze*.

Until well after the end of World War II there was no such thing as an Oriental pianist. But suddenly conservatories in America and Europe seemed to be taken over by Japanese, Taiwanese, and Korean pianists. More recently, after the end of the Cultural Revolution, Chinese pianists have started to appear. They all arrived with a work ethic that kept them practicing hour upon hour each day. Western observers marveled. These pianists developed amazing techniques, and diminutive young ladies would flip through such finger twisters as Liszt's *Feux follets* with complete aplomb. What they did not seem to have was a resonant sound and real identification with the music. One of the few who has made an impression on Western musicians in Hiroko Nakamura, who studied at the Juilliard School with Rosina Lhevinne. Most of her playing since then has been confined to her native Japan, with some appearances in Eastern Europe. She has a brilliant technique, temperament to spare, and an affinity for romantic music.

XXXV

After the Thaw

BETWEEN THE RUSSIAN Revolution of 1917 and the thaw that resulted during the Khrushchev dictatorship in 1955, the Russian school was an enigma. In the early days of the Revolution, a few artists emigrated to the West—notably, among the pianists, Prokofieff, Rachmaninoff and Horowitz. Then, as Stalin achieved ultimate control, few Russians were allowed to leave the country. There were rumors about such great pianists as Vladimir Sofronitzky, Maria Yudina, Jacob Flier and others. There even were recordings to back up the flattering estimates. Finally, in 1955, three of the Soviet Union's finest musicians were allowed to tour the West. In the 1955–56 season New York heard Emil Gilels, David Oistrakh and Mstislav Rostropovich. Russia led with its best. Shortly to follow were Sviatoslav Richter and Dimitri Bashkirov, and then came Vladimir Ashkenazy and, eventually, Lazar Berman. The stream became a torrent. Some Jewish pianists, such as Bella Davidovich, managed to get exit visas. Some defected while on tour. Most remained loyal to their country, playing in Western competitions or concertizing but always returning home. There was a hiatus, however, after the Russian invasion of Afghanistan, when the Soviet Union and the United States stopped any form of cultural interchange. In 1986 there was a second thaw, and interchange was resumed.

As one listened, in the concert hall and on recordings, to the early group of Russian pianists in the 1960s, it was apparent that Russia at that time was the last outpost of romanticism. Of course, individual artists differed. Gilels was a strong, clear, healthy player, rather objective in outlook, who did not allow himself to become emotionally overthrown by the music. Richter was altogether the opposite—introspective, unpredictable, erratic, capable of great flights of imagination and also of inexplicable gaucheries. The young Ashkenazy was, at the beginning, a fusion of the two—a poetic pianist who coaxed his instrument along, who produced voluptuous sounds, who had a good deal of Gilels's steadiness and Richter's imagination.

But varied as the pianists were, they all concentrated, as the romantics did, on tone, on phrase, on the cantabile quality of the instrument. They were all spiritual heirs of Anton Rubinstein, Scriabin, Rachmaninoff. Their repertoire, too, was concentrated mainly on the nineteenth century and on the twentieth-century Russians (primarily Prokofieff and Shostakovich). When they played Mozart and Haydn, their playing tended to be restricted, dutiful and rather stilted, in accordance with their ideas about the "classic" nature of the music. Little of the significant contemporary literature had touched them. They played no Copland or Stravinsky, no Bartók, no Schoenberg, Berg or Webern, no Hindemith or Poulenc. Decadent bourgeois composers, these were called. The 1950s were still the days of Socialist realism, and it could be perilous to breach the ideological line.

All of this resulted in a provincialism highly noticeable in the playing of the first group of Russian pianists to visit the West. It was provincial in that it reflected only a specific school. Admittedly, there are various schools of pianism—the Slavic, the German, the French and, more recently, the American. But all Western artists, whatever their origin or training, cannot help but reflect a cosmopolitan point of view. As they travel the world, they automatically take in the best that their colleagues everywhere have to offer. They have access to the latest musicological research. They live and move in a world of ideas, taking from the pool what they find necessary.

But, until 1955, the Russians were isolated, and musically their culture was in a state of all but suspended animation. Not having been exposed to the trends of contemporary Western thought, their pianists necessarily had to fall back on a tradition that had its roots in Anton and Nicholas Rubinstein. This was a tradition admirably suited to certain types of music but, at the same time, it impressed trained Western observers as being inbred and even rather naïve. Russian teachers such as Heinrich Neuhaus, Alexander Goldenweiser and Konstantin Igumnov produced formidable instrumentalists; there was no getting away from that. Nevertheless, those superbly trained instrumentalists often appeared anachronistic to Western musicians.

It took about ten years for a change to manifest itself. As more and more Russian musicians traveled to the West, they brought new ideas to their colleagues on their return. Most of them also were teachers—all important Russian instrumentalists and singers are expected to teach—and they introduced to their classes something about new musical trends, both in composition and in performance practice, that they had encountered in the West. In Stalin's day, Russia was a prison camp. In Khrushchev's time, Russia, although by Western standards anything but a free society, allowed the intellectuals and artists a little leeway.

As the decades went on, Russian musicians became as informed as musicians anywhere. All of the Russian musicians listened on their short-wave radios to the latest scores and the newest musical figures from Paris, Vienna and London. All had up-to-date audio equipment with which they could tape broadcasts off the air. The inevitable happened. Russian musicians today are trained according to international standards. Their teachers are as interested as any Juilliard, Paris Conservatoire or Vienna Conservatory teacher in producing competition winners. The result is a new generation of musicians in the Soviet Union, who are indistinguishable from musicians elsewhere, as Vladimir Ashkenazy ruefully noted in 1980. Russian pianists, he said, were well prepared, "but for what? I tend to think that Russia creates good musical sportsmen rather than great artists. They play well, but I don't think they say very much." The new Russian pianists represent the new international conformity. Pianists from the Moscow Conservatory play very much as pianists from the Juilliard. In the late 1980s, national styles of music making seemed all but extinct. The only survivor was the French school. Pianists from the Paris Conservatoire still favored the top-of-the-keys approach and the fast tempos that stemmed from Herz, Zimmerman, Saint-Saëns and Isidor Philipp.

Immediately after his first Western appearances in 1955, Emil Gilels was unanimously hailed as a master pianist. He was a short, powerful man, and the *New York Times*, thinking back to Eugen d'Albert, promptly dubbed Gilels "The Little Giant." Born in Odessa in 1916, he studied there with Bertha Reingbald, won the first All-Union Contest of Musicians and Performers in 1933, and then went to the Moscow Conservatory as a pupil of Heinrich Neuhaus. In

Emil Gilels, "The Little Giant." His playing was strong, logical and un-affected.

1936 he took second prize in a Vienna competition and two years later won the first prize at the Queen Elizabeth Competition in Brussels. He settled down to teaching and concertizing in Russia, and when he was sent abroad to concertize in 1955 he captured the West.

He played in an easy, natural manner, with strong but unassuming musicianship. His technique was brilliant; years later Neuhaus, still astonished, was to recall Gilels's incredible octaves in Liszt's *Spanish Rhapsody.* Yet Gilels was never looked upon as a mere virtuoso. As a matter of fact, his programs did not often include music *pour épater le bourgeois.* He played a steady diet of Beethoven (the *Hammerklavier* was a work that strongly engaged his last years), Schubert, Schumann, Chopin and Brahms. In many respects, the great virtuoso who put his authoritative stamp on whatever he played was, at the same time, a thinking man's pianist.

If Gilels was in the mainstream tradition of piano playing, Svia-

Sviatoslav Richter, the reclusive, introverted Russian who hypnotizes audiences.

FOTO KLAUS HENNCH ZÜRICH

Klaus Hennch (Zurich)/Angel Records

toslav Richter belongs with the great individualists. Alkan? Busoni?
Michelangeli? All represented a kind of maverick approach to music
and the keyboard, marching to a different drummer. For a while
there seemed to be some question as to whether Richter would ever
be a pianist. He was tremendously gifted as a child and could read
anything at the piano, but he spent more time going through scores
than practicing repertoire. His parents were German, and his father
was his first teacher. During World War II, according to *Time* magazine, Richter's father came under suspicion because of his German
name and because he had taught piano at the German consulate in
Odessa. He was arrested and killed by the security police. Richter's
mother fled to West Germany and settled there. Following his love
for opera, Sviatoslav became an accompanist at the Odessa Opera
Theater when he was fifteen and was chief assistant conductor
three years later. Not until 1934, when he was nineteen, did he
make his debut as a pianist, and not until he was twenty-seven did
he enter the Moscow Conservatory to study under Neuhaus. Thus,
he never followed the usual pattern of great concert pianists, who
are generally completely trained and already concert veterans at
eighteen.

At the conservatory, his magnetism, his dedication, the aura that
always has surrounded him made themselves felt. His teacher was
bowled over. "I do not take pride in Sviatoslav Richter as a pupil of
mine," he said. "The least I can do is take pride in having been
chosen as his teacher." Richter repaid the compliment, saying that
Neuhaus had freed his hands, "really freed them." When Richter
started concertizing, in 1942, he did not tour with only one or two
programs. He had twenty-five. Everything he did was different from
what other pianists did. His enormous hands could span a twelfth—
C to G. A compulsive practicer, he was sometimes known to work
twelve hours a day. He would even practice after a recital. Or he
might not touch the piano for months. In all things he was *different*.
Neuhaus was struck by the way Richter adapted his mind to that of
the composer. "When Richter plays different compositions it seems
that different pianists are playing." He developed an enormous repertoire, from Bach and Handel (he is one of the few who plays the
Handel Suites) to Prokofieff, Shostakovich and Benjamin Britten.
He played the world premieres of three Prokofieff sonatas—Nos. 6,
7 and 9.

An unusual man, obviously—and he was recognized as such, winning the Stalin Prize in 1950 and the title of People's Artist in 1955. His behavior could be eccentric in the extreme. As a juror in the 1958 Tchaikovsky Competition, he was required to rate the candidates on a one to ten numerical basis. In the first round he gave Van Cliburn one hundred instead of ten and all the other competitors zeros. He continued this throughout the competition. He was never asked back.

In 1960 he started playing in the West. He quickly became a legend, as much for his reclusive and rather mysterious personality as for his piano playing. It is not that Richter has had trouble making friends. But he has been secretive about his private life, refuses to give interviews, does not enjoy robust health and cancels concerts at whim. He awes his colleagues as much as he awes audiences. Ashkenazy has described the impression Richter made on him:

Richter magnetized me, like he did so many others, and I wouldn't have missed his concerts for anything.

I think he communicated more than anyone else complete devotion and sincerity to his art. When I look back, this is what attracted me most to him then, and continues to do so today. I now understand that the strongest element in his magnetic appeal to audiences is his conviction that what he does is absolutely right at that particular moment. It comes from the fact that he has created his own inner world, absolutely complete in his mind, and if you argue with him about anything it's almost no use. He might say "Yes, perhaps you're right, but I just don't feel it that way. This is what I feel and this is the way I play." And that's it.

Then Ashkenazy says something that puts a finger exactly on the nature of a Richter performance. "I don't often agree with him after the performance, but during it I can see that everything fits together and is completely sincere and devoted, and that wins me over." The point is that Richter on stage exudes such magic, such fierce concentration (his protégé, Andrei Gavrilov, has described him as a "biofield") that he carries everybody, the doubters included, along with him. It is not until later that the listener can have nagging doubts and questions. Ashkenazy, incidentally, claims that Richter is the greatest living Debussy player, with unmatchable imagination behind the beautiful sonorities.

Vladimir Ashkenazy, the first of the postwar Russian pianists to leave his country.

Several years before his American debut, Richter records were available, and they prepared audiences for his highly idiosyncratic playing. At his first series of concerts in Carnegie Hall—seven concerts plus an appearance with the New York Philharmonic—professionals noticed wrong notes and sloppy passages, but these were not important. What was important was the way Richter illuminated the music. He was one of the original slow-tempo men (and, especially in the Schubert sonatas, his tempos became progressively slower as he grew older), but the force of his personality, his laserlike concentration, held the music together. One was always conscious of an original, unusual mind behind the music. His American appearances became rare and finally ceased. Richter preferred to appear in small, intimate festivals, such as the Aldeburgh in England (where he enjoyed playing four-hand music with Benjamin Britten, a friend and skillful pianist).

Vladimir Ashkenazy was the first important Russian pianist to break from his homeland. He was playing fluently and reading music with equal fluency at six, when he entered the Central Music School (from which the best talents were taken into the Moscow or Leningrad conservatory). He stayed there until he was eighteen. In 1955 he entered the Moscow Conservatory as a pupil of Lev Oborin. He took second prize in the Chopin Competition in Warsaw and in 1956 won the Queen Elizabeth in Brussels. An American tour, in 1958, followed. Forced against his will to compete in the 1962 Tchaikovsky Competition, he shared first place with John Ogdon from England. "I was told officially," he says in the autobiography he wrote with Jasper Parrott, "that unless I agreed to participate, my whole future career would be in jeopardy, not just abroad but also in the Soviet Union. This was my first explicit experience of blackmail from the authorities."

While at the conservatory—he did not graduate until 1960—Ashkenazy and a young pianist from Iceland, a classmate in Oborin's class, fell in love and got married. She traveled to England with him during his 1963 tour, and they both announced that they would not return to Russia. An international incident followed. Ashkenazy never asked for political asylum and, indeed, they both returned to Russia, leaving their children with the wife's parents. Ashkenazy played a few concerts in Russia and worked out a deal in which he would live in the West but retain Soviet citizenship. He said it was not a political move, but rather a personal one. He and his wife did not wish to bring up their children in Russia. Later, Ashkenazy became an outspoken critic of the Soviet Union: "I would call Russia a country of lies. . . . By the time you are a grown-up person you're so utterly brainwashed that you don't know anymore what you like and what you don't like."

He became one of the most popular pianists on the international circuit, even though his style changed perceptibly. As a young pianist, he had a fine technique but never a bravura one; a big tone but never a brazen one. Bravura playing did not interest him. His repertoire was predominantly romantic, with excursions into such music as the Bartók concertos. He played with sensitivity, a singing line and plasticity of phrase. As time went on, he became more "modern" in his musical approach. There was less poetry, more concentration on the formal elements of music. The critic Peter Davis called his playing "rootless . . . cosmopolitan and impersonal." Was it, Davis conjectured, because Ashkenazy had severed all cultural and ethnic ties? Ashkenazy has admitted that he has never identified either with his Russian or Jewish heritage. In any case, the impersonality mentioned by Davis has not gone unnoticed by other critics, and a record reviewer for the *New York Times* described Ashkenazy's playing as "limpid, intelligent, elegant. . . . It represents the best of the modern style, which means that the pianist offers no more and no less than what the notes say." Could it be that Ashkenazy arrived at the point where piano playing bored him? Certainly in recent years he has been concentrating on the baton. He started conducting at a music festival he organized in Iceland and, in recent years, has devoted more and more time to the orchestra, even working up the beginnings of a sizable discography. He would not be the first pianist to end up in front of an orchestra. Daniel Barenboim is as famous a conductor as he is a pianist. Many great conductors of past and present, such as Georg Solti, Bruno Walter, Dimitri Mitropoulos, Erich Leinsdorf and George Szell could have had major careers as pianists had they been so inclined.

A Russian pianist who has attracted considerable attention, pro and con, is Lazar Berman. He started playing at the age of two, was in the Central Music School of Moscow at nine, studied with Alexander Goldenweiser there and at the Moscow Conservatory, started touring in 1958 and made his American debut in 1976.

In Russia he is regarded primarily as a technician, and nobody takes him very seriously. It is a feeling shared by many critics and

Lazar Berman, spectacular technician who concentrates on the romantics.

musicians in the West, and Berman himself admits that when he was young he would let his fingers run away. At best, it is felt, he can play the virtuoso music of Liszt as very few can. But Mozart? Beethoven? Don't be ridiculous!

As a matter of fact, not even Berman's admirers subscribe to his Beethoven playing. But he has a technique on the Barere or Lhevinne order, and it is a technique ideal for certain kinds of romantic music. His recording of the complete *Années de Pelerinage* by Liszt is an example of technique coupled to superior artistry; nobody plays Rachmaninoff with more style and elegance; few have equal authority in Scriabin. Perhaps this is a segment of the repertory not valued by all musicians, but is there not esthetic gratification in the work of a pianist who can not only make the Liszt *Transcendental Études* sound easy but also make them sound musical? One problem faced by supertechnicians is that their more serious brethren refuse to admit that supertechnicians have anything more than fingers. Their belief is that the fingers are uncoupled to a brain. Berman has had to fight that concept all of his life, and the fact that he is not notably successful in Beethoven and Mozart gives ammunition to his critics. But, in certain aspects of the repertoire, only a handful of pianists can come near matching him.

Berman was the last of the "big" Russian pianists. The ones emerging from the Soviet Union in recent years have not made the impact of Gilels, Richter or Ashkenazy. Gregory Sokoloff, Alexander Slobodyanik, Dimitri Bashkirov, Nikolai Petroff, Mikhail Pletnyov, Vladimir Krainev—they have come and gone, making no particular impression. In more recent years, there has been much talk about Andrei Gavrilov, winner of the 1974 Tchaikovsky Competition. He is a virtuoso, sometimes an explosive one, who has Horowitz instincts that are not yet under full control. At least, he has temperament, and temperament is in short supply among today's pianists. Another pianist who could mature into an important artist is Evgeny Kisin, born in 1972, who at twelve was playing Liszt études and both of the Chopin concertos with a remarkable combination of bravura and musical understanding: a thin, nervous, shy child, but a fearsome one with untold potentialities.

XXXVI

Bach à la Mode

IN THE PERIOD just after World War II, it became unfashionable to play Bach on the piano. The new musicology was in vogue, and all agreed that to play Bach on the piano was *nykulturny,* a violation of the holy spirit, probably worse even than the super-virtuoso Bach-Tausig or Bach-Liszt arrangements. Harpsichordists proliferated, headed by Wanda Landowska, the reigning empress of the instrument. Nobody made too much of the fact that Landowska played a Pleyel instrument that was the next thing to a concert grand piano or that her registrations and musical approach were highly romantic. The important thing was that Landowska made music, and she convinced audiences and critics that there was only one way to hear Bach—on the harpsichord and preferably in a Landowska performance. Bach on the piano all but vanished. There was only one major holdout—the respected Rosalyn Tureck, an admirable artist, a woman who had devoted her life to Bach and Bach performance practice, an instrumentalist with an independent left hand ideally suited for Bach's linear strands. Yet even Tureck was regarded with a certain suspicion. She was playing the *piano.*

Then in 1955 Glenn Gould appeared.

His was one of the stranger careers in pianistic history. One of the great eccentrics of music, he nevertheless was a supremely gifted instrumentalist whose ideas changed the way musicians looked at Bach. His first recording, the legendary *Goldberg* Variations that appeared in 1955, was revelation to many. It had a combination of personality, finesse, new ideas, bouncing rhythm, fast tempos and technical security that was a new approach to Bach playing. It had authority. Maybe musicologists could pick it apart. No matter. It made listeners *believe*. Above all, there was the linear quality of the playing. Gould had an extraordinary ability to sort out the contrapuntal lines, weight them, contrast them with each other and run them in tandem. In hindsight it is possible to wonder just how "authentic" this *Goldberg* really was. But every age, as has been noted, makes music its own way, and Gould's way exactly suited his age, just as his last recording—by coincidence, another look at the *Goldberg* about a generation after his epic recording debut—suited the 1980s. For this was a completely different interpretation. It observed many more repeats, the tempos were much slower, it was philosophical and even mannered.

Glenn Gould, whose legendary Bach playing forced a revision of the composer's piano music.

Don Hunstein

To many musicians today, Glenn Gould is a symbol, a sort of Bobby Fischer of the piano. Like the eccentric chess genius, he was an amazing talent who retired early and went into seclusion. Like Bobby Fischer, Glenn Gould made his own rules, went his own way, did not care what the world thought of him, and ended up bending the world to *his* will. No wonder he represented something to which all young musicians aspired. Just as Bobby Fischer was a legend after he conquered Boris Spassky in Reykjavik in 1972, so Gould has remained a legend among those who never even heard him play. To his generation he still represents revolt against authority, contempt for the Establishment. This is especially true in Russia, where Gould is revered. (So is Bobby Fischer.) Any pianist or piano specialist who visits the Soviet Union is besieged by Russian pianists wanting to know everything about Glenn Gould. They have as many of his records as can be purchased, borrowed, stolen, copied, or pirated. They have copies of his television appearances. They imitate his physical mannerisms and model their Bach interpretations after his, and they believe him to have been the most stimulating musician of his time.

This *enfant terrible* was born in Canada on September 25, 1932. He started playing at the age of three and was first taught by his mother. At six he heard a recital by Josef Hofmann and never forgot the experience. Many years later he recollected that, when he was being driven home, "I was in that wonderful state of half awakedness in which you hear all sorts of incredible sounds going through your mind. They were all orchestral sounds, but I was playing them all, and suddenly I was Hofmann. I was enchanted."

His next step was the Royal Conservatory in Toronto. There, between the ages of ten and twenty, he studied with Alberto Guerrero. Music was his entire life; he never even finished high school. When he started to concertize, it was as a finished artist with highly unusual programs. He played very little romantic music. His programs, of course, had Bach. He played some Beethoven, notably the last three sonatas. He also took a look at composers not normally associated with piano recitals—Sweelinck and Gibbons, to mention but two. Then there was a grand jump to Berg and Webern. "I have," he explained, "a century-long blind spot approximately demarcated by *The Art of the Fugue* on one side and *Tristan* on the other—everything in between is at best an occasion for admiration rather than love."

He said of Chopin, "I don't think he is a very good composer." But there was little in romanticism that he did like:

The whole first half of the nineteenth century—excluding Beethoven to some degree—is pretty much of a washout for me as far as solo instrument music is concerned. This generalization includes Chopin, Liszt, Schumann. . . . You see, I don't think any of the early romantic composers knew how to write for the piano. Oh, they knew how to use the pedal, and how to make dramatic effects, splashing notes in every direction—but there's very little real *composing* going on. The music of that era is full of empty theatrical gestures, full of exhibitionism, and it has a worldly, hedonistic quality that turns me off. Almost every criterion that I expect to encounter in great music—harmonic and rhythmic variety, contrapuntal invention—is almost entirely absent in these pieces.

As for Beethoven, he was a composer "whose reputation is based entirely on gossip." To Gould, Beethoven was "the supreme historical example of a composer on an ego trip." Gould liked the early works and a few late ones, especially the *Grosse Fuge*, which he considered "not only the greatest work Beethoven wrote but just about the most astonishing composition in musical literature." As for the symphonies, the Violin Concerto, the *Waldstein* Sonata, Gould was "absolutely at a loss" how they ever became popular.

On the other hand he had his wild enthusiasms—Schoenberg, Hindemith and especially Richard Strauss. Gould went so far as to record Strauss's *Enoch Arden* and some early piano pieces, all of those works a crashing bore. Yet, in his brilliant and provocative articles about Strauss, he made a strong case for the composer. Gould wrote a good deal—enough to fill a large, 461-page book edited by Tim Page. The program notes to Gould's records were invariably his own, and he contributed to many magazines. His writing illustrates the paradox that he was. His observations on music, and on life in general, are a mixture of profundity, cleverness, adolescence, heavy-handed humor that does not come off at all, and actual nonsense. Gould just loved to startle, to fizz off ideas without thinking them through. Often he deals in paradox. Once in a while there is a becoming humility. In short, his writings are like Gould the musician—at their best infuriatingly brilliant and brilliantly infuriating.

No wonder musicians were up in arms. Did Gould really mean all that? Or was it that, in the words of Lewis Carroll, "He only does it to annoy because he knows it teases"? Rudolf Serkin once heard Gould utter these kinds of comments on a radio broadcast. "He said ridiculous things which made me mad. But then at the end he played, and everything was all right." On the other side of the coin, there were musicians and critics who idolized Gould and all he represented. To them, he was the one young pianist with a real mind and real individuality.

He had only nine years as a concert pianist, but those nine years made him a superstar. In constant demand, he played in Europe, Russia and Israel as well as the United States. At the age of thirty-two he retired. Years previously, he had announced that he would stop playing in public when he was thirty, to devote himself to making records, and he kept his word. He gave his last concert in Chicago on March 28, 1964. He died tragically young, after a stroke in 1982. He was only fifty years old.

During his years away from the concert stage, he was fascinated by the communications media, about which he wrote a great deal. He continued to record, made radio and television appearances, and created some television shows. He was voluble on the importance of electronic technology, and he gave it as one of the reasons for his early retirement. "Technology," he said, "has the capability to create a climate of anonymity and to allow the artist the time and the freedom to prepare his conception of the work to the best of his ability. It has the capability of replacing those awful and degrading and humanly damaging uncertainties which the concert brings with it." He said that when he played concerts he felt like a vaudeville performer.

Part of the Gould mythology was his eccentric path through life, and his eccentricities were gleefully recited by musicians and the public. He never would shake hands with anybody for fear of contamination. Even on the hottest summer days he wore a sweater. On cold days he wore gloves and had a pair with the fingers trimmed that he would sometimes use for concerts. Interviewers loved it; he was such good copy. "It was not a cold day," wrote one, "but Gould was wearing a beret, ear muffs, a scarf, an overcoat and a pair of sturdy leather mittens. In the restaurant, when he had peeled these off, he was still wearing a thick woollen shirt, a heavy sweater, a shaggy tweed sports jacket, woollen slacks and a pair of knit gloves from which the fingers had been cut." He was very much a night person and slept through the day. Highly reclusive, he would spend hours with people on the telephone instead of seeing them. He was a hypochondriac. He took innumerable pills. He cancelled concerts arbitrarily—as many as one out of five.

Of course, his way of life made him a natural for publicity. During his concert days, he carried his own chair with him because no normal stool was low enough for his unusual position at the keyboard. This chair was built so that it was exactly fourteen inches off the floor. But it still was a shade too high for him, so as often as not he would insist that the legs of the piano be put on blocks to raise the instrument about an inch and a quarter. Stories about Gould and his chair made the rounds. Once, so the story goes, he kept George Szell and the Cleveland Orchestra waiting interminably during a rehearsal while stagehands juggled with chair and piano. Gould looked at the impatient Szell and said something to the effect that he did not know what to do with his chair. Szell told him exactly what he could do with his chair.

His concert mannerisms included swaying, humming and beating time with free hands. At one performance of the Beethoven Piano Concerto No. 4 in New York, he carried a glass of water to the piano. He adjusted himself, played the opening solo and then, while the orchestra was in its tutti, crossed his legs and had a few refreshing gulps. The *Times* critic congratulated him on his informality and suggested, for Gould's next performance of the concerto, a bottle of beer and a ham sandwich.

How much of this was calculated? Nobody will ever know. But Gould had a knack *pour épater le bourgeois,* and he well knew the advantages of publicity and how to manipulate the press. Did he purposely carry his eccentricities into his piano playing? Some of his performances outraged musicians as much as some of his oral and published statements. His eccentric recording of the last three Beethoven sonatas all but started lynching parties among musicians, so mannered and *outré* were they. When he recorded some Mozart piano sonatas, he brought out the Alberti bass figurations to a point where they assumed equal importance to the melodic line. And many considered his tempos downright crazy—much too slow or much too fast. Mozart specialists were outraged. But, then again, Gould was on record as saying that he did not really like Mozart very much.

It is as a Bach player that he will live and his recordings constitute his permanent legacy. Sometimes, as in the Partitas, he forced professionals, music lovers and critics to reconsider the music, throwing overboard all preconceived notions. It was not only that he had wonderful fingers and an ability to clarify the linear elements of the music. Other pianists—admittedly, not many—could do that too. But none had his particular kind of firmly centered sonority; a sonority that Piero Rattalino, the Italian specialist on pianists, compares to the sound evoked by the great colorists—Horowitz, Richter and Michelangeli. Above all, Gould's Bach interpretations made the music sound different—different in tempo, in phrase, in dynamics, in conception. Elements nobody previously had paid much attention to suddenly sprang into high relief. But there was nothing eccentric or mannered about the performances. The music was passing through a mind that took nothing for granted. It was an original mind that worked on a different set of premises and principles from other pianists. One could not describe it as traditional Bach playing, or romantic Bach playing, or neoclassic Bach playing, or modern Bach playing, or musicological Bach playing. Whatever it was, it breathed a life and spirit unique in the history of Bach performance.

XXXVII

Two Cult Figures

IN THE 1970s two pianists emerged as the archetypes of the modern style, to a point where they became cult figures—their concerts breathlessly received, each surrounded by an aura, each receiving the devotion paid to such pure musicians of the past as Clara Schumann and Artur Schnabel. The modern style that these two pianists represent is objective, literal, severe, impersonal, dedicated to an accurate blueprint of the architecture of the music. Color, charm and emotion mean much less than a stringent exposition of the form and relationships of a piece. The modern style takes Stravinsky's injunction to heart: don't "interpret" me, just play the notes as I have written them. Alfred Brendel and Maurizio Pollini met all the requirements of the modern style and more than any other pianists represented the spirit of the age. On the occasion of one of his Beethoven cycles in London, where he has lived since 1972, Brendel even got awed editorials from the *Times*, couched in prose normally reserved for the Deity.

Brendel (born in Austria in 1931) and Pollini (born in Italy in 1942) share many of the same traits. Both are constantly being described as "intellectual" musicians. Both have completely discarded the entertainment aspects from their recitals. In romantic pianism, entertainment played a fairly large role; programs almost always contained flashy pieces that were calculated to stun the public. These kinds of programs were not for Brendel and Pollini. Where the big virtuosos of the past paid little, if any, attention to contemporary music, here was Pollini playing the Piano Sonata No. 2 by Boulez, or the complete piano music by Schoenberg, or works by Stockhausen, Webern and Berio. In 1985 his program, which he

Alfred Brendel, the latter-day Schnabel who also plays Liszt.

played all over Europe and America, consisted only of Book I of *The Well-Tempered Clavier*. Not even Rudolf Serkin, the exponent of pure classicism, had ever done that. Pollini did, and audiences rushed to hear the Pollini-Bach combination, listening to the program as though attending a holy rite. Brendel also had Schoenberg solo works in his repertoire, as well as the piano concertos by Schoenberg and Bartók. Such atypical behavior alone made them heroes to what Virgil Thomson used to describe as "the intellectual audience." Top pianists normally never touch such repertoire. The avant-gardists, especially, felt that in Brendel and Pollini they had an eloquent and important pair of spokesmen, and they became the darlings of the intelligentsia.

Aside from his excursions into contemporary music, Brendel's repertoire was, and has continued to be, confined largely to the great Austro-German classics—Bach, Haydn, Mozart, Beethoven and Schubert. He plays no French music, no Chopin, no Russian music (although many years ago he recorded the Mussorgsky *Pictures* and a few other Russian pieces) and, curiously, little Schumann or Brahms (he has recorded some major Schumann works, but they seldom appear on his concert programs). Even more curiously, he has from the beginning played a great deal of Liszt—and this in the days when Liszt was equated with everything despicable in romanticism. It was received opinion that the music of Liszt was, ugh, virtuosic, vulgar, shallow, meretricious, not to be discussed in polite society. Since then, however, Liszt has been rehabilitated, and Brendel's contributions have had a good deal to do with the new estimate of one of the most fascinating composers of the nineteenth century. "I believe," Brendel once said about Liszt, "he was a person of great nobility. . . . I treat Liszt as a complement to Mozart, Beethoven and Schubert."

At the beginning Brendel, unlike Pollini, did not set the world on fire. Of course he started young, playing at six and composing at seven. Brendel never considered himself a prodigy. He studied in Zagreb and then in Graz. Later he attended master classes of Paul Baumgartner, Eduard Steuermann and Edwin Fischer. Brendel considers Fischer the greatest influence on his style. He also came under the sway of Fürtwängler. Brendel says that after the age of sixteen he never had a regular teacher. "Self-discovery is a slower process but a more natural one." At seventeen he made his debut. He also entered a competition, the Bolzano in Italy, 1949, and came out third. It was his one and only competition. Virtually every important pianist after Brendel has been a competition winner. Ever since Van Cliburn captured the first Tchaikovsky Competition in 1958 and won fame and fortune, competitions have been a way of life for pianists. Much has been written about the pros and cons of competitions, and both sides make sense, but of one thing there can be no doubt: competitions provide a sensational launching pad for their winners.

If Brendel did not go the competition route, he found another way: recordings. His career—certainly in the United States—was made through records, years before he first played there. The LP record came into existence in 1948. At that time only two American record companies—Victor and Columbia—dealt to any large extent with classical music. But within five years after the introduction of the LP disc there were thousands of record companies in America alone and, of these, several dozen concentrated on serious music. The leaders were Vox and Westminster. Thanks to the new process of recording on magnetic tape, the record companies could go to Europe, buy or lease tapes from radio stations, or engage young artists for a modest fee. Brendel, Paul Badura-Skoda and Jörg Demus were three pianists who benefited from the early days of LP. For Vox, Brendel recorded a great deal of Beethoven and Liszt. When he made his first tour of America in 1963, it was as a known quantity.

Known—but not universally admired. There were exceptions. Such critics as Michael Steinberg in the Boston *Globe* immediately greeted Brendel as the new Schnabel. It was the Steinberg view that eventually was to prevail, but from the very beginning of Brendel's career there have been critics and specialists who never could warm up to Brendel's austerity or, to use a less hedged word that comes up again and again in association with Brendel, pedanticism. It also was pointed out that Brendel never had the spectacular, infallible technique of, say, a Pollini. It so happens that Bendel has a fine technique, but he has never worried much about pure finger work. "If I miss a few notes, I don't care as long as the musical purpose is clear," he says. "Perfection has done too much harm already in music." Here, Brendel may have been alluding to the impact of records, which magnetic tape techniques have made an inhumanly perfect process. Wrong notes can be eliminated and correct ones spliced in at will. Various effects can be added by the engineers. In the old 78 rpm records, on the other hand, the listener can be confident that he is hearing exactly what the artist put on it. There was no way of correcting a disc; the only thing the artist could do, if he were not satisfied with the result, was to play the entire side over.

As early as 1958, a *New York Times* record reviewer, listening to a Liszt record played by Brendel, noted that the pianist had a great deal of skill. "But he takes the music too seriously, something that Liszt himself (it is certain) never did. The one thing lacking in his armament is the sportive quality that the great virtuosos have—the quality of flexibility coupled to an enormous mechanism plus the ability to revel in the technical wonders and toss them off with the éclat of a magician producing rabbits from a hat. . . . Mr. Brendel, who appears to be possessed of a very musical mind, seems to find it difficult to enter into the extroverted quality of the music. If only he had let himself go a little more, his disc would have been outstanding."

Clearly, this reviewer was one who responded to romantic pianism, and Brendel is not a romanticist. His playing has always given trouble to those who look for color and suppleness, and many dismiss him out of hand as a Liszt pianist, if only because of his hard, rather percussive tone. Even Brendel's generally admired Beethoven was described by Donal Henahan of the *New York Times* in his review of a 1983 concert as ". . . rather brittle. It was as if Mr. Brendel were projecting an X-ray picture of each sonata onto a screen for our admiration rather than luring us into the heart and soul of the composer."

Brendel is perfectly aware of this kind of criticism, but he insists he is not an intellectual pianist. "That is not right at all," he told an interviewer in 1983. ". . . Feeling must be alpha and omega. It's a question of thinking with the composer, like Schenker tried to do, and not going along blind, like Schnabel. . . . Every piece of music makes its own rules, and you have by a great effort to understand those rules and then play within them, like playing roles—within those psychological barriers you can do almost anything." Heinrich Schenker was an Austrian theorist who in the 1920s developed a new kind of musical analysis. It may have brought some musicians up short to learn that Schnabel, one of the pioneers in textual examinations of Beethoven's music, was "going along blind." And the very fact that Brendel cited the formidable apparatus of Schenkerian analysis supported those who were firmly convinced of Brendel's "intellectualism."

As for the Brendel tone, he says that he has never attempted to make the piano sound like a traditional virtuoso instrument. "There is a certain idea," he told the *New York Times*, "of 'good,' 'beautiful,' 'appropriate' piano playing which reduces everything to pianistic terms. I try to do exactly the opposite, to remove music from these limitations and to make people forget the piano." In other words, the message is much more important than the instrument. But what, one can ask, if message and instrument are irretrievably linked, as they are in Liszt?

In any case, romantic sound or no, Brendel's ideas about Liszt cannot be easily dismissed. He has found things in the music that the romantic pianists either ignored or did not know were there. In emphasizing the intellectual side of Liszt, he brings into prominence Liszt the twentieth-century harmonicist, the man who in so many respects was a hundred years ahead of his time. The turn-of-the-century Liszt pianists played him with aristocracy, floating sounds, a singing line and controlled tempo fluctuation. Brendel's is a twentieth-century Liszt, metrically strict, tonally hard and verging on the percussive, much more interested in the organization than in the color of the music. In some of the problematic late works—which the older generation of pianists did not even know existed—Brendel attains an impressive focus of concentration that can make these prophetic pieces actually scary.

Maurizio Pollini, even more than Brendel, more than anybody, is the very paragon of the modern style. As a technician, he is perfect, and his cool, flawless performances of anything he plays strikes envy or fear in his colleagues. He can do anything he wants to do at the piano, and he does everything much the same way—objectively, standing outside the music, refusing any fervent emotional commitments, just producing beautiful, well-organized, impersonal sounds.

He has a much wider-ranging repertory than Brendel. It covers most of the literature, and he plays it all with the same cool perfection. He probably was doing that at five, when he started his piano studies, making his debut six years later. He went on to work with Carlo Vidusso, a highly respected Italian pianist, and, after 1960, with Arturo Benedetti Michelangeli. Each gave him, in Pollini's guarded words, "useful technical advice." That is all he is willing to grant. Among pianists who played a part in his development, he cites Cortot, Backhaus, Fischer, Gieseking, Haskil and Rubinstein.

Competitions occupied him for a while. He won an award in his

Maurizio Pollini, archetypal pianist of the modern school.

DG/G. Brandenstein

home town, Milan, in 1957, took second prize in the big Geneva Competition the same year, and first at Seregno in 1959. In 1960, at the age of eighteen, he capped it all by winning the Chopin Competition in Warsaw, and his career was launched—but not immediately. Pollini gave very few concerts during the next five years; he spent most of his time studying by himself and expanding his repertoire. When he resumed concert life, he was an immediate success. He could have been like Arthur Rubinstein and played some two hundred concerts a year, but he has never accepted more than seventy. He says that he needs time to think.

A shy man who grants very few interviews, he nevertheless has been in the news on subjects unrelated to piano playing. He was a former member of the Communist Party and engaged in some political activity during the Vietnam War. When he attempted to read an anti–United States manifesto before one of his concerts, he was hissed, and the story was duly reported in the newspapers. Otherwise he lives a very private life.

The jury of the Chopin Competition must have been bowled over by Pollini. He was the perfect type of competition pianist—a player with a vast but never show-off technique; a musician who observed all the amenities, whose tempos were sensible with never a trace of eccentricity. Competition judges dote on this kind of pianist. Thus Pollini was, and thus he has remained: a pianist who represents computerlike total control. As such, he is the ultimate pianistic symbol of his age, and thus an ideal to young pianists who think along his lines and wish they could realize their goals as successfully as he has. To many of them, Pollini is by far the greatest living pianist.

XXXVIII

Made in America

AMERICAN PIANISM is a relatively new phenomenon. It is true that before World War II there was a handful of Americans who were accepted on the international scene as admirable and, in some cases, brilliant artists. A few names that come to mind are Frank Sheridan, Beveridge Webster, Leonard Shure, William Masselos and Sidney Foster. But it remained for the period after 1946 to see the handful suddenly swell into an army. What kind of Cadmus had been sowing to produce such a crop? The concert halls were swamped, and still are, with young pianists, many of them very good (and, unfortunately, apparently with no place to go). There are far too many to mention in this book, just as there were too many in 1961 when Abram Chasins's *Speaking of Pianists* appeared. Chasins took several chapters to list the American scene, and even that book, concerned mainly with twentieth-century pianists, does not pretend to any kind of exhaustive analysis. Often names are merely listed.

The most promising of all the American postwar pianists was William Kapell, who died in an airplane crash in 1953. Kapell had won a Naumburg Competition award, and he went on to impress an international public with a spectacularly honest technique (never any bluff or cover-up with the pedals), a forthright musical approach and a fierce integrity. His playing had those indefinable things known as charisma and command, and he was well on his way to becoming one of the century's most important pianists when his plane from Australia went down during its approach to San Francisco.

In winning the Naumburg, Kapell was typical of his generation. Until the 1970s, America had two major competitions (and many lesser ones) that helped virtually every important pianist of the last half-century. The two major competitions were the Leventritt (no longer in existence) and the Naumburg. Among Naumburg winners, in addition to Kapell, have been Jorge Bolet, Abba Bogin, Dalies Frantz, Leonid Hambro, Constance Keene, Theodore Lettvin, Joseph Schwartz, Abbey Simon, Zadel Skolovsky, Ralph Votapek, André-Michel Schub (who went on to win the prestigious Van Cliburn Competition), Peter Orth and Stephen Hough—a goodly company. Equally impressive are the Leventritt winners, among them: Michel Block, John Browning, Van Cliburn, Sidney Foster, Malcolm Frager, Gary Graffman, Eugene Istomin and Anton Kuerti. Cliburn won his Leventritt in 1954 and was respectfully received at that time. It took his 1958 victory in the very first Tchaikovsky Competition in Moscow, however, to make his name a household word and also to make all musicians competition conscious. When Seymour Lipkin won the first and only Rachmaninoff Competition in 1948, triumphing over the pick of American pianists, or when Leon Fleisher won the Queen Elizabeth of Belgium competition in 1954, over an unusually strong field, their feats passed virtually unnoticed by the public. But in the post-Cliburn age, when Ivan Davis carried the Liszt Competition in New York in 1960, when in the same year Malcolm Frager followed on the heels of his Leventritt with first prize at the Queen Elizabeth, when Agustin Anievas took top honors at the first Dimitri Mitropoulos Competition in New York in 1961, when in 1962 Ralph Votapek won the first Van Cliburn Competition in Fort Worth (beating out two Russians), when in 1970 Garrick Ohlsson won the Chopin Competition in Warsaw, their feats were on everybody's tongue.

It was Cliburn who, more than any other pianist of his time, captured the American imagination. Though, one wonders, what would have happened had not Max Frankel, the Moscow bureau chief of the *New York Times*, followed the competition on a day-to-day basis, building it up like a suspense story, to the point that when Cliburn won it was front-page news all over the United States and, indeed, the world. When Cliburn returned home, it was to the accompaniment of ticker-tape parades, mountains of publicity and an equally mountainous raise in fees. He was, for a while, the highest-paid musician of his time, the hottest thing in show business. He had everything working for him. Had he not gone to a strange, exotic and (in many American minds) hostile country and conquered,

Van Cliburn, America's hero after the 1958 Tchaikovsky Competition.

Galahad-like? Was not this apple-pie, Deep South, gangling, inno-
cent-looking boy a typical American? All of which was true, but
there were other, more important, factors. Looks do not win major
prizes, and Cliburn, a pupil of Rosina Lhevinne, had brilliant pianistic credentials, including a technique that could take care of anything (his big piece was the Rachmaninoff D minor Concerto) and a
golden tone. Of all the Americans of his generation, Cliburn was
able to produce the most sensuous of sounds—rich, never percussive, a real piano sound that reminded old-timers of the great romantic pianists of the past.

For reasons that he has never made clear, Cliburn retired in the
mid-1970s. Perhaps he never learned how to handle his sudden
fame. Perhaps he was torn two ways. On the one hand, he had such
natural gifts that he could have played any repertoire, could have
developed into a supreme artist. On the other, he was constantly
asked to repeat his competition concertos—the Tchaikovsky B flat
minor and the Rachmaninoff Third—and he acceded. He played up
to his role as America's favorite son to the point of starting every
concert with the national anthem. His playing got limper and
limper, and toward the end his performances sounded perfunctory,
bored and even sloppy. Could he have felt a certain unhappiness,
even disgust, with himself? Whatever the reason, one of the most
brilliant talents in American pianism called it quits.

Not all American pianists, of course, have been competition winners. Some, indeed, never had as big a success in America as they would have liked and went overseas to gather acclaim. Julius Katchen was one; he went to Paris, where he died young. Rosalyn Tureck spent much time in Europe before returning home and cementing her position as one of the great Bach specialists. Many other Americans have become specialists. Among those who have concentrated on contemporary music have been Leo Smit, David Tudor, William Masselos, David Burge and Paul Jacobs (another fine artist who died young). Some have achieved special identity with a particular composer or school—Grant Johannesen in French music, Philip Evans in Bartók, Raymond Lewenthal in Alkan. The popular Byron Janis has won no major competitions, and neither have Earl Wild, Jacob Lateiner, Lorin Hollander nor Claudette Sorel.

Most of the postwar American pianists represent the objective modern school, and none of them can properly be called a romantic player. It is to such veterans as Jorge Bolet and Earl Wild that romanticism belongs; and also to the Russian-born but American-trained Shura Cherkassky. These three pianists represent the teachings of an older generation. Bolet, born in Cuba in 1914 but a resident of the United States since childhood, studied with David Saperton, Moriz Rosenthal, Leopold Godowsky and Abram Chasins. He also had some lessons from Josef Hofmann. Wild, born in Pittsburgh in 1915, worked with Egon Petri. Cherkassky, born in Odessa in 1911, came to America to study with Hofmann and was a resident for many years. Later he moved to London.

Bolet is a pianist who achieved success late in life, thanks as much to the romantic revival as to his own fabulous gifts. He was playing at six and was sent to the Curtis Institute in Philadelphia when he was twelve. At Curtis he was a star. He could play anything, read anything, memorize without effort and already had a world-class technique. Indeed, it was too great a technique—so all-encompassing that Bolet was typed as one of the technical wizards without too much style or substance. He went to Europe after graduation in 1934, gave some concerts and returned to the United States as a teacher at the University of Indiana music department. Later he succeeded Rudolf Serkin as head of the piano department of the Curtis Institute.

Jorge Bolet, exemplar of the suave, elegant side of Romantic pianism.

He had some bad years in the 1940–1950 decades. His style of playing was completely out of fashion, and no manager or, indeed, public was interested in what he had to offer. It could well be, without sounding overly romantic about it, that those bad years helped his intellectual growth. He had time to think, experiment, and work on repertoire. It also could be that not until relatively late in life did he develop into the great artist he became. And there also was the romantic revival. Musicians suddenly started to become interested in music that only a few years previously had been universally derided. With that came the beginnings of an interest in romantic performance practice, an area that had been completely neglected. Bolet gave a series of New York recitals in the 1970s that created a sensation. Suddenly, the time was ripe for his kind of playing. Then he went to London, to Paris, to Berlin. Everybody went wild. Suddenly, Bolet became a star attraction, in demand everywhere.

His is a refined, aristocratic kind of piano playing. With his equipment he could out-thunder Vladimir Horowitz if he were so inclined, but that is not his style. If anything, he tends to underplay. Perhaps a psychological factor is involved here; he is so determined not to be known merely as a bravura pianist that he sometimes throttles down when in fact he should be damning the torpedos. He plays with delicate mixtures of color; his interpretations are perfectly proportioned; he can achieve big sonorities without banging; and he has mastered the romantic secret of tempo fluctuation. And, of course, there is the stupendous Bolet technique. Everything sounds easy under his fingers. In many respects he is a sort of latter-day Josef Lhevinne.

The job of a musician, he says, is to turn the printed note into a living experience. "Pianists who consider the score as being the Bible," he dryly adds, "turn out to be excellent craftsmen." He works on the premise that there is no absolute. "Everything in music must be sifted through one's mind and personality. That is what music-making is all about."

In his day Bolet has played everything, but the area in which he is supreme extends from the early romantics through Rachmaninoff. As such, he represents the Hofmann-Godowsky-Lhevinne school of Slavic pianism. Bolet and Cherkassky are the last living active exponents of that school; the only ones whose playing actually reduplicates the sounds made by the great romantic pianists of the nineteenth century.

Shura Cherkassky is a more eccentric player than Bolet, in that he uses much more tempo fluctuation to a point where the basic meter can become unsteady. But he too has the golden sound, the color, the infallible technique, the personality and, at his best, the musical ebb and flow of the romantic tide. His interpretations are always highly idiosyncratic and always interesting.

Earl Wild first became known as a Gershwin specialist, and that soured his reputation among many critics and the intellectual audience. How could any pianist who ran around playing the Gershwin Concerto in F and the *Rhapsody in Blue* be taken seriously? But professionals appreciated Wild's craft. They knew that he had an utterly spectacular technique, on the Horowitz-Bolet stratospheric level; that he was a serious musician who was all but unapproachable in certain aspects of the literature, especially Liszt. Like Bolet, Wild was playing Liszt long before it again became fashionable to do so. In the 1985–1986 season, on the occasion of the centenary of Liszt's death, Wild celebrated with a three-concert series that he played in the United States and Europe. He named the programs Liszt the Poet, Liszt the Transcriber and Liszt the Virtuoso.

These pianists of an older generation aside, the American school remains an objective and eclectic one. On the face of it, that is strange. For Americans until only a short time ago were studying with foreign-born teachers whose roots were in the nineteenth century. Among those teachers were Isabella Vengerova, Rosina Lhevinne, Nadia Reisenberg, Rudolf Serkin, Egon Petri, Rudolf Ganz, Sascha Gorodnitzki—all settled in America from overseas. Of the generation before *them*, Arthur Schnabel, Josef Lhevinne, Alexander Siloti, Josef Hofmann, Heinrich Gebhard, Leopold Godowsky —name almost any important teacher—were foreign born. And if not foreign, they had, like Olga Samaroff and Beveridge Webster, studied abroad. One would have thought that American products of such teaching would automatically respond to the same kind of literature that their mentors had represented.

But it did not work out that way. The great flowering of American pianism after World War II was not successful in allying itself to the romantic tradition. Perhaps the very sophistication of young American pianists is part of the explanation. Americans tend to be pragmatic and eclectic and to ride with the prevailing intellectual trend. As the trend remained antiromantic, so did the pianists. When the romantic revival of the 1970s got under way, it was too late. The teachers who could have drilled some of the concepts into the new generation were long gone. American pianists are awesome when it comes to playing contemporary music. But in romantic music they have to counterfeit an emotion they do not feel. For they have been trained to respond primarily to the intellectual content of music— form, structure, the solution of technical problems.

But, since much the same thing is happening everywhere in the world, it may not be fair to blame the problem only on the Americans—except that there is every indication that the Americans started it. Now, thanks to the incredible speed with which ideas are transmitted and bodies hurtled around the world, we have an international school of music-making rather than national schools. Pianists of today's international school are eclectic in approach, clear in outline, metrically rather inflexible, tonally hard. They tend to be literalists who try for a direct translation of the printed note. As a matter of fact, they make a positive fetish of the printed note, observing the values the way accountants study a balance sheet. This they do very well. What they do not do is read *between* the notes. In a way, they are junior executives, company men, well trained, serious, confident and efficient, and rather lacking in personality. One of the most prevalent complaints about today's piano playing is that there is such deadening uniformity that it is next to impossible to distinguish Pianist A from Pianist B from Pianist C. They all tend to sound alike.

On the whole, their playing tends toward caution. That is, despite strong technical equipment, they curb their temperaments to a point where they seldom will take a chance. The great artists of previous generations were always taking chances. If what they aimed for came off, the effect was stupendous. If it failed—well, it was a magnificent failure. This is not encountered very often today. Planning is substituted for personality and daring.

Their repertoire is all-embracing. Bach and Scarlatti on the piano, as opposed to the harpsichord, have been restored to favor. Beethoven and Schubert fascinate them. The Beethoven test pieces are the *Hammerklavier* and C minor (Op. 111) Sonatas, and the *Diabelli* Variations. Pianists today rush to play them as soon as they think

Horacio Gutierrez: tone, technique, temperament.

Murray Perahia:

serious, stylish, sensitive.

they are mature enough—say, eighteen years old. The early Brahms pieces have enjoyed a great revival. Liszt has come back into favor. They fall with great shouts of joy on the impressionists, especially on Ravel's *Gaspard de la nuit*, and they also are greatly attracted to Prokofieff. A surprisingly large number of the new school of pianists have dedicated themselves specifically to the avant-garde. No matter how difficult the music, how abstruse the notation, they seem to learn it practically overnight. Americans are especially good at this; in their ability to handle the intricacies of modern composition they lead the world. On an all-around basis the American pianist is the best trained in the world today, and the same applies to singers (ask any European impresario).

In the United States, a few pianists are beginning to break out of the straitjacket. Chief among them are André Watts, Horacio Gutierrez and Murray Perahia. Watts, born in 1946 of a black American father and a Hungarian mother, is the first black pianist to have achieved a major international career. He studied in Philadelphia and attracted the attention of Leonard Bernstein, who featured him in one of his televised series with the New York Philharmonic. Watts, then sixteen, played the Liszt E flat concerto and immediately became famous. He displayed an unusual flair, backed by a brilliant technique. He also was a handsome, photogenic youth. Watts went on to concertize and play with orchestras all over the world and to make many recordings. More than most pianists of his generation, he displayed a feeling for the grand line, and his interpretations have continued to contain a controlled kind of freedom that may eventually result in making him an Old Master.

Gutierrez, born in Cuba in 1948, studied in Los Angeles and at the Juilliard School. In 1970 he won the silver medal of the Tchaikovsky Competition. He not only has the technique demanded of a competition winner but also an extroverted, even flaming temperament. It is hard to imagine anybody playing such pieces as the Prokofieff Second Piano Concerto with an equal combination of abandon and control. In romantic music, Gutierrez is still a little too much a child of his time; he has not been fully acquainted with the conventions, and his metrics remain too regular. Nevertheless, he has unlimited potential and is recognized as one of the major talents of his time.

Perahia, born in New York in 1947, won the important Leeds Competition in 1972. He is a representative of the modern school—

with some differences. A serious pianist who avoids any suggestion of flashiness in his playing, he has concentrated on Mozart and Beethoven. Something of a cult has grown up around him. Musicians and an international public admire the finish of his playing, his warm sound, his obvious dedication. Unlike Watts and Gutierrez, he does not have it in him to be a heroic pianist, and he has been wise enough to confine himself to a repertoire in which he excels. Recently (1986) he has started to play some Chopin, and it is possible that he could develop into a convincing Chopinist, especially in the shorter pieces. His sensitive ear allows him to weight chords so that they float, and he has a feeling for the inner voices and coloristic textures of the music.

To discuss the future of pianism is sheer guesswork. Perhaps a new romanticism may be emerging, in which the Russian style, already cross-pollinated with the international style, will bear fruit. One thing seems sure, however. The day of the super-virtuoso-showman is gone—at least for the time being, and perhaps forever; the last living holdout is Vladimir Horowitz. The emphasis today is on "musicianship": clarity, proportion and the other contemporary virtues. The concept of the Artist-as-Hero has been abandoned. Accuracy is more important than temperament. A Paderewski or a de Pachmann would not be allowed to graduate from a reputable conservatory today, and the chances are that even an Anton Rubinstein would have trouble getting through (too many wrong notes, too much exaggeration in tempo and dynamics). Whether this be progress or retrogression, the fact remains that standards have shifted, and that today's international standard calls for an entirely different set of values from the standards on which the romantics operated.

This contemporary emphasis on musicianship means that the good old days were, according to current thought, really the bad old days. Previous ages saw themselves differently. The point has long been made clear, it is to be hoped, that we in our infinite wisdom are apt to blame our predecessors for the very things for which they prided themselves. Which leads to the question: is there, can there be, an esthetic truth? If much nineteenth-century pianism would not be approved today, is not the converse true, that most of today's pianism would not have been approved by the nineteenth century?

In any case, all of the old pianists, from Mozart on, have played their part. They may be the *neiges d'antan*, but from them did spring the present race of pianists. The past is always impinging on the present (more today than ever before, because scholars are more interested in the past than ever before). In the racial subconscious of every living pianist are all the old knights in armor: Dussek and his profile; Steibelt and his tremolos; Liszt simultaneously shaking the hair from his eyes and the hearts of his ladies; Chopin gliding over the keyboard; Henselt playing the *Well-Tempered* while reading the Bible; Dreyschock and his octaves; de Pachmann and his antics; Herz titillating the Americans; Thalberg imitating three hands; Godowsky juggling polyphonies; Hofmann releasing surges of energy.

For, in pianism, as in physiology, ontogeny recapitulates phylogeny.

Index

503